"Even those who lean a little to the left will find this intimate portrait of Justice Scalia fascinating, funny, and deeply loving. A Scalia–Garner collaboration based on a ferocious dedication to the language of the law leads to a friendship that is challenged at times by comic misunderstandings, almost disastrous arguments, and the foibles of both men. The ending of this vivid story is almost unbearably poignant."

—DR. BETTY SUE FLOWERS
DIRECTOR EMERITUS, LBJ LIBRARY
PROFESSOR EMERITUS OF ENGLISH,
UNIVERSITY OF TEXAS

"Justice Scalia was one of the most controversial and influential jurists of the late 20th and early 21st centuries. He was lionized by the political right, and often demonized by the left. In this memoir, he is humanized by Bryan Garner, who paints a sympathetic but frank portrait of their friendship in the justice's twilight years. The justice is often cranky or peevish, but he can also be warm and funny, and Garner's story shows the broad spectrum of his intellect and temperament—and offers a rare glimpse into the intellect and private persona of a man who, whether you love him or hate him, helped shape American law for decades."

—BRIAN R. MELENDEZ
PARTNER, BARNES & THORNBURG
MINNEAPOLIS

"One day on the way to the Forum, Bryan Garner met his modern-day Cicero, Justice Antonin Scalia. Their friendship blossomed, and it is celebrated with obvious enjoyment in *Nino and Me* (not *Nino and I*, you'll be pleased to read). At every step of his conversation with Justice Scalia, Bryan Garner is alert to language issues, and one of the triumphs of the book is the manner in which—together—they prod, and examine, and then demystify many of the totems of legal English."

—JOHN SIMPSON
CHIEF EDITOR OF THE *OXFORD ENGLISH DICTIONARY* (1993–2013);
AUTHOR, *THE WORD DETECTIVE* (2016)

"Bryan Garner's first venture in biography is both erudite and witty, and the influence he and the Justice had on each other makes for a wonderful and profitable read."

—HON. ROBERT HENRY
FORMER CHIEF JUDGE (RET.),
U.S. COURT OF APPEALS FOR THE TENTH CIRCUIT
PRESIDENT, OKLAHOMA CITY UNIVERSITY

"Bryan Garner's elegant *Nino and Me* captures both the essence and the details of a historic man as only a confidant could. Garner illustrates Justice Scalia's generosity and his temper, his panache and his idiosyncrasies, his charm and his fastidiousness—and nothing more completely than the Justice's love of English, the 'mother tongue,' which Garner reveals through private vignettes recounting the pair's many discussions spanning a decade. Those who have enjoyed the books that Justice Scalia and Garner jointly produced will find a new appreciation for the effort that those works required. Those who have not will learn what a fortunate pairing the two proved to be. And all will enjoy the benefit of what those who knew Justice Scalia wished for after he passed: a few more hours with the Justice, faithfully provided by a man who loved him well."

—JUDD STONE
MORGAN, LEWIS & BOCKIUS
LAW CLERK TO JUSTICE SCALIA, 2014–2015

"Bryan Garner has written a unique book steeped in affection for a truly mesmerizing person. It is deeply illuminating about the persona of 'Nino' Scalia. All future biographers will need to consult this book. But it is also a heartfelt, moving, and sometimes quite funny tale of a deep friendship forged initially by Garner's and Scalia's shared status as what David Foster Wallace labeled 'snoots,' obsessives about lexicography and grammar (about which Garner is a world-class expert with strong views). One does not have to be a snoot oneself—or even a devotee of Justice Scalia's jurisprudence—to appreciate the humanity of this book."

—SANFORD LEVINSON
W. ST. JOHN GARWOOD PROFESSOR OF LAW,
UNIVERSITY OF TEXAS
AUTHOR, *FRAMED: AMERICA'S 51 CONSTITUTIONS AND
THE CRISIS OF GOVERNANCE*

"Early in *Nino and Me*, one learns that a 'snoot' is someone who cares obsessively about words. Antonin Scalia and Bryan Garner were both snoots. This sparkling memoir of Professor Garner's collaboration with the Justice provides innumerable insights into grammar and usage, the law and advocacy, and how two strong-willed professional sticklers can nonetheless make a joint project work. Through it all, one comes to see the qualities that drew people to Justice Scalia regardless of whether they agreed with his jurisprudence."

—ERNEST YOUNG
ALSTON & BIRD PROFESSOR OF LAW,
DUKE LAW SCHOOL

"We all think we know Mr. Justice Scalia, whether as the hero of conservative jurisprudence or as the bogeyman of liberal nightmares. Bryan Garner, though, gives us Nino Scalia the man. It's refreshing to get a glimpse of the human side of one of our age's true intellectual giants, who could be equally passionate about the principles of constitutional interpretation and the merits of different editions of *Webster's* dictionaries.

"Garner gives us a portrait of the collaboration, and the occasional clash, of two champions of the English language—or 'snoots,' as they're called. *Nino and Me* is a surprisingly touching account of two friends who shared a legal philosophy, a devotion to clear communication, and a passionate commitment to 'snootitude.'"

—JACK LYNCH
PROFESSOR OF ENGLISH,
RUTGERS UNIVERSITY–NEWARK
AUTHOR, *YOU COULD LOOK IT UP* & *THE LEXICOGRAPHER'S DILEMMA*

"By the end of this book, those who never met the Justice will feel they know him well. But Garner's entertaining book does so much more: it explores the challenges and rewards of scholarly collaboration, it explains and defends the textualist approach to statutory and constitutional interpretation, and it captures the sheer joy that the two main characters derived from mastering the English language. Their shared ability to communicate with precision, concision, and verve makes this book a real page-turner."

—THOMAS R. PHILLIPS
FORMER CHIEF JUSTICE (RET.),
SUPREME COURT OF TEXAS
BAKER & BOTTS L.L.P.

Other Books by Bryan A. Garner

Reading Law: The Interpretation of Legal Texts with Justice Antonin
  Scalia

Making Your Case: The Art of Persuading Judges with Justice
  Antonin Scalia

*Quack This Way: David Foster Wallace and Bryan A. Garner Talk
  Language and Writing*

Garner's Modern English Usage

Garner on Language and Writing with foreword by Justice Ruth
  Bader Ginsburg

Black's Law Dictionary

The Law of Judicial Precedent with 12 appellate-judge coauthors,
  including Justice Neil M. Gorsuch; foreword by Justice
  Stephen Breyer

The Chicago Guide to Grammar, Usage, and Punctuation

Garner's Dictionary of Legal Usage with foreword by Judge Thomas
  M. Reavley

The Winning Brief

The Redbook: A Manual on Legal Style

Legal Writing in Plain English

The Elements of Legal Style with foreword by Charles Alan Wright

Guidelines for Drafting and Editing Legislation with foreword by
  Judge Harriet Lansing

Guidelines for Drafting and Editing Court Rules

The Winning Oral Argument

Ethical Communications for Lawyers

The Chicago Manual of Style, ch. 5, "Grammar and Usage"

HBR Guide to Better Business Writing

Securities Disclosure in Plain English

The Rules of Golf in Plain English with Jeffrey Kuhn

Bertie Gets It Right: Good Grammar for Kids and Their Parents

NINO
AND
ME

My Unusual Friendship
with Justice Antonin Scalia

BRYAN A. GARNER

THRESHOLD EDITIONS

New York   London   Toronto   Sydney   New Delhi

Threshold Editions
An Imprint of Simon & Schuster, Inc.
1230 Avenue of the Americas
New York, NY 10020

First Threshold Editions hardcover edition January 2018

THRESHOLD EDITIONS and colophon are trademarks of Simon & Schuster, Inc.

For information about special discounts for bulk purchases, please contact Simon & Schuster Special Sales at 1-866-506-1949 or business@simonandschuster.com.

The Simon & Schuster Speakers Bureau can bring authors to your live event. For more information, or to book an event, contact the Simon & Schuster Speakers Bureau at 1-866-248-3049 or visit our website at www.simonspeakers.com. For Bryan A. Garner in particular, contact LawProse Inc. at 214-691-8588 or visit www.lawprose.org.

Manufactured in the United States of America

10 9 8 7 6 5 4 3 2 1

Library of Congress Cataloging-in-Publication Data

Names: Garner, Bryan A., author.
Title: Nino and me : my unusual friendship with Justice antonin scalia /Bryan Garner.
Description: New York : Threshold Editions, 2018. | Includes index.
Identifiers: LCCN 2017037066 (print) | LCCN 2017037925 (ebook) | ISBN 9781501181504 (ebook) | ISBN 9781501181498 (hardback) | ISBN 9781501181511 (paperback)
Subjects: LCSH: Scalia, Antonin—Friends and associates. | Garner, Bryan A.—Friends and associates. | BISAC: BIOGRAPHY & AUTOBIOGRAPHY / Lawyers & Judges. | BIOGRAPHY & AUTOBIOGRAPHY / Personal Memoirs. | BIOGRAPHY & AUTOBIOGRAPHY / Political.
Classification: LCC KF8745.S33 (ebook) | LCC KF8745.S33 G37 2018 (print) | DDC 347.73/2634—dc23
LC record available at https://lccn.loc.gov/2017037066

ISBN 978-1-5011-8149-8
ISBN 978-1-5011-8151-1 (pbk)
ISBN 978-1-5011-8150-4 (ebook)

The names and details of the U.S. Marshals Service have been changed so as not to compromise their important work. Also, for the sake of simplicity, no distinction has been made between the U.S. Marshals Service and the Supreme Court Police; only insiders would notice, anyway.

Suggested musical pairing for those who read with background music: Edvard Grieg's *Peer Gynt*, Suite No. 1, Op. 46, and anything by Luigi Boccherini.

To the memory of
David Foster Wallace
(1962–2008),
without whose intervention the events recounted
after page 12 of this book could never have occurred

snoot /snüt/, n. (2001) [Acronym for either *syntax nudnik* (or *nerd*) *of our time* or *Sprachgefühl necessitates our ongoing tendance*] A person who cares intensely about words, usage, and grammar, and who adheres to a kind of enlightened prescriptivism that assesses language for its aptness, clarity, succinctness, and power. • The term was first used in print in the April 2001 issue of *Harper's Magazine*, in an essay entitled "Tense Present," by David Foster Wallace, who described it as familial jargon with more-positive connotations than the dysphemisms *grammar Nazi, usage nerd, syntax snob*, and *language police*.—Sometimes written as *SNOOT*.

Contents

Prelude

This story begins with three professional snoots: a novelist, a lexicographer, and a textualist judge. The novelist wrote a long essay entitled "Tense Present" about the lexicographer and his usage dictionary. As a result of that essay, the novelist and the lexicographer soon became friends, and the judge, having read the essay, became a fan of the novelist. Appreciating from afar the judge's linguistic virtuosity, the novelist suggested that the lexicographer seek out the judge. Those two soon became friends—and, what is more, collaborators. The lexicographer in turn suggested that the judge should meet the novelist. Those two liked each other as well. But soon there were only two snoots left: the lexicographer and the judge. Although some of the events that ensued in the following years may seem far-fetched, they are in every respect true—to the best of the lexicographer's ability to recollect and record.

Introduction

Antonin Scalia was a man of strong likes and dislikes: one was that he relished long paragraphs and recoiled from single-sentence ones.

He was at once conservative but nonconformist; temperamental but companionable; epicurean but admiring of asceticism; passionate but dutyconscious; thoughtful but unremorseful; rotund but athletic; ultracompetitive but compassionate; serious but often impish. At turns he could be jovial or tetchy; demanding or forgiving; taciturn or talkative; curmudgeonly or resigned; pugnacious or agreeable; stubborn or acquiescent. With his expressive, almost perfectly symmetrical face—his high forehead accentuated by hair neatly combed straight back, his ruddy cheeks that would crease into dimples when he grinned, his long philtrum above a protuberant lower lip, and the slightly cleft chin punctuating his squarish jaw—he was quick to smile when amused, and predisposed to guffaw with unreserved gusto. At five feet nine, he had a stocky frame with rounded shoulders, and he moved always with purpose, even determination. His burly, sun-spotted hands gesticulated with Sicilian flair. If something displeased him, his visceral reaction would almost instantly be clear to all present as a matter of body language before manifesting itself in words. He put a great deal of stock in a person's conversational skills: he appreciated good discussions and resented poor ones that wasted his time. He was a gifted raconteur whose mind was well stocked with pertinent stories and jokes, but he consciously avoided repeating any to listeners who had already heard them. He dreaded the idea of seeming trite and banal. He liked most things classical and detested most things newfangled. Upon the mere mention of the composer Edvard Grieg, he would burst into a boisterous rendition of "In the Hall of the Mountain King," a rousing movement of Grieg's *Peer Gynt*. His taste in popular music, on the other hand, ran only as far as the Andrews Sisters' "You Call Everybody Darling" (1948), and he felt impelled to leave a 2010 wedding reception when the band began playing something as "rock-'n'-rolly" as an early Beatles song. He liked unpretentious refinement and deplored the manners of what he called "yabbers"[1]—especially the incorrect grasping of a fork at table and the epidemic of men's wearing hats indoors, particularly at restaurants. He was a proudly old-fashioned man who took pleasure, upon mention of the latest fad, in declaring absolutely no knowledge of it.

Yet with nine children having entered various fields—including law, the clergy, the military, the humanities, and business—he was hardly out of touch: he well understood the more enduring features of American life. He was skeptical of people's motives but moderately susceptible to flattery. Although his mind was suspicious, his heart was welcoming—and the latter won most close conflicts. He was an intellectual *enfant terrible* of the right who relished "teaching against the class"—that is, affronting the complacent notions of politically committed people by pointing out uncomfortable truths incompatible with their ideas—especially if their ideas were left-leaning. His favorite rhetorical device was the *reductio ad absurdum*, and he was a relentless debater who could be defeated resoundingly only when he wasn't present. Bad press seemed to affect him not in the slightest. Never outwardly diffident, in private he was an intellectual pugilist who would sometimes retreat when confronted by a knowledgeable opponent

---

1   This noun seems to have been an idiosyncratic Scalianism*—one he used often. The closest recognized word is the Briticism *yobbo* (= a lout, yokel, or hoodlum). As an Australianism, the verb *yabber* means "to babble, jabber, or prate."

*   This will be the only footnote to a footnote—a nod to David Foster Wallace. As you will come to see, I am not a fan of substantive ("talky") footnotes, at least not in everyday lawyerly writing. But this isn't everyday lawyerly writing. My purpose here is to explain why I'm using the spelling *Scalianism* instead of either *Scaliaism* or *Scalia-ism*. The answer is partly that the English language is generally inhospitable to vowel clusters. *See Garner's Modern English Usage* 951 (4th ed. 2016) (s.v. "Vowel Clusters"). It is also partly that midword hyphens, when not necessary to prevent ambiguity, are aesthetically repellent—or, at least, are perceived this way by most readers of the American variety of Standard Written English. *See ibid.* at 751. The adjectival *Scalian*, meanwhile, is well attested in American English from 1982, and it sprang to great popularity in legal circles in the late 1990s. *Scalianism* makes every bit as much sense as the noun *Americanism*. We don't, after all, say *Americaism* or *America-ism*—likewise with *Australianism, Europeanism, Romanism,* and *Victorianism.*

whom he trusted. He was prone to what one of his colleagues called "summer thunderstorms"—temperamental outbursts that would pass quickly, leaving no remnant. What he admired he praised freely, but he never gave empty compliments. He reveled in words and knew their power, and his strong aesthetic sense flexed itself as much with language—even penmanship—as it did with music, architecture, and art. He had as many close female friends as male ones. He enjoyed the "manly" activities of hunting, cigar-smoking, and hearty eating and drinking. He was a trencherman. But he also knew his limits, disapproving gluttony and lauding those with the self-restraint to curb hedonistic pursuits.

He liked bright-line distinctions and clear rules; he abhorred blurred lines and fuzzy indecisiveness. Adoring of his parents, he rebelled against his father—if he rebelled at all—by becoming an even more devout Roman Catholic at a time when his father was an unbeliever. He preferred a Latin Mass on Sunday and bristled at Masses featuring folk music. As a teenager in New York, he had been something of a heartthrob on a TV show about adolescent etiquette. In a way that he could never have imagined then, he later became an intellectual heartthrob to many. But despite all the beautiful law-student devotees who sought him out for pictures and autographs at every public event, he was a husband of unwavering devotion with nothing but an amused chuckle and a signature for his young admirers. "Maureen knows all about my groupies!" he'd say with a grin. He loved the routine of doing yardwork alone and of playing poker regularly with friends.

Those who loved him did so with fervor and devotion; those inclined to loathe his ideas were more often than not disarmed by how much, upon meeting him, they were drawn to him—and at how cogent and intelligent his ideas were when fairly presented.

In perhaps the unlikeliest collaboration in the recent history of legal writing, we wrote two books together. We appeared onstage together more than 40 times, teaching, exhorting, admonishing, and trading gibes. We dined and traveled together. This book is my remembrance of him and our time together.

When he died in February 2016, we had before us three unbegun (or barely begun) projects: a series of ten or so videotaped interviews in which I would ask him *everything* about his life and philosophy (to be published posthumously in book form, we agreed); a three-volume collection of his speeches, which I had agreed to edit and had already sorted for him into three categories (law, religion, and civics); and a two-night engagement at Carnegie Hall, to be called "An Evening with Justice Antonin Scalia," in which he agreed to a pedagogical interview before a live audience: he would answer any question I might ask him in the two-hour presentation. Profits would be quietly given to Legal Aid because fundraising was not allowed (the gift would not be publicized in advance). Having begun our performances at the Kennedy Center for Performing Arts in 2008, we were both eager to book Carnegie Hall.

"Bryan," he told me when I agreed to edit his speeches, "the important thing is that we continue working together." This memoir is undertaken in the spirit of making good on that commitment. Although death ends a life, it doesn't end a friendship.

❧ ❧ ❧

In reflecting on her classic biography *Yankee from Olympus*, about Justice Oliver Wendell Holmes, the biographer Catherine Drinker Bowen wrote that many old friends of the great Justice resented her writing about him. In her words, they "owned Justice Holmes, or thought they did, lock, stock, and barrel."[2] Perhaps that comes with the long friendship of a great person. I certainly encountered it with some of Justice Scalia's friends and acquaintances. I've met many who knew him much longer than I did. One, a law professor, told me outright that she had tried to talk him out of collaborating with me because she thought he shouldn't have "conferred equality" on a non-Justice. Another told me that Justice Scalia detested his projects with me: "He's always complaining about working with you," she said.

I make no claims about the intensity of our friendship relative to others, and I certainly don't claim that the Justice Scalia I present in these pages is the only or the definitive version. He was a complex man. He was also a simple man, paradoxically enough. But he was definitely his own man. Nobody owned him.

It was one of the most fortunate and unlikely events of my own life to become his coauthor and, what is more important, his friend. This resulted, as you will see, from an audacious proposal on my part. And it almost went bad before it really started—through a serious misunderstanding. But I get

---

2   Catherine Drinker Bowen, *Adventures of a Biographer* 58 (1959).

ahead of myself. Having shared the relationship that I did with the man, I would feel remiss if I didn't share with his many admirers—as well as with anyone else who cares to learn more about him—the Antonin Scalia I came to know so well.

You will notice that the book is replete with direct quotations. While it would be foolish to claim that they are all verbatim, I can say with assurance that all the conversations took place, that many are indeed word for word, and that the rest are at least close. I had the benefit of diaries and notes I've kept over the years. Also, as I often told Justice Scalia, I considered every visit or trip with him an important event. So I was exceedingly alert to him and have a vivid recollection of our discussions. I invoke the astute admonition of the English writer C. P. Snow, who observed in reference to a memoir: "When I report remarks in direct speech, I believe that my memory is accurate, and that they were said in those words, or in words closely similar. I have a pretty good memory, but not a freakish one. I have never met anyone who can totally recall a long conversation over a period of hours, much less of years."[3] Nevertheless, Snow said, the remarks had stuck in his memory, and he could vouch for them even though they had been made in the course of long conversations. The decision to include dialogue in this book was an easy one: without Justice Scalia's spoken words, the book would have presented a sterile, abstract picture of an immensely dynamic man—which in itself would have been an unjust portrayal.

I mean to follow the example of Samuel Johnson's biographer, James Boswell, who insisted that his subject should "be seen as he really was."[4] He explained: "I profess to write, not his panegyric, which must be all praise, but [a part of] his Life; which, great and good as he was, must not be supposed to be entirely perfect. To be as he was, is indeed subject of panegyric enough to any man in this state of being; but in every picture there should be shade as well as light."[5]

The pages of this book firmly disprove what George Bernard Shaw's biographer wrote: "The later years of any great man are known to everybody who reads newspapers."[6] Little of what is printed here would be known

---

3   C. P. Snow, *Variety of Men* xi (1967).

4   1 *Boswell's Life of Johnson* 30 ([1791] George Birkbeck Hill ed., L. F. Powell rev., 1934).

5   *Id.*

6   Frank Harris, *Bernard Shaw* xx (1931).

to posterity but for its appearance in these pages—although some might say that the broad strokes were pretty apparent. Even that is questionable. Everything that matters emerges from the details, and readers should be able to make up their own minds. Perhaps all that can be asked—all that I ask, and I believe all that my late coauthor would have asked—is that if the text is to be read, it should be given a fair reading. Of course, "fair reading" is the method of interpretation about which he and I ended up writing copiously.[7]

---

7   See generally Antonin Scalia & Bryan A. Garner, *Reading Law: The Interpretation of Legal Texts* (2012) (especially pp. 33–41).

1

Preliminary Glimpses

(1988–2005)

In December 1988, at the age of 30, I was a featured speaker at the British Embassy in Washington, D.C., introduced by the British ambassador, Sir Antony Acland. Oxford University Press had agreed to join forces with the University of Texas to create the Texas/Oxford Center for Legal Lexicography, and I was named its director. In its most imposing, highly decorated hall, the Embassy was helping to promote this Anglo-American enterprise. I had brought the deal together by negotiating to have the Press and the university sponsor what was planned to become *The Oxford Law Dictionary*—which would have been the first and only historical law dictionary, something along the lines of *The Oxford English Dictionary*. At this event, I'd have about ten minutes to explain the project.

For me, one of the most exciting prospects of that evening was that Justice Antonin Scalia would be attending, and I looked forward to meeting him. Although he had been on the U.S. Supreme Court only two years, he was already acknowledged to be its most adroit wordsmith. For example, in a judicial opinion just months before, he had used the lexicographer's arcane phrase *hapax legomenon* (denoting a word that appears only once within a corpus of writings). He was famous for his command of the English language, his flair for metaphor, and his unremitting argumentative rigor.

As I spoke that evening, Justice Scalia stood toward the back of the audience of 100, flanked by Robert Strauss, the powerful Dallas/Washington Democrat, who had somehow managed to drape himself across the top of a couch, and Senator Lloyd Bentsen of Texas, who at the vice-presidential debate just months earlier had delivered the memorably scathing riposte to the young Senator Dan Quayle: "I knew Jack Kennedy. Senator, you're no Jack Kennedy." So there was a good deal of excitement about Bentsen's presence as well—even though he and Michael Dukakis had just lost the presidential election.

People at the event seemed enthusiastic about this monumental lexicographic undertaking. At the conclusion of the speakers' remarks, I was determined to meet Justice Scalia and shake his hand. Drinks had been served, and I was being approached all around by lawyers and academics. I made my way to the back of the chatter-filled room, where the Justice was deep in conversation with Strauss and Bentsen. Closed off in a triangle, they were chuckling among themselves. I paused about ten feet away, thinking that great affairs of state might be their subject, and I shouldn't intrude.

A few people were beginning to leave, but I was still being greeted by well-wishers: I had simply brought them to the back of the room with me. Finally, I excused myself from my immediate company and walked up to the three men. I was, after all, the reason for this get-together, and I thought they might welcome my greeting them. "Senator Bentsen, I'm Bryan Garner. So glad you could come." I shook hands with all three. "Mr. Strauss. Justice Scalia, it's great to know of your interest in the dictionary project."

"It sounds promising," Justice Scalia said, smiling politely.

They immediately turned back into their triangular huddle and resumed their discussion. A theater director would describe their "blocking," or positioning of their bodies, as discouraging any further interruptions. And I believe there were none for the next ten minutes, until the cocktail party broke up.

Two years later, the Texas/Oxford Center for Legal Lexicography and *The Oxford Law Dictionary* broke up, too—quietly and unceremoniously, for insufficient funding. I would continue my work on dictionaries, but in different forms and without university sponsorships. I came to know Robert Strauss pretty well while teaching seminars at his D.C. office in the 1990s and early 2000s, but I never again saw Senator Bentsen. And I figured I might never again see Justice Scalia.

In late 1990, after the ignominious scuttling of the dictionary project, I turned entrepreneurial and founded the Dallas-based LawProse Inc., under whose aegis I began offering seminars on advocacy and transactional drafting. LawProse became an early success: within the first year, demand became fairly constant, and I was flying throughout the United States to lead seminars at law firms, corporate legal departments, and government agencies. These engagements—and, more important, the several books I published on legal writing and advocacy, as well as on English grammar and usage—raised my profile in the legal community. By the mid-1990s, I was invited to become editor in chief of *Black's Law Dictionary*. Over the several unabridged editions that followed, I tried to make *Black's Law Dictionary* a reputable source of legal scholarship. Essentially, it's now close to what I would have produced had I completed *The Oxford Law Dictionary*.

Although I had no contact with Justice Scalia during this time, I admired him and his writing. Like every American lawyer, I read about him whenever he would write or say something noteworthy—which was often.

In 1995, I was asked to revise the Rules of the Supreme Court of the United States—not quite by the Court itself, but by an arm of the U.S. Judicial Conference. I had just played the lead role in revising the Federal Rules of Appellate Procedure, and some of the federal judges, appreciating my work, "volunteered" my services to the Supreme Court. One major feature of my revisions had been to eliminate the word *shall* from the rules: it is notoriously ambiguous in legal drafting and therefore a frequent source of argument and even litigation. I apportioned its various responsibilities among *must*, *will*, *is*, and *may*, depending on context and meaning. To explain my editorial approach, I had written a little booklet for the U.S. government: *Guidelines for Drafting and Editing Court Rules*.[8]

Upon submitting my handwritten edits of the Supreme Court Rules, I learned that Justice Scalia and Justice Ruth Bader Ginsburg, the latter of whom I had known since 1992, were on the Court's rules committee, along with Justice John Paul Stevens. I imagined they might have spent a day or so combing through my copious hand-marked edits, with marginal annotations keyed to my *Guidelines*. They rejected almost all my edits on the first few pages and then accepted almost all of them after that. I was fascinated: it was as if their resistance to being edited had been gradually worn down.

---

8   http://www.uscourts.gov/sites/default/files/guide.pdf.

Chief Justice William H. Rehnquist alerted the lower federal judges who had offered my services that Justice Scalia was staunchly opposed to my deletions of the word *shall*. Today, *shall* has been almost entirely removed from the various sets of federal rules—except for those of the U.S. Supreme Court.

I never use the word myself.

2

The Breakfast and the Interview

(2006)

Over the years, nearly 200,000 lawyers and judges have attended my various seminars. Teaching and traveling allowed me to make friends in all the major American cities, most of which I visit several times a year. For someone with a schedule like mine, Dallas is the perfect place to live: I can lecture from 9 o'clock to 4 almost anywhere in the country and still see my family that night. Travel is comparatively easy for someone whose routine entails it and whose bags always stay packed.

By 2006, I'd been going at this pace for 15 years and had written more than a dozen books. In my teaching, I began doing something I had long yearned to do: incorporating short video clips of interviews I'd conducted with judges, influential lawyers, and major writers. The snippets reinforced the points I was making about language and writing. I'd started the project of filming interviews in 2004, and by the spring of 2006 nearly 180 interviewees were in my film archives.

In early 2006, after filming my interview in Los Angeles with the noted novelist and essayist David Foster Wallace, David and I went to eat at McCormick & Schmick's restaurant, then on South Hope Street.[9] David had driven 90 minutes or so from Claremont to downtown Los Angeles. He seemed contented that evening, and I was happy to see him in such good form. He'd given up his trademark bandanna, and he seemed much calmer and more confident than when I'd seen him before. We had a good long talk. He seemed like a regular guy—not like the most revered novelist of

---

9 The full events of that evening are recorded in the book *Quack This Way: David Foster Wallace and Bryan A. Garner Talk Language and Writing* (2013).

his generation, the author of the famously thick and difficult book *Infinite Jest*.

Reflecting on the interview and thinking of other potential interviewees, he volunteered that he'd like to help me get an interview with his friend Jonathan Franzen. Then he said: "Have you interviewed Justice Scalia?"

"No. I've thought of that."

"Do you know him?"

"Met him once at the British Embassy—years ago."

"You should interview him."

"If only I could. Well, I'll try. Maybe I'll write him."

That casual conversation firmed up my resolve: I'd invite the Justice to do a filmed interview. After all, I'd already interviewed federal judges on all the circuit benches and lots of state appellate judges. I'd interviewed such august names in the legal field as Frank Easterbrook, Alex Kozinski, and Richard Posner. Perhaps I should be aiming at the U.S. Supreme Court. I assumed it might be considerably harder. With most federal judges, I'd just call chambers, get through to the judge (usually by identifying myself as the editor in chief of *Black's Law Dictionary*), and ask for an on-camera interview. I served as my own camera crew, and I had gotten pretty good both at filming and at asking questions that would elicit useful, sometimes dramatic answers. There was no reason I shouldn't use the same techniques for Supreme Court Justices, even if the initial approach had to be more formal than my usual 24-hour notice.

So on March 26, 2006, I faxed and mailed a letter requesting an interview:

Dear Justice Scalia:

In November of last year, I started a project of interviewing federal and state judges on the art of writing—on everything from briefs to law reviews to judicial opinions. I intersperse brief video clips in my lectures to law students, lawyers, and judges.

 I'm on record as saying you're our top judicial stylist (see Oxford Companion to the U.S. Supreme Court [2d ed. 2005] at 710). *So naturally I'd very much like to interview you.*

 Although I'd be willing to travel any weekend to conduct an interview with you, the ideal times for me right now would be 4:30 or 5:00 p.m. on a day when I will be giving seminars in Washington: June 21, June 22, or June 23. Might you be available on one of those dates? The interview will last about 45 minutes.

Enclosed are two of my recent books. The first is The Winning Brief *(2d ed. 2003), which I believe has much material that will interest you. Second is my* Modern American Usage, *an alphabetically arranged treatment of grammar and usage. I know that you're a fan of Fowler. So am I, and I try (in what is undoubtedly an inferior imitation) to do the kind of work that Fowler would do if he were still alive.*

Please let me know if an interview would be possible. It would be great seeing you again: I haven't seen you since we met at the British Embassy in 1988.

Sincerely,
Bryan Garner

His response came more than a month later, in a letter dated May 5, 2006—by which time the invitation seemed to me like a distant memory. He thanked me for the books, especially *Modern American Usage*, and expressed admiration for "anyone who holds firm on *imply* and *infer*." But he said he'd pass on the video interview. Nevertheless, he said he'd like to speak with me informally about *shall* vs. *must* (calling my position "Jacobin") and suggested that I get in touch with Angela, his secretary, to arrange for a lunch.

Hmm. He wanted to talk about *shall*—or, rather, about my mostly successful efforts to supplant it with *must* in federal rules. Surprisingly, I thought, he seemed open to the possibility that I might convince him of the inadvisability of using *shall* in rule-drafting. Although I was disappointed about his declining a filmed interview, I figured that having a meal with him would be fun.

We agreed to meet for breakfast at 10:00 a.m. on June 23 at the Four Seasons in Georgetown. He also agreed that my daughter Caroline, who was interning at the U.S. Senate that summer, could join us. A mature 19, Caroline was a self-possessed young woman whose interest in history and literature, together with her affable ease, meant she could hold her own in any conversation.

The Most Important Meal

Caroline and I arrived at 9:30 and went to the restaurant early to ensure that we had a more or less secluded table. We tipped the hostess $20 and asked her not to seat anyone else near us, if possible. Then we went back to the front of the hotel and waited. At precisely 10:00, a black SUV drove up, and Justice Scalia emerged from the backseat. Caroline and I walked out to meet him.

"Hello, Justice Scalia."

"Hello, Bryan. Good to see you."

"This is Caroline. She's just completed her first year at Yale."

A loyal Harvard man, he grinned. "Sorry to hear that. Are they brainwashing you there, Caroline?"

"Probably. But I had a good year."

"What are you studying?"

"History, mostly European."

On our way down to the restaurant, Caroline mentioned that she had recently attended a lecture at the Supreme Court that Justice Scalia had given for Washington interns. I added that I'd heard that some of the questions he'd received were boneheaded. No, he said, they really weren't so bad. Our conversation was easy. He wasn't a self-conscious man.

"I'm curious about what you do," Justice Scalia said as we reached the table. "You must be awfully proud of *Black's Law Dictionary*. The seventh and eighth editions have been superb. But you're not one of these anything-goes dictionary writers, are you, like the people who did *Webster's Third*?"

"Far from it," I said, "but in *Black's Law Dictionary*, the question of prescriptivism versus descriptivism doesn't come up much. In my usage dictionaries, that question is very much at the fore. And in those books I'm unabashedly prescriptivist—though I use descriptive methods by citing lots of evidence."

We had plunged straight into this conversation, barely interrupting ourselves to order coffee and breakfast.

"Caroline," I said, "did you notice just now Justice Scalia's reference to *Webster's Third*? He much prefers *Webster's Second*."

"Yes, I do!" he said. "It had standards. *Webster's Third*, the 1961 edition, eliminated most of the usage labels. The editors accept *infer* as a synonym of *imply*!"

"We're a *Webster's Second* kind of family," said Caroline.

"Really?" Justice Scalia asked with mild surprise.

"Yes. I'm afraid I've spent hundreds of hours with it," she said.

"How can that be?" asked Justice Scalia, looking as if he was on the verge of laughter.

"Starting when I was 11, my dad hired me to mark a copy of *Webster's Second*—underlining every legal term in the book. I was looking for 'Law' tags."

"What?" he said, chuckling incredulously. "That sounds like child exploitation."

"I got a dollar for every legal term I found," Caroline said.

"She loved the J's," I said. "And the L's weren't bad. She made quite a bit of money."

"Why would you do that?" Justice Scalia asked me.

"Because *Webster's Second*, first published in 1934, is particularly strong in its treatment of legal terms. The great Roscoe Pound of Harvard Law was special consultant to Merriam-Webster, and he did an extraordinary job."

"So your work, Caroline," said Justice Scalia, "was helpful to your father in *Black's Law Dictionary*?"

"Well, I sure hope so!" she said, laughing.

"You must have learned lots of things just spending hours and hours scouring the pages of that great dictionary."

"I think so—though I couldn't tell you what."

"So," Justice Scalia said, turning back to me, "*Webster's Second* was reasonably prescriptivist, and *Webster's Third* became wildly descriptivist—without any judgments about right and wrong."

"The point," I said, "is simply to make linguistic assessments that accord with linguistic realities. In the past, lexicographers often just guessed, and grammarians recommended wordings that no significant part of the population actually used. It's no use saying that *self-deprecation* is wrong and *self-depreciation* is correct if no one actually says it."

"*Self-depreciation*? Who recommends that?"

"Fowler, for one."

"I *love* H. W. Fowler."

"So do I," I said, "but he's quite dated on lots of points, like the term *self-depreciation*. I have essentially the same sensibility as Fowler, but I write with the benefit of more linguistic data."

"But Fowler was so *witty*. No one compares to him there. 'The writer who produces an ungrammatical, an ugly, or even a noticeably awkward phrase, and lets us see that he has done it in trying to get rid of something else that he was afraid of, gives a worse impression of himself than if he had risked our catching him in his original misdemeanor.' That's fantastic."

"Yes, it is," I said. "Fowler's my hero. That's from his entry 'Out of the Frying Pan.'" I was astonished that he could recite it by memory.

"You know that!" Justice Scalia leaned back and grinned.

"Of course. It's classic."

"How do you know Fowler so well?"

"By 18, before leaving for college, I had committed to memory about everything in the usage books by Fowler, Bernstein, and Partridge. I was obsessed by their writing."

"You know this stuff much better than I do."

"I do it professionally. But you're the legal writer everyone admires."

Justice Scalia chuckled. "You know, I got it from my father," he said. "He was a professor of Romance languages in Brooklyn. He really inculcated in me an appreciation for language. Even when I became a judge on the D.C. Circuit, he would correct my opinions after they were published."

"He must have been awfully proud. Did he live to see you become a Supreme Court Justice?"

"No. Both he and my mother died shortly before. I've always regretted that."

"Oh, I'm so sorry to hear that. How did your father correct your opinions?"

"He was a stickler for the subjunctive mood of the verb. The D.C. Circuit had a form order that said: 'It is ordered that the district court's judgment *is* reversed.' My father insisted that it should be subjunctive after the verb *ordered*. So it should have been *It is ordered that the district court's judgment be reversed*. You see?"

"Yes. Your father was right."

The conversation continued in this vein for quite some time. Caroline asked how much of the writing in opinions is actually done by the Justices, noting that in senators' offices, all sorts of papers and letters get sent out without the senators' direct knowledge. Justice Scalia said that conditions aren't anything like that at the Court, but he acknowledged that he used clerks to do his first drafts. I remarked that he certainly put his own stylistic stamp on opinions to a greater degree than any other Justice.

He agreed, but added that law clerks at the Supreme Court often come up with good stuff on their own—they are top students who have proved their talents, and they're trying hard to match his voice. He mentioned an opinion that would soon be coming out in which he used the phrase *turtles all the way down*. He asked whether either of us knew the allusion. We didn't.

He explained that it's part of our cultural heritage, with a long provenance in religion and philosophy. It alludes to a myth that the world rests on the back of an elephant, and the elephant is said to rest on a turtle. "And what's under the turtle?" comes the inevitable question. "Well, it's turtles all the way down." Justice Scalia had used the phrase a week before to characterize the reasoning in a concurring opinion by Justice Anthony Kennedy as a sort of infinite regression.[10]

I ventured my assessment that Justice Kennedy's writing is prone to errors such as his misspelling of *de minimis* (he wrote *-us*) during the previous term, followed by a subject–verb agreement error in the very next sentence. Justice Scalia was discreetly noncommittal about these points. I took it that he would not be drawn into any private criticism of a colleague—whatever he might say in dissent. He suggested that I call the Reporter of Decisions to get these errors cleaned up before they appeared in the *United States Reports*.

Lightening the conversation for a bit, Justice Scalia turned to my daughter and said: "You know, Caroline, I think breakfast is the most important meal of the day. It's my favorite. What do you think?"

"I've never been big on breakfast," she said.

"I just *love* breakfast. If I don't have it, I'm unhappy for the rest of the day. How about you, Bryan?"

"Well, I know it's supposed to be an important meal, but I often write early in the morning, and I tend to get so caught up with it that I end up missing breakfast."

"Hmm. I can't do without it."

But Justice Scalia wasn't finished with our conversation about language and writing. "Now, back to Fowler," he said, resuming our earlier thread. "I

---

10 *Rapanos v. United States*, 547 U.S. 715, 754 (2006).

give copies of *Modern English Usage* to my law clerks every year. You know, there's a word for people like you and me—people who care a lot about words. What is it? It was in a magazine a few years ago. Do you know it?"

"Snoot," I said.

"Yes, *snoot*! This man wrote an article about it."

"Yes, in *Harper's*."

"Right! It's the most amazing piece. My son Christopher is getting his Ph.D. in English at Wisconsin, and he put me onto it. Have you read it?"

"Yes, it's by David Foster Wallace."

"Right! That's the guy. I *love* that piece. And it's a perfect word: *snoot*." He gestured with thumb and forefinger as the word left his lips, adding: "We didn't really have a good word for it."

"No, we didn't."

"Have you read this article, Caroline?"

"Yes, sir." She smiled knowingly.

"You're smiling," Justice Scalia said.

I explained: "That Wallace essay is really a long review of my book, *A Dictionary of Modern American Usage*."[11]

"What? Really? Ooooh. Your stock has just gone *way* up in my eyes."

"Thank you. It was a very flattering piece, and I was honored that he wrote it. We've become friends since that was published."

"My son Christopher would love to hear that."

This seemed like a good time to bring up one matter I wanted to hash out with him. I asked whether he really disliked the word *must* in place of *shall*. He replied that *shall* has been used as an imperative for hundreds of years without any problem at all, and he asked for my objections.

There *have* been problems in statutes and contracts, I said. Lots of them. I cited some typical sentences in which *shall* has variously meant "is," "is entitled to," "will," and "may." I even cited the opinion by Justice Ginsburg in which she noted that *shall* has been held to have all these meanings.[12] I told him that at least half the *shall*s in U.S. statutes don't mean "is required to." They're not mandatory at all.

---

11 A very slightly different account is that I said, "Sir, that essay is a review of my book." Alex Carp, "Writing with Antonin Scalia, Grammar Nerd," *The New Yorker*, 16 July 2012, http://www.newyorker.com/news/news-desk/writing-with-antonin-scalia-grammar-nerd.

12 *Gutierrez de Martinez v. Lamagno*, 515 U.S. 417, 434 n.9 (1995).

Justice Scalia seemed a little surprised.

I reminded him that the U.S. Supreme Court had issued new rules in 1996—and that I had been asked to help in that revision. He nodded, as if remembering. I said that I had understood that the Court wanted to keep *shall* but that I had tried to ensure that in every instance it meant "is required to." Even so, I remarked, the Supreme Court Style Committee (which he served on) had allowed at least one instance of *shall* meaning "may" to persist in the rules. He was curious about that—and noticeably skeptical.

When I said that lawyers aren't educable on the subject of *shall*, he agreed rather provisionally: "Well, you're probably right. But *must* is a harsh word that doesn't fall well on the ears."

As our conversation went on, Justice Scalia began reeling off word issues that he thought I should touch on in my writings about English usage and legal usage, including *such that* (where *such* has no antecedent) for *so that*, and *susceptible of* vs. *susceptible to* (which I told him I'd written about). He explained to Caroline that *susceptible of* means "capable of" whereas *susceptible to* means "vulnerable to."

I mentioned that he is more fastidious than most of his colleagues about hyphenating phrasal adjectives. He replied that many people who write stylebooks are unknowledgeable and don't understand that *well done* shouldn't be hyphenated because *well* is an adverb. I explained the *-ly* exception to the phrasal-adjective rule, positing that *well done* should in fact be hyphenated when it's used before the noun (*well-done steaks*) because flat adverbs like *well* don't immediately reveal themselves as adverbs, but *-ly* adverbs do. He didn't like the distinction.

Motion for Rehearing

There was a pause in the conversation as we ate our breakfast. "You must be busy just about now, getting out opinions for the end of the term," I said.

"Yes, though mostly now it's dissents. I'm going straight to the office after we finish, to work on some dissents."

We had nearly cleaned our plates, but I didn't want this breakfast to come to an end.

"Justice Scalia . . . is there really no way I could persuade you to sit for an interview?"

"I don't want to do an interview. I'm sorry. But I do want to stay in touch . . . Well . . . what kinds of questions would you ask?"

"What are the most common failings in briefs? Should judicial opinions be shorter? Why are transitions so important? What do you think of footnotes in different types of writing? How could law reviews be improved? Why do you begin so many sentences with *and* and *but*?"

Then I stumbled onto a breakthrough: "I think Chief Justice Roberts is going to do an interview." I had been working on scheduling that interview as well.

"I'll tell you what. If you get the Chief Justice to do an interview, I'll do an interview."

I said nothing. I just smiled and looked him in the eye.

"Ah, what the heck," he said. "I'll do an interview. You can set it up with Angela, my secretary."

"Thank you, Justice Scalia."

There was an awkward silence for about 30 seconds as Justice Scalia finished his eggs Benedict. When he was done, he asked Caroline more about her experience at Yale. He explained that he had stopped hiring law clerks from Yale because the school didn't give reliable grades: 40% of the class received H, meaning "honors," so it was hard to tell exactly what quality of clerks he was attracting, he said. I asked whether grades are the best predictor of success. He said they are.

Somehow we got around to the subject of judicial pay. I mentioned how horrible it is that clerks get paid more, right after their clerkships, than Justices themselves do. Not only that: according to Justice Scalia, they each get bonuses of $220,000 when accepting those jobs. That was 2006. It's more now. But even then, the law clerks were making three times the salaries of their former bosses.

Justice Scalia called Congress "craven" when it comes to raising judicial salaries, or even their own salaries.

I told him that I'd been in Thailand when President Reagan appointed him to the Supreme Court—and that I'd never forget the announcement on Bangkok radio. He mentioned again that his parents had both died within a short period just before the appointment. "You know, you accomplish something really good, and you want to share it with your parents. That was really the only thing that cast a pall over that period in my life."

Changing the subject, after a respectful pause, I ventured that there was one thing he might do to make his judicial opinions appreciably better. That piqued his attention. I suggested that although I'm generally against footnotes, he should start putting all citations in footnotes. I took him through the history of Spottswood Robinson (once his chief judge on the D.C. Circuit), John Minor Wisdom, and Alvin Rubin, and how they all footnoted citations so as to remove all the bibliographic gunk from their paragraphs.

"I might just be the only one on the Court crazy enough to try it."

"My thought exactly," I replied.

He gave a big belly-laugh.

"Well," I said, "I mean that you might be the only one on the Court *bold* enough to try it."

I told him that as the Court's stylistic bellwether and the most influential stylist in modern legal writing, he could precipitate a huge stride forward in legal writing by relegating bibliographic data to footnotes. He said he'd experiment with it.

But then he backtracked, saying that readers sometimes get important information from those citations. I conceded the point but said that all the truly important information could be—even should be—worked into the text. I pressed a bit hard. He said he'd try it.

Changing the subject, Justice Scalia asked Caroline about her sister, Alexandra. Caroline said that Alexandra was in middle school at the Hockaday School in Dallas—where Caroline had also gone. I asked about his children. He had nine: five boys and four girls. He said it's hard to raise that kind of family on professorial and then government salaries. He kiddingly suggested that my wife and I weren't doing our job in keeping up with the 2.3-children average in American households, adding that he and his wife had more than made up for our slacking.

"Now I need to get to work on some dissents!" Justice Scalia said. He seemed suddenly restless. It was 11:30 a.m. Although we'd been talking for about 90 minutes, it hardly seemed like 20. Justice Scalia invited Caroline to be his guest at Supreme Court proceedings and to sit in one of his "box seats." He gave me his home address. This, he said, would work better for correspondence because anthrax screening seemed to hold up all Court mail for up to a month. He also gave me his office phone number, saying: "Call Angela and set things up with her. I've enjoyed it. See you again soon." The marshals whisked him away in the SUV.

The next day, I penned a handwritten note and enclosed a copy of David Foster Wallace's *Consider the Lobster*:

Dear Justice Scalia,

Caroline and I thoroughly enjoyed our breakfast with you yesterday at the Four Seasons. What splendid conversation. Thank you for taking the time.

I'll be in touch soon about two points (interview, citations), but I hasten to send you the locus classicus *for SNOOT, in its unexpurgated form (Harper's had foreshortened it severely). See esp. pp. 69–70. Don't take pp. 118–20 too seriously. That part is turtles all the way down.*

How nice of you to invite Caroline to Supreme Court proceedings.

All best,
Bryan

Justice Scalia immediately made good on his invitation to Caroline. On Wednesday, June 28, he had her in the box seats reserved for the Justice's guests. Opinions were announced from the bench that day. Two days later I wrote a letter thanking him for his generosity, adding: "She thoroughly enjoyed the proceedings, especially since the Texas redistricting case was on the calendar that day. That afternoon, she visited for 45 minutes in chambers with Justice Ginsburg. It's been a heady summer for her."

Planning the Interview

On July 1, Justice Scalia wrote me a two-page letter in which he agreed to be added to my "Rogues' Gallery of videotaped judicial writers." He went on, at some length, to say that I had persuaded him on neither the eradication of *shall* nor footnoted citations. He closed by thanking me for *Consider the Lobster*, adding: "I look forward to seeing you soon."

In a fascinating footnote to his letter, he suggested something to replace my campaign for footnoted citations. If I was going to insist on pursuing "Jacobin novelties," he proposed including parentheticals to indicate both great judges and judges who are "notoriously stupid and result-oriented."

He explained that when federal circuit-court opinions dealing with some areas of the law were cited, the names of certain authors—"I shrink from identifying them, but you know who they are"—flagged the opinion as almost certainly wrong. Because, of course, one man's dummy may be another man's genius, we would necessarily have to indicate our flattering or deprecatory intent—perhaps by appending "a 'G' or a 'D' to the name, thusly: '(Smith, J. [D]).' "

I refrained, in response, from pointing out that *thusly* is a barbarism, *thus* itself being an adverb. That would have involved pointing out that in the 1995 edition of my legal-usage book, I had taken him to task on this very point.[13] Given the many things that we were going back and forth on, the "genius"/"dummy" designation, which I was sure he meant tongue in cheek, is something we never pursued further.

By August, we had arranged the date for the interview: October 2, 2006. That was the first day of the new Supreme Court term. The interview would take place in the Lawyers' Lounge, just opposite the Marshal's Office. In the run-up to the interview, I spoke mostly with the Public Information Office (PIO, as they say), run by Kathy Arberg—a real pro, and a friendly one at that.

I remembered Ms. Arberg, but I wondered whether she remembered me: we had been mentioned alongside each other in the *New York Times* five years earlier, in July 2001. The *Times* had run a front-page article about my urging judges, especially appellate judges, to put their citations in footnotes—the very point that I had discussed with Justice Scalia during our breakfast. It was somehow controversial enough and interesting enough to make the front page in a Sunday edition—above the fold! When someone had noted that Supreme Court Justices don't footnote their citations, I commented: "Although I have the highest respect for the Justices of the U.S. Supreme Court, most of their opinions cannot be held up as literary models by any means." When the journalist responsible for this lead article, William Glaberson, had called the PIO to ask Ms. Arberg about the issue, she declined to comment. Here we were five years later, I thought.

The interview was to take place at 2:00 p.m., and I was to arrive by 1:00. All I had was a video camera, two pages of questions (not disclosed in advance), and my briefcase with an Antonin Scalia bobblehead inside. I

---

13   Bryan A. Garner, *A Dictionary of Modern Legal Usage* 881–82 (2d ed. 1995).

had brought it, together with a Sharpie pen, to ask Justice Scalia to auto-graph it for me.

It turned out that the PIO official who met me wasn't Kathy Arberg after all but instead her amiable chief deputy, Patricia McCabe (now Patricia Estrada). She took me into the Lawyers' Lounge, showed me where to plug in my camera, and chatted with me as I got my equipment set up. She made sure that both Justice Scalia and I had side tables with water, that his chair would be comfortable, that the camera angles were acceptable (I put Chief Justice William Howard Taft's portrait squarely in the shot's background), and that signs outside the door warned passersby that an interview was in progress. She was perfectly genial, and though I was keyed up about interviewing Justice Scalia, she made me feel at ease. We had ten minutes before showtime.

Pulling out a box from my briefcase, I said, "I brought along Justice Scalia's bobblehead to ask him to sign it."

The Supreme Court bobbleheads had been commissioned by the *Green Bag*, a law journal edited by Professor Ross Davies of George Mason School of Law. The Scalia bobblehead is a pretty good likeness. It shows him wearing wire-rimmed glasses, standing in his judicial robes atop a copy of *Webster's Second New International Dictionary* (1934). In his left hand is a red pencil plunged down into an enormous lemon, symbolizing his skewering of the *Lemon* test for assessing Establishment Clause violations. In his right hand is a copy of volume 483 of the *United States Reports*, which contains his memorable words about the negative commerce clause. A wolf stands at his side, recalling his statement that in draining the powers of the executive branch, a particular statute wasn't a wolf in sheep's clothing: "This wolf comes as a wolf."[14]

Patricia frowned a little. "What? What's *that*?"

"The *Green Bag* makes these," I said. "Haven't you seen them?" I lifted the box so she could have a better look.

Without answering, she rushed from the room. Oh no, I thought. I've done something wrong. I put the bobblehead back into my briefcase. She stayed gone until 2:00 p.m., when she opened the door for Justice Scalia, who bounded in ahead of her: "Hello, Bryan! Where do you want me to sit?"

---

14 *Morrison v. Olson*, 487 U.S. 654, 699 (1988).

The Interview

"Right here, Justice Scalia."

"You're by yourself? No camera crew?" He sat down.

"All by myself. We're just going to have an informal conversation on camera. It'll be best if you simply look at me while we talk, not at the camera. The perfect answer is 30 to 90 seconds. But please be expansive whenever you like."

"Okay. I can do that."

"I'll turn the camera on, if you're ready."

The interview was scheduled to last 45 minutes, but he seemed to enjoy it so much that he extended it twice—which I welcomed, naturally. It was a meaty interview with a lot of thoughtful discussion about legal advocacy.[15] We also had some lighthearted exchanges. At one point, I asked him whether current opinions of the Supreme Court could be cut in half with a benefit. "Some . . . Some," he replied, nodding. "You don't want me to name names, do you?" We both laughed.

At one point I got off a zinger he'd never heard. He was complaining about legalese such as *nexus* and *instant case* and *informs our consideration*. Then he mentioned the "terribly trite" *Marbury v. Madison and its progeny*. He hated "progeny."

I deadpanned, "What do you think about the law-review author who wrote about '*Roe v. Wade* and its progeny'?" It took him a second, but then he chuckled without further comment.

We spent some time talking about David Foster Wallace and his term *snoot*. He had remembered our first discussion about the term when we'd met for breakfast, and he began to elaborate. "Snoots are those who are nitpickers for the mot juste, for using a word precisely the way it should be used—not dulling it by misuse. I'm a snoot, I confess." He explained that he acquired this trait from his father and asked, "Can I tell a story?" He wanted to repeat for the camera the story he'd told over breakfast.

"Absolutely," I answered. I was delighted that the interview was going so well. Justice Scalia was settling in and seemed to be enjoying it, too.

"My father was a linguist. He taught Romance languages at Brooklyn

---

15 All the interviews of Supreme Court Justices can be seen at http://www.lawprose.org /bryan-garner/garners-interviews/supreme-court-interviews/.

College. He used to read my opinions when I was on the court of appeals and correct my grammar," he said with a chuckle.

"The D.C. Circuit used to conclude all of its opinions with a formula: 'For the foregoing reasons it is hereby ORDERED'—solid caps—'that the judgment of the District Court is affirmed' or 'is reversed.' This used to drive my father up the wall. He would write to me: 'Son, you cannot order that 'it is affirmed.' You have to use the subjunctive: 'It is hereby ordered that it be affirmed.' So I ended up being the only judge on the D.C. Circuit who wrote: 'It is hereby ORDERED that the judgment of the District Court be affirmed.' But I don't think that's pedantry; I think that is *snoot*."

"Are there any other snoots on the Court?" I asked.

"I think the biggest snoot on the Court used to be Harry Blackmun, and Harry and I joined forces to try to police the Court's opinions." He laughed and continued, "On the current Court, I think probably David Souter is a snoot. Ruth [Bader Ginsburg] is too polite to be a snoot, but she cares a lot about proper use of the mother tongue."

"Do you think it'd be a good thing if more lawyers became snoots?"

"Oh, absolutely. I cannot imagine why any lawyer would not be a snoot. It's the tools of your trade, man! It's what you work with. Why do you want to abuse them?"

Later in the interview, I asked him about book authorship. I was thinking of his short book *A Matter of Interpretation*. "When you go about writing an article or a book . . . I'll let you take a sip first." He was on film, after all, and I was asking a question right as he was taking a drink of water.

"I can sip water and listen at the same time, contrary to what Lyndon Johnson thought." We laughed at the allusion to Johnson's famously saying that someone was so dumb he couldn't walk and chew gum at the same time.

"How would you describe your writing process? How do you go about writing an article or a book? You get a germ of an idea?"

"You've got to outline it first."

"Do you?"

"Yeah, I always do."

"Does anything happen before you outline?"

"Well, I think about it a lot," he said. "There has to be a lengthy germination process. You don't just sit down cold and say, 'I'm going to do this.' You think about it. You think about it when you're driving home, when you're exercising at the gym; ideas go through your head. Then, when you think you have all of the ideas, all of the points you want to make, then you sit down and organize them. You say, what's the proper approach, what order to put them in, and so forth. And then just sit down and write it. That's the hardest part. Sit down and write."

We were nearing the end of our time on film. I said, "I take it you really enjoy what you do."

"Ahh. Love it. I can't imagine anything I would enjoy more." As I began to thank him for his time, he said, "I enjoyed being here, and I thank you for your . . . I think you're something of a snoot yourself, and that makes me happy."

Precisely 63 minutes after we began, I thanked him and concluded the filming. I felt exhilarated.

"That was great!" I said.

"You know, I learned some things from this interview—just from listening to your questions. They made me think about things I hadn't stopped to consider before. I *enjoyed* that."

"Well, me too. I think that's the finest interview I've ever conducted. You're an astonishing repository of knowledge about rhetoric. I learned things from listening to your answers." I was putting my camera and tripod back into their pouches.

"I understand that you have some kind of *doll*. Is that true?"

"It's your bobblehead. Haven't you seen it?"

"Yes, I've seen it. I have one."

"I was hoping you'd autograph mine."

He hesitated and looked doubtful. "If I sign this, am I going to see it on eBay? I've signed a lot of things that end up going for sale on eBay, and I don't do that anymore. I resent it."

"Justice Scalia, believe me. I'd never let go of this bobblehead. It's mine forever, and I'll never forget this day."

He pulled a fountain pen from his pocket.

"This Sharpie will be much better. Let's use it instead." He signed with a big flourish—a beautiful signature. "Thank you, Justice Scalia. I collect Supreme Court memorabilia, and I'll treasure this." I also had him sign his book *A Matter of Interpretation*.

Indignantly, he said, "You know, I don't make a penny off this book!"

"What? Really?"

"Not a penny. Princeton University Press continues selling it, and they're making a good deal of money. I don't see anything from it."

"How can that be?"

"They paid me a flat fee—a nominal fee. And that was it. No royalties."

"That's a shame. Royalties are great, particularly with evergreen books—books that will sell year after year."

"Especially *Black's Law Dictionary*. It's such a classic."

"Thank you. The publisher allowed me to remake that book from scratch."

"I'll bet that was a big project."

"Humongous. It took many years for each of the two unabridged editions I've done. I won't say 'edited,' because I've really *written* them—with lots of good help."

Patricia McCabe was standing nearby, waiting patiently for us. I suggested, "You ought to write books the way Chief Justice Rehnquist did. You're the best writer on the Court, and that's a way to supplement your income without limit, isn't it?"

"Yes. Bill Rehnquist did it, but I don't think he made a lot of money from it. What did you think of his books?" he asked.

"Not much. I think they're supposed to be scholarly, but they're not; and I think they're supposed to appeal to a popular audience, but they don't."

He nodded slowly as if in thought, but then said dismissively, "Anyway, I don't have the energy. As I was saying during the interview, writing is really difficult for me."

"Well, you're an extraordinary stylist. Justice Scalia, it's been a great honor having this time with you. Thank you for the interview. I'll send you DVDs as soon as they're ready."

"I won't watch them," he said bluntly.

"Maybe your law clerks will. Thank you again." We shook hands.

"Goodbye, Bryan." He smiled and walked away decisively with Patricia. That was that.

Moments later, Patricia came back in with Kathy Arberg. "I hear you had a tremendous time with the Justice!" said Kathy.

"Yes, indeed." We chatted a few minutes, and I told her that I was hoping for interviews with the other eight Justices as well.

3

Making Your Case: Part I

(2006–2008)

Settled into my American Airlines seat after taping the interview, I felt euphoric. I'd done the interview of my life. More important, I'd made a new friend. After the plane had taxied to the runway, I drifted into a semi-sleep, as I often do in the moments before a plane takes off. That's when I get some of my best ideas.

Suddenly it hit me: Justice Scalia and I should write a book together. Our thoughts about rhetoric aligned almost perfectly, and he seemed so much more insightful on the subject than anyone else I had ever met. His impromptu thoughts were just superb. Imagine being able to capture all that in a book. It would be called *The Art of Persuading Judges*. This book on legal rhetoric would be broader than *The Winning Brief*. It would be a book, I thought, the likes of which only the two of us could produce. He seemed so interested in my books that, in retrospect, I believed he might even have been hinting at something after the interview. Or maybe not. But what the heck, I thought I should try. So I drafted this letter on the airplane—and elaborated it the next morning at the office before leaving on another trip:

Dear Justice Scalia:

That was a fabulous interview this afternoon. Thank you. I'll send you a DVD soon (when I get a little time in Dallas—I'm off to Atlanta now).

Afterward, when you were signing your books for me, I was struck by what you said about the 1997 Princeton book: you received a small flat fee for that work, and no royalties. That's a pity.

So I've had a brainstorm. You may know that I have some 18 books in print. I derive a third of my income each year from book royalties. I have a good sense of what books will sell.

I suggest that we write a book together: The Art of Persuasion, *or perhaps* Persuading Judges. *For some months now, I've been working on a plain-English update of Aristotle's* Rhetoric. *I'll still do that someday, but why don't you and I write a book elaborating the major propositions about persuasion? I've written around this subject a good deal, and I have a huge library on the subject. All that remains is to distill the major points and develop essay-like treatments of them for a modern audience.*

I'm pretty sure that I could obtain a favorable royalty rate. I'd propose to divide advances and royalties 66% for you and 34% for me.

Please tell me whether you're interested. It would be a delight to work together, I think, and I can tell you that royalties are wonderful: one derives income for work done many years before, and over time the sums become significant.

It would be great to strengthen and deepen our friendship.

> *Sincerely,*
> *Bryan A. Garner*

This letter was self-testing: could *I* persuade a judge—in this instance to collaborate on a book about persuading judges? Of course, it was an appeal unlike what any advocate could make to an adjudicator: I praised him, then appealed to his financial self-interest, then appealed to prospective friendship.

The next morning in my office, I had it typed up and edited by my then-staff of two lawyers and two paralegals, who have always been a critical part of my team. Jeff Newman, one of my lawyers, seemed quizzical and doubtful about the idea; Tiger Jackson, my other lawyer, said it sounded like a great project. After four drafts, it was ready. I sent it FedEx to Justice Scalia's house.

The following morning, my father called to ask about the interview. By this time I was in Atlanta.

"How'd it go, Bryan?"

"Dad, it was just great. You wouldn't believe it. He extended the interview twice, and we got on so well."

"That's wonderful to hear."

"His ideas about advocacy are so profound—and they align more with my own than anyone I've ever met, even though he seems not to know much about my work."

"How exciting."

"Yes, and you'll never believe what's happening just about now. I have a letter being delivered to the Scalia house—a letter inviting him to become a coauthor with me."

"What?"

"We hit it off so well personally. The interview was a dream. It was amazing, Dad. So I've invited him to write a book with me about legal rhetoric."

"What?! That's absurd."

"You think so?" I suddenly felt chastened.

"The sheer chutzpah of it. You should be embarrassed. You have an interview with the man, you get excited, and you think he's going to coauthor a book with you?"

"Well, I think he might, Dad." My heart sank.

"You've really outdone yourself here. I'd try to prevent it from being delivered if I were you."

My embarrassment deepened. What had I done? Why hadn't I seen this before? It was clear, though: my father was right. "Let me call FedEx right now," I said hastily. "I'll see whether I can get the delivery canceled. Thanks, Dad. I love you."

"I love you, too, Bryan. See if you can cancel that delivery."

I immediately called my assistant, Brandy, to see whether she could stop the delivery. She called FedEx and soon reported back that the piece had already been delivered just 30 minutes earlier. So be it, I thought. At least the embarrassment would be only between Justice Scalia and me. I tried to forget about it and go on about my day.

A busy two weeks followed. I was teaching three to four seminars per week—all of them out of state. Then, nearly three weeks later, I received the most extraordinary letter, dated October 18, 2006. It was from Justice Scalia, and it said that he had mislaid my letter and so was responding without having it before him. He had been "chewing over" my proposal and had concluded that he should "gratefully accept."

He wanted it to be a truly joint enterprise and stood ready to commit to the time this might take. He suggested that every section should be jointly authored—so that no sections would be individually signed. Then he signed off with a *shall* and (for the first time) with his nickname: "I shall await further word. Best regards. Sincerely, Nino."

I could hardly believe my eyes.

I would later learn, from Mrs. Scalia, that their son Christopher—the newly minted Ph.D. in English whom Justice Scalia had mentioned at our breakfast meeting—had been staying at the house when my letter arrived. When his father opened the letter and showed Christopher, the son was reportedly enthusiastic and encouraged his father to accept. He was a fan of David Foster Wallace, who less than a year before had published *Consider the Lobster*, the book containing "Authority and American Usage," the long encomium to my *Dictionary of Modern American Usage*. True serendipity.

A Meeting of the Minds

Having received the acceptance letter, I called Justice Scalia at his office to set up dinner the next time I'd be in Washington: Sunday, November 4, with an in-chambers planning session the day after. The phone call was warm but businesslike: we agreed that we'd need to settle on a plan of attack. For dinner the night before, we confirmed that he'd make a reservation for 6:00 p.m. at his favorite Italian restaurant, Tosca.

When the day came, I went to the restaurant at the appointed time, but he didn't show up. When I checked with the maitre d', he said he had no reservation for Scalia. So I ate alone. I figured there must have been a mix-up—and though disappointed, I didn't feel particularly slighted because in the past year I'd done the same thing to someone else. It was the mortifying by-product of spending so many nights per year on the road and of having three people responsible for updating my calendar. So I was pretty understanding.

The next morning I called to ensure that our 10 o'clock meeting was still on, and Angela Frank, his omnicompetent secretary, said our dinner must have slipped his mind because she hadn't been told about it. She said to come on over to the Marshal's Office.

It was with a sense of high purpose that I entered the Supreme Court building on November 5. I went through the north entrance, on Maryland

Street. A marshal stopped me as I was walking from the front plaza toward that entrance. "What's your business?"

"I'm here to meet with Justice Scalia."

"Your name?"

"Bryan Garner."

He said something into the line dangling from his earwig. Then to me: "Go ahead."

I went through the metal-detector screening near the door. One of the police officers said, "You're here to meet with Justice Scalia?"

"Yes."

"Go ahead. Have a good day."

I went to the Marshal's Office, where the reception room is long and narrow with lots of fine millwork. All the furniture and walls matched, and they seemed to be finely crafted. I would later learn that the Supreme Court has its own mill in the basement, with carpenters who perpetually have cabinetry projects.

"Hello," I said to the woman sitting closest to the counter. There were four workstations there, and all four were occupied. Four faces looked up at me. "My name is Bryan Garner. I'm here to see Justice Scalia." I smiled, and two of them smiled back.

But they were all business. "One moment." One of the marshals called through to say I was there. Then to me: "Someone will be here in a moment to escort you."

There were two chairs for guests in the Marshal's Office, opposite which were the individual photographs of the nine Justices. I took a chair and studied them for what they might show. Chief Justice John Roberts had a boyish grin; Justice John Paul Stevens an avuncular look; Justice Scalia a subdued but happy smile; Justice Samuel Alito a somber look that bordered on sullen; Justice Ruth Bader Ginsburg a serene sort of smile so slight that it resembled the Mona Lisa; Justice David Souter a look of humorless earnestness; Justice Clarence Thomas a good smile with the upper lip slightly curled; Justice Stephen Breyer an air of patrician erudition; and Justice Anthony Kennedy, lips slightly parted as if expressing wonderment. One unexpected thing was the way in which they were hung: rather too high and not quite even. This was a do-it-yourself job of hanging art.

"Mr. Garner, I'm Angela." I hadn't even seen her walk in. She was about five feet four inches tall, brunette, with a broad smile. I liked her instantly.

"Oh, good to meet you. Please do call me Bryan."

"All right. Bryan it is. Please come this way."

She used a code to get us through a locked passageway into the secured parts of the Supreme Court building. We walked down two long halls past doors with signs on them reading "Justice O'Connor" and "Justice Stevens," finally coming to an office designated "Justice Scalia."

She gave three rapid knocks and then immediately opened the door. "Justice, Mr. Garner is here to see you."

The spacious office itself was impressive: federal-style maple woodwork throughout, floor to ceiling, with neoclassical designs around the built-in bookshelves and drawers; a handsome Chippendale desk and side chairs; a black-marble fireplace with two silver plates that looked as if they'd been inscribed as mementos for him; an old, seemingly 18th-century oil paint-ing of George Washington; two 19th-century oil paintings of Justices, one of whom I recognized as Stephen J. Field; the head of a 12-point buck mounted high on the wall; a complete set of the *United States Reports*; a duck decoy and a lap desk atop his coffee table, which sat on a Persian rug; and bronze busts of Abraham Lincoln and Theodore Roosevelt, the latter of which I noticed had recently been presented to Justice Scalia by the Union League Club as recipient of the "Theodore Roosevelt American Experience Award."

He swung around in his swivel chair and rose with an outstretched hand: "Bryan! How good to see you. I'm so sorry about last night. Forgot all about it. Can I make it up with dinner *tonight*?"

"Of course! That'd be great. You know, it's so great to be here. This is an exciting project. And happy Guy Fawkes Day, by the way."

"It is Guy Fawkes Day, isn't it? Tried to blow up Parliament."

Angela said, "Would you like Fernando to bring you some coffee, Jus-tice?"

"No, I think I'd like a root beer. Bryan, do you like root beer?"

"I do, but I'd like a Diet Coke even better if you have one of those."

"We do indeed," Justice Scalia said. "Fernando! Fernando! Is he there, Angela?"

We settled into the sitting area near his desk, he on a Chippendale chair and I on his leather couch. A Filipino man of slight build appeared at the door, nodded at me, and then focused intently on Justice Scalia. "Fer-nando, please bring me a root beer and Mr. Garner here a Diet Coke." As

Fernando walked out, Justice Scalia said, "Fernando is my tipstaff. That's what I've decided to call him. For years each Justice has had a 'runner,' but 'runner' just doesn't sound good. In England, a judge's factotum is called a 'tipstaff.' So Fernando is my tipstaff."

"Great word. I didn't know it."

"Yes. It's a great word. So we're going to write a book! I'm looking forward to it. You know, I've never really written a book. *A Matter of Interpretation* was really just an essay with other essays tacked onto it so it looked book-size. But this will be a real book." He exuded enthusiasm.

"Yes."

"Tell me, you've written lots of books. How do you go about it?"

"Well, I've gotten better at it over the years. It's about as you said last month in our interview. We'll do the outline first."

"Right."

"I'm convinced that the best way to approach a didactic book like ours is to work out the table of contents first, but to do the table of contents in complete sentences only."

"What do you mean?"

"We'll figure out the propositions and then write essays in support of them. If you look at my book *The Winning Brief*..."

"I like that book. One of my lawyer sons showed me that one."

"Oh good. *The Winning Brief* has 100 propositions about brief-writing. Some are small points, and some are hugely important. But it's divided up that way, point by point—each with a full-sentence heading."

"I don't want our book to be *The Winning Brief Lite!*" Justice Scalia said. "You've written so well and so fully about brief-writing."

"Thank you," I said. "But I don't think that's a danger. You and I are going to write more about argumentative strategy—the way Aristotle did. But you know that Aristotle's *Rhetoric* is an architectural mess. The organization makes no sense at all. We don't want that."

"I agree," he said.

"That means that we'll need to work out the main propositions first, order them appropriately, and then write in support of them later."

Fernando came in with a tray: two glasses of ice, a bottle of root beer, and a can of Diet Coke. He set the drinks down carefully beside us and slipped noiselessly out of the room.

I continued: "What I propose to do in this meeting is to agree on the main lines of the book. I've worked out a preliminary outline, and I was hoping perhaps this might prompt you to think of things I've missed. Or perhaps you'll want to reorganize the points I have. Or maybe modify them entirely."

After handing him my three-page draft table of contents, I waited for a reaction. It came about 60 seconds later. Justice Scalia said: "You've missed the starting point. Number one must be to ensure that the court has jurisdiction."

"Ah."

"I can't tell you how many litigants get into trouble because their lawyers don't verify that the court has jurisdiction. It happens in the Seventh Circuit all the time. Point number one should be jurisdiction!"

"How would you like to word it?" I asked.

"Be sure that the court has jurisdiction."

"That's good. I've put all the blackletter section headings in the imperative mood, as injunctions, and that fits perfectly."

"I'm glad," he said with a purposeful nod.

"One fundamental point we need to deal with," I said, "is the purpose of the book. We're not confining ourselves merely to appellate practice. Right?"

"Right. And certainly not just United States Supreme Court practice. That would limit the book too much. We need a bigger audience."

"Yes, so we include trial practice. But shouldn't we also be considering arbitral panels and other types of forums like that?"

"Wait. You use the plural *forums*?" he asked me.

"Yes, I think the Latinate plural *I* is pretentious, don't you?" I said.

"I don't know. It's a Latin word. You know I was a good student in Latin."

"Great training, isn't it?" I said.

"No better way to improve your English than to learn Latin. It's a shame it's dropped out of the schools. Did you have Latin?" he asked me.

"Two years in college. Four years of French but only two of Latin."

"I had seven or eight years of Latin, and I use it all the time," he said.

"I know you once used the phrase *hapax legomenon*, but that's Greek."

"I used that phrase? Remind me."

"It means a word or phrase that appears only once within a language or only once within a single writer's corpus of work. You used it in your first term on the Court—in reference to the adjective *material*. You wrote, 'The term *material* . . . is no *hapax legomenon* in our jurisprudence.'"

"I think you're wrong about the meaning. I think it's only once within the language as a whole," said Justice Scalia. "Is that really what I wrote?"

"I'm pretty sure. Let's look it up."

He did this often, calling my hand over a word's precise meaning. So did I, for that matter. We were kindred spirits when it came to words. We were both snoots.

"You have a *Webster's Second* right there," I said, pointing to the dictionary stand some ten feet from the chair behind his desk. "Let's have a look." I went over to his dictionary and read: "hapax legomenon. Said or used but once, as a rare word, verbal form, etc., evidenced by a single citation."

"Aha! A single citation. It doesn't say a single author." He was on his computer.

"You know," I said, "it's strange *Webster's Second* defines the phrase as if it's adjectival. Most linguists treat it as a noun. In my book on usage, I define it as a noun: 'a word or phrase that is used . . . ,' not the past participial 'said or used,' as if the term were always used as an adjective."

"You define the term?" he said.

"Yes, in my usage book."

"Let's see." He jumped up eagerly, not as if to challenge me but more to indulge his curiosity. He grabbed the book from behind his monitor and started flipping through the pages. Suddenly his lower lip jutted out. "Buh-buh-buh-buh-buh." These rapid-fire syllables were a habit of his that I would soon become accustomed to whenever he was thumbing through a book to find a particular page. "You give two meanings: '1. A word or phrase found only once in the written record of a language. 2. A word or phrase found only once in the work of a particular author.' You have support for that?"

"Sure. *The Oxford English Dictionary* defines it in more or less that way. It also defines the phrase as a noun. I think *Webster's Second* gets that wrong."

"You're undercutting *Webster's Second*?"

"Are you kidding? I love that dictionary. It was my booster seat when I was a kid—whenever I visited my grandfather, the judge."

"Your grandfather was a judge?"

"Justice Meade F. Griffin, on the Supreme Court of Texas for almost 20 years—from 1949 to 1968. When I was four or five, he had me sit on *Webster's Second.*"

"That's something."

"I now own about 15 copies of it, and I keep them placed conveniently around the house and in the office for my employees—for emergency look-ups, not booster seats. I have only about 6 copies of *Webster's Third.*"

"Ooooh," he grumbled, shivering and shaking his head. "*Webster's Third* is an awful book."

"Well, it's actually a good piece of lexicography. It's just that people need to know how to use it. It's too bad that Philip Gove, the editor, didn't include enough usage labels to warn people against using certain terms."

"Like misusing *infer* for *imply.*"

"Right. And *ain't.* Gove actually took the position that educated Americans routinely use the word *ain't.* You ought to see what I say about that."

"Your usage book? You've written about this?"

"Yes."

"Let me see. Buh-buh-buh-buh-buh. Page 31: 'ain't. Is this word used orally in most parts of the country by cultivated speakers? In 1961, *Webster's Third* said it was, provoking a firestorm of protests from journalists and academics.' Understandably so. I remember that. '*Webster's Third*'s assessment was quite a change from that of *Webster's Second* (1934), which had given it a tag: "Dialectal or Illiterate." The editor of *Webster's Third*, Philip Gove'— by golly, you name him right here, heh, heh, heh—'explained the change by conceding that he had no large files of empirical evidence: "Knowledge of some kind of language behavior comes through contact with its observers and is not always documented because there seems to be no reason to collect additional evidence." If that's the method, then one can confidently say that *Webster's Third*'s treatment was flawed in its incompleteness.' Wow. You really called him out."

"Read the next paragraph," I said.

"'In 1962, the year after *Webster's Third* was published, an apt cartoon appeared in the *New Yorker*. It's hilarious. A man is standing in the reception area of G. & C. Merriam Co., Dictionary Division, as the receptionist says to him, "Sorry, Dr. Gove ain't in."'"

"Ha! Ha!" Justice Scalia bellowed with delight. "Boy, you really skewered him. Did he live to see that?"

"No. I'm afraid he died a few years after *Webster's Third* was published. *Webster's Third* isn't a bad book: it just requires discernment. Still, for traditional terminology—rhetorical and legal terminology—I do prefer *Webster's Second*."

"My father introduced me to *Webster's Second* when I was a young man," he said. "I've liked it ever since. But let's get back to the point! Where were we?"

"*Hapax legomenon*, and whether it can refer to a corpus smaller than the entire language. If you think about it, your own use of the phrase in your 1988 opinion used a corpus smaller than the entire language: '*Material* is no *hapax legomenon* in our jurisprudence.' The corpus you're referring to was just the *United States Reports*—not the whole English language."

"I don't think I said that."

"I'm quite sure you did."

"Well, let's look it up right now," he said. We did, and I was wrong.[16] He hadn't used the phrase *in our jurisprudence*. I had misrecalled the wording in the case.

"So your memory is failing you, eh?" he said with a smile.

"I suppose so," I replied, suppressing a grin. "But my point still stands. You can have a *hapax legomenon* for a subset of the language, I assure you."

"Let's get back to *forum*," he said. "It was the word *forum* that got us off on this tangent!"

"Oh, yes," I said. "The word *forum* has been completely naturalized. We don't italicize it unless referring to it as a word. And the plural has been fully anglicized: *forums*."

"Are you sure? Is it in your usage book?"

"Yes."

"Let's see. Buh-buh-buh-buh-buh. Page 365: 'The preferred plural is *forums*, not *fora*.' Is it in Fowler?"

"I seem to recall that both the original 1926 Fowler and the 1965 Gowers revision are silent on the question."

"Let's just check. I have the 1965 edition right here. Buh-buh-buh-buh. Here it is. Nope. It's not there. How do you *know* all this stuff?!"

"I'm a lexicographer. I live and breathe this stuff."

---

16 See *Kungys v. United States*, 485 U.S. 759, 769 (1988) ("The term 'material' in § 1451(a) is not a hapax legomenon.").

"Hey, listen, we need to get back to our *book!*"

He was right. "The point is," I said, "that we want our book to be useful to people in arbitrations and even city-council meetings as well as police courts, family-law courts, and even the U.S. Supreme Court—every forum. So I think we should use the word *tribunal* in point number one."

" 'Make sure that the tribunal has jurisdiction.' I like that. We'll start with that. Then we can go to the points you already have."

"Let's look at them closely and see whether you agree with the general principles—the first 20 points or so."

We ended up working through those first 20. He rearranged the points in my draft and reworded them as I took careful notes. He also had a few other observations throughout the table of contents. But the close scrutiny on the 100 or so points after the "General Argumentation" section would have to wait. Time was getting short for this particular meeting.

"What do we do next?" he asked.

"Let's discuss something I might have brought up earlier," I answered. "Whenever I write a book, I must learn the literature through and through. I believe it's important to try to know the existing literature in the field as well as any human being has ever known it. That means we must do lots of reading as we collect points and elaborate them."

"Okay, tell me what you want me to read."

"I'd like you to start with Quintilian's book on rhetoric and Cicero's book called *Orators and Oratory.*" He was taking notes with a pencil.

"What else? I'll look at whatever you say."

"Piero Calamandrei's book *A Eulogy of Judges.* Have you heard of it?"

He smiled. "No. You like the Italians, don't you?" He then picked up the telephone: "Angela, have the library get me three books—Quintilian's book on rhetoric, Cicero's book on orators and oratory, and Calamandrei's book on a eulogy of judges. Thank you." Down the receiver went. "I'll turn to those this weekend, Bryan. Anything else?"

"One last thing. It's a practical problem about collaborating—and I have a proposed solution to it."

"What's the problem?"

"I've been thinking that if I do the first draft and you just edit what I write, then you're just reacting to my material. We won't have the full benefit of your creativity. If *you* do the first draft of a section, I might be too deferential to whatever you write. Do you see the problem?"

"I want to make one thing clear with this book. You are not my law clerk. You're my equal—for purposes of this book, anyway. Let's have no signed sections in the book. What's your proposed solution to the problem?"

"I propose that we each write every section once we approve the outline. Let's write the same sections simultaneously, as if we were independent authors, and then I'll meld your work with mine. We'll have the benefit of your creativity as well as whatever modicum of creativity I bring to it. I'll bet it'll work perfectly."

"Could we try this on some sections of the book we've agreed to today?" he asked.

"Great idea. Why don't you send me two sections each week beginning this Friday. So we'll each draft sections 1 and 2 this week, 3 and 4 next week, and 5 and 6 the week following. Then I'll be in charge of blending the two drafts of each section together. If it works, we could do the whole book that way."

"We have our weekly conference on the cases on Fridays. What time on Friday?"

"How about 4:30 Eastern Time?"

"That's good. So 1 and 2 are due to you at 4:30 this Friday."

"Yes, sir. And I'll finish my first draft of those sections by the same deadline."

Angela came in. "Justice, your reservations at Tosca are in 30 minutes. The marshals are in the car in the garage."

"Yes." To me: "Let's call it a day and go have dinner. But you don't want to go to Tosca again."

"Sure I do. It's great. I'd never been there before last night. If it's your favorite, let's go there."

Guy Fawkes Day Dinner

When we arrived at Tosca, we were ushered to the back, where Justice Scalia's favorite table was. He ordered a Campari and soda and suggested I do the same. "You'll like it, I think." And I did. The waitstaff and Paolo, the manager, were especially solicitous.

"We're off to an excellent start. Thank you, Justice Scalia. I think it's going to be a good book."

"I agree. I'm most happy about it. Now tell me about your family."

"I have two daughters. You met Caroline, who's at Yale, and Alexandra just turned 15. She's at the Hockaday School in Dallas."

"That's a private school?"

"Yes. It's perhaps the finest girls' school west of the Mississippi—one of the best in the country."

"Ah. Very good. And tell me about your wife."

"I'm going through a divorce right now."

"Oh my. How long have you been married?"

"Twenty-three years. It's a very difficult time for me."

"What's your religious tradition?"

"I was raised an Episcopalian, but I'm not a churchgoer." I shrugged. "I never thought I'd be someone who'd get a divorce."

We discussed my predicament at some length, and he was sympathetic and understanding. "That's too bad. Sometimes there's just no other option," he said. "Look, we're friends now, and you let me know if you're ever in need of help. Maybe just someone to listen."

"Thank you."

Meanwhile, the gourmet fare at Tosca, together with the wine, was superb—even better than the night before—perhaps because I was in better company. The waiter brought us tiramisu and grappa on the house, and we were both thoroughly satisfied. He insisted on having the marshals drop me off at my hotel before taking him home. It was a chilly, wintry night.

"Thank you, Justice Scalia. That's very kind. By the way, I'll be back in town next Sunday," I said. "I'll be interviewing Justice Ginsburg the following day."

"You're flying in again Sunday?"

"Yes."

"Well, let's have dinner again then!" he said. "You can show me the revised outline."

"Excellent."

"I'll get it on the calendar this time! But let's try Bistro Bis next week. Sunday at 7. You'll like Bistro Bis."

I made a note of it, as well as a note to call Angela so that she could remind him.

As the marshals' car approached the Mayflower Hotel, on Connecticut

Avenue, Justice Scalia said, "Okay, Bryan, goodnight. You'll have my first writings on Friday."

"Thank you! Goodnight. Best Guy Fawkes Day ever."

Technical Difficulties

The next day, I called Angela to ensure that Bistro Bis was on his calendar for Sunday at 7:00 p.m. Good thing, too: she hadn't yet heard anything about it.

That Friday, at precisely 3:30 Central Time, I was in my office in Dallas. On my computer screen popped a message that I'd received an e-mail message from "Scales" at the Supreme Court. "Attached is my first crack at the initial sections." That was it. No sign-off. A Word document was attached.

Even in 2006, I was considered a dinosaur for clinging to WordPerfect and MS-DOS instead of switching over to Microsoft Word on Windows. WordPerfect was a great word-processing program. The pages looked more beautiful, and I had mastered all sorts of macros that made composition easier for me. Here's what shocked most people: I used WordPerfect 5.1, which had been essentially discontinued in the 1990s. That software allowed me to type and execute all sorts of commands without ever leaving the keyboard. No mouse clicks. Everything was by keystrokes. I was convinced (and still am) that my letters and manuscripts had a more pleasing look than anything produced with Word.

In any event, it was no trouble opening Justice Scalia's document in WordPerfect. But as I would soon learn, his opening my documents in Word was a different matter—and a major annoyance to him.

I had more immediate problems, though. His attachment perplexed me. Although I could tell that the first two paragraphs went with section one, the rest of the materials seemed jumbled. It wasn't clear what sections he was writing on. It looked as if he'd written on the first six sections—two or three paragraphs for each—but nothing was designated, and no point headings were given. It looked like a mishmash. The writing was good, of course, but the presentation baffled me.

By e-mail, I acknowledged receipt and said some complimentary things. But I couldn't quite bring myself to acknowledge how confused I was by the intended placement of his contributions. I tried to figure out how to integrate his paragraphs with mine, but trying to do that only intensified my frustration. I just couldn't tell where he wanted his paragraphs to go.

I decided we'd talk about these points over dinner Sunday at Bistro Bis. I took a cab from the Mayflower at 6:45 and arrived at the restaurant five minutes before our 7 o'clock reservation. He still wasn't there by 7:30, when I asked to go ahead and be seated. Once again, he didn't show up at all. I felt disappointed but somehow not entirely surprised. I worked on my questions for the Ginsburg interview instead.

The next day, I arranged to meet with Chief Justice John Roberts's assistant to schedule his interview the following March, recorded a half-hour interview with Justice Ginsburg, and then met with Justice Scalia late that afternoon. He was profusely apologetic for standing me up a second Sunday in a row, saying that he'd unwittingly double-booked the night before. We had a productive meeting: we improved the outline a little more, and we both liked the new organization. I had proposed adding a new major section on legal reasoning, and he approved of that as well.

That evening, it occurred to me how we might simplify the preparation of the manuscript. Perhaps I could ask him to handwrite his paragraphs. He could use one of my favorite techniques: I would print a manuscript-development copy of the book—call it a workbook—in which each point heading would appear in boldface type at the top of a separate page, with the rest of the page left blank. That way, he could handwrite his paragraphs there, or he could simply print the manuscript, hole-punch it, and put it behind the section to which it belonged. Then it would be clear to me what went where.

This assumed, of course, that he was as comfortable with handwriting as I am. Having seen him jotting things with a pencil when we were in chambers together, I knew that his penmanship was quite legible. Anything would be better than these disembodied paragraphs with no discernible place where they belonged.

On December 29, I had one of my assistants prepare such a three-ring binder. I handwrote a letter to accompany the binder, explaining how he could use it by jotting down paragraphs as they occurred to him. Here I acknowledged pretty candidly that his first batch of materials was proving a challenge to sort out, and I assured him that I thought this "manuscript-production binder" might make the writing easier for him. Here's what my letter said:

29 Dec. 2006

Dear Justice Scalia,

The 14 pages of manuscript you sent last week are superb. Thank you. I'm thinking that it might be easier, though, for you to hand-write your paragraphs on the sheets in these notebook pages, and to add sheets when necessary. I'd be happy for you simply to send me your longhand manuscript. That will make it easier for me to tie your passages to the particular section of the book (that's taking some judgment with the parts I've already received).

We're off to an excellent start.

Our lunch on January 10 must be postponed: I'm to testify in St. Louis as an expert witness midday that day—and I recall that you're leaving town just after lunch.

At some point I certainly hope to meet Mrs. Scalia. My best wishes to the entire Scalia clan for the new year.

Sincerely,
Bryan

With this letter stuck into the front of the binder, my assistant and I sent off the package by FedEx the following Monday, for Tuesday-morning delivery. Meanwhile, I worked on sorting out the embryonic manuscript as best I could.

That Friday, more material arrived in much the same condition as the last batch: unnumbered, undesignated paragraphs to be plugged in some-where in sections toward the beginning of the book. As promised, I had been writing in those sections. I tried to integrate his drafts, which I edited moderately. The writing was excellent, and the melding of his materials with mine was going smoothly.

I attached the first five or so sections to an e-mail and sent it before New Year's Day so he could savor the material over the holiday. I imag-ined him reading it over during the occasional lulls that must occur in the Scalia household even with so many children and grandchildren around. If I heard nothing back for a while, that would be understandable: I'd wait and see whether I'd heard from him by the end of the first week in January.

It was a good 18 pages' worth of manuscript. I had massaged it, amplified it, rearranged it a couple of times, and run it by my in-house editors. They subjected it to the normal level of LawProse editing—which is quite a lot. Once we had it polished, I asked Tiger and Jeff, my colleagues, to try to identify what Justice Scalia had written and what I had.

They told me it was too easy. They marked the manuscript with an S or a G indicating who they thought had written each paragraph—and they both got it wildly wrong. Although they'd both been working with me for nearly seven years, they attributed most of his work to me, and most of my work to him. That was encouraging. What was more important, though, was that they were unusually enthusiastic about this manuscript. Normally, Tiger and Jeff are subdued in reacting to a manuscript that I think sizzles. But this time was different: both more or less gushed about it.

What remained was to get a reaction from my coauthor. Having heard nothing in a week, I sent a brief message on January 6: "Dear Justice Scalia, I trust you received the manuscript I sent you shortly before New Year's Day. How do you like it?"

This had been my first attempt at combining our work into one cohesive text, and I was excited about the results. But as more time passed with no response, that excitement turned into anxiety.

The Breakup

In the middle of the afternoon on January 17, I decided to call his office. I'll never forget where I was: in the Driskill Hotel in Austin as an unusual blizzard was beginning to hit. Travel would be impossible. I lay on my belly on the hotel bed—my usual posture for writing—and called his office. Angela answered. "Justice Scalia's chambers."

"Hello, Angela! It's Bryan Garner. Is Justice Scalia in?"

"Yes, he is." She sounded a little hesitant. "Please hold a moment."

After 45 seconds or so (it felt like an eternity), he came on the line: "Hello, Bryan." He sounded a little somber. "How's the weather down there?"

"I'm in Austin, in the midst of a blizzard. How's the weather up there?"

"It's sunny and fine. Beautiful for this time of year."

"Have you had a chance to look at the manuscript I sent?"

"Yes, Bryan, I have. I'm not going to be able to do this book. I'm sorry."

"You didn't like it? Everyone I've showed it to is raving about it—my staff, I mean."

"I don't think so. It's not for me."

"Oh, no. Well, how can I fix it?"

"You can't. You're not using my stuff. Frankly, I think you just wanted my name on your book, and I don't want to be used that way. Lookit, this is your book, not mine. I've enjoyed getting to know you a little, but a collaboration just isn't in the cards. I'll tell you what. Next time you're in Washington, come by and we'll have lunch in chambers. But I'm not doing the book."

I fumbled for words: "May I at least have another chance?"

"I don't know what good it would do. I've made up my mind."

"Did I edit your material too heavily? Is that the problem?"

"You're not even using my material. I don't even recognize it. This is your book."

"Please give me one more shot. I'll send it to you shortly."

"Send it along, if you like. You know my thoughts."

"Thank you."

"Goodbye, Bryan." Click.

Needless to say, I was stunned. What had I done? Was it that he just wasn't used to having his work edited by someone else? I know sometimes people are shocked by having others edit their work, but here he was at least seeing a clean manuscript, not all my hand-marked edits (which might indeed have shocked him). Obviously, I'd gone too far.

Immediately, I went down to the Driskill business center and began composing a letter to him:

Dear Justice Scalia:

Of course I can accept your decision not to continue on our book project, but I can't help thinking there's been a miscommunication.

My intention had been to use every word of what you sent to me. It's just that some of those paragraphs (I thought) were intended for sections later in the book, and I had inserted those paragraphs where I thought they belonged. The drafts on using cases and using statutes are wonderful, and I've been working on ranging them suitably through the chapters.

Perhaps my editing was heavy-handed in some way. But I believed that our intention was to meld our drafts into single, cohesive sections.

What I had in mind, all along, was a working relationship similar to that of H. L. A. Hart and Tony Honoré—as they composed Causation in the Law. *While writing their book, they'd work through their material (mostly independently), each week adding a tad more in new sections and embellishing their earlier work. In the end, they had a classic. I would be Tony Honoré to your H. L. A. Hart.*

I also knew that there would be some sections that I'd have to write (the detailed stuff on syllogisms and enthymemes), and some that you'd inevitably write (such as a few sections on oral argument).

Also, I'm not indissolubly wedded to the idea about responsive arguments—§ 8, where I quote Aristotle to the effect that a responder must begin by undercutting. I only recently discovered this passage in Aristotle, and I wanted to see what you thought about that idea. I have no problem with totally rethinking a section.

Mostly, I'm sad about not having the opportunity after all to work with you—and to learn from you.

Coincidentally, yesterday after we spoke I received an e-mail from West, in Eagan, Minnesota. West has worked hard over the past six weeks to develop a special proposal for us, and when I spoke with Pam Siege Chandler this morning she said that the company has a firm offer for us. It's unprecedented. The offer has been approved at the very highest levels within the company.

So there we have it: West stands ready to pay an acquisition fee tomorrow, if we'll do it, and the royalties would be a whopping 20% (both the fee and the royalties subject to the 66–34% division we originally agreed on).

I never had the idea for this book until after our interview—so it's not something I'd otherwise have been working on. I've already arranged my 2007 schedule to be in D.C. much more than usual, in hopes of some work sessions with you.

I know you're extremely busy (it hardly needs saying), but there's no rush on the project: we could complete it gradually over the next two years.

So I humbly beseech you to reconsider. We'd learn from each other, mostly I from you. And I still think we'd thoroughly enjoy it.

Sincerely,
Bryan

Then I waited. Nine days.

Back in Dallas, the snow having melted, I called his chambers at 11:00 a.m. January 26. Angela Frank answered: "Justice Scalia's chambers."

"Hi, Angela. It's Bryan Garner. Is Justice Scalia in today?"

"One moment, please."

"Hello, Bryan, how's the weather down in Texas?"

"Not like a week ago in Austin. Things have cleared up. The snow has melted. How is it up there?"

"It's getting nasty, I'm afraid. Cold and wet."

"Did you receive my letter?"

"Yes, but I'm afraid my answer hasn't changed. Lookit, you're not using my work at all!"

"Justice Scalia, I don't know how you can say that. I've included every single sentence you've written! I edited them, but they're all there."

"I'm not seeing any of it. Lookit, I think I know what you're doing. You want my name on this book just so it'll sell better. You just want my name. You're trying to capitalize on my supposed involvement. Well nobody uses me that way."

"That's not so, and it's not fair of you to say that, Justice Scalia." I'd been caught totally off-guard. "I've used all your work."

"Lookit, this book has absolutely no intellectual content. I'd be a laughingstock if I put my name on this. I'd be ashamed within the academy to put my name on this."

My head was spinning. "I don't know how you can say that. We quote Aristotle and Cicero."

"I'm not seeing that." He sounded indignant. "The book has zero intellectual content. It's as if you expect people to be satisfied with 'Thought of the Day on Advocacy.' Nope. I'm out. I'm not doing this. I'm sorry. Goodbye." Click.

Solving the Mystery

How could this be happening? I was stunned by the accusatory tone and by the idea that the book wasn't "intellectual" enough. I was hurt on the one hand, and yet calm and clinical on the other because I knew that there was no real basis for what he had said. And I was hungry. So I left the office for an early lunch. I drove to Rafa's Tex-Mex on Lover's Lane, asked for a seat in the corner near the kitchen, and ordered two cheese enchiladas. While eating chips and salsa, I replayed the entire conversation in my head. Over and over. "Zero intellectual content." "Laughingstock." "Ashamed within the academy." "You're using me."

How could he say these things? How could he think this? Although I was chagrined, I knew something about this just didn't add up. He must not be seeing the real manuscript. What could he be looking at? My enchiladas were served, and as I took the first bite, I stared blankly, shaking my head, and thought again: "Thought of the Day on Advocacy."

Then it hit me: he must have been looking at the workbook—the binder I'd sent to help him generate handwritten notes for the manuscript, the one with nothing but headings at the tops of the pages. He was taking those headings as "thoughts of the day" blurbs. That *had* to be it! I could think of no other explanation. Without finishing my lunch, I rushed back to the office, determined to get the true manuscript in front of him. I called his chambers from my car.

"Justice Scalia's chambers."

"Angela. It's Bryan Garner again. I think Justice Scalia hasn't been looking at the real manuscript. If I fax a few pages to you, can you get it before him?"

"He's leaving town today, and he'll be leaving the office in 45 minutes."

"I'll have the fax to you in five."

I printed the first 15 pages (single-spaced), which had already gone through about ten drafts, and typed out a cover letter:

26 Jan. 2007

Dear Justice Scalia:

Is the attached manuscript what you've been looking at? I've marked with S the parts you wrote and with G the parts I wrote. It's pretty evenly split, isn't it (apart from § 6)? After we spoke, it occurred to me that you might not have seen this.

Even if this is what you've been looking at, I'll be working more with might and main on other sections—and perhaps rethinking these.

As ever,
Bryan

The fax machine made its connection, and I watched anxiously as each page fed through.

I was excited and agitated as I told Jeff and Tiger what I thought had happened. Justice Scalia hadn't even opened my WordPerfect file that was attached to my e-mail; I had forgotten that he uses Word. He had received my "manuscript-production binder" but hadn't read the letter, or had misplaced the letter and forgotten about it. That had to be what had happened. Jeff was doubtful; Tiger hoped I was right. They had watched the ups and downs of this seemingly abortive collaboration.

Soon my cellphone rang. It was Angela: "Mr. Garner, please hold for Justice Scalia."

"Bryan, this is *wonderful*! This is *not* what I've been looking at—not at all. This is just brilliant. I *love* it."

"Gosh," I sighed. "I'm so glad to hear you say that. My staff loves it. So we're back on?"

"Yes, we're back on. This is first-rate work. I really *like* the way you've blended what I wrote into what you've written. It all jibes perfectly."

"I'm so relieved," I said. "I'm looking at it right now. We could improve on it, perhaps, but I think it's close to what we want."

"Me, too!"

"Listen," I said, "I know you're leaving for a trip, so let's talk when you get back. I can't tell you how happy I am."

"Thank you, Bryan. I'm glad we're back on. Glad we've cleared up this misunderstanding."

"Yes, indeed."

"Goodbye, Bryan."

It occurred to me that both the unpleasant conversations that month had begun with, "How's the weather?" Never again did that happen.

Within minutes of hanging up, I realized that he had said he was on his way to Claremont before visiting Hawaii. So I called him back.

"Justice Scalia, are you going to speak at Pomona College?"

"Well, yes, there are three of them, I believe. The Claremont Colleges. Maureen and I will go there for a speech and a faculty luncheon, and then off to Hawaii."

"Are you going to meet David Foster Wallace—the man who coined the word *snoot*?"

"Oh, is he there?"

"Yes, he's the Disney Professor of Writing there. Why don't you ask the administration to invite him and his wife to your luncheon?"

"Good idea! I'll have Angela call them."

"Excellent. I'll say a word to David so that he might expect an invitation."

"Okay. Gotta go. Thank you, Bryan. I'm glad we'll be working together. I'm excited."

"So am I."

Back on Track

I sent him a quick handwritten note by fax, hoping that it might reach him before he left the courthouse:

Dear Justice Scalia,

Here are the materials for starting on oral argument. Each section begins with a blank page for your jottings, etc., or full paragraphs if they come to mind. Then there are research materials for that section—some of which will doubtless trigger good thoughts, and some of which may actually be quotable.

I'm so glad we cleared up our miscommunication. West will be sending us a contract next week, I'm told. My editor was relieved to hear that the project is on after all.

Have a great trip to the West Coast and Hawaii. All best wishes to you and Mrs. Scalia.

Sincerely,
Bryan

Having rescued a project that had gone awry through a gross misunderstanding, I felt enormous relief. Just hours before, he had accused me of some pretty severe misbehavior and bad intentions, but now we were collaborators again. Despite this roller-coaster ride, I felt pretty certain that I could see the book through to success, especially given his ardor for the sample sections—once he had the real ones.

By the way, my plan for having Justice Scalia handwrite a few paragraphs under this or that heading never materialized. He just didn't work that way. Instead, he liked to type passages on his computer and then, when I confirmed that I had received them, delete them from his machine. I never quite understood why he was so keen to delete things, but he was. Often, there would be only one extant draft of a passage he had typed— the one cut out and taped into my master copy for insertion at a particular point in the book. Whenever I had such a draft in my briefcase—it happened many dozens of times—I'd feel nervous until the edits had been entered and verified back in Dallas.

Shortly after our contretemps, I was having dinner with one of Justice Scalia's former clerks near the West Coast. When I recounted what had happened, he told me this story: Justice Scalia had once lost his temper and excoriated the clerk mercilessly, making him think he'd lost his job. Just an hour later, the Justice summoned him back and said: "I once had an uncle, Antonino. I knew him as Uncle Nino—in fact, my nickname came from him. He would sometimes lose his temper. He had a tempestuous nature, and he'd sometimes get furious. But then he'd get over it quickly. We never doubted that Uncle Nino loved us. He really loved us. Now get back to work."

Justice Scalia and I never spoke again about our misunderstanding and his vow to withdraw. I came to understand, however, that I might need to show a heightened sense of fortitude, tenacity, and understanding in this particular relationship. I might occasionally feel visceral shocks coming my way. Only time would tell.

David Foster Wallace

As promised, I called David Foster Wallace on January 19 to alert him to the Scalias' visit to Claremont. He knew about the event but hadn't expected to be included. I told David that Justice Scalia would particularly like to meet him and that the president of the university might well be call-ing with a request that David and his wife, Karen, attend. I said I hoped he'd enjoy the experience. David replied, "We have very little in common politically."

"It was your idea that I meet with him in the first place," I reminded him. "You're both snoots," I said. "Avoid politics and discuss language!"

Apparently that's just what they did. A few days later I received a voice-mail message from David saying just how much he and Karen had enjoyed the luncheon. They were seated directly with the Scalias and found the conversation scintillating. So did Justice Scalia. In an interview with the *Wall Street Journal*, Justice Scalia would later be quoted as saying, "He was a very personable fellow. As co-snoots, we got along very well."[17]

David told me that he felt a little baffled by just how drawn he was to Justice Scalia—how disarmingly likable the man was. I could understand that.

Hitting Our Stride

Justice Scalia and I needed to get into a working groove. "Just tell me what you want me to work on," he said in a February 2007 phone call.

"I've been thinking about our plan to write the same sections simul-taneously. We have a good draft of the first several sections. Let's jump to the middle of the book, on oral argument, and work from there to the end."

"Why would we do *that*?"

"Lots of books get very lopsided because writers run out of steam at the end. Lots of these oral-argument sections will be short, and they'll be relatively easy to write. Let's do them first and then circle back around to general principles."

"If you say so," he said.

"This will help get us into a working pattern. Can we stick to two sections a week until the book is done? Keep with the Friday-afternoon deadline?"

---

17 Jess Bravin, "How David Foster Wallace Prompted a Scalia Book," *The Wall Street Jour-nal*, 23 July 2012, https://blogs.wsj.com/washwire/2012/07/23/how-david-foster-wallace -prompted-a-scalia-book/.

"Sure. That's a plan," he said. "And you'll adhere to the same deadline?"

"Yes. Each weekend I'll spend time melding what you've written with what I've written, just as you've seen in the first seven sections."

"Sounds good. Which sections for this week?"

"How about 61 and 62—toward the beginning of the oral-argument section?"

"Okay," he said.

"One point. If you're working on a given section, please type out a few words of the blackletter heading just above your paragraphs. Our sections will probably shift some, and I must know precisely which sections you're writing about."

"Why must I do that? I'll just put the number of the section before what I type. Don't make me retype the blackletter!"

"My experience with writing books of this type tells me that the section numbers will shift as we go. We'll consolidate sections and develop still more sections, and the numbers will shift from week to week. If you type a bit of the blackletter, it'll be unmistakable where your paragraphs are intended to go."

"That makes sense. Okay."

"We're getting into a routine, and there'll be lots of drafts going back and forth. I want to keep this all orderly so as not to waste one minute of your time."

"I appreciate that."

"This'll be fun."

"I think so, too."

Friday afternoon, precisely on schedule, an e-mail popped up on my screen. The cover memo said, "I hope you likee." In 30 minutes, I wrote back, "I likee very much. Next week, 63 and 64." I thought he was using *likee* as some sort of jocular expression. It turns out it was only a typo that I mimicked, as I would later discover over a laugh during dinner.

Both of us remained assiduous in completing our weekly allotment of sections, and I'd combine his writing with mine each weekend. In May 2007, when we next worked alongside each other in chambers, we had assembled drafts of most sections on oral argument.

During that session on May 10, we tackled a few underdeveloped sections for which I suggested that he write an extra passage. We also reviewed the redesigned table of contents so that he would see how I'd reorganized things; he made further changes, all excellent. It was a full, productive day. We had lunch in chambers and dinner that night at Tosca.

"When are you going to be back?" Justice Scalia asked.

"June 19."

"Let me call Maureen and see whether we can have you out to the house. Is Caroline in town?"

"Yes, she'll be working this summer at a law firm in D.C."

"We'll have the two of you over for macaroni. But let me just check with her." He was dialing. "Maureen? Can we have Bryan and his daughter Caroline over for macaroni on June 19? Are we already committed to anything that evening? Oh, good. Let's have dinner, just the four of us." He hung up. "Can we work here that day?"

"I'm afraid I'll be teaching a seminar until 4 o'clock."

"Okay. Then just meet us at the house at 5:30. How does that sound?"

"Great."

"You're going to love Maureen's macaroni. She's a wonderful cook."

"You mean mac and cheese?"

"No," he said matter-of-factly. "In the Scalia family, when we say 'macaroni,' we just mean pasta of any kind. It could be spaghetti; it could be tagliatelle. Our generic term is 'macaroni.' I don't know what she'll be making."

Macaroni with the Scalias

When the day came, Caroline and I met at my hotel to take a cab to the Scalias' home, an impressive Georgian revival. When Mrs. Scalia opened the door, it was our first meeting, and she greeted us warmly. She's a diminutive woman, soft-spoken with a winning smile. She led us back to the kitchen, saying, "Where's Nino? Nino? *Nino?*" Her crescendo would go only so high. "Oh, I know, you'll find him out on the back porch. You can go see him there. Caroline, why don't you stay here and help me?"

I went back to their porch, where he was puffing on a cigarette. "Hello,

Bryan! I had to have a cigarette. Maureen hates it when I do this, so I sneak out here on the porch."

"I didn't realize you're a smoker."

"I don't do it much. Sometimes one a day. They don't like it when I do it at the Court, either. But . . . how was the trip over here? Did you find us all right?"

"No problem."

"Say, let's go in and I'll mix some drinks."

As we alighted at the kitchen door, Mrs. Scalia said, "Nino, I know what you were doing back there!"

Without acknowledging that comment, he walked into the small bar area beside the kitchen, smiling and resting his hands on the counter, making a kind of shrug.

"I'm going to mix some drinks, dear. Would you like one?"

"Not just yet. Still cooking."

Then he looked at me. "Campari and soda?"

"Yes, thank you."

Justice Scalia reached beneath the counter and put the Campari on the bar. "Wait a second. Maureen, where's the soda? I thought I bought some soda!" he said emphatically.

"You did, Nino," Mrs. Scalia said in a low voice. "It's in the refrigerator. Right where you put it."

"Oh."

After retrieving the soda, and washing his hands, he scooped some ice into our glasses. "Bryan, there's something I've been meaning to tell you. I don't think we can continue working together . . ."

He paused, and my heart sank.

". . . if you keep calling me 'Justice Scalia.' Please call me 'Nino.' I'm Nino."

"Okay, Nino. Thank you."

He handed me my drink and said, "Here's to our book." As we toasted, I knew we were marking a milestone in our relationship. He was Nino to me now.

Mrs. Scalia turned from the stove and said, "You know, he's very excited about it. He's enjoying your various writing projects."

"So am I, believe me. I've never had any experience like it."

"You know," Justice Scalia said, "neither have I. Well, that's not quite true. I did some work as an editor on the *Harvard Law Review*—some work with a classmate, David Currie, who's now a professor at Chicago. What we're doing reminds me of those days working with David. I really like this. It makes me happy."

"Me, too."

At dinner, Justice Scalia said a brief prayer. We engaged in a kind of convivial conversation while getting to know one another, with the full understanding that an alliance had already been formed.

"Caroline, are you old enough to drink wine?"

She stole a glance at me and said, "I'm only 20."

"That's true," I said, "but under Texas law a parent is allowed to serve a child wine even in a restaurant—as long as the restaurant staffers don't do it. I don't know about Virginia law, but I'll bet the rule is the same here."

"Really?" said Justice Scalia.

"Since she was 18, I've usually poured Caroline half a glass of wine."

"Well, then. I guess we can. Caroline, would you like some wine?"

"Yes, sir." He poured meticulously.

The "macaroni"—in this instance, spaghettini—was as promised: as superb as any I'd ever had, with a tomato-based meat sauce. Mrs. Scalia beamed as all three of us expressed our admiration for her cooking.

"Did you learn from Nino's mother?" I asked.

"Some, but mostly from cookbooks."

"And boy, did she master it," he added. "She knew how much I like Italian cooking, and she's as good as anyone I've known. Not bad for an Irish girl." Mrs. Scalia blushed.

Late in the evening, Justice Scalia couldn't help shifting the conversation back to the book: "Bryan, I've been thinking we should use shaded boxes throughout the text."

"Shaded boxes?"

"Yeah. You've been coming up with good quotations from noted authors. We're not going to be able to use all of them. I think we should put the ones we're not using into shaded boxes and have the text wrap around."

I was skeptical. "I've never seen such a thing."

"Well, I have, and I think it works really well. It adds a whole new dimension to the page. Just try it with a couple of sections, and see what you think."

At dinner's end, about 9:30, Justice Scalia said, "Let me drive you back to your hotel!"

"No, of course not. We'll just call a cab."

"Nonsense. I want to drive you back. No sense in paying a cab fare. I'll drive you back."

He was generous to take us back. We had to drop off Caroline first, at her apartment in Georgetown, and then me at the Mayflower, and then he would have to make his way all the way back home—a round trip of about 30 miles in 45 minutes.

In the garage, we climbed into a 1990s-vintage BMW with a stick shift. He said he loved driving standard-transmission cars. "You feel more connected to the engine!" A fast driver, he was impatient with less-efficient drivers sharing the road. And he was aggressive in traffic, so the ride had its moments of excitement.

The next day, after a second day of teaching in D.C., I was at Reagan National Airport when an e-mail came through from Justice Scalia. He sent me what he thought of as his final installment on oral argument. He had scanned a formally prepared cover letter in which he said he was sending me all the remainder of his materials on oral argument. He said that if he hadn't written on a given point, that meant (1) he didn't agree with it, (2) he didn't understand it, (3) he thought the point had been dealt with elsewhere, or (4) he simply had nothing to say. He hastened to add how much he'd enjoyed dinner with Caroline and me the night before.

This letter caused me to jettison some sections on oral argument, combine others, and write on the remaining ones that had no text from him, with the hope that he'd see merit in a section and add to it.

The end of the 2006–2007 Supreme Court term was nearing, and Justice Scalia would soon be heading to Innsbruck to teach in a summer-school program. By the end of June, before he packed up for Europe, I sent him some sample pages incorporating his idea of using shaded boxes. We both liked the way they looked, and I came to think of this feature as one of the most attractive elements in the typography and layout of the book. An example appears on the next page.

By this time, we had agreed to a new title—one that Justice Scalia devised: *Making Your Case*. My original title, *The Art of Persuading Judges*, became the subtitle.

Briefing

The Writing Process

33. Spend plenty of time simply "getting" your arguments.

Good briefing is the product of lengthy thought. The raw material for that deliberation is the facts of your case as you contend them to be or as they have already been conceded or determined. Each one of those facts may be the basis for a legal claim or defense, or the means of establishing or defeating the relevance of governing cases. Review them in detail and prepare a timeline—a chronological listing—of the pertinent ones that must be included in your Statement of Facts.

Don't start writing until you've turned the case over in your mind for days—thinking about it while you're driving to work, discussing it with other lawyers in your firm, even talking it over with friends and family. New ideas may occur to you as you read the leading cases and scholarly authorities. And think not just about your affirmative case but also about the case you can expect from your adversary and the responses you have available.

> "[T]here can be said to be three kinds of author. Firstly, there are those who write without thinking. They write from memory, from reminiscence, or even directly from other people's books. This class is the most numerous. Secondly, there are those who think while writing. They think in order to write. Very common. Thirdly, there are those who have thought before they started writing. They write simply because they have thought. Rare."
> —Arthur Schopenhauer

Working in Chambers

Our days together composing and editing were exhausting, often 9–4 o'clock or 1–5, depending on what my D.C. schedule allowed. That is, every one of these working days was scheduled around a teaching engagement I'd have with a D.C.-area law firm or government agency. I'd just schedule an extra day for writing and editing with him. "Who are you teaching on this trip?" the Justice would often ask with a bit of exuberant admiration. The answer might be the Department of Justice, the FDA, EPA, HHS, HUD, the FCC, the FTC, the PTO, or any one of a few dozen D.C. law firms. He'd always respond as if hopeful and marveling at the answer.

"You're teaching them to write better?"

"You bet I am."

"That should help us—the judges!"

By the time *Making Your Case* was completed, we had worked together in his chambers more than 100 hours. Sometimes we'd work on Saturdays or Sundays, but more often on weekdays. Fernando would prepare a trestle table with a white tablecloth, two chairs side by side, plenty of pens and pencils, a pair of scissors, and a roll of tape. Dictionaries were within easy reach.

Meanwhile, Justice Scalia would also have an extra chair for me beside his own at his keyboard. We'd spend most of our time at the trestle table, going page by page examining passages I'd selected in advance for his further consideration. We'd often read passages back and forth to each other and handwrite in a sentence here and there. We wanted the cadence of each passage—as well as its substance—to be just right. If an addition grew to the length of a paragraph, he'd jump up from the table, walk over to his computer, and begin composing. Typically I'd go to the chair beside him, behind his desk, and watch as the words he was typing appeared on the screen. I'd stay silent until he had reached a stopping point. Then I'd mention any typos that needed fixing, and he'd make the corrections. I'd often suggest another sentence or two. He would type them as I dictated. I'd finish, and then he'd modify one or two of my word choices. Often we'd have our little word-battles over those choices.

Then he'd print two copies of our new two-paragraph insert, and we'd independently edit in silence for three minutes or so, after which we'd sit down at his computer while he entered his edits first, then mine. We'd usually repeat this process, printing out two more copies, reading it again, sometimes aloud to each other. Or there would be more editorial adjustments. Those made, he'd print out just one copy for me to insert into the master version of the manuscript (always labeled "BAG Master," from my initials, on the front cover) using scissors and tape. Upon my return to Dallas, I'd have the insertions retyped into the master.

As we'd work through the text, I'd carefully show him all the new passages I had composed to fill out sections that had seemed underdeveloped. Half he would approve verbatim. But then he'd stop on one, and our exchange—it became a ritualistic exchange—would go something like this:

"Do we really need to say this?"

"I think we do. It's an important point."

"Hmm. I just don't like the way you've said it."

Then his eyes would close as he'd lean back, fingers steepled across his belly. He'd start staring at a spot on the ceiling—a spot that would become part of our personal lore in collaborating. That spot—always the same one—seemed to be the source of his inspiration. Perhaps 30 seconds would pass in silence, and then he'd dash over to his computer with my draft in hand. He'd begin typing out the same idea in his own words, often using little of what I'd written. Almost always these passages contained some bold metaphor or striking phraseology. One that sticks in my mind is the tasseled-loafer passage: "You can bet your tasseled loafers that some judges, like Lord Denning, will be disposed to change the law to accord with their 'moral sense,' and that many more will, like Chancellor Kent, base their initial decision on their 'moral sense' and then scour the law for some authority to support that decision."[18]

Once he had completed his rewrite, we'd go through our editing routine as I described above, culminating in ceremoniously taping the replacement passage into the "BAG Master." He'd take a pencil and put a huge X through the passage to be replaced.

We fell into these patterns quite naturally. Instinctively I knew not to speak when he was staring at his spot or composing a sentence, and he would do the same when it fell my turn to write something in his presence.

If the passage was short, or just a few words were to be changed, he'd

---

18 Antonin Scalia & Bryan A. Garner, *Making Your Case: The Art of Persuading Judges* 27 (2008).

make the change in pencil—either red or Number 2. (By contrast, I habitually edited in ink.) With anything longer than a sentence, he'd prefer typing. He was a fast typist, and he knew how to touch-type—a skill he'd acquired in high school. Unlike me, he wasn't inclined to write out paragraph after paragraph in longhand.

He was often physical. When he'd get an idea while we were sitting alongside each other, he'd nudge me with his elbow. At the outbreak of a disagreement, the jabs would be sharper. Sometimes we'd argue for five or ten minutes on some point or other, but usually we'd find a way of reconciling our views. When we couldn't, we'd call a circuit judge's chambers to seek his or her views. At various points, we called Judge Frank Easterbrook, Judge Edith Jones, Judge Alex Kozinski, or Judge Thomas Reavley to ask their opinions. Invariably these calls helped us. Each time, though, the judges seemed quite surprised to be getting a call from the Supreme Court seeking their views on advocacy.

One dispute between us had to do with the summary of argument in a brief. I already knew his idiosyncratic stance from the interview I'd conducted with him in October 2006.

"It's a waste of time and space!" he said, elbowing me in the shoulder.

"Nino, your views on this are out of step with those of most judges. You wouldn't want to read a book without reading the dust jacket first."

"I always do that. I hate dust jackets! I never read the dust jacket. It's a waste of time."

"Are you kidding?"

"Absolutely not. Throw them right away."

"Well, please stop that. Dust jackets have important information on them. And books are more valuable to collectors if they have dust jackets. Our book is going to have a dust jacket, with our mugs on it!"

"That's true. But the summary of argument in a brief is completely unnecessary. Just read the argument in full!"

"You're an outlier. Other judges don't agree with you!"

"How do you know that?"

"Through interviews. You know I've interviewed judges all over the country. You're the only judge who's ever said that. Alito and Thomas say precisely the opposite."

"They do?"

"You bet. I can show you."

I powered up my laptop and showed him a brief video clip of Justice Alito stressing the importance of writing a good summary of argument because that's one of the best ways of first learning about a case.

"Well, I'll be," said Justice Scalia, sitting down at his computer. He began typing a passage that ended up appearing on page 97 of the published book. I sat in a chair beside him and watched as the words appeared on the screen: "Some judges never read the Summary of Argument, which will precede the Argument section of your brief. Why read a cut-down version when you're about to read the real thing?" So he'd stuck to his dust jacket view. I remained silent as he bit his cuticle for a moment. Then he continued typing: "Other judges, however, consider the Summary of Argument indispensable—indeed, the most important part of the brief. As long as judges of the latter sort exist, and the judge you're appearing before has not publicly committed, you must include the Summary."

"That's good, Nino."

"You think so?"

"Well, much better than your initial position!"

Then we explained something that all too few advocates understand: "Unlike the Introduction, the Summary of Argument is not just a preview of the topics of argument that are to follow. It is a short version of the substance of the arguments under each topic. . . . State the main lines of thought without embellishment, omit quotations, and cite only key cases (if any at all)."

We spent probably ten minutes considering whether to capitalize the names of the parts of the brief, and throughout the day we vacillated. In the end, we decided that capitals helped demarcate the discrete sections we were referring to at any given point in the discussion. We wrestled with countless tiny decisions like this throughout the project—and Justice Scalia wanted to be fully involved with all the minutiae.

We kept up our pace of weekly assignments from late July through September, both of us working on the same sections at the same time. Then I'd combine our two versions, meanwhile editing his work just as I would anyone else's. That meant, among other things, contracting his instances of "do not" and "does not" and "is not"—so that they generally (not invariably) became "don't" and "doesn't" and "isn't." Little did I know that these particular changes would threaten to wreck our collaboration.

Invasion of the Apostrophes

Early on in our work, I noticed that all my coauthor's negative advice (and there was an abundance of it) was couched as "Do not do this," or "Do not do that." As had been my stylistic habit since the early 1990s, I changed "Do not" to "Don't" in all instances—partly to regularize the style and partly to improve the tone. But then I noticed in the batches that he'd returned to me, *Don't* was crossed out in pencil, and *Do not* was written above. I figured that we were in for a discussion of the issue, but I had no idea what a source of ferocious conflict this would be, and what a serious impasse it would create.

"We cannot use contractions!"

"But we must!" I insisted. "A lot of our advice is negative. We can't keep saying 'Do not do this, Do not do that.' It sounds stilted."

"I never use contractions. I don't like them. They're *infra dignitatem*."

"You just used a contraction in that statement!"

"Lookit, I'm talking about formal writing. You know what I mean."

"And why do you say *infra dignitatem*? Most scholars say *infra dig* for short."

"That's a colloquialism. And it's a contraction! It's beneath one's dignity."

"I used to have a bias against contractions myself. But look how the best nonfiction writers of our day write: they use contractions."

"What do you mean?"

"*The New Yorker. The Atlantic Monthly. Harper's.*"

"They're a bunch of lefties."

"Okay, then *National Review!*"

"They're magazines. We're writing a *book*."

"I can cite readability studies showing that contractions make writing more readable. They really help. We want people buying this book and reading it."

"Well, I admit you know about that. I'll conditionally go along for now, but I'm not happy about it. What really upsets me is what you're doing on gender. You're neutering my prose."

"I've made it gender-neutral, yes."

"That's Jacobin, absolutely *Jacobin*," he said while walking into the private restroom adjoining his office.

I wasn't quite sure what that word meant—even though I recalled that he'd used the word a few times before—but I didn't want to confess my ignorance. So while he was out of view, I sneaked a look at *Webster's Second*: "violently radical." But *Jacobin* was defined as a noun; *Jacobinic*, the big book suggested, would have been the right adjective. Naturally, though, I managed to suppress my urge to correct him—which, in any event, would have been insufferably pedantic. After all, I had been unfamiliar with both words.

When he came out, I said, "Nino, this isn't radical at all. Half our readers are going to be women. Why offend them—or risk offending any of them?"

"Everybody knows that the masculine pronoun includes the feminine."

"Well, we all used to be taught that, it's true. It's a rule that first appeared in the work of a grammarian named Anne Fisher, writing in 1745."

"You see! A woman came up with that rule," he said.

"But very few people in the world know that, and it doesn't matter. The fact is that people don't really see it that way. The English language is inherently sexist without an epicene third-person singular pronoun."

"It is *not*. Grammatical gender is arbitrary, just as in all the Romance languages. If I say 'Everyone can think for himself,' everyone knows that includes women. You're just caving in to the PC police!"

"I am not," I said. "I'm just being practical and just."

"Many women don't care, and they prefer the generic *he*."

"Of course that's true of some. People don't fit stereotypes. Many men are bothered by the generic *he*."

"What kind of men are they? Namby-pamby men? They're being ridiculous."

"Nino, I'm conservative in matters of language. You know that. The point is that we can write this thing without having the question of sexism even enter anyone's head. Why make some readers suspect that we're sexist troglodytes?"

"The problem is you *can't* write around the problem. Readers will see through it."

"No, they won't," I said. "And I don't think they could if they were prompted to try."

"I totally disagree," he said. "Your rewrites are awkward."

"Instead of 'Everyone can think for himself,' all you have to say is, 'All of us can think for ourselves.'"

"But there are many other sentences that aren't so easy. Believe me, I've seen it."

"Nino, if I recall correctly, at some point early on you said that nothing we say should gratuitously contradict your jurisprudence."

"That's right. What of it?"

"Well, I have a jurisprudence of writing. I've written at least four books saying that it's highly desirable to write in a gender-neutral way."

"You have? Let's see one."

"You have three right here behind your monitor: *The Winning Brief*, *The Elements of Legal Style*, and *Garner's Modern American Usage*. Let me show you *The Winning Brief*, section 56."

"Buh-buh-buh." He flicked through the pages of the second edition of *The Winning Brief* and began reading aloud: " 'Shun sexist language, but do it invisibly.' Hmm." I pointed to the words of Chief Judge Judith Kaye of New York: "I believe that gendered writing . . . will one day be immediately recognized as archaic and ludicrous. My only message to brief-writers is that, to many brief-readers today, it already is."

"You see?" I said.

"You devoted three full pages to this subject?"

"It's really important in many people's minds—and it's important to me."

"It's balderdash. But I'll go along for the time being. You see what an agreeable coauthor I am?"

"You're a great coauthor, Nino."

Proto-Draft

By early September we had a rough draft. I suggested that we send the manuscript to lawyer friends for their comments on possible improvements. In the end, he sent it to 15 friends of his and I to 30 of mine. As the comments trickled in, I'd incorporate many of their suggestions into the manuscript. If his commenters suggested new avenues of argument or analysis, he'd write an additional paragraph or two.

Meanwhile, the two of us edited the book independently. On September 19, I received a voluminous pile of his edits that he had made while visiting his place at the Outer Banks. Many of these were buttressed by his usual summer visitor, the learned and urbane Judge Marty Feldman of New Orleans. Justice Scalia would often annotate his edits with, "Marty agrees!" Justice Scalia lightly reorganized the table of contents, containing the 108 sections we then had in the draft (it would grow to 115). He moved paragraphs around, added new ones, deleted lots of sentences, and generally gave the manuscript a heavy massage.

For what became section 31 of the book ("Set timelines for the stages of your work"), I had given a hypothetical example in which the brief-writer produces the first draft on Sunday afternoon. Justice Scalia wrote in the margin: "Some readers would disapprove of working on Sunday. Can we revise the time schedule? Use Sunday as the cooling-off period." Naturally, I made the adjustment.

His marginalia (besides "Marty agrees") were often wonderfully colorful. "WORDY WORDY," he'd admonish, or "I do not agree (vigorously)," "UGH!," and even "BULLSHIT!" On the whole, though, the edits were more restrained and easily entered.

We scheduled a marathon session to complete the book: November 2–3, along with November 4 if necessary. The idea was to work through the more difficult comments we'd received and to approve the final selection of shaded boxes (I had collected some 400 quotations, but we agreed we'd use only about 85). And of course we'd have dinner both nights to decompress.

While we were working together on November 2, I suggested, "We should have some type of photographic record of how we work together."

"What do you mean?" he asked.

"Well, when I'm with you, I feel as if it's a historic event. Why don't we have Angela or Crystal [his other assistant, Crystal Martin] snap a couple of photographs? I just want to remember the way you've set up this table, how we sit together, and so on."

"Just a moment," he said, going to his phone behind his desk. "Angela, send over the Court photographer."

Ten minutes later, Steve Petteway, from the curator's office, appeared with a camera and introduced himself. "Steve," Justice Scalia said after introducing me, "we want some photographs of us working together. We're just going to carry on as if you weren't here. Just document more or less what we're doing."

That's what Steve Petteway did. In our decade-long writing partnership, Petteway's photographs on this day are the only ones that show us actually composing paragraphs together. Although Justice Scalia didn't like most of them because he thought he looked mean, we used two of the better ones in the preshow for our various presentations.

The Inner Child

At one of our dinners at Tosca during those sessions, Justice Scalia and I traded stories about our past.

"How did a kid from Texas become a snoot?" he asked me.

"My parents cared a lot about language. My mother would call the local television station every time the weatherman would call himself a 'meterologist.'"

"Oh, that's a bad one," he said. "Leaving out the first *o*: /mee-tee-uh-ROL-uh-jist/. It has six syllables, not five."

"Right. And then I had an early run-in with *shall*."

"You did?"

"Scarred me for life."

"What happened?" he asked.

"I can't really talk about it without getting emotional." Indeed, to this day I cannot.

"Tell me."

"I really shouldn't. I might cry. I don't want to embarrass myself. Besides, *Webster's Third* ends up being the hero of the story. And contractions come into play."

"Oh, now I've got to hear it. You won't really cry, will you?"

"I might. I regress."

"Well, I won't force you. But if you'll tell me that, I'll tell you why I never learned Italian."

"Okay. I grew up in the Panhandle of Texas on the High Plains, near Palo Duro Canyon—the second-largest canyon in the country."

"No kidding."

"It's 1968, I'm in the fourth grade. And we had this wonderful teacher, Mrs. Pearcy, whom I really liked—my mother thought a little too much."

"Ha!"

"That year, a student teacher shadowed Mrs. Pearcy: Miss Phillips. She was a college student trying to earn her teacher's certificate. I remember her as cold, sour, sullen, and constantly disapproving—especially of a certain child named Bryan Garner."

"Can't imagine why," Justice Scalia said, eyebrows raised, sipping his Campari and soda.

"One day a professor of education walked into Mrs. Pearcy's classroom. I knew him. He was a friend of my father's. Mrs. Pearcy went to the front of the room and explained that Miss Phillips would now be teaching the English lesson for the day while the professor of education observed. This was a required element in Miss Phillips's teacher certification."

"This is a long story, Bryan."

"Yes. Bear with me. Miss Phillips came to the front of the class, stood nervously, and scowled. She then announced in a very artificial way, 'Children, today I am going to teach you about contractions. Can anyone name a contraction?' "

"I was sitting on the first row. My hand shot into the air, and she called on me: 'Bryan.' "

"*Shan't,*" I said.

" 'No, that's not a word.' "

"It is, Miss Phillips. It's a contraction for *shall not.*"

" 'No. That's not a word. Can anyone name a contraction?' "

"Other kids started shouting out *isn't* and *doesn't* and *wouldn't* and *couldn't,* and she was saying, 'Good, children, good. Now *those* are contractions.' Or at least that's the way I heard it."

"This really happened?" asked Justice Scalia.

"Exactly as I'm describing it. October 1968. I was nine. I clammed up for the rest of the class."

"Is that the end of the story?"

"Of course not. I started eyeing the dictionary stand in the corner of the classroom. And my nine-year-old self thought, 'I'm going to look this up.' I didn't know it at the time, but it was *Webster's Third.* I felt certain it would vindicate me by showing that *shan't* is a word."

"I suppose *Webster's Third* has its uses."

"It certainly did to me that day."

"Wait a second. How did a kid from a small town in West Texas know the word *shan't?*"

"Mr. French!"

"Mr. Who?"

"Don't you remember the television show *A Family Affair,* with Buffy and Jodie and their English butler, Mr. French?"

"Oh, of course! 'Children, we shan't be going out today.' " Justice Scalia mimicked an upper-class English accent.

"Precisely. So I was sure of my ground."

"Did you confront Miss Phillips with *Webster's Third*?"

"I tried. At the end of class, I looked up *shan't*, and there it was: 'contraction of *shall not*.' I lugged the book over to where she was standing."

"And . . ."

"It was an inconvenient moment. She was speaking to the professor of education, who of course had come to evaluate her performance."

"Ooh. She should have been marked down for her quick dismissal of your suggestion."

"Well, I wish he'd seen what happened next."

"What happened?"

"When he left, and I tried to show her the dictionary, she refused to look. I said, 'Look, Miss Phillips, it's a word! *Shan't* is in the dictionary! It's a word!' I was genuinely excited. This was no attempt at a comeuppance." I got a little choked up as I told the story.

Justice Scalia reached over and put his hand on my forearm. "This really affected you deeply, didn't it?" he said.

"Yes," I said. "I told you I still get emotional when I tell this story. Anyway, she said, 'Bryan Garner, that's not a word, and I'm not looking at that book. Now you go run and play.'"

"You must have been a sensitive child."

"I suppose. That was one of the most important incidents of my life—my first encounter with anti-intellectualism. In retrospect, it probably put me on the road to lexicography. I'm sure that my entire career has been some twisted, protracted psychological attempt to get back at Miss Phillips."

"Ha! Well, I don't have anything in my background with quite so much anguish tied to words. It was just something I shared with my father. But I can see now why you're a word-nut."

"Okay. Now tell me why you never learned Italian. I don't get that. Your father was a professor of Romance languages."

"That's true. But the way he spoke Italian was something he wasn't proud of. It was dialect. It was considered low-class Italian. It would have sounded like an uneducated yokel, the equivalent of 'Hey, youse guys!'" He was affecting a loutish gangster voice from a James Cagney movie.

"That's so strange. He was teaching Italian. You'd think he'd have picked up the cultivated Italian accent."

"I know. But he was convinced he hadn't, at least not for everyday talk."

"Yet he was teaching Italian to other American students."

"It is kind of strange, isn't it?" he mused.

"I think there was something else going on," I said.

"What's that?"

"In your parents' era, ethnic assimilation was an extremely strong value. Parents were ambitious for their children, and no matter how proud they were of their heritage, they wanted their children to be thoroughly American."

"You know, that's true—unlike today, when assimilation is seen to be a bad thing," he said.

"I'll bet that's why your parents didn't speak Italian in the home. They were practicing their own English, and they perhaps feared they might retard your progress in English."

"You don't know that," he said, scowling and sounding skeptical—and almost as if I'd hit a nerve.

"No. I'm just playing amateur psychologist. I'm probably quite wrong. Or maybe they didn't want you speaking English with an Italian accent."

"Hmm. Maybe not." He was chewing on his lower lip quite a bit that evening, and he seemed lost in thought once we started talking about his past.

"What part of Italy did your mother come from?" I asked.

"She was born here in America. Her parents came from Italy." He didn't quite answer my question directly.

"Maybe that explains it as well. Her dialect might have been quite different from your father's, and maybe that would have complicated things."

"He wanted me to study Italian in college, but I never did. I think I really disappointed him there."

"Don't feel bad, Nino. He'd have made things painless for you if he'd spoken Italian to you whenever the two of you were together before you were ten years old. Painless." I was referring, of course, to the natural facility that young children have for language acquisition—whereas it's much more difficult for a college-age student. "A famous linguist, Max Black, said that young kids can acquire a new language as effortlessly as they catch the measles. You shouldn't feel bad."

"But I still do," he said. "I disappointed my father."

Greeting Justice Souter

During one of our sessions that month—November 2007—a curious thing happened. To put it into context, though, I must explain that from the preceding October to March, I had filmed interviews about advocacy with eight of the nine sitting Supreme Court Justices—all but Justice David Souter. In the end, the project was considered newsworthy enough to receive front-page notices twice, once when the interviews were released as videos on the Internet[19] and once when the print transcripts appeared.[20] Although Justice Thomas initially declined by letter, a word from Justice Scalia persuaded him to reverse that decision—and the interview went exceedingly well. Only Justice Souter's letter politely declining the invitation remained firm.

In fact, Justice Souter didn't acknowledge my follow-up letter to him, and Justice Scalia's friendly word on my behalf had no effect. So by late 2007, I'm sure I had resigned myself to not getting an interview with the famously introverted Justice.

A chance happening confirmed that result. As Justice Scalia and I were leaving for lunch one day, walking down the ornate marble corridors of the Court, we rounded a corner where a heavy, elaborately decorated gate separated the public from the private areas. Justice Souter walked through the gate just as we were approaching. The gate clicked shut behind him. Before he saw us some 50 feet away down the hallway, I whispered to Justice Scalia, "Lookee there. You know, I'll never get that interview. Would you introduce me?" I'm certain my comment was audible only to my companion, who suddenly kicked into a highly extroverted mode of good-natured hectoring as we walked up to him: "David, give this man an interview. C'mon! You ought to do an interview!"

This wasn't the introduction I'd expected. I stuck my hand out and said, "Hello, Justice Souter, my name is Bryan Garner."

---

19 Tony Mauro, "Interviews of United States Supreme Court Justices," *Legal Times*, 20 March 2008, at 1. To watch the video versions, go to http://www.lawprose.org/bryan -garner/garners-interviews/supreme-court-interviews/.

20 Adam Liptak, "Keep the Briefs Brief, Literary Justices Advise," *New York Times*, 21 May 2011, at A1, A12. For the full transcriptions, see *Scribes Journal of Legal Writing*, vol. 13 (2010).

Justice Souter pursed his lips and looked down at my hand, which was poised awkwardly in midair. Then I added, "I'm not asking for an interview—just to shake your hand."

He hesitantly withdrew his hand from behind his back and shook mine. Justice Scalia had become silent, I think in disbelief.

"Good to meet you," I said.

"Likewise," I believe Justice Souter might have said as he continued on his way.

He wasn't unfriendly. Doubtless he felt as if he was being aggressively pressured. And Justice Scalia's playful badgering seemed to make him withdraw.

"That was really strange," Justice Scalia remarked as we got onto the elevator. Although I knew that the Justices liked each other, I couldn't help thinking that if they'd been two of several children at a playground, they'd have been the least likely to be playing together.

Passive Aggression

Soon we were back in chambers having a lengthy argument about passive voice. Justice Scalia wanted the very first line of the introduction to read: "Judges can be persuaded only when three conditions are met." That, in fact, was his suggested rewrite of my sentence: "You can persuade judges only when you satisfy three conditions."

"I like mine better!" Justice Scalia insisted.

"But it's passive voice!"

"There's nothing wrong with passive voice."

"Not always, that's true. But it's best to avoid it when we can."

"We're going with passive!"

"You use a lot of passive voice," I said. "In fact, I was surprised at how much passive voice you use. For such a bold writer, and one with such a reputation for flair, you use it astonishingly often."

"When it's right, I use it."

We argued about this leadoff sentence for perhaps five minutes. Again, the argument continued as he was in the restroom, shouting to me. "You're just trying to change my style!" he said in a very accusatory tone.

"I am not! You're the one who changed *my* sentence! But if I am changing your style, it's only because it needs changing!"

Suddenly I became aware that I was shouting back at him. Everybody had gone home for the day, and here we were—alone and shouting at each other. I made a mental note to modulate my voice and vowed never to shout at him again. But when he emerged from the restroom, he seemed unperturbed. If anything, he seemed to enjoy the argument.

"Okay," I said, "if I can't budge you on this one, we'll leave it your way. The sentence is ten words either way. But I promise you there are going to be other sentences that need a passive-to-active transformation."

"We'll see when we get there."

I could tell these were going to be long sessions. We had hundreds of edits to go through. I had my "BAG Master" with some 20 of these commenters' remarks in the margin, all color-coded to tell us who made each comment. Among the most copious substantive commenters were Justice Scalia's friend Professor Michael R. Devitt of San Diego and Justice Scalia's son Eugene, a D.C. lawyer. We remarked again and again how grateful we were for the voluminous annotations.

We extended our weekend editing session through Sunday, meeting at the Court before noon. I showed him a comment from one of my readers, Steven Hirsch of San Francisco. Hirsch had said that the book was recognizably Garner but that there was scarcely any hint of Scalia. Upon reading this, Justice Scalia grew quiet with concern and worry.

"I think we just need more of your metaphor and verve in general. We *do* need more Scalia personality in the book."

"Well, you've rewritten my work all in *your* style."

"No, I haven't. It's just that we need to massage more paragraphs to put more color in the work. Now that we have a complete draft, it's time to do that."

"This is hard work," Justice Scalia said, "harder than I figured when I signed up for it."

"I know. Writing a book is always hard—really hard. It's a lot harder than people think."

"You're telling me. I think we need another weekend together. Can you come back next weekend?"

"I can be here Sunday and Monday, the 11th and 12th."

"Let's see how the next draft looks."

It was 3 o'clock. "I want to call it a day," he said. "Can I drive you to the airport?"

"No. Don't worry about me. Get back to Maureen. She's been without you for three solid days."

"She's probably glad about that!" he said, laughing. "I'm looking forward to dinner with her tonight. How are you going to get to the airport?"

"I'll take a cab. It's easy to find cabs in front of the Court."

We packed up our things, he called a marshal to take me to the exit, and he took the elevator on down to the garage. He was still noticeably bothered by the comment that the manuscript showed little of the Scalia vitality.

More Blowback

My observation, as it turned out, wasn't ill-founded. Late the next morning, on Guy Fawkes Day 2007, I received a four-paragraph e-mail from Justice Scalia. Unlike all the earlier substantial messages I had received from him, this wasn't printed on letterhead and then scanned. Instead, it was typed as an e-mail with the subject line: "Mag. Op." That reminded me that he'd taken to calling *Making Your Case* our "magnum opus."

But the message was not a happy one. He said he was having "buyer's remorse" after our weekend session. He lamented that we had "cast the whole thing" in what was unmistakably my style, not his. Again he was resisting contractions, which he said were "not what a scholar and a Supreme Court Justice ordinarily uses." He moved on to gender-neutralizing, which he said "everyone knew" he abhorred. And he resented my changing each instance of his using *upon* to *on*, calling his own two-syllable preposition "a perfectly acceptable style preference." My small stylistic victories had left him unsettled: "If we had set out to make this look like a book that you wrote and I lent my name to, we could not have done much better. (Note that even in this informal message I do not naturally say 'we couldn't have done much better.')"

He wasn't dictatorial in his approach to me, but instead was trying to persuade: "I hope you will give some thought to this, especially in light of the remark from one of your commenters that there doesn't seem to be much of me in the book." I had been hoping to cure this shortcoming with more of his striking metaphors, similes, and other turns of phrase—not by changing *don't* into *do not*. Nevertheless, he said: "I am currently inclined to delete a lot (not all) of the contractions. That is a fetish of yours and not of mine. I should think you would *want* a book with a Supreme Court coauthor to have a somewhat more formal tone."

Yet he was conciliatory on one point: "I will continue to yield on your gender-neutralizing, but not cheerfully."

When it came to style, though, he said that he was not disposed to accept any more editing of his prose, adding "verb. sap. sat.," meaning "a word to the wise." Then came a clear direction: "Do the next draft the way we agreed (unless you want to eliminate most of the contractions). But I reserve the right to renege. Regards. Nino."

I called to discuss his concerns, and I broached a further problem: my conviction that citations ought to be footnoted, not interspersed throughout the main text. We'd already started quarreling about that. In September I had written a passage about footnoting citations, and that was where he had written "BULLSHIT!" in the margin. Now he was considering moving the citations up into the text of our book—a move that I couldn't have accepted. We were at serious loggerheads.

"I'm just not comfortable with the way things are going," Justice Scalia said.

Neither was I, and I began to worry. In a few hours he followed up to say that he'd make himself available Sunday the 11th and Monday the 12th. I booked my flights that afternoon.

The Trimble Solution

Over the course of the evening, I fretted about what to do. I called my good friend John Trimble, a professor emeritus of English at the University of Texas who, over many conversations with me, had been following my progress with Justice Scalia. John saw things my way on all the points of conflict (contractions, sexist language, and footnoted citations)—in fact, he had influenced me on adopting contractions way back in the spring of 1991, when he and I began teaching LawProse seminars together. After I related to John the most recent developments in the Scalia–Garner collaborations, he suggested a novel idea: Justice Scalia and I should simply debate our three disagreements in the book itself. We'd set forth the Garner view and then the Scalia view, or vice versa.

The next morning, I suggested this solution to Justice Scalia, who enthusiastically embraced the idea. "That's great, Bryan. You write first, and then you let me write a dissenting opinion. I love that."

But after hanging up, I suddenly felt less sanguine about the idea. I'd be debating one of the most famous debaters of all time. And he'd be using his strongest rhetorical weapon—the blistering dissent.

Within 24 hours, I had sent him all three of my "pro" positions. I imagine he read them with rapt pleasure, finding each opportunity I'd presented him for rebutting my points. That very afternoon, a scant four hours later, he sent me a message saying: "Bryan: Here are my dissenting views. I had fun. Nino."

Did he ever. He talked of how contractions "vulgarize." And he wrote this clincher (which I still consider exaggerated): "I guarantee that if you use contractions in your written submissions, some judges—including many who are not offended by the use of contractions in the *New Yorker*, *Time*, *Vogue*, *Rolling Stone*, *Field and Stream*, and other publications not addressed to black-robed judges engaged in the exercise of their august governmental powers—will take it as an affront to the dignity of the court." That's enough to scare any lawyer away from contractions.

On sexist language he injected even more vim: "I find it incomprehensible that my esteemed coauthor, who has displayed the inventiveness of a DaVinci and the imagination of a Tolkien in devising circumlocutions that have purged from my contributions to this volume (at some stylistic cost) all use of 'he' as the traditional, generic, unisex reference to a human being—incomprehensible, I say, that this same coauthor should speak disparagingly of 'shibboleths,' and feign inability to come up with an acceptable substitute for the clumsy 'Do you not think?' "

He was doing what he loved.

At one point when I was making a passage gender-neutral, he exclaimed in exasperation, "You're doing the same thing in this book that Ruth does to my opinions!" I responded, "Well, it's a good thing she's there!"[21]

As for footnoting citations, Justice Scalia had this to say: "Whatever the merits of this debate, the conclusive reason not to accept Garner's novel suggestion is that it is novel. Judges are uncomfortable with change, and it is a sure thing that some crabby judges will dislike this one. You should no

---

21 See Garner, "War of the Words," *American Lawyer*, Feb. 2009, at 56 (recounting this anecdote).

more try to convert the court to citation-free text at your client's expense than you should try to convert it to colorful ties or casual-Friday attire at oral argument."

These passages had the dual effect of spicing up the text and allowing Justice Scalia to vent his otherwise stifled frustrations about compromising with me on questions of style.

When we started working together that Sunday afternoon, I mentioned to Justice Scalia that he likes a good argument.

"I *do* like a good argument. I think the book is much better now."

"Me, too. Have you ever heard Monty Python's skit 'The Argument'?"

"No. But I've heard of Monty Python."

"I should play it for you."

I ended up getting out my iPod and playing the audio skit for him, much to his delight. It's about a man who walks into an office to pay for an argument with someone. When he gets to the room where the argument is to be held, his interlocutor begins contradicting everything he's saying, including the fact that he has paid for an argument. There ensues an argument about whether mere contradictions amount to an argument at all, and by the time it gets interesting the interlocutor rings a bell and says that the time is up. Then there's an argument about whether the customer got his money's worth—whereupon the interlocutor refuses to argue any further until the customer pays more.

"That's *really* funny," Justice Scalia said.

"You'd probably pay for an argument if you couldn't otherwise get one."

"I might indeed," he said, smiling.

In the end, we decided to add a fourth argument. I took the position that nothing of substance should appear in footnotes—in particular, no complete sentences that readers would be expected to read. I backed this up with ten citations (in footnotes) to appellate courts saying they wouldn't consider any argument raised exclusively in a footnote. Justice Scalia took a softer position here, since our differences weren't great: "I know of no court that will categorically not consider substantive footnotes. The citations in my coauthor's scary footnote pertain to the raising of fundamentally new claims or new arguments."

After the point/counterpoint arguments had been set in stone, I happened to receive an e-mail from a lawyer in Utah who had noticed a major trend toward contractions in the opinions of then–Tenth Circuit Judge

Neil Gorsuch. She sent me 11 examples of *could've, might've, should've,* and *would've* from his opinions, including this: "While I do not doubt for a moment that additional investigation would have been a good idea, asking whether the officers might've, could've, or should've done more investigation before effecting an arrest is not the test."[22] I responded to the lawyer by saying: "Interesting: Watch for the Scalia–Garner book due out soon—Justice Scalia objects to contractions, and I defend them." Meanwhile, I sent a blind copy to my coauthor.

He responded with just two words: "Sounds godawful."

An Outré Request for Testimony

In that second long weekend together, over our Sunday-evening dinner, I broke some bad news of my own. My divorce case had now been pending for 15 months, and my soon-to-be-ex-wife's lawyer was saying he wanted to take Justice Scalia's deposition. My lawyer had asked me to get some convenient dates. This embarrassed me greatly, as I could see no real reason for it. I told Justice Scalia about the imbroglio.

"My deposition? But why?"

"He's saying he needs to investigate the financial arrangement between us for the book."

"Why would it matter?"

"It doesn't, really. But Texas is a community-property state."

"So what?"

"Even though I had filed for divorce and moved out before interviewing you and before getting the idea for this book, I'm creating it while still legally married. So she may technically have rights in it as a matter of community property."

"That's crazy. Why not give them a copy of the contract?"

"We've given it, but her lawyer says he wants the deposition anyway. I think this may be just a bizarre form of gamesmanship. Or maybe he just wants his day in the Supreme Court. I can't imagine what they want other than to embarrass me in front of you."

"Lookit, bring it on. Tell them to come depose me. It doesn't bother

---

22 *Cortez v. McCauley,* 478 F.3d 1108, 1139 (10th Cir. 2007) (Gorsuch J. concurring in part & dissenting in part).

me. You're my friend, and I'm standing by you. If they want to waste my time, and it helps you, I'm glad to do it."

"I'm so sorry this is happening."

"Don't worry about it. I want to see you through this. I know it's hard. Call Angela and get some dates."

"Thank you, Nino."

In the end, the deposition never took place. But I was gratified by my coauthor's unflinching resolve.

We had been working weekends together, and Justice Scalia was cheery. In mid-November 2007, he sent me this e-mail message: "Bryan: Great session this weekend. I think one more two-day session should do it. Excelsior! Nino." We agreed that our final two-day session would be December 27 and 28. He and some friends would leave the next day to go hunting for geese—but he offered to skip the trip if those two days didn't fit my schedule.

Breaking News

Meanwhile, the legal reporter Tony Mauro had gotten wind of our project and called me. Because I'd known him for years and trusted him, I spoke to him at some length—making the snap judgment that neither Justice Scalia nor West would mind my talking to a reporter even though the book wasn't to be published until mid-spring. Mauro asked whether I could get Justice Scalia to talk with him, and I said I'd try. But my coauthor was resistant.

"I don't want to talk with that man. I won't talk to him!"

"Nino, he's a friend of mine. I've cooperated with him on past stories, and I think he's kindly disposed. Don't assume that it's going to be negative."

"It will be, believe me. It always is." Doubtless he had been conditioned to react quite differently to the press through his own bad experiences.

"Not this time. I'm involved. He'll be square with me. Let me help you on this aspect of media relations. Sometimes you just need to cooperate with them. If you're nice to the media, they'll generally be nice to you." This might have been my callowness talking.

"No, they won't. Lookit, I'm not talking to the guy."

"Can you at least issue a written statement about the book through the Public Information Office?"

"I'll do that, but no more."

Later that day, Justice Scalia had the PIO send this message to Tony Mauro: "The object of the book is to make available, in a compact and (we hope) readable format, what we think to be the best advice on how to argue a case. It covers both brief-writing and oral argument. And it includes both advice from modern sources and advice from ancient sources adapted to modern American circumstances. We hope it will be helpful to the bar; if so, it will benefit the bench as well."

Tony Mauro's lead in the *Legal Times* (26 Nov. 2007) read this way: "While Supreme Court Justice Clarence Thomas has been out publicizing his best-selling memoir, fellow conservative Antonin Scalia has been quietly writing a book of his own. But Scalia's probably won't be a chart-topper—except among lawyers." Then he zeroed in on the nature of the enterprise: "Without fanfare or publicity, Scalia and Bryan Garner, the legal-writing guru, have joined to coauthor a book on the art of persuading judges, both orally and in written briefs." Mauro quoted me as saying that we had spent 4 of the past 14 days side by side in Justice Scalia's office to write and rewrite chapters in the book.

The article continued: "Scalia 'defers on all kinds of points,' Garner laughs, adding that with all the changes and rewriting, 'we can't tell any-more which of us wrote which sentences.'" The point about deference caused me some trepidation, given our recent turbulent debates about whether the book had enough Scalian style.

I also announced to the world the identity of "Justice Scalia's new hero": Quintilian, the Roman rhetorician who wrote books on oratory nearly 2,000 years ago.

On the Monday when Mauro's piece appeared, Justice Scalia wrote to me: "The Mauro piece was fine. Whets the appetite."

Final Editing

On December 26, I traveled with my two daughters, Caroline and Alexandra, to Washington, D.C., for what we thought would be our final joint session on *Making Your Case*. After our first day, Mrs. Scalia, Caroline, and Alexandra met us for dinner at Tosca. It was a happy occasion. The Scalias had just had a large family gathering, the girls and I were having a good trip, they were excited to be with the Scalias, and we coauthors felt we were on the verge of a literary coup.

On our way out of the restaurant, Justice Scalia called me aside to say, "Your daughters are beautiful and intelligent. Congratulations." Then he paraphrased the Roman poet Lucan: "But you know that to have children is to give hostages to fate."

"You should know," I replied, "since you have 4.5 times as many as I do."

Our sessions during this trip were largely occupied with considering, and mostly accepting, edits by my old friend John Trimble, whose watchwords as an editor were *tighten*, *sharpen*, and *brighten*. He tried to implement such edits throughout the manuscript. He'd trim sentences and find more stylish phrasings for all sorts of ideas. Some pages were heavily marked, and Justice Scalia was losing patience.

"Now hold on, Nino, just look at this one," I'd say, trying to get him to see the merits in one of Trimble's reworkings. After about 50 pages with only a couple of edits rejected, Trimble had earned Justice Scalia's respect. "Okay, you just make the edits, but be careful. You know what I like and don't like by now."

"Yes, I do. I know which kinds of edits to reject."

"I'm just having to trust you."

By January 3, I had sent all the final corrections to Justice Scalia. Three days later, he sent me his final revisions to the pro-and-con sections. He noted: "I think I owe you nothing more—and good thing, too, since I will be sitting the next two weeks. I like the book. Regards. Nino."

Fortunately, I was traveling a good deal to D.C. during this period, and we had another afternoon to work together on January 8, 2008. We also posed for dust-jacket photos that day. The photo shoot had us inside his office, in one of the four rectangular courtyards at the Court, and in front of the Supreme Court building. Justice Scalia was insistent that we mustn't use any background that recognizably had anything to do with the Supreme Court. A plain marble wall would be acceptable, or a wood-paneled wall—but not, for example, the famous front edifice.

After a few photos in the office, the photographer took me aside to say there was a problem. I was towering over Justice Scalia in most photos because of our four-inch difference in height. She wanted to know whether we could find a stepstool. "Trust me," she said, "I've taken pictures up here at the Court before. Important men don't want to appear short in photographs. He's not going to like any of these. Can you help me do something about it?"

I decided to be direct when I walked back to Justice Scalia. "Nino, there's a problem with the photos. For dust-jacket purposes, we need our heads to be even . . . on the same level."

"I agree."

"Is there a step in the courtyard that we can use?"

"Let's go see." We walked down the hall with a retinue of five—Justice Scalia's assistant Angela, two Public Information Office employees, a lighting assistant, and a makeup assistant.

The step in the courtyard worked perfectly, and for the back of the book we used one of the photos taken there. Many astute observers have noted that although Justice Scalia appears about an inch taller than I in that photo, my torso appears much longer than his. They wondered how this happened—whether he didn't have preternaturally long legs or I preternaturally short ones. In fact, it was just a five-inch step.

During the session, Chief Justice John Roberts caught sight of us and came out into the courtyard to say hello. "You guys are looking good out here!" We said hello, shook hands, and he was back striding down the walkway almost as soon as I could realize what had just happened.

That afternoon, the question of dedicating the book came up. "Why don't we dedicate it to our parents?" I asked.

"I'd like to dedicate it to Maureen."

"Okay. Well, I'll dedicate it to my parents. I've just been divorced, so I'm not in a position to dedicate it to a significant other."

"It should be parallel. Okay, let's dedicate it to our parents."

"Well, my father is alive, but our other three parents are dead. Should we dedicate it to their memory?"

"No. Dedicate it to them directly—all of them," Justice Scalia said. "Our parents live on in a different life. That's how I see it."

Production and Publicity

The book was scheduled to appear in bookstores in mid-April. At the end of January, I still had the index to prepare. On January 25, I wrote to Justice Scalia: "Nino—To celebrate the publication of our book, let's plan dinner one night from April 21 to April 24. It looks as though that'll be my only stint in D.C. this spring."

His response was curt (as he could sometimes be). It read in its entirety: "Bryan: Sorry. I'm out of town that week. Nino."

By February, things started moving fast. On the first of the month, Justice Scalia wrote to tell me he'd met in chambers with Lesley Stahl of *60 Minutes* and her producer, Ruth Streeter, about a segment on the book. Then he added: "I liked Lesley Stahl and her staff people, and I think they liked me. More important, I trust them not to make this a gotcha event. It is a go. They will want to have you on with me—but probably not for the entire segment." Their approach made sense to me. He said: "As I should have anticipated, they want to speak with me about my general judicial philosophy and biographical stuff. That was probably inevitable; the show would not be much of a draw without it. But the book will be enough of a focus that I'm sure it's worth the time." He said he'd send me a copy of the letter agreements that he was entering into with CBS News.

A week later, he wrote to me that he'd returned from England and that *60 Minutes* had filmed two speeches he'd given: one at the Inner Temple and one at the Oxford Union. They'd sent only film crews—no Lesley Stahl. He added: "Maureen didn't come. I had an OK time." I took that to mean that he'd have had a much better time had she been along. "London is the land of $100 cab rides. Hurry the galleys. Nino."

On February 11, I sent Justice Scalia a message: "Because we're preparing the index now, I'm trying to do nothing that will affect pagination. Please confirm that you're overjoyed with the page design."

He responded: "I've just printed it out. I am overjoyed with the page design. Good work! Nino."

A couple of days later, we had a two-hour phone call in which he gave me edits orally. He had caught some typos, he wanted to move around the shaded boxes (with great meticulousness about precisely what lines of text they would appear beside), and he wanted to replace a few paragraphs with new paragraphs of his own. He faxed these to me within the hour after we hung up. Many of the rewordings we negotiated during the phone call. They were all definite improvements. Often he streamlined. For example, our draft contained this passage on oral argument:

A noted barrister, F. E. Smith, had argued at some length in an English court when the judge leaned over the bench and said: "I have read your case, Mr. Smith, and I am no wiser than I was when I started." To which the barrister replied: "Possibly not, My Lord, but far better informed." Smith, who later became a famous judge as the Earl of Birken-

head, could spontaneously carry off such statements with aplomb and, reportedly, without prejudice. Anyone else who tries this sort of thing is likely to maim the client's case.

Justice Scalia thought everything after the name Birkenhead wasn't quite right, and he replaced it with this: "could reportedly carry off such snappy rejoinders with impunity. We doubt that, but in any case we don't recommend that you emulate him." The contraction *don't*, of course, had to be negotiated.

By the end of the day, Jeff sent a new draft reflecting these corrections to both Justice Scalia and me.

Two days later, Justice Scalia asked to see the index. After pressing my staff, I sent him the 26th revision of the index four days later. He wrote back an hour later: "Just so you know: I think the index needs lots of work. It's about 5 times too long, and many of the entries are not at all helpful. . . . Needs a lotta work. Nino."

That same day he called LawProse to speak with me, but I was on the road teaching. So he spoke to Jeff. In a 45-minute call, he dictated a whole series of new edits. His level of assiduity and attention to detail astonished us all. And again, he wanted to tinker with the precise placement of boxes.

Tussles with Indexing

On February 21 and 22, Justice Scalia wrote two long e-mails complaining about the draft index. I was away from the office that whole week and couldn't respond until late midday on the 22nd. I said, "Please give me your proxy. We must submit pages next week, and a major reworking of the index could be disastrous." I asked him to trust me.

"Can't trust you on this," he responded by e-mail. "Not if you think that the current version is 'on the whole' a good job. I think it is godawful. . . . I have put in too much work on this to see it spoiled at the last minute." He added: "If need be, I will take some time this weekend to prevent that. Send me a copy of your revision and I will attend to it at once."

His final words, just after this, were most worrisome, given that the book was ready to go apart from the index: "Who would have thought that this is the point which would bring our happy collaboration to an end?!?! Just kidding. But I do want to see the damn thing before it goes."

He kept me on tenterhooks. We had a long, testy telephone conversation in which we debated the purpose of an index.

"Who would want to look up Aristotle in the index?" Justice Scalia wanted to know. "It's preposterous to have individual authors listed, as opposed to a subject index."

"I would for one. Nino, believe me, there are rhetoric teachers throughout the country who will want to know how many times we cite Aristotle, and for what purpose."

"You really think so?"

"I'm sure of it. And if we're citing current lawyers or rhetoricians, it appeals to them. They're more likely to assign the book if they can point to an index entry listing their name."

"That makes sense. I can see that."

"But quite apart from that, most books today are inadequately indexed. We need a comprehensive index as part of our scholarly impedimenta." (Yes, I actually used that word in conversation.)

"*Impedimenta*? What's that?"

"The traveling appurtenances, more or less. The equipage, you know."

"I want a two-page index—no more!"

"Nino, you can't do that. If I have any fame as a legal writer, it's partly because of my indexes. People can find what they want. I pride myself on thinking about how someone might look something up, and providing the apparatus for doing that easily."

He then started picking holes in my 30-page index, suggesting cuts throughout. I made notes. Occasionally I argued. Often I relented immediately. But he was making many exacting points about subentries.

"Never did I dream, Nino, that you'd be so perfectionist about minute points in the index!"

"Well, I'm teaching the so-called perfectionist a thing or two about perfectionism."

"Indeed you are," I said.[23]

In the end, we wound up with a 26-page index. Together we pruned out 4 pages or so. On Tuesday, February 26, he wrote to me: "I feel good about the index—and about the whole book."

---

23 See Garner, "War of the Words," *American Lawyer*, Feb. 2009, at 56 (acknowledging that from our wrangling over the index, "I learned the true meaning of the word *painstaking*.").

On March 4, I sent the book to West for printing—one day after getting Justice Scalia's final corrections to the index. In the publishing business, this kind of schedule is remarkable: only six weeks from the release date, the book went into production.

60 Minutes arranged to film the dust jackets being put onto the hardcover books as they were rolling off the presses, and the producers used that film clip in the segment that aired.

60 Minutes

Just before sending off proofs, I happened to be flying from New York to Dallas on a flight with my old friend Merrie Spaeth, a media consultant, and told her of the forthcoming *60 Minutes* segment. She was aghast. "They'll make mincemeat of him! Bryan, you have real cause for concern." He was to be interviewed in Queens in March, and then he and I were to be jointly interviewed later that month for an airing in April.

I asked whether she'd help prep him for the interviews. Of course she would. I called Justice Scalia about it, and he agreed that he could use some preparatory work. He marked off a few hours through lunch on March 6, and I arranged to spend the day in the Ulysses S. Grant Suite at the Willard Hotel. Like all the presidential suites at the Willard, it's a magnificent room, with an oval office.

That morning, Merrie and I flew up and met Justice Scalia in the lobby of the Willard Hotel. The preparation consisted mostly of asking Justice Scalia difficult "gotcha" questions and seeing how he'd respond. When he was defensive, we suggested better body language and a more positive message. When he denied a negative, we suggested reframing the answer as a positive assertion that didn't repeat the negative idea. Merrie and I filmed him, and Merrie played back his responses to show what a difference it could make to recast the question before answering. He was impressed. He seemed to have learned some valuable lessons (and so did I). Merrie and I both stressed the importance of having the interviewer *like* him. But Merrie emphasized that it's not the *interviewer* so much as the *producer* who must like him. That was a lesson for me as well. When we finished up an hour early, Justice Scalia thanked Merrie for her help, assured her that he'd benefited from the session, and vowed to remember her lessons.

The *60 Minutes* interviews were done in two parts: one in early March, when Lesley Stahl did a series of interviews with him in his boyhood neighborhood in Queens; and one on March 28, filmed in the Lawyers' Lounge at the Supreme Court. I participated in the final part of this last interview. Never have I seen so many cords strewn over a floor—all for lighting and cameras.

Stahl began interviewing Justice Scalia at 2:00 p.m., and the plan was for me to join the interview at 3:00. But at 3:35, she was still going at him, lights glaring in his now-sweaty face. She was beginning to ask him probing questions about abortion, the Ten Commandments, and gay rights. He had been sitting more than 90 minutes, and I could tell that his energy was flagging just as she was asking these "gotcha" questions. One of 30 or so observers from the perimeter of the room, I walked over to Kathy Arberg and suggested that the Justice might need a break and that she cut off the questions. She agreed, and did so within five minutes. He had said nothing intemperate or ill-considered.

Ruth Streeter, the producer, announced that we'd be resuming with Justice Scalia and me together at 3:55. She told me privately that Justice Scalia had really won over everybody on the *60 Minutes* team.

Back in chambers, I told Justice Scalia that what I'd seen had gone really well. He had done just what we had talked about with Merrie.

"She kept me under those hot lights so long."

"I know. That's all, though, and you did really well. Now we'll be talking about the book."

That's just what we did, for 30 minutes or so. It went really well, and I had the opportunity to say how disarmingly deferential Justice Scalia had been on certain points, such as contractions. Then they took a group photo with producers, staffers, and court personnel, followed by video clips of Justice Scalia, Lesley Stahl, and me in front of the Supreme Court. They wanted shots of Justice Scalia and Lesley Stahl walking along the sidewalk in front of the Court. As the sun was setting, they also got a shot of me walking around one of the fountains.

That night we went to the restaurant Bebo in Crystal City to celebrate what seemed like a successful encounter with a major news organization—a venture that Justice Scalia had rightly seen from the beginning as fraught with danger. Afterward, he had the marshals drop me off at the airport for my late-night return to Dallas.

The *60 Minutes* piece ended up airing on April 27, and everyone seemed happy with it. It was part biography, part judicial profile, and part book promo. The whole thing was positive.

A few days later, I heard from a CNN producer who wanted us to appear on the morning show. I passed it on to Justice Scalia, saying: "Apart from *60 Minutes*, it'll be our only joint media appearance for the book."

He responded: "Bryan: I do not want to do the CNN interview. The morning audience is not fertile ground for our book, and I don't want to overdo my exposure. I will be doing Brian Lamb, and Laura Ingraham, and perhaps Charlie Rose. That should be enough. Sorry to say no."

Dallas Bar Association Filming

Two nights after the *60 Minutes* piece aired, Frank Stevenson, president of the Dallas Bar Association, threw a party at the Belo Mansion in Dallas, the association's headquarters, to commemorate the publication of *Making Your Case*. This was April 29, 2008, the day after the official publication date. Precisely a week before, I'd been in chambers with Justice Scalia, and we had recorded a film that I played for those attending the party. Here's how it went:

SCALIA: So, Bryan, this is the Dallas Bar Association, is that right? Am I supposed to look at the camera, or at you?

GARNER: At me.

SCALIA: All right. Good.

GARNER: These folks have gotten together to celebrate the book.

SCALIA: And to buy it I hope! [*chortles*]

GARNER: We hope! [*laughs*] Now why did we write this book?

SCALIA: Why does anybody write a work of nonfiction? To transmit useful knowledge to somebody else. Right? I mean, I've been doing this judging thing for, what, 26 years now and have learned a few things. And, more important, a lot of friends of mine have learned a *whole* lot of things. It would be a shame to let it all go to waste.

GARNER: Our friends were really very helpful to us on this, weren't they?

SCALIA: Oh, yeah! Probably more helpful than you or me. [*chuckles*]

GARNER: Well, it was a great process wasn't it. We had probably 40 people look over the manuscript, didn't we?

SCALIA: It must have been that many. Well, you have the credits there in the beginning. Was it that many? Forty?

GARNER: A lot of federal judges; a lot of friends.

SCALIA: And practitioners—successful practitioners.

GARNER: What are we going to tell people when they ask, "Why a new book on advocacy?"

SCALIA: Because you assured me—you know, I had never surveyed the field—that there was not a modern handbook, post-Cicero, that was very helpful. Things have changed a lot, even in the last 40 years. I mean, the nature of the appellate practice, with 20-minute appellate arguments, and a lot of questions from the bench—that's all quite different from what it was 40 years or so ago.

GARNER: Much more active questioning.

SCALIA: [*laughing*] Oh yeah! Sometimes nasty.

GARNER: Do you like the idea that you're continuing a tradition of Italian thinkers on rhetoric—namely, Quintilian . . .

SCALIA: [*smiling*] Oh, come on! Get out of here! I mean . . .

GARNER: And Cicero, and then we skip a couple of thousand years, but we have . . .

SCALIA: They're Italian? I don't know that they're Italian. You know, Rome was empty for several decades after all you northern barbarians came down and destroyed it. I'm not sure I'm a descendant of Quintilian. Nobody ever told me that.

GARNER: Now you and I had some disagreements in the book, didn't we?

SCALIA: [*looking innocent*] Did we? Did we have disagreements?

GARNER: I think we had disagreements.

SCALIA: They're all set forth there. The only ones we had are set forth and described—at least the only ones we couldn't resolve.

GARNER: We resolved a lot of things, didn't we?

SCALIA: I yielded more than you did, probably.

GARNER: But we were able to work most things out.

SCALIA: I'm that kind of guy. Go along to get along. So I don't write many dissents.

GARNER: But when you do write them . . . You're kidding about not writing many dissents, right?

SCALIA: Of course I'm kidding.

GARNER: You can be very forceful. I think in a way, being your coauthor on this book, and having you dissent, I think I've experienced something that only eight other human beings have probably ever experienced.

SCALIA: [*big chortle*] I don't know. I had colleagues on the court of appeals. [*continues laughing*]

GARNER: I guess that's right.

SCALIA: I was sort of sharp.

GARNER: You throw a mean punch.

SCALIA: You took some good hits.

GARNER: Right on the chin! Well, is there anything that you'd like to close with for the members of the Dallas Bar Association?

SCALIA: Yes. You know that's my circuit down there [the Fifth Circuit]. I'm the Circuit Justice for Texas, Mississippi, and Louisiana, and I'm delighted to serve in that capacity there. They're good folks down there, and so different from New York City.

GARNER: I'll bet they are. You've got a lot of friends in Texas.

SCALIA: I hope so.

GARNER: Well, thanks very much for taping this.

SCALIA: Always a pleasure to talk to you.

GARNER: And now, in Dallas, we're going to get back to drinking.

SCALIA: [*laughs*]

GARNER: It's a cash bar.

SCALIA: Have a bourbon and branch water for me!

But then we kept the tape rolling, and we talked some more about the work we had done on *Making Your Case*. We reflected on the process of writing and editing:

SCALIA: As you noted from our collaboration, I am not a facile writer. And I tend to suspect that whoever is isn't a very good writer.

GARNER: But once you got into it, you were a pretty facile writer. I mean, once we got writing, I thought it flowed pretty easily—off your fingertips.

SCALIA: Oh, so many times we'd sit down, put it one way, delete that, and put it another way. And if I went through the book another time, I'd still be making changes. You probably would too, because you're as much of a nerdy perfectionist as I am.

GARNER: Well, we will do that in future editions, won't we?

SCALIA: Oh, I think we will.

GARNER: Well, I really enjoyed working with you.

SCALIA: I did too, Bryan. It was great fun.

Further Plans

After filming that short video in Justice Scalia's chambers, we went to dinner, again at Tosca. Meeting us there was the woman I'd begun dating, Karolyne Cheng. Born in Dallas to immigrant parents, one from Taiwan and one from Hong Kong, she was reared from the age of seven in North Attleboro, Massachusetts. After receiving a degree in philosophy from Boston College, she attended Texas Tech School of Law—which is coincidentally in the city of my birth, Lubbock. Karolyne had joined an intellectual-law boutique law firm in Dallas, where she was both prosecuting patents and litigating them.

Justice Scalia wanted to know how we'd met. Karolyne explained that at the behest of her boss, she had attended a LawProse seminar in March 2007, and then we'd met when she came to another in June. Smitten, I'd soon persuaded her to be my guest at yet another. Because she's smart, gregarious, polymathic, down-to-earth, quick to smile, and contagiously vivacious, Justice Scalia seemed to like her instantly.

"Should I call you 'Lyne,' as I've heard Bryan do, or 'Karolyne'?"

"Only close friends and a few family members call me 'Lyne,'" she said. "So I think you'd better call me 'Lyne.'"

He smiled. "Lyne it is."

After the introduction that night, he was always as eager to see her at any social occasion as he was me. Okay, more so.

That night, we discussed at length the possibility of a second book on the interpretation of legal documents. He was mildly interested but skittish. The second book would involve a lot more work than the first, and the first he considered almost unbearably difficult. Still, he said he'd think about it.

Within a couple of weeks, on May 11, I'd sent him a draft contract that our publisher had sent for *Reading Law*, thinking he'd accept. But the next day, he called to decline.

By e-mail, we talked about publishing his essays and speeches, and I offered to serve as both agent and editor. He formalized our agreement by writing: "I gladly accept your offer. I would prefer Knopf." Unfortunately, logistical difficulties arose, and this became a back-burner project for both of us until 2014.

Kennedy Center

Shortly after the publication of *Making Your Case*, Karolyne suggested that Justice Scalia and I team-teach from the book. She thought we could promote the book and further lawyers' training (one and the same, really) by holding a major seminar in Washington, D.C. She rather ambitiously suggested having it at the Kennedy Center for the Performing Arts. When I called Justice Scalia to see whether he'd be interested, he liked the idea and especially liked the Kennedy Center as our venue. My staff at LawProse soon booked the Kennedy Center for us—no easy task in itself—for July 25, 2008. Thomson/West agreed to videotape the entire event with the understanding that LawProse would hold the copyright. Profits would be quietly donated to Legal Aid.

On the morning of the event, Karolyne and I met Justice Scalia at 9:45 at the Kennedy Center and were taken by staffers to the greenroom, where we'd spend our time before the show and on our lunch break.

Justice Scalia and I were both nervous. People had flown in from all over the country for this seminar, and we wanted to make it worth their while. We were to lecture for five hours (with a 90-minute lunch break), covering all 115 points in *Making Your Case*. We'd arranged that he'd do the odd-numbered sections, and I'd do the even, each briefly amplifying the other's sections as we thought desirable. It was a lot of material, and we'd never lectured together before. Justice Scalia had never given such a lengthy presentation—and for my part, I wasn't at all sure whether I'd be playing the straight man or supplying the humor. It turned out to be a little of both.

Onstage

If I was worried about precisely how to warm up the audience, Justice Scalia removed any qualms by taking control. He said, with a perfectly timed delivery that was punctuated with laughter:

> *I always wanted to be center stage at the Concert Hall. Actually, I'd prefer the Opera House, but you do what you can. This is probably— apologies to LawProse and my coauthor—the dullest act ever to play here, although I can think of some atonal music that would bomb better. There's the famous New York joke about the tourist who asks, "How do you get to Carnegie Hall?" And he's told, "Practice, practice, practice!" So here we are.*

As we got into the substance, we relaxed and soon established a rhythm. Justice Scalia stuck pretty closely to the book, whereas I simply took the blackletter point and talked briefly about what it meant and why it was important. On the whole, we both seemed fairly extemporaneous. And once Justice Scalia started cracking jokes—some at my expense—the audience really warmed up. If I went on a little too long, he'd say, "Are you finished now?!" with mock irritability. People liked that.

"I'm quite finished," I'd say.

"Next point, then!" And he'd move on.

At one point he thought I was getting a little abstruse. "What in the world are you talking about?!"

"Let's move on," I said, as the crowd erupted in laughter.

But then sometimes I'd needle him instead. "Well, that's not what you told me in chambers!"

"I do think I did."

"I don't recall it that way."

"I certainly did. And here's what people must remember. . . ."

So there was a lot of good-natured raillery running throughout our presentation. It was a type of jocularity we'd employ in all our future presentations. People sometimes said they thought it was all fastidiously rehearsed shtick, but in fact all of it was off-the-cuff humor. Justice Scalia and I thoroughly enjoyed ourselves when performing.

During the lunch break, we had sandwiches backstage with Karolyne, my daughters, and my friends Eric English and Dick and Shelley Walinski. Everyone seemed exhilarated about how the presentation was going. But Justice Scalia was concerned that we'd gone through much less than half the book in half our time. I assured him that we could make up time in the second half.

I asked him over lunch, "Is this the first time you've performed here at Kennedy Center?"

"Not quite. I've been onstage as an extra in an opera."

"First time as the main feature?"

"Yes, it certainly is. This is fun."

In the final 30 minutes of our 90-minute lunch break, I had arranged for Tony Mauro to talk with us, and for West's videographers to interview us. Justice Scalia still didn't want to do either one.

"I don't want to talk to Mauro!" said Justice Scalia.

I felt almost as if I'd experienced this before—as if he was challenging me to persuade or cajole him to do something he might in the end actually enjoy.

I told him that Tony Mauro was waiting next door.

"I don't care. I won't talk to that man. He won't be fair to us."

Now I was beginning to doubt my instinct from a moment before.

"Yes he will, Nino. He wrote a good piece about us in November. Remember that? Please talk to him."

"I won't!"

"Nino, if you want good press, you have to cooperate with the press."

"No."

"You can be charming. Ask him about his family. I learned some years ago that if you want good press relations, you have to show interest in the journalists. Ask how long they've been reporters. Ask about their jobs. It's pure Dale Carnegie."

"Really?"

"I've had only one bad experience with the press, years ago. I was preoccupied, and I showed no interest in the guy. He wrote a snarky piece about me in *Texas Monthly*. That's never happened since. I learned to show interest in *them*."

"You think he'll treat us fairly?"

"I know he will. I have no doubt. But you must talk to him. Be your charming self."

"Okay. Let's go over."

Next thing I knew, Justice Scalia and Tony Mauro were in deep conversation about Mauro's daughter going off to college. I could barely break them apart when it was time for us to resume.

In the afternoon session, we put our four debates to the audience for a show-of-hands plebiscite—on sexist language, contractions, substantive footnotes, and footnoted citations. Justice Scalia was a formidable debater, and here his competitive streak came out strongly. I felt he all but browbeat the audience into siding with him, and of course he had a strong argumentative advantage as a Justice urging lawyers in a debate against a mere lawyer. As best I recall the votes of our audience, they were as follows: 80% to 20% on not making language gender-neutral (hence a Scalia victory there); 75% to 25% on banishing contractions from briefs and opinions (another Scalia victory); 90% to 10% on occasionally allowing substantive footnotes in briefs and opinions (yet *another* Scalia victory); and 50% to 50% on footnoting all citations (a modest moral victory for me).

"You have to be dismayed by that," I said in reference to the final vote, getting a laugh from the audience.

"I am a little," Justice Scalia admitted grudgingly. "They're not thinking it through!" Then he cracked a wry smile and we went on with the program.

Decompressing Afterward

When it was over, I announced that we'd be signing books for those in attendance. In the front foyer of the Kennedy Center, a line snaked on and on outside the building. We began signing books at 5:05 p.m. and stayed for 90 minutes. We signed more than 550 of them—a record, the Kennedy Center staffers told us, the previous record having been set by the great Placido Domingo.

This was the first of many times we'd sit together and sign books. It was here that I learned that Justice Scalia would sign only on the half-title page. He'd sign just below the title of the book, and then I'd sign just beneath his signature. If people didn't have the book open to the half-title, he'd get annoyed, so Karolyne helped the Kennedy staffers alert people in line to open the book to the proper page before they approached the table. It was an assembly line, more or less, and he would only occasionally look up. At first, when participants wanted to take a photograph with us, he'd invite them to come around the table. But after a while, the line seemed so long that he insisted on moving things along: "No photographs!"

"Would you please inscribe this copy to Darla?" someone would ask.

"No inscriptions," Justice Scalia ruled. "It's not fair to the people behind you. Sorry."

Soon everybody in line was told by staffers not to ask for inscriptions, and things ran more smoothly.

We'd chat between ourselves as people came through. "Your signature is beautiful, Nino. Did you cultivate that?"

"You know, I did! After I got on the Court, I spent an afternoon working on what my signature would look like. This is what I arrived at. You've got a fine signature, too."

"Well, thanks. It has to be decent if it's appearing alongside yours!"

Occasionally I'd recognize someone that I'd introduce to Justice Scalia. He was unfailingly gracious. But if I said something like, "Where do you practice?" he'd be bothered if the answer was prolix. "You're getting behind, Bryan! You're slowing us down! You're being Chatty Cathy."

"Sorry, Nino."

And then we'd get back into the quick assembly-line signatures. This was the first time that I realized how much Justice Scalia enjoyed autographing books. He seemed to relish it.

When it was all over, Karolyne and I had a small reception in the JFK Suite at the Willard Hotel—complete with wine, hors d'oeuvres, and Campari. Justice Scalia stayed only briefly. Before the guests arrived, he told us how much he had enjoyed the entire experience, and I assured him the feeling was mutual.

The Lifetime Achievement Award

On August 8, 2008, Justice Scalia flew from Norfolk (he had been at the Outer Banks) to join me in New York City for the annual meeting of the American Society of Legal Writers—also known as Scribes. I'd been on the board of directors intermittently for 18 years, and the organization had decided to bestow upon him its highest honor: the Scribes Lifetime Achievement Award for Excellence in Legal Writing.

He and I met beforehand at the Harvard Club, where the luncheon would begin at noon. We sat down in the bar to have club sodas, knowing we'd soon have a glass of wine. It was the first time I'd seen him since the Court had handed down its historic *Heller* opinion, in which it declared a personal right to keep and bear arms. He had written the majority opinion—one of the most noteworthy opinions of his career.

"Have you read my *Heller* opinion?"

"Of course I have!"

"Do you think I got it right?"

"Well, I'm a textualist, like you, so of course I do. I think the policy is horrid, but your majority was much more compelling than Justice Stevens's dissent."

"What do you mean?"

"I wish the Second Amendment could be repealed. It's just awful what we've done in this country—arming everyone so heavily."

"But you liked my historical analysis?"

"It seemed impeccable to me."

"And my textual analysis?"

"Well, you omitted to say that the preamble is a mispunctuated nominative absolute."

"What?"

"The whole phrase 'A well-regulated militia being necessary . . .'—that's a nominative absolute."

"That's what it's called?"

"Yes. And there should be no comma after *militia*. It's as if you were to say, 'This bar being clean, we can put our elbows on it.' There's no comma after *bar*."

"It's called a 'nominative absolute'?"

"Right. You didn't say that in your opinion."

"I can't believe I missed that! Why didn't you tell me?"

"I didn't know you were working on that case. We never talk about cases."

"But you knew the Court had the case, and you knew it involved a nominative absolute."

"Didn't any of the brief-writers point that out?"

"Not a single one! Damn. I thought I'd covered every single aspect of that amendment, both historically and grammatically, and here you give me the name for it just off the cuff. I can't believe I didn't know it."

I smiled. "I can't believe you didn't either, Nino. A nominative absolute is a noun or pronoun followed by a nonfinite verb or an adjective phrase. It's grammatically independent from the rest of the sentence."

"Give me another example."

"He having left, we were all relieved."

"You having told me this, I'm now wishing I could revise the opinion. But tell me, you think the opinion was substantively correct?"

"Of course! I just hate the result."

"If you'd been on the Court, you'd have voted with me?"

"I'm a textualist, so of course. It's hard to read the words 'the right of the people to keep and bear arms shall not be infringed' contrary to their plain meaning."

"It's a good illustration."

"Of what?"

"You show me a judge who always agrees with the results he reaches, and I'll show you a bad judge. Bryan, you detest the result, yet you'd vote that way."

"Right. Your textual and historical analysis was compelling."

"But I missed that it's a nominative absolute!"

I chuckled. "You're funny. Let's go to the lunch. There'll be lots of people eager to meet you."

And there were. One of the first was my old friend John Wierzbicki of West Publishing. When I introduced John, first and last name, Justice Scalia said, "That's a strong name!"

There were dozens of others standing in line for autographs and photographs. Justice Scalia was particularly solicitous this day. He was unusually patient standing for staged photographs.

Soon the presentation began. I was to introduce him and give him his award. He would then make his acceptance speech on a topic relating to legal writing. I had no idea what he'd say.

I began by remarking that chairing the selection committee was the best assignment I'd ever had. At the annual Scribes meeting in Las Vegas that spring, the Scribes president had appointed me to preside over the committee—a panel that, as it turned out, would never even meet. I asked the directors who they thought the greatest living legal writer was—someone in the tradition of Oliver Wendell Holmes, Learned Hand, or Robert H. Jackson. By acclamation, they chose Justice Antonin Scalia. I told them, "But wait a second, is there anybody else who should be considered for this award?" A few other names were suggested and considered, but the board agreed that Justice Scalia stood apart. My assignment was completed in less than five minutes.

Introducing Justice Scalia, I tried to give some perspective on his writing style and how it compares with other legal writing I'd encountered in more than 25 years of teaching and consulting in the field:

> In his book Marble Palace, the scholar John P. Frank wrote about the United States Reports and said that that set of books constitutes a vast literary wasteland. And for the most part, it does. Certainly there are exceptions—mainly, John Marshall, Oliver Wendell Holmes, and Robert H. Jackson, who was probably the greatest writer ever to sit on the United States Supreme Court. But I think his equal is Justice Antonin Scalia, and so it's great to be able to give him this lifetime achievement award. We've all benefited from the lucidity and the bold metaphors that he brings to his writing. He is like no other. And so Justice Scalia, if you'll please come forward.

Justice Scalia was in particularly good form on this day, and the audience was especially warm. He began in low tones by saying: "I am very honored to receive this award. I happen to sit in the chair once occupied by Robert Jackson and by the second Justice Harlan, and I'm very proud of both of those predecessors. I share the judgment that Jackson was the best legal stylist of the 20th century." After applause, he got a hearty laugh when he said: "Incidentally, I'm going to join the Society. I'm not going to just take your award!" Then he added: "I do care a lot about legal writing. I ought to belong to this organization!" That won him another hearty ovation.

But he wasn't done warming up the audience: "You ought to get a new name for this award. Lifetime Achievement Awards are best known at the annual Oscar ceremonies, where they are awarded to some old-time actor who never won an Oscar but should have, just for sheer persistence and endurance. [*laughter*] The awardee usually crosses the stage on a cane. I assume that your award has none of these connotations, and therefore I accept it with great pride. [*laughter*] But get a new name. [*more laughter*]"

Justice Scalia proceeded to make some interesting observations about legal writing, the first of which was that legal writing doesn't really exist as a separate genre of writing. Legal writing, he said, is nonfiction prose, an "unglamorous category of writing" that requires its writers to handle the subject with almost as much mastery as a good writer in any other field, such as theology or economics. As an example, he said, "C. S. Lewis would have been a magnificent legal writer." So would economists such as Ronald Coase and John Kenneth Galbraith, who, he said, wrote lucidly on the subject before the field sank into "esoteric regression analyses and mathematical formulae," becoming cluttered and opaque.

"Oops," Justice Scalia said, "I used the word 'cluttered,' which has set my esteemed coauthor Bryan Garner a-twitching." Clutter is rampant in legal writing, he said, pointing to my campaign both to eliminate substantive (sentence-containing) footnotes and to "banish to footnotes the case citations that so disrupt the flow of legal writing." The stuttering prose that results is almost unique to legal writing, he conceded, even though many fields require "constant appeal to authority" for their assertions. Almost no other field inserts them in the prose itself, but instead footnotes or endnotes keep the narrative flow unimpeded. "The only other type of writing coming to mind that is similarly afflicted," he said, "is theological writing in a religion based upon revelation." But even there, he added, "5 Kings 9" is more attractive than the typical legal citation, which can fill two or three lines before the text resumes.

He talked about his two years of teaching legal writing to first-year law students at the University of Virginia. It became immediately clear to him, he said, that what students lacked wasn't the skill of legal writing but the skill of writing at all. He thought that it's probably too late to undo this impairment during postgraduate studies. The best thing to wish for, he said, was to teach an appreciation for the vast difference between writing and good writing (that realization had come to some of his students as "an astounding revelation," he said), and then to persuade them to dedicate the time and sweat it takes to master the skill.

Time and sweat. He emphasized that. He said he was put on the road to good writing as a freshman at Georgetown, when his English professor, a "damned hard grader" named P. A. Orr, gave writing assignments every weekend. In the beginning, the future Justice was receiving B-minuses—marks that provoked "many nervous hours" of writing and rewriting the Orr assignments. Justice Scalia said, "I am grateful to this day."

"Finally . . . ," he said as though wrapping up. But instead he decided to tuck in an extemporaneous anecdote, smiling during almost his entire delivery:

> *I was going to tell a story . . . It doesn't have a whole lot to do with our subject, but it's such a good story, so what the heck. I was teaching in Galway this summer. On one of my first days there, the Chief Justice of Ireland gave me a book about practice in Cork, in what was called the Munster Circuit in the early years of the 20th century. It's a delightful book. One of the stories it tells is that it's good practice to use good, hard, brief Anglo-Saxon words instead of Latinate puffery. The story was told of this one barrister in Ireland who was a very boastful fellow. He made a bet that he could argue an entire case using only one-syllable words. One of the other barristers readily took the bet because he knew, of course, that you always begin your argument to the jury saying, "Gentlemen of the jury." So he thought he had a sure winner.*
>
> *So this barrister gets up and says, "Now you twelve men good and true. . . ."* [laughter] *It's irrelevant to everything else I was saying.* [laughter]

Justice Scalia next addressed a point of great interest to those who pursue the art of writing: Is high intelligence a prerequisite for great legal writing? It's not enough by itself, he answered. He recalled making law review at Harvard and being awestruck at the raw brainpower of his new colleagues. But he wasn't as impressed with their writing skills. He was convinced that he could "write rings around" many others who were much smarter than he was. So he concluded that intelligence alone wasn't the answer. But was it necessary to being a prose stylist? He didn't think so, he said, though it's necessary to handle the substantive content legal writers must deal with. Such things as good grammar and a knowledge of Latin can be learned, he said. "The less-than-brilliant mind may take longer to master those elements," he said, "but it's doable."

One thing probably can't be taught, he continued, and that has nothing to do with having a high IQ: genius. "There is no reason to believe that

Mozart was a genius in the ordinary sense of being brainy," he said. "He was a musical genius."

Then he came to the central point—a point not often publicly associated with Justice Scalia: empathy. He expressed the necessity that writers have empathy as pithily, I believe, as I've ever heard anyone do. Writing genius, he said, consists in "the ability to place oneself in the shoes of one's audience; to assume only what they assume; to anticipate what they anticipate; to explain what they need explained; to think what they must be thinking; to feel what they must be feeling."

On the other hand, he concluded, there is one reliable connection between good writing and intellect: "A careless, sloppy writer has a careless, sloppy mind."

He thanked the organization for its award and, amid sustained applause, sat back down beside me.

"Great job, Nino!"

"You liked it?"

"It was spoken like a snoot of the first order."

No More Infinite Jest

A little over a month later, on September 12, 2008, David Foster Wallace—the self-deprecating literary hero to more than one generation; the master of clear, distinctive, hyperintelligent, high-voltage prose; and the friend who had encouraged me to pursue an interview with the feistiest word-lover on the Supreme Court of the United States—committed suicide. The literary world mourned an incomparable mind; I mourned an irreplaceable friend.

The next day, I called Justice Scalia.

"Nino, did you hear the news?"

"About David? Yes. Very sad. Did you suspect anything?"

"No, not really. He'd gone silent for a while."

"It's such a shame."

"You know, he's the one who brought us together."

"He did?"

"He encouraged me to interview you. He knew you were a snoot."

"He was right about that."

"And then you were drawn to me more when you knew David's long essay about snoots was really a review of my usage book."

"That's right. You know, you're right!"

"So he's really responsible for our partnership."

"I hadn't thought of that, but I'm sure that's right. I liked him. He was an excellent writer, and he seemed like a good man. If you talk to his parents, please send my condolences. How did he die?"

"Apparently he hanged himself," I said falteringly. "I can't believe it."

"Did you know he was suffering from depression?"

"I knew he had in the past, but he seemed upbeat when I last saw him. We spent a long evening together two years ago. Damn."

"There's nothing you could have done, Bryan."

"I could have been a better friend. I shouldn't have let the whole evening be about my impending divorce. We should have talked more about *him*."

"Don't beat yourself up," said Justice Scalia. "You had no idea. When someone commits suicide, everybody close to the person wants to blame himself. Don't do that. No good comes from it."

I said, "In terms of our correspondence, he just went silent over the past year. I thought I'd struck a wrong nerve or something." I was suppressing audible sobs.

"No, he was surely descending into depression. It's all very sad, Bryan. You were a good friend. I'm glad you had me meet him. I thought he was delightful. I'm sorry I didn't get to know him better. You have my condolences, Bryan, as his friend."

I was so choked up I could barely speak. "Thank you, Nino."

"You take care, Bryan. I'll see you soon. You okay?"

"I'm okay, Nino," I said, with halting speech. "Lift a glass tonight in memory of David."

"I will, Bryan. You, too."

4

Making Your Case: Part II

(2009)

A lthough it was quite some time before we'd give another joint performance, the invitations to do so were rolling in—always many months
in advance of the events. The American Business Trial Lawyers group in
Los Angeles asked us to present *Making Your Case* in March 2009. The
Texas Law Review, where I'd served as associate editor during my third
year of law school, asked me to enlist Justice Scalia to speak the following
month in Austin. He readily accepted both. The president of the State Bar
of Texas wrote to both of us asking that we make a joint presentation at the
Bar's annual meeting in late June. This one he accepted only conditionally:
"June is always hectic. If you have received an affirmative response from
Bryan Garner (I have not spoken with him concerning the invitation),
and if you are willing to list Bryan and me on the program with the real
possibility that Bryan may have to do it alone, I will be happy to accept. If
you require an absolute commitment that I will be there, I must decline."
They accepted.

My friend David Battaglia of Los Angeles introduced us at the March
2009 meeting of the American Business Trial Lawyers. It was a packed
room at the Biltmore Hotel in downtown Los Angeles, and Mrs. Scalia was
present on that trip. I think it may have been the only time that she saw
us speak together—in fact, perhaps the only time that any Scalia family
member ever did. Battaglia introduced us as if we were boxers: "Tonight's
card features, in the *left* corner, standing five feet nine inches in height,
with a 27-inch reach, straight from the District of Columbia, none other
than Justice Antonin Scalia. Best known for his ferocious right cross." He
gave some familial and judicial stats, and then noted: "His birthday is at

the stroke of midnight tonight, on March 11. We are obviously quite honored to have him here."

And then my intro: "In the *right* corner, standing a healthy six feet one inch tall, with a 29-inch reach, direct from Dallas, Texas, we have . . . Bryan Garner. Best known for his pugnacious prose."

Then, with Battaglia's patented wit, he gave the audience a ten-question quiz on quotations. Who said this? Scalia or Garner? Six examples (don't look at the footnotes until you've taken the quiz yourself):

1. "The main business of a lawyer is to take the romance, the mystery, the irony, the ambiguity out of everything he touches."[24]

2. "As you might already suspect, I don't shy away from making judgments. I can't imagine that most readers would want me to."[25]

3. "Bear in mind that brains and learning, like muscle and physical skill, are articles of commerce. They are bought and sold. You can hire them by the year or by the hour. The only thing in the world not for sale is character."[26]

4. "[Judges] expect meandering, aimless briefs that take seemingly forever to get through. I say that you shouldn't give judges what they expect; instead, give them a pleasant surprise."[27]

5. "In a big family, the first child is kind of like the first pancake. If it's not perfect, that's okay, there are a lot more coming along."[28]

6. "Some people, it must be said, are inherently likable. If you're not, work on it."[29]

---

24 Antonin Scalia, Symposium at the Juilliard School (2005).

25 Bryan A. Garner, *A Dictionary of Modern American Usage* xiii (1998).

26 Antonin Scalia, College of William & Mary Commencement Speech (1996).

27 *Garner on Language and Writing* xxxiv (2009).

28 Antonin Scalia, as reported in *Newsweek* (1986).

29 Antonin Scalia & Bryan A. Garner, *Making Your Case: The Art of Persuading Judges* xxiv (2008).

If the audience had fun with this introduction, Justice Scalia and I had fun over the course of the evening, trading points from *Making Your Case*—and occasional barbs. We were both in good form.

Afterward, the Scalias and I had drinks with David and Julie Battaglia and a law-school friend and his wife, David and Marty Pendarvis. Upon meeting David Pendarvis, Justice Scalia asked what kind of law he practiced.

"I'm at ResMed, which is a company that makes C-PAP machines for those suffering from sleep apnea."

"Listen, I snore, and it bothers Maureen. My doctor has said I should get tested."

"You really should. Sleep apnea can be a dangerous condition. You ought to get tested."

At this point, Mrs. Scalia got involved, wanting to know whether a C-PAP could cure her husband's snoring. This topic dominated our conversation for about 15 minutes. Midway through, Justice Scalia vowed to be tested the very next week.

A couple of months later, when I was working with him in chambers, I asked him about the sleep-apnea test. He said he now had the C-PAP and loved it. He was sleeping better than ever as a result.

Austin City Limits

For the *Texas Law Review* banquet in April 2009, three events were scheduled: a faculty luncheon in which Justice Scalia would speak, a brief presentation in which he would speak to the local chapter of the Federalist Society, and then a book-signing together with his keynote address for a group of 300 or so law-review members and alumni. I was to introduce him for the keynote.

Karolyne and I met Justice Scalia in the lobby of the Four Seasons Hotel about 11:00 a.m., an hour before the luncheon was to begin. He was cheerful and eager to get underway. Accompanied by marshals, he, Karolyne, and I went to his room to chart the day's program: faculty lunch (noon–1:30), Federalist Society (5:00–6:00 p.m.), law-review banquet (7:00–9:00 p.m.). When Karolyne realized we had a three-hour gap from 2 to 5 o'clock, she suggested that we should go to the spa and get a massage.

"Do you like massages?" she asked Justice Scalia.

"I think I do," he said. "I haven't had one in decades. In fact, I think I've had only one in my entire life."

"You'll love it, Nino," I said. "Lyne and I have them all the time."

Karolyne said, "Why don't I see if I can schedule one for each of you?"

"I think I could use that," said Justice Scalia. "I'm awfully tight, and Maureen has been talking about getting me either a massage therapist or a certified stretcher."

"Is that a form of torture?" I asked, grinning.

The head marshal, who was also in the room, interjected: "We'll need to sweep the entire spa. We'll have the canine unit come by."

"Is that really necessary?" asked Justice Scalia.

"Yes, sir. We'd feel more comfortable in such a space if the canines checked it out. Also, we'll run background checks on the therapists."

"They're always very professional," I said.

"Nevertheless . . . ," said the marshal.

"Lyne," I said, "why don't you get a massage, too? You and I can get a room together."

"No, it's going to be hard enough to get two massage therapists at the same time. The Four Seasons spa usually stays pretty well booked. Let me schedule it for both of you. I'll go down now."

"Can I send a marshal along with you?" asked the head marshal.

"Sure," she said.

Soon Justice Scalia and I went downstairs to the ground-floor banquet room reserved for the event with the UT law faculty. Staff organizers had stacked copies of *Making Your Case* in piles on a reception table. They asked whether we'd be willing to autograph them.

"Of course!" said Justice Scalia. "We like signing books."

We managed to sign all 50 books before the faculty members started to arrive.

It was a warm event for us both. He was seeing old friends—people like Lino Graglia, a conservative constitutional-law professor who, like Justice Scalia, had grown up in New York, and Larry Sager, the dean, a liberal constitutional-law professor who had spent many years in New York. And I was seeing old teachers and colleagues—Sandy Levinson, the prolific constitutional-law professor whose teaching assistant I had been back in 1983–1984; David Sokolow, the effusively friendly expert in business associations; and Stanley Johanson, the legendary teacher of wills and trusts.

Only one junior faculty member made things unpleasant—a young man I'd never met. He was an anti-originalist who was keen to show up Justice Scalia by trying to point out contradictions in his jurisprudence. He hadn't been slated to sit at the head table, but he forced a clinical professor to give up his seat there. When I asked the clinical professor, my friend, why he wasn't sitting with me, he said that the new constitutional-law prof had pulled rank and insisted on switching. This in itself was annoying, given that I'd carefully arranged the seating. Then I noticed, when we were seated, that the new professor was nervous; his eyes were darting around erratically. So I remained aware of him.

Once the salads were served, he caught Justice Scalia's eye and blurted out, "Isn't it true that in *A v. B*, you said this, but in *C v. D* you said that, and in *E v. F*, you voted with a majority opinion that said something else entirely?"

Accustomed to counteracting people eager for a "gotcha" moment, Justice Scalia was particularly adept at deflecting here: "These are obscure cases you mention, and I imagine I'm not the only one at this table who has no idea what you're talking about."

Taking the cue, Professor Graglia then turned to Justice Scalia and said, "How's Maureen? And how are the kids? You have nine of them, right?" With that line of conversation, our table of eight was rescued from the obtusely disputatious professor, who seemed to be looking for another opportunity to interject a new contention.

Which he did. As soon as there was a lull in the Scalia–Graglia reminiscences of their salad days in New York, the bumptious young intellectual, short on social graces, said: "Isn't it true that in *Heller* you essentially read the preamble out of the Second Amendment?"

"Not at all," said Justice Scalia without a hint of irascibility. "My opinion takes account of the preamble, which grammatically, as Bryan would tell you, is a nominative absolute having no grammatical relation to the rest of the sentence."

"Fifteen legal historians, all with Ph.D.s in history, disagreed with your conclusion," the young man asserted.

"But others agreed," I said, as Dean Sager stood to introduce the guest of honor.

It's anyone's guess whether the purpose of the truculent junior professor was to rankle Justice Scalia, to provoke him to some intemperate rejoinder, or to engage in what he thought would be a scintillating dialectic. In any event, a senior faculty member had a word with him, and after that he was effectively squelched.

Justice Scalia's short talk was about the most important thing that goes on in law school: *teaching*. It was a quintessential example of his "teaching against the class": staking out a position that a large element of his audience would be likely to disagree with. He posited that U.S. law schools had long ago strayed from their core mission of training students to become lawyers—focusing instead on scholarship at the expense of teaching. When they do teach, he said, they teach skills that aren't peculiarly legal. He criticized the upper-division legal curriculum that had become preoccupied with "law-and" courses: law and feminism, law and literature, law and poverty, law and economics, and so on. He argued that faculty members should be better gatekeepers and that untrained students should never be allowed to determine what they should study.

Then he broadsided the law reviews, which, he said, publish professorial esoterica that is out of touch with anything related to real-world lawyering. He spoke of legal scholars' "self-indulgent posturing," "useless blather," and "abstruse writing." He noted—with disapproval lost on nobody—that 40% of the Harvard law faculty have no experience in practicing law and that only 25% have as much as five years of experience in practice. Several Harvard faculty members don't even have a law degree.

In the end, he made a strong pitch for a renewed appreciation, within legal academia, for the value of effective pedagogy. He said it wasn't too late for law schools to rededicate themselves to teaching law students to become good lawyers.

Toward the end of the talk, Karolyne texted me that she'd made our massage appointments: shiatsu for him, deep-tissue for me. Justice Scalia and I lingered only briefly to say goodbye to the faculty members, all of whom (as far as I could tell) were genuinely appreciative and enthusiastic. I'm excepting, of course, the argumentative con-law prof, who seemed to just disappear.

After changing clothes, I went by his room. "I'm looking forward to this," he said, smiling, as he stepped into the hall in his white robe and slippers. We matched. When we got off the elevator in the lobby, Karolyne was waiting for us. She escorted us to the spa, one floor down, where a marshal was leaving with a dog just as we walked up. Two marshals stayed behind, one at the main entrance and one at the door to Justice Scalia's treatment room. Karolyne went for a run along the river.

As it happened, we were the only customers in sight during our visit. We checked in, confirmed the massages we'd be getting, met our therapists, and walked down the hall to our side-by-side rooms. "Knock on the wall if you need anything, Nino," I said.

"Don't worry about me," he said. "You're the one getting deep-tissue. It's going to make you sore."

"We'll see," I said.

The time passed quickly. When it was over, we met up again in the hallway.

"That was great, wasn't it?" I said.

"There's nothing like it in the world," he said.

"Glad you liked it."

"Oh, yeah. So glad Lyne thought of it."

"Me, too. We can take a shower now, or go into the sauna or whirlpool."

He said, "Let's just take a shower and rest up a little."

"Do you want to shave?" I asked.

"I tend to get a 5 o'clock shadow," he said.

"Well, I don't. I'm blond. But let's shave." And so we did, using the spa's shaving cream and razors. As we stood side by side in front of the mirrors, removing the shaving cream one stroke at a time, I said, "I think the faculty really liked that speech."

"Think so? I've given it before. Seems like an impressive faculty."

"They are, except for that one guy. You handled him with equanimity."

"Ah. I've seen worse. Just a junior guy trying to play gotcha," he said, finishing up. "Piece of cake."

A minute or so into my shower, I heard him singing what sounded like snippets of an opera, perhaps Verdi or Puccini. In between the lyrics, which I couldn't make out, there would be a loud "Oooh," or "Aaah," as he ran his face under the showerhead and blew air, horselike, between his lips.

It was quite a long shower for me, perhaps ten minutes, but when I finished he showed no signs of drawing to a close. I got out, dried off, and glanced to see him running the shower over his head, singing all the while. He seemed utterly uninhibited.

I had delayed so long that I couldn't find any excuse to wait longer. So I went near his shower stall, interrupted his singing, and said, "Nino . . . Nino, I'm all finished, so I think I'll go on up to the room."

"This is a great shower!" he said.

"Yes. Wonderful."

"I'll be finished soon."

"I'll come by your room at ten to 5 for the Federalists."

"I'll be ready. What time is it now?"

"It's 4:35."

"Okay. See you then. Oh-soh-luh-mee-yoh!" He was singing again, the tones muffled somewhat by the stream of water pouring onto his face.

My Law Review's Banquet

If the Federalist Society event was quick and uneventful, the law-review banquet was something else entirely. Usually held at the Four Seasons, where we were staying, the event was held this time at the UT Stadium, in one of the public spaces that would fit 300 seated guests (though awkwardly arranged: in fingers jutting out from the speaker's position). I had warned Justice Scalia that the crowd was notoriously unruly, with an open bar that contributed to mass inattention to the speakers. I had seen many a circuit judge simply ignored as tables continued to talk over speakers. This year would be no exception. The din in the room grew long before I began to introduce Justice Scalia—but that moment didn't arrive until well after the night was supposed to be over.

The evening was badly planned. There were long pep talks for the incoming board members about how much hard work would be involved in editing the review. It was full of inside jokes that no one but the current staffers could understand. The parts that were comprehensible were just embarrassing: "You're going to have to work hard. Really hard. There may be all-nighters. There may be several all-nighters. That's what it means to be a member of this board—because we care about the high quality of the *Review*." Etc. Etc.

Justice Scalia and I were seated precisely 15 feet in front of the lectern, which wasn't raised. The speakers were essentially looking directly at the Justice.

"Is this for real?" Justice Scalia asked, leaning over to me. Not even whispering.

"No, it isn't," I said. "This is a joint nightmare."

Then came student awards, and they dragged on for a long time. The food consisted of three "mystery meats." We couldn't discern what was fish or fowl; it all seemed to be pork. So we fasted. And it was getting late.

"This is very inconsiderate," Justice Scalia said to me. "They ask me to come down here to sit through two hours of this."

He was exaggerating only slightly about the time.

"I know, I know," I said. "I'm sorry. I can't imagine how this is happening. There's just one more award, and then you're on."

It was now 8:45, and a quick award was to be given in the name of a famous expert on torts. Then it would be Scalia Time. I had expected the award recipient, a noted trial lawyer who was sitting at our table near Justice Scalia, to take the stage, say a quick thank-you, and sit down for the main event, but that's not what happened. He proceeded to try to deliver a learned discursus on two theories of causation in tort law—the minority view having been espoused by the person for whom the award was named. All the while, the crowd was growing rowdier and rowdier, completely ignoring him. Justice Scalia and I had our arms folded, at once bemused and further annoyed by the surreality of it all. He leaned over and said to me, aloud, "This guy is a *trial lawyer*? Are you kidding me? He can't read people at all!"

The group was so loud that the speaker stopped, completely flustered, and said, "May I have your attention, please? Please!" But the roar continued anyway, and he plodded on, reading his prepared remarks to an audience that could hear barely a word if they were straining to. A second time he stopped and shook his head, pausing several seconds to no effect. His faux-erudition was captivating to nobody.

I leaned over to Justice Scalia. "I told you it's a difficult crowd, Nino. I'm afraid they're thoroughly inebriated."

The bar, inconveniently enough, was *behind the speaker*, and a steady stream of people were lined up behind him as everyone ignored the man at the microphone. People were talking at their tables in full voice. I dreaded what would happen when Justice Scalia stood up. I felt regret that I'd gotten him into this horrible predicament.

Finally, at 9:10, I was being introduced as an alumnus of the law review and coauthor with Justice Scalia. Remarkably, the crowd grew quiet. They stayed pretty quiet during my three-minute introduction in which I talked about what it had been like to write with my coauthor. Then, after Justice Scalia took the stage amid perfervid applause, there was absolute silence and stillness—which reigned until he finished his speech 20 minutes later, although it was punctuated with frequent outbursts of energetic laughter.

His talk that night, on advocacy, was one that he'd given many times before—one that long predated *Making Your Case*. It was a tongue-in-cheek talk in which he joked about the irony of using the word "brief" for 50-page documents; insisted that it's impossible to exaggerate the importance of having a brief with the right color on the cover, since the Supreme Court votes on the basis of the color of the briefs; that at least two major points in every brief should be treated exclusively in footnotes; that judges should never be credited with having an ounce of wit; that no good advocate should rest his case on a precedent with a silly title like *Newman v. Piggie Park Enterprises*, since a case called *Piggie Park* just can't be taken seriously; and that if you want to succeed as an advocate, you should take on clients with names like *Marbury, McCulloch, Brown,* and *Miranda*.

The audience relished it, and he received a standing ovation. People rushed to thank him afterward. He called me over to say we must make a quick exit, and I alerted Karolyne and instructed the marshals of his wish. We were out in four minutes.

Once we were in the marshals' car, I said, "That was an extraordinary event, wasn't it, Nino?"

"I've never seen anything like it!" he answered.

"You had them in the palm of your hand."

"Well, so did you, in your intro. But before that point, they were rowdy and raucous," he said, shaking his head.

"I thought it was going to be a catastrophic evening."

"Actually," said Karolyne, "that took a lot of charisma and skill to do what you two did in turning the crowd. But listen, are you as hungry as I am?"

None of us had eaten the banquet food. When Karolyne and I suggested that Austin is famous for Mexican food, one of the local marshals urged us to try Guero's Taco Bar on South Congress Avenue. The marshals radioed ahead and had an advance team reserve a table for us—no mean feat, as we would learn, since there was a line extending way outside the restaurant. But when we got there 15 minutes later, we walked right in to a corner table that the advance team had staked out, and soon we were ordering the crispiest things we could find for Justice Scalia, who demanded no "mushy" food. "Mexican food is too mushy, I've always thought!" he said. We ordered crispy tacos for him, and he liked them.

Two young blonde women in sundresses came over to our table. "Justice Scalia! We can't believe you're here. We're UT law students, and we'd like your autograph! We're so excited to see you."

A marshal came over to see whether we wanted them escorted away. No, we said, they should stay.

"You're law students, are you?" Justice Scalia said.

"Yes. We're freshlaws!"

I said: "That's the UT slang for first-year law students, Nino. Don't read anything into 'fresh.'"

Justice Scalia said to them, "This, by the way, is my coauthor, Bryan Garner, and Karolyne."

"It's good to meet you, sir," they said, almost in unison.

"What do you want me to sign?" Justice Scalia said.

"Would you sign my arm?" one of the young women said. "I don't have anything else."

"You want me to sign your arm?" Justice Scalia asked.

"If you would. I wouldn't wash it off for a week!"

"I can't do that," he said. "I don't sign body parts. Get a piece of paper and I'll sign it."

"We don't have anything," one of them said. "We don't have a seat yet. We're still standing in line outside. We just followed you in."

I handed over my paper menu, and Karolyne handed over hers. I gave Justice Scalia a pen, grinning at him. "Here, Nino. This'll do." He signed them both.

As he was doing his calligraphy, I said to the women, "You'll have these menus permanently. Now don't lose them."

"Oh, I won't," one of them said. "Justice Scalia is my favorite. I'll always remember this."

As they walked away, I said, "Nino, I think those are the most beautiful Scalia groupies I've ever seen."

"Don't worry," he said, grinning. "Maureen knows all about my groupies. She's never had a thing to worry about, and she knows it."

"Bryan's groupies don't look anything like that!" Karolyne said.

"I'm sure they don't," Justice Scalia said. The two of them laughed. I saw nothing funny about it—nothing at all.

The Burton Awards

In June 2009, we spoke together twice, first at the Burton Awards in D.C. and later at the annual meeting of the State Bar of Texas. Bill Burton, founder of the Burton Awards, said he wanted to present us with the Law Book of the Year award. The Burton Award ceremony was a lavish black-tie event at the Library of Congress, where we were to be interviewed jointly.[30]

We spent that day, June 15, working together in chambers. In the afternoon, Karolyne and my daughter Caroline would be coming up to the Court to join me while I presented Justice Ginsburg with the Scribes lifetime-achievement award—the award that Justice Scalia had received the previous year.

"Ruth's getting the award this year?" asked Justice Scalia. "That's wonderful. She's *such* a good writer."

"Yes. It's a richly deserved honor," I said, "just as yours was last year."

"Why are you giving it to her *here*? Isn't it going to be a big public event, like mine?"

"She can't make the trip to Chicago in August. So I'm filming it here in her chambers. The film will be played at the annual meeting. Why don't you come with us to be a part of it?"

"I think I will. That'd be great . . . On second thought, maybe not."

"Why not?" I asked.

"I got the award last year. This is Ruth's year. The focus should be on her."

"Oh, I see what you mean," I said. "Do you know who taught Justice Ginsburg how to write so well?"

"No, who?" he asked.

"You'll never believe it. Vladimir Nabokov."

"You're kidding," he said. "How do you know that?"

"It came up in my interview with her. He was her undergraduate literature professor at Cornell."

"You're serious?" he asked.

"Absolutely. And he taught her a crucial principle: nobody should ever have to read a sentence twice to get its meaning. That's good, isn't it?"[31]

---

30 The joint interview can be seen at http://www.youtube.com/watch?v=oNcCQT_x4NU.

31 My interview with Justice Ginsburg can be seen at http://www.lawprose.org/bryan-garner

"That's awfully good," he said.

Soon Karolyne and Caroline arrived and came back to chambers to greet Justice Scalia, who chatted with them briefly and then saw us off to present the award to Justice Ginsburg. After a successful bit of cinematography in her chambers, we were back in his chambers again. Justice Scalia and I secluded ourselves in his office to change into our tuxedos. Then Karolyne came in and tied both my black tie and his, which was a chore because his was too tight for him. But she made it work.

The four of us walked next door to the Library of Congress for the Burton Awards. Red carpets had been rolled out. This was as close as things got in law to the Academy Awards. Once inside, we were shepherded backstage to the greenroom, where we enjoyed lively banter with David E. Kelley, creator of *Boston Legal,* and his wife, Michelle Pfeiffer, among others. I told David how much Karolyne and I had enjoyed the *Boston Legal* finale just six months before. In that episode, "Justice Scalia" (Jack Shearer—not a good likeness) ends up performing a same-sex wedding between Denny Crane (William Shatner) and Alan Shore (James Spader) at Nimmo Bay in British Columbia. The Scalia character is coincidentally there on a fishing trip, and he is implausibly (but hilariously) persuaded to administer the vows. David seemed surprised at how good-humored and exceedingly amused Justice Scalia was upon hearing about the episode.

Onstage at the Burton Awards, Justice Scalia and I were interviewed by the journalist Bill Press. He began with the very question I'd posed to Justice Scalia 14 months before, when taping in his chambers for the Dallas Bar Association: Why did we write the book? His answer here was very different from the one he'd given me privately (though on film [see p. 90]), but doubtless both were true and accurate. On this evening, before the crowd of lawyers and judges in formal dress, he said: "Anyone who has been a judge for any amount of time becomes more or less exasperated at the errors that lawyers make in their presentations to the court, both written and oral. I thought it was worthwhile—not only a boon to the practice, but also a boon to the bench—to try to eliminate some of those errors."

I added my own motivation: "My thought was there is a lot of literature on how to improve advocacy—a lot of articles—but that the really good advice is scattered. Nobody had ever pulled it together in a very brief and cohesive way, as I thought Justice Scalia and I could do. At first we thought it was simply going to be a restatement of advocacy, but it ended up having a lot of original ideas."

Justice Scalia said he was a bit surprised at the originality himself: "It's hard to believe that there are any new thoughts. Ever since Aristotle, there have been judges and other people giving advice about how to persuade judges. Literally it goes back to Aristotle, or Hammurabi, for all that I know. It's hard to believe that there was anything new to be said. But as it turns out, at least in our distinctive American system of law, there are some new things."

We continued for some 20 minutes in this vein. Toward the end, Justice Scalia was asked to pay homage to Justice David Souter, who had just left the Court, and he spoke touchingly of their friendship.

Bill also brought up the subject of the confirmation of Supreme Court Justices, saying: "In 1986, Justice, you were confirmed by the United States Senate by a vote of 98 to nothing."

"Right," said Justice Scalia.

"Any advice for Sonia Sotomayor?" Bill asked, referring to President Barack Obama's then-pending nominee.

Justice Scalia laughed, and then said: "What was the year?"

"Nineteen eighty-six," Bill said.

"My advice would be go back to 1986." There was lively laughter from both the crowd and the stage.

"Things have changed," Justice Scalia added, "and I think the reason things have changed has to do with the 'evolving Constitution.' What has happened is that the people between then and now have figured out that, under the new theory that the Court has been using since the Warren Court [of the 1950s], the Constitution does not have a fixed meaning, but it changes to comport with the times. When it changes and how it changes is up to the Court. Once you have that theory, who you pick as a judge should not depend mostly on who is a good lawyer or who has judicial temperament. I mean, all that stuff is good. But the main thing you want to know is what kind of a Constitution is this person going to write. That's what's happened since 1986. So I think I was a good lawyer in the days when that mattered a whole lot. And I think it matters less now—and it's unfortunate."

The State Bar of Texas

Justice Scalia flew to Dallas on June 28, 2009—the first time we'd gotten together in my hometown. I had arranged a book-signing event at the LawProse office for a select group of Dallas lawyers and judges, as well as 60 international lawyers from all parts of the globe. They were attending the annual academy of the Center for American and International Law in Plano—where I teach every summer—and they, along with my law students from Southern Methodist University, were excited to meet and speak with Justice Scalia. My father flew in from Amarillo to participate in the festivities. The SMU law dean arranged a dinner for ten at a local steakhouse.

Over dinner, when the subject of a forthcoming second book came up, the dean proclaimed that he wanted SMU Law to host the "world premiere" of our inevitable teaching engagements about the new book. Justice Scalia and I agreed that it would certainly be an early gig, if not the first.

The next day, our State Bar of Texas event was scheduled for 9:00 to 10:00 a.m., and this time we suffered from Karolyne's absence. Because she had to be in Boston that day, she couldn't do any advance work with the event planners. They didn't have the PowerPoint presentation in advance, and the traffic in Dallas made us ten minutes late. In any event, Justice Scalia didn't want to arrive earlier than absolutely necessary. My father and I had met him in the lobby of his North Dallas hotel, and the plan was for the marshals to get us to the downtown Hyatt convention center by 8:45 a.m. Instead, we drove up at 9:05, were taken directly onstage before 800 lawyers in attendance, and I made the peremptory decision that we'd speak without visual aids. Justice Scalia was unfazed by this adjustment in plans, since he normally spoke without PowerPoint slides anyway. But he did normally like giving credit to my daughter Caroline for making our slides, and occasionally he'd rib her (mostly in absentia) about some of the clever visual associations she had made to illustrate our lectures.

By now we had our Click-and-Clack routine down pretty well, and we invariably injected extemporaneous humor into our presentations. I began: "You want me to warm them up, you say?"

"Go ahead. Get 'em warmed up."

Things as simple as that would make people laugh, and we in turn drew energy from the audience. We gave what had come to be our standard short presentation of *Making Your Case*. We traded points, occasionally commenting on each other's ideas.

Among his best moments was telling the audience: "Treasure simplicity. You don't get any extra credit for eloquence. Just make it simple and tell us your point. Your job is to make a complex case simple, not a simple case complex." He strongly endorsed the effective writer's stylistic habit of starting a fair number of sentences with a snappy *But* (no comma after) rather than a plodding *However* (which, as a contrasting word, requires a comma). He warned that briefs shouldn't be overloaded with italics, which can make them read like "a high-school girl's diary." His sternest admonition that morning, though, was about using case law carefully. He stressed that statements about precedents must be accurate: "When a judge sees you playing fast and loose with a citation, he is not going to believe the rest of your brief."

We debated footnoted citations for several minutes. Once we'd had equal time, I asked the audience for a show of hands. The numbers were about equal, just as they had been at the Kennedy Center. He barely concealed his momentary consternation. It was all I could do to suppress my pleasure in the vote, as I felt obliged to do. The other three votes I lost, as I had at the Kennedy Center.

We stayed for 45 minutes to sign books. Then, joined by my father, we had lunch at Fearing's restaurant in the Ritz-Carlton. Because my father is heavily interested in politics and likes to engage people in conversation, I felt almost like an interloper in an interview he was conducting with Justice Scalia. Perhaps the most interesting question was whether Justice Scalia thought it possible for anyone today to rise to high political office and still maintain a high degree of integrity.

"Including judicial office?" asked Justice Scalia.

"Yes," said my father.

"Of course it's possible, even if the press impugns you mercilessly."

"What about excluding judges? Just politicians: can they rise to high office and still keep a high degree of integrity?"

"I think Ronald Reagan had integrity. Lincoln certainly had integrity."

"Bryan once had a colleague," my father said, "who worked with and admired Reagan, but his answer was no—politicians cannot under the current system achieve great heights while preserving their integrity."

"I suppose that might be right," Justice Scalia conceded, but seemingly on a theoretical basis, not that of personal knowledge.

As soon as we had finished our lunch, Justice Scalia was headed for the airport. The marshals had planned and timed his route, they said, and he was leaving just in time to make his flight. We said a quick but warm goodbye.

Upon returning to D.C., Justice Scalia wrote: "Enjoyed the visit with you, your daughter, your father, and your staff at LawProse. And I thought that the program went over very well."

The Book on Tape

Our work on *Making Your Case* wasn't fully complete until we made the audiobook, which took two full days in October 2009. A sound engineer set up equipment just off the Court's main conference room. It didn't take long for us to decide that we'd read separate sections sequentially. We'd listen closely to each other and occasionally stop each other to correct the other's pronunciation or emphasis. In fact, we had so many disputes over pronunciation that we soon had to send out for *Webster's Second New International Dictionary*, *Garner's Modern American Usage*, *The American Heritage Dictionary*, and my *Dictionary of Modern Legal Usage*. For example, at first Justice Scalia pronounced *gravamen* /GRAH-vuh-muhn/, when the traditional pronunciation is /gruh-VAY-muhn/. I persuaded him to do a second take with a corrected pronunciation. He also pronounced *appellee* with the accent on the second rather than the third syllable. We skirmished over that: he analogized it to *appellant*, which stresses the second syllable; I analogized it to *mortgagee* and *obligee*, with the third-syllable stress. The dictionaries bore out my preference, so he re-recorded the passage. On the other hand, his Latin pronunciations of the legal phrases *inclusio unius est exclusio alterius* and *noscitur a sociis* and *ejusdem generis* prevailed over mine: my knowledge of Latin couldn't hold a candle to his. Soon we were keeping score on who prevailed more often on the dozen or so matters of contested pronunciation.

Most of our readings were done in a single take. His reading voice was emphatic, strong, and deliberate. We tried to read at about the same pace. The process convinced us that we had done well with the prose.

At the very end, I suggested that we record a bonus track in which we'd extemporaneously discuss what we had just done. Here's part of it:

SCALIA: So what do you want to talk about?

GARNER: Well, it was kind of fun reading the book, wasn't it?

SCALIA: [*laughs*] Well, you know, I think that says something about the writing of the book. I don't know what other people do, and my wife often makes fun of me for this. I often read aloud, beneath my breath, a passage or a paragraph that I've just written. After all, these are words, and saying them aloud sometimes points out whether they're put together clumsily or gracefully. It's probably a good practice to read stuff aloud. If this audiobook sounds good, I think that's because the book itself was written well. And if it sounds bad, the reason might be that it wasn't written well.

GARNER: Well, you remember when we wrote the book. After we had a draft done, and we would add a paragraph, frequently we would deliver it orally.

SCALIA: You're absolutely right. You're absolutely right.

GARNER: And the listeners should probably know that it wasn't a matter of my reading Garner passages and your reading Scalia passages. Except for the signed debates, there's no such thing as a Garner passage or a Scalia passage.

SCALIA: Right. Except for that, I frankly, with a few exceptions, cannot recognize which ones I wrote the initial draft of and which ones you wrote the initial draft of.

GARNER: And we both so heavily revised the book that every sentence was truly coauthored, wouldn't you say?

SCALIA: I would say that.

GARNER: My own calculation is that you wrote about 52% of the book, and I wrote about 48%.

SCALIA: I can't cut it that fine. But I do think it was about 50–50. I can't slice it any thinner than that.

GARNER: Now, I'm just curious. We love our little debates. And we've given our debates live in New York, Washington, L.A., and Dallas. And we really enjoy having those debates. But I'm just curious. Do you really not have any misgivings about those points you've taken against me?

SCALIA: Absolutely not. [*laughs*] And, when we put it to a vote at those sessions, who wins? Who wins on all the points? Tell the audience who wins on all the points!

GARNER: You win on contractions. You always win on contractions. It just amazes me how timid the audiences are.

SCALIA: [*sarcastically*] Yeah, yeah.

GARNER: You win on no substantive footnotes. But our differences are very slight on that. You do prevail, much to my amazement, on sexist language—even though we made the book gender-neutral, and you were very acquiescent about putting up with me. I think you were partly tolerant because Justice Ginsburg has done that with some of your opinions, right?

SCALIA: No, I think I was tolerant because I know how punitive especially law schools can be for failure to observe the Code of Unisex. I think that's the main reason I receded. In other words, I think your position, while intellectually abominable, is commercially reasonable.

GARNER: And then on this question of citations in footnotes, it always surprises you what the votes are. I think the votes in almost every forum have been right down the middle, 50–50.

SCALIA: No, I don't think that's true. I've won in *every* case. Now on that issue it was closer than on the other ones. Come on! Come on!

GARNER: I think you conceded at the Kennedy Center it was 50–50.

SCALIA: No I didn't! I did not at all. [*laughs*]

GARNER: Well, I think standards are going to be changing on that point. But you have to be bothered by having 50% of the lawyer groups, having heard that question vented, think footnoted citations are the better way.

SCALIA: I think when they will come to consider it more thoroughly they will understand that we lawyers have gotten very used to just having these citations in the middle of the sentence. Well, not in the middle of the sentence, but in the middle of the paragraph anyway, and go on to the sentence. It is very clumsy to have to keep looking down. And it doesn't solve that keep-looking-down problem to try to put all the essential information into the text. [*impatiently*] Anyway, we're just redoing the argument.

GARNER: I do want to say one other thing, though, and that is . . .

SCALIA: Yeah, yeah, yeah.

GARNER: One of the great things about collaborating with you was that our literary styles really melded perfectly—seamlessly—wouldn't you say?

SCALIA: I think so, and that is partly because, as you informed me, early on in our relationship, we are both snoots.

GARNER: Snoots, yeah.

SCALIA: Snoots. Tell them.

GARNER: Syntax nudniks of our time [David Foster Wallace's term].

SCALIA: I thought it was nerds.

GARNER: Or syntax nerds.

SCALIA: Yeah, there are some people who care about pronouncing things correctly, and using *imply* instead of *infer* [when that's appropriate], saying *nuclear* instead of /noo-kyuh-luhr/, and all those little technicalities which a lot of people couldn't be bothered less about. But you and I care about that stuff, right?

GARNER: Why don't more lawyers care about that?

SCALIA: I don't know. I don't know. Anybody whose business is words ought to. But many do, I think, many do.

GARNER: Well, this has been a lot of fun.

SCALIA: It has been a very enjoyable collaboration. I will put it that way.

GARNER: And we're going to do it again.

SCALIA: I hope we will. [*laughs*]

Night at the Opera

The night we finished recording the audiobook, Justice Scalia, Karolyne, and I had dinner together.

"Guess what I'll be doing tomorrow," Justice Scalia said.

"What?" I asked.

"Ruth [Justice Ginsburg] and I are going to be supernumeraries in *Ari-*

adne auf Naxos—the Strauss opera—at the Kennedy Center. You know what a supernumerary is?"

"I know the word," I said. "As an adjective, it means 'superfluous' or 'surplus.'"

"It's an operatic term. You don't know it, do you?"

"I confess I don't. Is it a kind of theatrical extra?"

"You've got it! Ruth and I are going to be onstage for much of the opera as people in the crowd. There are lots of crowd scenes."

"Have you rehearsed?"

"No. It doesn't require that. We just sit there as the performers interact. We'll be in modern dress—our own clothes. We have a few stage directions to follow."

"That's great."

"Can we get tickets and come see you?" Karolyne asked.

"I'm sure you can," he said.

"Good," she said. "Let me see if I can book them right now online. Do you mind?" She got out her iPhone and within a couple of minutes had booked us some good seats in the orchestra. Justice Scalia was amazed that it could all be done so quickly from a handheld device.

"You need to teach me how to do that!"

"I wish she'd teach me," I said. "People of a certain age struggle with these things."

"You're right about that. Listen, you'll need to look for Maureen in the audience. She'll be sitting with Marty Ginsburg."

And so we did. The next evening, we texted Mrs. Scalia's cellphone to tell her where we were, and Karolyne and I had a good short visit with her and Marty Ginsburg—both of whom were excited for their spouses. During the opera, the actors interacted with both Justices quite a bit. There was an opera-within-the-opera, rather like Shakespeare's play-within-a-play in *Hamlet*. The actress playing Zerbinetta, a feisty coquette, came and sat on Justice Scalia's lap and embraced him—much to the crowd's delight. And a couple of male actors were particularly flirtatious with Justice Ginsburg. The Justices, doubtless a major attraction for much of the audience, enjoyed sitting feet away from virtuoso opera performers. They had the best seats in the house.

Afterward, we waited in the foyer of the Kennedy Center with Maureen Scalia and Marty Ginsburg while their spouses were backstage taking off their makeup. We had hearty congratulations for them as they walked out together. Never before had I seen the two Justices so ebullient.

An Exuberant Phone Call

Not long after, as I was sitting in my office in Dallas, I received a phone call from Justice Scalia.

"Bryan: People are listening. People are really *listening!*" He sounded giddy.

"What do you mean?"

"You know how we say, in *Making Your Case*, not to use up all your time at oral argument but to sit down early if there's nothing left that's useful to say?"[32]

"Yes."

"It happened this morning in our Court. *Both sides did it!* The Justices couldn't believe it. We got out 20 minutes early."

"That's amazing!"

"I haven't seen it in nearly 30 years on the bench—and certainly not in the 25 years I've been here at the Court."

"Wow."

"They got it from our book, Bryan."

"Of course they did!"

"They got it from our book. They're paying attention. The petitioners did it, and the Justices all glanced at each other. Then the respondents did it, and we were stunned. We were all buzzing about it afterward in the robing room."

"Did your colleagues acknowledge that it was because of our book?"

"Well, no."

"Did you tell them?"

"Of course not. I didn't want to claim credit. It would have been im-modest. But you and I know. That's why the first thing I did in getting back here to chambers was call you. You and I know."

"Yes, we do, Nino. Congratulations."

---

32 Antonin Scalia & Bryan A. Garner, *Making Your Case* 173–74 (2008) ("When you have time left, but nothing else useful to say, conclude effectively and gracefully.").

5

Reading Law: Part I

(2009–2010)

Even as we were putting the finishing touches on *Making Your Case* back in 2008, I had begun to realize how much I'd soon miss the side-by-side work at Justice Scalia's trestle table and his computer monitor.

"Aren't you going to miss this?" I asked him one day as we were sitting in his chambers.

"Are you *serious*?" he replied. "This is hard work—harder than I ever thought it would be."

"Elmore Leonard once said that writing is the hardest work there is that doesn't involve heavy lifting."

"That's exactly right."

"But look what we've created. From *nothing*!"

"It's a good book," he said. "We can be proud of this."

"What we really need to do is a second book, on textualism. Something like a playbook for litigators—how to make a textual argument. And for judges—how to evaluate statutes. No such thing exists."

"I've already written all about that in my opinions."

"True. But I'm thinking of something more systematic."

"Lookit, if this book on advocacy is hard, the one you're suggesting would be much harder."

"But who else could do it? You're the greatest living expositor of textualism, and I'm supposed to be the great expert on legal language."

"Don't undersell yourself—the English language generally."

"We're two modest guys, aren't we?" I said with a smile.

"We're a lot alike."

"Some egos are deserved," I said. "But nobody who really knows you could say you're full of yourself."

"I hope not. You know, I've resolved to be a better person. I went to a men's retreat not long ago—a Catholic retreat. I do that every few years. You ought to try it sometime."

"What's involved?" I asked.

"Fellowship. Contemplation. The study of Scripture. That might not be for you. Anyway, I've resolved to be a better person—to be a kinder person, and more patient with people. Never to take Maureen for granted—or my children. I want to be kinder to my colleagues. You ever think about that kind of thing?"

"All the time, Nino. I may not be a churchgoer, but I'm a spiritual person—in an ethical sense. I just don't go for the mysticism."

"Ah, but that's where greater truths lie, if you're a believer. Anyway, when do you have time for quiet contemplation?"

"On airplanes, in hotels. I have my noise-canceling headphones. I sit back and listen to Mahler or Janáček and shut out the rest of the world. So I guess it's not entirely quiet contemplation."

"But that's good. You like classical music?"

"Of course. As you know, I come from a family of professional musicians."

"But somehow you became a writer."

"Yes, I'm a writer. So are you. And that's why I want to do a second book with you, on your greatest intellectual love: legal interpretation."

"I've done that already in *A Matter of Interpretation.*"

"You skimmed the surface there. It's an important book, but it's really just an essay followed by other people's essays. Think of all the canons of construction that you've never written about."

"Too hard. That would take a major treatise."

"You'd learn a lot from doing it."

"What do you mean?"

"I know you're worried about the amount of work. But you'd discover things that you don't know right now. That always happens when you write."

"True."

"Think about how much more clearly you think about advocacy now that we've written *Making Your Case.*"

"That's true. You really think I'd learn things about textualism?"

"Sure. You'd become even better at it. We would probably discover things that nobody has ever written about."

"Like what?"

"The exceptions to the *ejusdem generis* canon. Do you know what they are, or how many there are?"

"No idea. Nobody's written about that?"

"People have written *around* it. But nobody has done it as systematically or with as much acuity as we could. Are you sure I can't convince you?"

"Let me think about it. Let me talk to Maureen. I'm kind of doubtful about a second book."

The week after this conversation, Justice Scalia called me—it was June 2008—to say he'd decided against the second book. He simply had too much to do already, given his day job. He was tired of extracurricular writing. Disappointed as I was, I said I understood.

A Change of Heart

Although Justice Scalia and I were doing a fair number of speaking events together in late 2008 and early 2009, we weren't seeing each other nearly as often as we had during the two previous years, when we were writing together. We had dinner together only a handful of times, and we'd go several weeks without talking at all.

During the first week of March 2009, as I was working in my office, my assistant buzzed to say that Justice Scalia was on line two.

"Hello. Nino?"

"No, it's Angela. Let me put the Justice on the line." There was a 15-second pause.

"Bryan, my friend!"

"How are you, Nino?"

"I miss you, Bryan. I've really missed you."

"Well, I miss you, too, Nino. You know, there's a cure for that. Let's start the second book."[33]

---

33 A close variant of this bit of the dialogue was quoted in Alex Carp, "Writing with Antonin Scalia, Grammar Nerd," *The New Yorker*, 16 July 2012, http://www.newyorker.com/news/news-desk/writing-with-antonin-scalia-grammar-nerd.

He chuckled. "Okay. Let's do it," he said.

"Terrific," I said, fairly stunned at this reversal of fortune, given what he had told me a few months before.

"You know I loved working on our book. I think we could do it again."

"Well, I agree. It *is* great working together," I told him. I was having to collect my thoughts quickly. "Now this second book is going to be more ambitious, and it'll take time."

"I realize that. But I really care about interpretation, and I think we can contribute to the field."

"I'm sure we can," I said. "As with the first book, it'll be something only the two of us could write. This is great news."

"How do we start?"

I had hoped for this moment for a while, so I already had a semblance of an outline in hand. "I have an outline," I said. "Let me pull it together and send it to you, along with a sample section. I won't be up in D.C. until June."

"What's the date in June? I'll get it on my calendar. You still traveling the country?"

"Yes. You just happened to catch me on my one day in the office this week. Okay, it's June 15. We could work that day and then have dinner afterward."

"Let me see. . . . Sure. Tosca?"

"That'd be great. Glad we're going to be working together again."

"Me, too," he said. "Makes me happy."

A few days later, I sent him the outline and a first draft of the *ejusdem generis* section. The Latin name (meaning "of the same kind") intimidates people, but it's a simple idea. It's a doctrine of legal interpretation saying that broad words at the end of a list are necessarily narrowed by the types of things listed—"turkeys, roosters, hens, doves, quail, and other animals," for example. Despite its normally broad meaning, the word *animals* in that list might well be limited to birds—because only birds appear in the preceding list.

I sent a six-page draft citing about 30 cases and many scholarly authorities. So we had a start that he could elaborate on. I had somehow forgotten, I suppose, that Justice Scalia didn't have the habit of opening e-mail attachments—or perhaps I figured that he'd acquired it. In any event, he didn't actually see my draft until late August. He liked it, and he added a good deal to it.

Meanwhile, I started working with West to get a contract in place for *Reading Law*. When I called Justice Scalia to discuss the terms, he insisted that royalties should be split 50–50 down the line. "It should have been that way on the first book," he said. "You worked as hard as I did."

"But that's not the deal we made."

"Well, you're very generous. I think it should have been 50% to you."

So that's what it became for the second book. The contract had been signed by all three parties by April 3, 2009.

The Bard Hath a Way

Later that month, we started working hard on our table of contents, which consisted of complete propositions such as, "General terms are to be given their general meaning," or "The text must be construed as a whole," or "A statute is not repealed by nonuse or desuetude [a long period of disuse]." I had collected nearly 200 of these propositions, and we were organizing and reorganizing them, as well as cutting many of them that we considered unsound for one reason or another. As we worked through them, we were steeped in books that had been conveniently sent over by the Supreme Court Library so that we could verify citations against original sources.

At one point, Angela interrupted us as we were hard at work. "Justice," she said from the doorway, "Jess Bravin of the *Wall Street Journal* is on the line. He'd like a comment from you about the authorship of Shakespeare's plays."

"I'll pick up in a moment," said Justice Scalia.

"Nino," I said, "you don't believe in one of those crackpot theories that William Shakespeare didn't write the plays, do you?"

"It's not a crackpot theory at all. I believe there's a good possibility that it's this man de Vere."

"Edward de Vere, the Earl of Oxford?" I asked.

"Yes," he said.

"That's so silly."

"Well, let me take this call, and then we'll discuss it," he said. He then got on the line with Bravin, a most capable journalist, and told him he had real doubts about whether the actor from Stratford-upon-Avon could have written the plays attributed to Shakespeare. He said that the intricate knowledge of the internal workings of the royal courts of Europe made it highly unlikely that someone who, for all we know, never left England and never went to Oxford or Cambridge could have composed the plays. It must have been someone with a good knowledge of the intrigues of courtiers.

When he got off the line, I ribbed him a little. "Nino, you're just spreading ill-founded rumors in the popular mind. There's zero evidence in favor of de Vere." Eyebrows raised, he took off his glasses and listened intently. I continued: "Nobody doubted Shakespeare's authorship until a century after his death. Even his chief rival, Ben Jonson, paid homage to the man as a great playwright. Many of the plays were published in his lifetime. If he hadn't written them, there would have been at least the whiff of contemporaneous scandal."

"I stand by what I said." He rubbed his lower lip with his right thumb.

"What if someone said that it's completely implausible that Scalia's opinions could have been authored by an Italian kid who grew up in a tenement in Queens and had absolutely no knowledge of the inner workings of legislatures?"

"Ha! Well, I suppose they'd have a point!"

"The point is," I said, "that *reading* makes all the difference. You and I can know about Socrates or Caesar or Chaucer because we can *read*. Shakespeare had Plutarch and other historians as his sources, but then he understood human nature more completely perhaps than any other writer ever has. De Vere was a mediocrity and an irresponsible popinjay. He died, if I'm not mistaken, in 1604—and more than a quarter of the plays were written after that."

"A popinjay? Lookit, I haven't studied the point closely, but many people who have think it was de Vere."

"And they're all dilettantes, Nino. The experts who've devoted their careers to Shakespeare studies—and I mean real experts—think it's not even a close question. We know more about Shakespeare's life than any other Elizabethan playwright except Ben Jonson—a lot more than we know about Christopher Marlowe."

"Really?"

"Sure. We even know what the curriculum was at the Stratford grammar school where he studied. We know where he picked up his not insignificant knowledge of Latin."

"How do you know this?"

"I started out writing about Shakespearean linguistics. I own more than 20 biographies of Shakespeare."

"Have you read them?"

"Of course not! I *use* them—I don't read them. The best is by Samuel Schoenbaum. It's called *Shakespeare's Lives*. I *have* read that one, and it's worth reading."

"These Shakespeareans have a vested interest in perpetuating the myth that little Willie Shakespeare from Stratford wrote those plays!"

"No they don't! Most Shakespeareans are just literary critics. They're glad we have the plays, regardless of the source. But they have a strong enough historical bent that they detest seeing this literary hoax foisted on the popular mind by amateurs when there's nothing to support it."

"John Paul [Justice Stevens] thinks it was de Vere."

"Well, Nino, I wish Justices wouldn't opine on literary and historical matters like this without looking into them closely."

"Okay, Bryan, you've convinced me to shut up about it unless I do more homework. But I think I've already given him a good quote!" He smiled mischievously.

We went on about our work.

The Writing Grind

For this second book, our working mode was quite different from what we had done before. We didn't try writing the same sections at the same time, as we had for *Making Your Case*. Instead, we wrote about whatever we felt moved to write about at the time. I did the initial drafts of the linguistically oriented sections, and he did most of the ones involving the types of legal doctrines that commonly arise in the Supreme Court.

As with our first book, we began by assembling a table of contents containing complete sentences, or full propositions. That way, each section became essentially a short essay in support of the blackletter proposition, just as we had done in *Making Your Case*. We agreed that the core principle of the book was that legal instruments should be given a "fair reading": an interpretation that a competent, sensible user of the language would ascribe to the words used.

I didn't receive any drafts from Justice Scalia until late July, when he wrote: "Bryan: I have started in earnest on the book, and wanted you to peruse [by which he meant "scrutinize"—the traditional sense] my first few jottings, to be sure they are in form along the lines you approve. Let me know what you think. Also let me know what other sections you want me to work on." He ended his e-mail with, "Long time no see. Nino." This despite our having spent two days together at the State Bar of Texas meeting less than a month before.

By the end of August, we were both going full throttle. I thought we were approaching a full rough draft. But Justice Scalia thought at most we were nearing a full rough draft of only the opening sections. His assessment was closer to the mark.

The work on *Reading Law* was much slower and more painstaking than it had been on *Making Your Case*. We wrote the book over a three-year period, and the research was far more labor-intensive.

On the many days when we'd work together, we'd go through a routine that became comically predictable. I'd show up at his chambers with a few problems for us to work through, usually based on specific criticisms of Justice Scalia I'd found in law reviews or books. Typically, Justice Scalia would try to deflect and say he'd like to ignore the criticism, but I'd persist and say I thought we should address the point to clear up any perceived weaknesses. Again he'd demur, and again I'd insist. I'd finally get him writing, if only reluctantly.

For example, that's how the refutation of Stanley Fish (arguing that there is no "textualist" method) made its way into the published book; and that of Robert Benson (arguing that there's no such thing as "following the law"); and that of Mark Tushnet (arguing that there's a constitution outside the written Constitution); and that of J. Harvie Wilkinson (arguing that judges should have no theory of interpretation). Those passages were written in separate sessions between 2009 and 2011, and Justice Scalia typed most of them at his computer. They were hard passages to write, and sometimes just two or three paragraphs would occupy us for an entire afternoon.

Because we cited so many Supreme Court cases, I thought it might be useful to identify the writing judge for each majority opinion. So I'd add "per Frankfurter, J." or "per Warren, C. J." after each citation. But my co-author phoned me to object to this practice.

"Bryan, it's well known in Supreme Court circles that the author of the majority opinion is never to be called out."

"I know that, Nino, but we have a special purpose here. Readers need to know that we're citing lots of judges of different backgrounds. We're not citing just the conservative bloc of the Court. We're certainly not citing just Scalia opinions. We cite Thurgood Marshall positively, and Earl Warren, and John Paul Stevens. We need people to see that."

"You have a point."

"If it's just a case name, people might suspect that you wrote every one of the recent opinions we cite positively, when that's not true at all."

"Okay, let me think further on it."

"Believe me, Nino, it'll make our text harder for our intellectual enemies to undercut."

"Then leave it in for now."

We left it in for good.

But much potentially valuable material was left on the proverbial cutting-room floor. In May 2010, I had the idea of analogizing statutory interpretation to musical interpretation—hardly a novel idea in itself. But I recalled the free-form cadenza typical of 18th-century compositions, and I thought this idea might be novel. Justice Scalia liked the opener. Here's how it read:

Introduction

Imagine if every legal instrument, toward what should be the end, trailed off with "and so on and so forth." Or perhaps any piece of writing, for that matter. Readers expecting coherent ideas would be baffled and disappointed.

But in music, there was a mostly 18th-century tradition of having composers include cadenzas, which were musical flourishes left to a soloist's imaginative improvisation, giving the "impression that the solo performer, worked up to an artistic frenzy, had burst away from his companions [the accompanists] *to indulge himself in the unrestrained expression of his enthusiasm."* In Jean-Pierre Rampal's most famous rendition of Mozart's flute concerto in G major,** for example, Rampal fills 85 seconds at the end of the first movement with supposedly extemporaneous playing. That's the proper way to play the piece. In fact, the most famous compositions requiring cadenzas have had various renditions written for them. By the dawn of the 19th century, though, most composers came to feel "that if anyone was to prepare beforehand such material for insertion in their music, it might as well be themselves."****

And in modern times it has not been considered a denigration of classical musicians to ask that they faithfully play the music set before them.

In legal instruments, there are no cadenzas. We don't have statutes or regulations or wills or contracts that conclude amorphously with the old King of Siam's favorite phrase: "Et cetera, et cetera, et cetera!" The notations on the page are expected to convey a determinate meaning. At least that's how it ought to be.

But within the common-law tradition, "idea-cadenzas" have abounded. Originally, they were necessary in the days when statutes were the exception. But today things have changed: statutes are the rule. But some judges have continued to want to improvise freely as interpreters of legal instruments. Mind you, it's not that the drafters mark "cadenza," with a blank, the way Mozart and others sometimes did; rather, some judges have simply decided to insert flourishes where an advocate for one party to a dispute has entreated them to do so.

This brings us to the single greatest challenge to sound legal interpretation: self-restraint. It's the refusal to usurp power that is available for usurpation. Because judges are the final interpreters of legal instruments, there is no constraint placed on "idea-cadenzas" except what the judges impose on themselves. Hence this book is largely about self-restraint—how to derive meaning from authoritative legal texts without undue embellishment.

---

*   Percy A. Scholes, *The Oxford Companion to Music* 130 (2d ed. 1939).

**   K313.

***   *Id.*

We read this aloud to each other one day in his chambers, trading paragraphs as I sat on his couch and he sat behind his desk. We gave the passage a "dramatic reading," much as if we were actors. We liked the passage. It appealed to our love of classical music; it provided an apt analogy; it was easy to follow. Afterward, from my iPod, I played a recording of Jean-Pierre Rampal playing the concerto, explaining that I'd grown up hearing my father, a university flute professor, play the piece. Justice Scalia knew well the convention of musical cadenzas, and he liked the comparison as well as I did.

It wasn't until after my wedding that I realized we wouldn't be able to use the passage after all. Cutting it was hard for us both.

6

The Wedding

(2010)

In March 2009, Karolyne and I had set a date to be married—a year and a half later. That would give her family in Hong Kong time to plan. Soon after, we asked Justice Scalia whether he'd be willing to officiate. "I'd be honored! Of course I will!"

By January 2010, we had picked a wedding site near Karolyne's hometown of North Attleboro, Massachusetts. It would be at the Rosecliff Mansion in Newport, Rhode Island, on August 8. As a young girl, Karolyne had gone on field trips to Newport, and she had always had fond memories of that beautiful place.

Justice Scalia warned us that we must ensure that he'd be properly credentialed to perform a wedding in Rhode Island. He hadn't done many weddings, and he didn't want to embarrass anyone by performing a wedding without following the proper formalities. I promised to find out more about what he'd need to do to conduct the ceremony in Rhode Island.

But the news was slow in coming. Although we had friends in state government who were "handling" the matter, there was essentially no word for months. In mid-May, when we sat down for lunch at Plume, the restaurant in the Jefferson Hotel, Justice Scalia was greatly concerned about having the proper credentials.

He also wanted to know what wedding service we'd be using. "How about the Catholic service?" he asked.

"But you know we're not Catholics," I said. "I grew up Episcopalian, and Karolyne is nondenominational. How about the Episcopal service?"

"Have a look at the Catholic service. I think you'll like it."

By mid-July, I had sent him our proposed service, based on the Episcopal Prayer Book. Given what he'd said about the Catholic service, I assumed that he'd be happy with a good dose of religion in the ceremony. And I knew Karolyne and her family would appreciate that.

Meanwhile, Karolyne and I kept hearing that we were in the clear for Justice Scalia's performing the ceremony—but we couldn't get any specifics apart from vague assurances. This caused us as well as Justice Scalia some consternation. Just six days before the wedding, he wrote to me: "Are you sure that I have authority under Rhode Island law to conduct the wedding? If not, we must clear that up at once."

We pressed our Rhode Island contact, who told us that we must have a special bill enacted by the Rhode Island Legislature authorizing Justice Scalia to conduct the ceremony. Only one day was left in which this could be accomplished, but our contact assured us that they would get it done. In the end, we learned that there was actually debate on the floor of the legislature about the matter. A Republican (!) legislator had stood up and said, "We don't need an out-of-state judge coming in to Rhode Island to perform a wedding! We have plenty of able judges in this State." Fortunately, his opposition was summarily squelched.

Meanwhile, just as the bill was being voted on, I received an e-mail from Justice Scalia: "No reply regarding my authorization under Rhode Island law. Should I start worrying? Nino."

We were all relieved when we got news that the legislative resolution had passed—only five days before the ceremony.

Then Justice Scalia raised his own objection in an e-mail: "Your proposed wedding ceremony puts me in a terrible position. You have to eliminate from the ceremony (or substitute for me) all parts in which I offer a prayer, invoke God or the Trinity, bless the rings, or do anything else that is priest-like. If you wanted a religious ceremony you should have gotten a clergyperson, not a goddam judge."

Then he added, "I hate to bother you at such a busy time."

I quickly removed all the religious references. I had been mistaken in assuming that he wanted them in the first place. In any event, we were to have a Chinese clergyman conduct the religious part of the rite in Mandarin—an acknowledgment of Karolyne's Chinese heritage and for her non-English-speaking family. Justice Scalia was glad to learn of that.

In the middle of the afternoon the day before the wedding, Justice Scalia arrived at the Westin Hotel in Providence, where the wedding party, family, and guests were staying. I met him at the front entrance when the U.S. marshals drove up. He wanted to go to his suite, settle in, and take a nap before the rehearsal dinner. We agreed to meet in his room at 5:30 for a drink (Campari and soda, of course), and then head off to the rehearsal just downstairs in the hotel. But on the way up to his room, I casually mentioned that I had a passage or two for him to think about for *Reading Law*. We ended up spending an hour on those before he took a short nap.

As usual, the marshals had an adjoining room. I introduced myself to each of them, learned their names, and offered my phone number. They already had it. I encouraged them to call if they needed anything at all.

The Wedding Rehearsal

At 6 o'clock that night, the wedding planners walked us through the ceremony. We were all dressed casually, the men with jackets but no ties. Justice Scalia greeted my father and my brothers. He also greeted Karolyne's mother, brother, and the rest of the wedding party. Everyone was excited and honored that he was on hand.

I took Justice Scalia aside to chat a little. "Have you performed many weddings?"

"Not many. About four—usually for one of my clerks in chambers. Not like this. The reason I was so nervous about the authority is that I didn't get it in Wisconsin, and so I had to have a shadow judge."

"What?"

"My son Christopher's dissertation supervisor was getting married when we were in Wisconsin for Christopher's graduation, and they wanted me. But I had no authority. So the chief justice of Wisconsin had to do the actual pronouncement of husband and wife at the end of the ceremony. Funny—and mildly embarrassing."

"Glad we took care of it here, just in the nick of time."

"Thank you for that!"

I explained that Karolyne's mother, Sandra Cheng, would be hosting our rehearsal dinner at China Inn, an excellent restaurant in Pawtucket. It was owned by a close family friend, Louis Yip, who would be standing in for Karolyne's late father at the wedding. Many of the guests spoke English as a second or third language, and a few spoke only Chinese. So Sandra, an accomplished translator (in addition to her day job as a hospital administrator), would be providing some translations.

"It won't be a long dinner, will it?" Justice Scalia asked.

"Not long and drawn out," I said.

"I have cert petitions to work on."

"It shouldn't be too long."

"How far is it?"

"About ten minutes away."

"You want to come with me?"

"Sure. Karolyne and I will ride with you and the marshals."

"Good."

About 80 people were invited to the dinner—half the wedding attendees. At the entrance to the restaurant, we met a middle-aged couple from Providence. The husband was eager to meet Justice Scalia.

"Judge, may I say what a true honor and privilege it is to meet you," the husband said.

"Thank you," Justice Scalia said.

Then the wife chimed in: "We donated to your campaign in the last election." There was an awkward silence. Her husband smiled uncertainly. Then she added, "Didn't you run for office in Providence?"

Justice Scalia just chuckled and smiled.

"No," I said, "he's a Justice on the Supreme Court of the United States."

"Well, even then," she continued, "I'm sure we donated to your campaign."

"Thank you for your support!" said Justice Scalia. "Well done."

And we walked in.

Friends from all over the country had converged on Providence for the wedding the next day in Newport. Most of them were lawyers, and all of them came by our table to greet Karolyne and me and of course to meet Justice Scalia. As people approached, I'd give him a quick background note to cue him for any remark he'd wish to make. "This is the daughter of Jacques Barzun; she's a New York transactional lawyer." "This is Sam Polverino, a criminal lawyer from San Jose." "This is Barbara Wallraff, the language columnist for the *Atlantic*." "This is Lynn Hughes, a federal district judge from Houston." "This is Bill Lynch, the influential lawyer who introduced the resolution enabling you to perform our wedding." And so on. That way, he could tailor and personalize his greetings.

"There's not going to be a lot of toasting, is there?" he asked nervously.

"Some, Nino. Please just grin and bear it."

"I don't want to sit through that."

"I can't blame you. But people will be talking about your friends, Lyne and me. You're marrying us tomorrow." I smiled at him.

"That's true. But let me leave before the toasts begin."

"Your old kill-me-first joke." I was referring to his favorite joke about the prisoner whose last request is to be hanged before, not after, a congressman delivers a speech.

"Ha! Exactly."

"People will notice if you leave, Nino, and that'll put a damper on the party. No doubt."

"Okay, but they'd better not last long."

"I'm sorry, Nino. I have no control over that. Please just be as gracious as you can be."

"Well, I'm not speaking."

"That's fine," I said as reassuringly as I could.

He grimaced at me when the toasts started, but all in all the speeches were heartfelt, apt, and fairly succinct. He laughed at various points when stories were told of my early fascination with words and dictionaries—especially when my brother Brad told how he'd warned our parents that his 15-year-old brother was spending hour upon hour copying words out of *Webster's Second New International Dictionary* instead of doing anything useful that might lead to a career.

Much to my surprise, but perhaps no one else's, Justice Scalia spontaneously took the microphone at the end of the evening and made several minutes' worth of generous remarks about Karolyne and me. "I've never known anyone more passionate about his work than Bryan," he said, "and in Karolyne he has a perfect match." Given his stated opposition to speaking at such events, I was touched that he felt moved to take the floor.

On our way out after the three-hour dinner, he said, "That wasn't so bad! I learned some things about you, Bryan. You're quite a guy. And of course Karolyne's quite something, too."

"Thanks, Nino," I said as the three of us piled in to the backseat of the marshals' car.

Freudian Slip-and-Fall

The next morning, Justice Scalia went to a Latin Mass we'd found for him in Providence, then met me in the lobby of the Westin to have lunch in the historic neighborhood known as Federal Hill. It was a beautiful, sunny day. The marshals took us to DePasquale Plaza for open-air dining at Constantino's Venda Ravioli. We were joined by my father and his companion, Mary Irene, a Santa Fe artist. The day before, my father had missed the rehearsal dinner because of a kidney stone; on a layover in Denver (en route from San Francisco), he and Mary Irene had taken an ambulance from the airport to a local hospital, where he was in excruciating pain until he passed the stone. Over lunch, the two of them recounted the traumatic events of the past 24 hours.

Probably casting about for something interesting to say to Justice Scalia, my father asked whether *Bush v. Gore* was a hard decision.

"Not really. Remember: it was Al Gore who took the case to the courts. The real question was who was to decide: a highly partisan Florida Supreme Court or the U.S. Supreme Court."

"But isn't the Supreme Court highly partisan these days?" my father persisted.

"It looks that way, which is unfortunate, but in fact we're not. It's just that presidents appoint Justices with a particular judicial philosophy, which ends up looking as if the votes go down party lines. That's misleading. In any event, most of our cases aren't political at all; we're doing mundane lawyer work involving patents and regulatory authority."

As we left the restaurant, we said goodbye to my father and Mary Irene, who headed toward a taxi line. Walking on the cobblestones of the promenade, I spotted the marshals at the car waiting on Atwells Avenue. I said to him joshingly: "Nino, you're so mollycoddled! You have these marshals taking care of you. Look at them. They make everything so easy for you. I'll bet you've forgotten what it's like to travel like a normal person."

"Not at all. I'm aware of what's going on. I'm not like Warren Burger, who was also known by insiders as Mr. Magoo!"

"He wasn't aware?"

"Are you kidding? He was a real Mr. Magoo. You know the cartoon, right?"

"I remember."

"The marshals would lead Burger around, and he was unaware of everything that wasn't three feet in front of him." He did a brief imitation of the Mr. Magoo character.

"Really?"

"Yeah." He did a silly walk as if holding a cane, squinting as he went. "He would bumble along, doo-duh-doo-duh-doo-duh-doo. Oblivious of everything." We laughed, and then he resumed his normal gait.

Justice Scalia started to get into the marshals' car, and a marshal was with him at the door. As I was going behind the car to get in on the other side, Justice Scalia fell to the ground and rolled. He was utterly silent. I saw him on the ground and ran over to help him up. It seems he hadn't gotten entirely onto the seat when he'd begun turning, and he slid out instead of in. Our waiter, who had been lingering at a distance as if starstruck, rushed toward him at the same time as I did but didn't touch him. With the marshal, I pulled him up to get him into the backseat. The marshals seemed embarrassed.

"You okay, Nino?"

"I'm okay. Guess I wasn't very careful."

I ran around and got into the backseat with him. "No broken bones? Check your knees, your wrists, your fingers." I gently squeezed both of his knees to make sure he felt no pain there.

"No broken bones. I think I'm probably just bruised."

"You're sure?"

"I'm okay. My elbow hurts."

"Give me your arm." But as I massaged his left elbow, he jerked it away. "Ow!"

"Let's just be sure you didn't dislocate your elbow or shoulder."

"I'm fine. Let's get back to the hotel."

"Let me feel your other elbow and shoulder."

"I didn't fall on that side, dammit!"

"Should we go see a doctor?"

"No! I'll be bruised. I'm sure it'll be sore for a few days."

"You're really lucky."

"I guess so. Dammit! My elbow's going to hurt for the next week."

"I'll give you some ibuprofen when we get to the hotel. That'll keep the swelling down."

"Okay. You sure? Ibu-what?"

"Ibuprofen. It's Advil. Maybe we should ask your doctor whether it's compatible with whatever other medicines you're taking."

"It'll be fine. I don't take many medications."

"Nothing incompatible with Advil?"

"Nah."

"Okay. I'll give you two Advils as soon as we get to the hotel."

"I'm a tough guy," Justice Scalia said, grinning in the backseat.

"I feel bad about the conversation we were having beforehand."

"How so?"

"About your being mollycoddled by marshals, and then your Mr. Magoo reference to Chief Justice Burger."

"What of it?"

"I don't know if you've read Sigmund Freud's *The Psychopathology of Everyday Life*, but he connects things like that. He might say that my kidding you about being pampered caused you subconsciously to be a little more footloose and incautious."

"Ah, baloney."

"Well, I'm glad you're okay. You're going to have a sore elbow, all right."

"I've had worse," he said, stretching his arm. "At least I'm in good enough shape to get you hitched tonight. You're absolutely sure I have the authority?"

"Yes. I'll even show you the legislative resolution granting it specifically to you for our particular wedding. Did I tell you that some Rhode Island legislator made a speech in opposition?"

"What?!"

"Yeah, a Republican started bloviating about how they have plenty of good, solid Rhode Island judges to perform weddings."

He laughed. "Did someone explain *why* I would be coming here to do it? That we're friends and coauthors?"

"I think so. The objections didn't last long. Let's run by my room so I can show you the resolution."

"Nah. Show me later. I trust you. Let's get to my room."

Walking through the lobby toward the elevator, I promised the bellman $20 if he'd get two ice packs into my hands quickly. One of the marshals said he'd wait behind and bring them to the room.

We got on the elevator. "Nino, let's stop at our suite first. We've got to get your Advil anyway, and if I don't show you the certificate now, you'll never see it. 'Later' will never come."

"Oh, okay." Soon we were at my door. "Hey, great suite!" he said as we entered my room. "Did you know they put a bottle of Campari in my room?"

"Of course! Lyne did that," I said, handing him two Advil tablets and a bottle of water. Then I showed him the fancy certificate.

"Pretty impressive. I'm endowed with full authority. I am, after all, a Supreme Justice!"

"You are indeed. Let's go over to your suite, relax a bit, and get those cold compresses on your elbow. I'll get you some sparkling water."

"Sounds perfect. I'll put my feet up. My right knee's a little sore, too."

We walked to his room. I helped him get his shoes off: at this point in his life (age 74), bending over to tie or untie shoes required a bit of effort. To get situated, he stripped down to his undershirt and boxer shorts. I put sofa pillows under his feet and got him lying back on the couch. A knock came at the door: the ice packs had arrived in less than three minutes. All was well. I felt as if we'd averted what could have been a disaster.

Free-Riding and Textualism

Although I might have left him alone, I decided to stay with him to make sure he was feeling all right. Soon he seemed to have forgotten about his elbow.

"I've been thinking about *Reading Law*," I said.

"Always working, aren't you?" he said, lying back. "For goodness' sake, you're getting married tonight!"

"Well, we have this time together. We may as well use it."

"If you say so."

"In the literature," I said, "some scholars are using the term 'legislative free-riding.' If the legislature can't pass clear legislation, they just rely on the courts to patch up their messes."

"That's right. They pass more and more of this junk. Courts shouldn't bail them out. Courts should either enforce the statutes as written or declare that they have no discernible meaning and hold them invalid. I wish we did that more."

"Wouldn't you agree that we have a syndrome right now of courts' not doing that and therefore encouraging more and more slipshod lawmaking?"

"I would agree. It should stop."

I handed him his Campari and soda—light on the Campari and heavy on the soda. "Well, I've written a couple of paragraphs for the intro. See what you think."

"I will. When can I get a new draft?"

"It's awaiting you back in chambers."

"You managed that? I imagine you've been busy this week. I don't know how you do it all."

"Well, I love what I do, just like you."

"We're lucky that way," he said.

Our conversation returned to Congress: "We should have a moratorium on new laws for a while," Justice Scalia said.

"What would happen if Congress passed no laws for five years—just had occasional hearings to keep themselves busy?" I suggested.

"That would be excellent. Our polity would flourish."

"And what if, instead of the congressional staffers who work with might and main to produce 'legislative history,' we had grammatically rigorous editors to proofread and refine the statutes that are passed?"

"People like you? There wouldn't be enough!"

I disagreed. "Oh, there are *lots* of highly qualified editors out there—highly skilled in grammar. They could work wonders, and the judges' jobs would get a little easier."

"They surely would—if they're textualist judges. If they're nontextualists, they're not paying too much attention to the enacted words anyway."

"Right. Of course, in the popular mind, textualists are pretty badly misunderstood."

"I agree," Justice Scalia said. "But why do you say so?"

"All the reporting is just about bottom-line results, especially when it comes to constitutional litigation. You're either for gay rights or else you're homophobic."

"The liberal press. I suppose that's right," he said.

"It's as if it's commonly understood that judges get to adopt whatever policy pleases them. Most people don't grasp the separation-of-powers problem."

"I see what you mean," Justice Scalia said. "So my liberal colleagues have convinced people that the Court will create new policies with hardly any restraint."

"Sort of. If a textualist judge refuses to gloss a statute in some newfangled progressive way, on the principled ground that that's not what judges are supposed to do, it never gets reported that way."

"That was the point of a speech I gave recently at the National Press Club."

"I remember that speech, but I thought you were making a different point—that the statutory wordings at issue are never reported in the press."

"Right."

"But you weren't emphasizing that under the separation-of-powers doctrine, the judicial power doesn't extend to amending the Constitution."

"Lookit, I've said that dozens of times in various ways."

"But those who oppose you have now conditioned the public to think otherwise."

"Well, if that's true, it's *very* disappointing."

"And your principled approach to judging is called a 'fig leaf' for conservative results."

"Ridiculous," said Justice Scalia.

"I know, but I think we can help set matters right in the introduction to *Reading Law*."

"The intro's already too damn long!"

"No, it's not! I found a quotation from George Washington saying that the prosperity and endurance of our nation depends on proper interpretation of the laws."

"I've never seen that. You found it?"

"Yes. You're going to love it. We must lay out a cogent argument in the intro before we get into the details of how to do textualism properly."

"I'll have a look when I get back," he said, closing his eyes.

Again and again, I replayed in my mind Justice Scalia's fall. The moment it occurred, I decided never again, when outside Washington, to leave it to marshals whom he didn't know well to see that he got safely into a car. Of course, they were also concerned with external threats to safety, so it was understandable that their attention might be focused on the immediate environment instead of on the Justice himself. In any event, unless a marshal stayed close to him, I would stand with him at his door to prevent a fall. From my wedding day, that became my usual practice.

Interestingly, the next day both the local TV news and the *Providence Journal* ran pieces about how Justice Scalia had tripped and fallen near his car on Federal Hill—and reported that he was unhurt. A reporter had called all the local hospitals to find out where he might have been treated. One even called the Supreme Court's Public Information Office to find out more about the fall. But of course the Court knew nothing of the fall: only he and I, the marshals, our waiter, and a few bystanders knew anything about it.

Travel Plans

"Say, where's Lyne?" Justice Scalia asked.

"She's getting her hair done with her bridesmaids. They're surely having a good time."

"I'm certain of that. What time do I have to be at the wedding location? Where is it, again?"

"Newport. Let me get the marshal and tell him." I stepped out into the hall to summon the lead marshal. "You know where the Rosecliff Mansion is in Newport?"

"We've already checked it out."

I asked him: "How long does it take to get there?"

"We timed it at 23 minutes," said the marshal.

"Good. Nino, we take over the mansion at 4:30, have photos at 5:30, and the wedding at 7:00, and then dinner at 7:45. There's a dragon dance in there somewhere."

"What time should I arrive?"

"I'd say 5:30."

"That early? Are you going with me?"

"No. We have a bus that's taking the wedding party from here at 4 o'clock."

"So I'll leave here about 5:30 and get there about 20 minutes later. I don't want to be there too early."

"Believe me, you won't be. Please leave at 5:15. You'll have friends there and people who'll enjoy talking to you. You'll like them, I promise."

"Okay."

Then I turned to the marshal. "How many of your men are going to be stationed around Rosecliff?"

"Four of us, sir."

"The wedding planners have asked me if you can manage to be discreetly placed so that we don't have marshals in all the wedding photos—earwigs always visible, that sort of thing."

Justice Scalia chimed in: "Oh, you don't want that!" He seemed horrified at the idea that our wedding photos would be marred by U.S. marshals lurking in the background.

"We'll be out of the way, sir," said the marshal, diplomatically excusing our wedding planners' anxiety.

"Thank you."

The marshal left. "Nino, thank you for coming all this way—interrupting your time at the Outer Banks with Maureen and the family," I said. "I know it wasn't easy. How's your arm feeling?"

"I'm gonna take this ice off! I don't need it. It isn't doing any good."

"It undoubtedly did some good. Rest up for the next couple of hours. It means so much to us that you're here."

"Well, you two mean a lot to me, so it's mutual. I'm honored to be officiating."

"It's gonna be a great evening."

"That it will, my friend. That it will."

"See you at the mansion."

"See you there. Break a leg . . . well, maybe I shouldn't say that."

Wedding Photos

At 5:45, as we were having photographs taken in the rosary outside Rosecliff Mansion, Justice Scalia approached the two of us.

"Look at you," he said, walking up to Karolyne. "You look beautiful." They hugged.

"Thank you. Thank you very much," she said.

Then I shook his hand. Seeing that he was in a black suit with a red tie, I said, "I thought you were going to wear shorts under your robe."

"Bermuda shorts," he said, grinning. "This is a nice location."

"Oh, it really is."

Most of the posed wedding photographs were taken before the ceremony. After Justice Scalia had donned his robe, the groomsmen stood with me and him for photos. He was getting impatient with the peremptory tone and bossiness of the photographer. As she made requests of us, I was constantly reassuring him, over my right shoulder, that she knew what she was doing. She was telling him to move his right foot two inches forward and his left foot to the right one inch.

"Why?!" he said with some irritation.

She said: "I'll explain it to you later. We'll have a whole conversation about it."

"Okay," he said, lightening up and placing his foot where she'd asked him.

Then she told us to look at each other laughing, without moving our feet.

"Ha! Ha! Ha! Ha! Ha!" he chortled rapidly, with his lips turned up in a kind of hardy-har-har caricature of laughter. All six of us engaged in artificial laughter, which soon led to the real thing. Justice Scalia then turned to me and said the manly words that are surely uttered to every groom right before the ceremony: "It's not too late to back out!" The laughter just continued.

The Ceremony

Soon we were proceeding down the sprawling, beautifully manicured back lawn of Rosecliff, down toward the ocean, with the sound of the wash just below the marble balustrade. Justice Scalia strode off the back porch, down the steps, lips pursed, leading me and the groomsmen. In his characteristic way, he swayed as he walked, holding in his left hand the scrolled-up service that he would be performing. After the entire wedding party had reached the end of the lawn, and my bride was standing beside me, he intoned, "Dearly beloved . . ."

He performed the ceremony with deliberation and high seriousness. After two scriptural readings, Justice Scalia said:

The script here says that I am supposed to give an impromptu homily about the couple. I had intended to skip that. But providentially I was at Mass this morning. Bryan very kindly found me a Latin Mass. I'm an old-fashioned Catholic and do the Latin Mass when I can. And the very first reading had a line which is so appropriate—the introit of the Mass begins Deus in loco sancto suo—*"God in his holy place."* Deus qui inhabitare facit unanimes in domo—*"God who makes those in a home to be of one mind"*—unanimes. *And that is my hope for you, Bryan and Lyne, that throughout your life, you be of one mind—in the most important things. Because it's not just a union of the flesh, as the Scripture says, but also, and more importantly, a union of the minds. So may you both be of one mind for many years.*

He came to what he called "the important part"—the vows—and he pronounced us husband and wife (as duly authorized by the State of Rhode Island, of course). A Chinese prayer by Dr. Pon Chan, a solemn "Amen" led by Justice Scalia, and the Lord's Prayer followed.

"Mr. Garner, you may now kiss the bride. Ladies and gentlemen, I now give you Mr. and Mrs. Bryan Garner." As we walked back up the aisle, toward Rosecliff, amid clapping, our mics were still on (though we didn't realize it). "That was fun, wasn't it?" I said.

"You look so handsome," Karolyne said.

"You're so beautiful."

But as Justice Scalia would say, "Enough with the mushy stuff!"

The Reception

At the reception afterward, a five-piece Chinese percussion band played the "Dragon Dance." Two men working in tandem in a large dragon suit (head and tail) taunted the onlookers, lingering a little with Justice Scalia, who found the cultural spectacle entertaining. Then the dragon taunted Karolyne and me. The tradition, for which I had to be prepped, is that the bride and groom put a head of lettuce into the dragon's mouth; after chomping it up, the dragon spits it into their laps—for good luck.

At dinner, Justice Scalia sat with our friends the Englishes from Portland, Oregon, and the Tietjens from Minneapolis. In planning the seating arrangements, I put him between two talented conversationalists: Elizabeth English and Susan Tietjen. He was always hungry for good conversation. Of course, he was the cynosure of the table, deeply involved in discussions—and he listened and laughed perhaps more than he spoke. At one point I saw him jump up from the table and walk to the bar, flanked by marshals who suddenly hopped to. Elizabeth came over and said, "He's getting us a drink called a Pimm's Cup, which involves something called 'bitters.' He can't believe we've never had one." Then he went back to his table, holding three cocktails at once, and had a toast.

Later, toward the end of dinner, he came over to me. "Bryan, I saw your wedding cake. It looks like Samuel Johnson's *Dictionary*!"

"Yes. The two bottom layers are a facsimile of the first edition of 1755."

"Very appropriate, but I don't think I'll eat any. The band's starting to get kind of rock-'n'-rolly." They were playing the 1963 Beatles song "All My Loving." He said, "I can't go for this music. I think it's time for me to leave. I hope you'll understand."

"I'll stop the band." I sent a friend over to stop the music. "My father's about to read an epithalamion written to us by John Simon. He couldn't attend. Can you wait to hear that? We'll be done in five minutes."

"John Simon, the guy who writes for *National Review*?"

"He used to write for it, yes. The film and theater critic."

"How do you know him?"

"We're close friends. He's a world-class snoot. We've known each other since the late 1970s."

"No kidding."

"You know, he wrote about language for *Esquire*," I said. "It was language that drew us together—kind of like you and me."

"Wait. Did you say *epithalamion* a second ago?"

"Yes. You know, it's a poem written in honor of a bride and groom. Simon wrote it specifically for us."

"I think the correct word is *epithalamium*. It's Latin."

"That's the more usual form, you're right. But Simon used the Greek form *epithalamion*, which is also recorded in unabridged dictionaries like *Webster's Second*."

"Why would he use that form?"

"To make the final rhyme work. The last two lines are, 'And may my words not shame me on, / This heartfelt epithalamion.'"

"That's clever."

"The poet Edmund Spenser also used that Greek form."

"Okay, I'll wait to hear it. But then I've got to leave."

"Understood. Thanks, Nino, for being part of this. I know it wasn't the easiest thing to come up here for two days. You made the whole thing especially memorable."

"Thank you for asking me. Glad to do it! You're a lucky man, and I'm happy to see you so well married. I'll say goodnight now, and then slip out when your father's finished."

"Goodnight. We love you, Nino."

He hugged Karolyne and then went over to the corner of the room as my father read Simon's poem. The earwigged marshals stood around him, and when I next looked up, after thanking my father, he was gone.

7

Reading Law: Part II

(2010–2012)

Immediately after returning to Dallas from our honeymoon, I resumed work on *Reading Law*. Soon the cadenza opener that I'd been so enamored of seemed less and less appealing. For one thing, I discovered that another writer on statutory interpretation had already used the cadenza analogy—so the idea wasn't as original as I'd thought. For another, one of my early critical readers, Sir Christopher Ricks of Boston University, insisted that we should use an actual case rather than an imperfect analogy.

That's when I hit upon using *James v. United States*,[34] which was decided less than a year before Justice Scalia took his seat on the Supreme Court. The difficulty here, I imagined, would be to persuade Justice Scalia that Chief Justice Burger and Justices Rehnquist, Powell, Brennan, White, and Blackmun had decided the case wrongly—and that Justices Stevens, Marshall, and O'Connor had gotten it right.

The case involved a 1928 statute with an immunity provision stating: "No liability of any kind shall attach to or rest upon the United States for any damage from or by floods or floodwaters at any place."[35]

The facts of the case were tragic. At a flood-control reservoir open for recreational water-skiing and other activities, a federal employee, perhaps acting maliciously, opened the enormous floodgates as skiers passed by, creating a strong current. Two female skiers fell and couldn't swim out of the current. Their husbands, operating the boat, tried to circle back to give their wives towlines, but the women couldn't hold on to them. One hus-

---

34 478 U.S. 597 (1986) (per Powell, J.).
35 33 U.S.C. § 702c.

band jumped in to help and drowned as the torrent sucked him through the gates. The women survived but were badly injured.

The question was whether the statutory immunity barred a lawsuit for personal injury or the loss of human life. The majority held that it did. There could be no recovery because of the absolute wording of *no liability of any kind shall attach*. But the dissenters astutely noted that it has to be *damage* of some kind. They cited dictionaries from 1928, and they focused on original meaning. In response, the majority said that *damages* are given for all sorts of injuries, including loss of life. In turn, the dissenters said that *damage* (harm) is a different word from *damages* (compensation for harm), and the two have entirely different meanings in law.[36]

Later, Justice Stevens would say that this was among the most torment-ing cases he'd ever sat on during his tenure on the Supreme Court.[37]

I pointed out all these things to Justice Scalia, who wanted to know how I knew the case so well and why I thought it to be a good illustration of textualist principles. I told him that the case had been decided correctly by the Fifth Circuit sitting en banc in 1985, that the legendarily erudite Judge Thomas M. Reavley had written an opinion distinguishing *damage* from *damages*,[38] and that I had clerked for Judge Reavley that year. I pointed out that praising Justices Stevens, Marshall, and O'Connor, who had ad-opted Judge Reavley's reasoning, would be rhetorically wise—and quite unexpected. My coauthor agreed that in the year before he was appointed to the Court, the majority in *James* had gotten the case quite wrong. And he agreed that we should open the book with this illustration of judicial interpretation. Cadenzas were out, and floodgates were in.

But soon we reached a possible impasse on something much less weighty. It was a point on which we'd both been stubborn for years: contractions. In late August, he wrote to me about some "fundamental differences" that we would have to resolve. The first was contractions. He said he would yield in this second book on gender-neutralizing, but not on contractions: "The difference is that here we are competing with serious, scholarly treatises, and saying 'don't' and 'isn't' makes us sound like amateurs among profes-

---

36 478 U.S. at 615–16 (Stevens J. dissenting, joined by Marshall and O'Connor JJ.).

37 John Paul Stevens, *The Shakespeare Canon of Statutory Interpretation*, 140 Univ. Pa. L. Rev. 1373, 1387 (1992).

38 *James v. United States*, 760 F.2d 590 (5th Cir. 1985) (en banc) (per Reavley, J.).

sionals. Like it or not, contractions convey a more folksy, and hence less weighty tone." I could hear him breathe a sigh of near-despair: "God, there is an awful lot more work to be done." Again, characteristically, he ended on a note that was half-modest and half-perturbed: "I hope you mostly like what I've done—and that it converts to your antiquated word-processing system [WordPerfect] (which remains a pain in the ass to deal with). Give me a call. Nino."

I relented on contractions without hesitation. Given how accommodating he'd been with the first book, I thought that reciprocating was only fair. Together, we made the contractionless style work without making the tone too wooden and hyperformal.

Three days later, he urged me to abandon about one-third of the book— all the points relating exclusively to the interpretation of contracts. I had already been noticing how intractable that material was. So this came as something of a relief to me as well. In any event, the first 37 canons dealt with all legal instruments, including contracts, so we were hardly abandoning that subject altogether.

I responded: "Nino—Okay. I'm persuaded. You see what a reasonable coauthor I am? [I was echoing the words he'd used with me when conceding about contractions in the first book.] It would make the book unwieldy, and the contracts stuff would overwhelm much of the rest of the book."

He came back: "*Deo gratias*. I'll concentrate on statutes."

The Judicial Juggernaut

My coauthor's energy was unwavering. On Wednesday, September 15, 2010, he wrote me a typical message that reflected the kind of schedule he kept. He said he'd be leaving the next day for "a gig in San Francisco," and wouldn't return until the day before our Sunday-afternoon session. He wanted a clean draft that incorporated all our cumulative changes to date. Maybe I just imagined a sense of excitement: "I am arranging to have a trestle table set up in my chambers, so we can edit side-by-side, as we did for the last book. Nino."

I took clean copies for us to use that Sunday afternoon—a binder for him and a binder for me—with all his proposed revisions entered, together with my own gentle revisions of his revisions. We liked how the book was shaping up.

As we were working on Sunday, he wanted to delete an insertion that I had marked for revision. It was a long block quotation of one of his own dissenting opinions, and he wanted to end the paragraph by saying, "The dissent stated," followed by a colon and then a three-paragraph block quotation that occupied more than one full printed page. My notation, inserted characteristically in double brackets, said: "[[Must supply informative lead-in.]]" When we reached this point in the manuscript, he said, "Get rid of that."

I said, "We have to lead into this quotation more deftly, Nino. It's your dissent in *Babbitt v. Sweet Home Chapter*."

"I know what it is," he said sharply. "What do you mean 'lead in more deftly'?"

"It's one of my rules of writing that you can't just say, 'The court stated,' and then plop a quotation on the page. We must entice the reader."

"I disagree. Leave it."

"We can't leave it, Nino. Many readers will notice."

"Why do you say that?"

"I spend 15 minutes in every seminar showing lawyers how to introduce block quotations properly. It's in all my books."

"Show me."

"It's point #76 in *The Winning Brief*. It's section 29 in *Legal Writing in Plain English*." I pulled both books off his shelf to show him.

"Ha! You know the sections that well?"

"I know our sections of *Making Your Case* that well, too. In fact, we make the point there, if only glancingly. Here, hand me your copy. I can find the page within 15 seconds, thanks to our thorough index."

He handed it to me. The pressure was on because he was timing me. I looked in the back of the book under "Quotations, Block," and ten seconds later announced: "Nino, it's on either page 128 or 135. I'm wagering on 128. Here, we say: 'Never let your point be made only in the indented quotation. State the point, and then support it with the quotation.' There." This, of course, was a subtle fillip for his having battled me on whether we'd have a thorough index in *Making Your Case*. It was a small triumph.

"I'm astonished," he said. "So what are you saying we need to do here, in this passage?"

"First, we need to be candid with our readers that you wrote the dissent. Second, we need to explain briefly why we're quoting it."

"I don't want to say I wrote the dissent," he said.

"But we *have* to. We must be frank about that. If we just say, 'The dissent stated,' and then have a two-page block quotation with a footnote that says 'Scalia, J., dissenting,' it won't look good."

"We have to say *why* we're quoting it?"

"Yes," I said. "Tell the reader why. That induces the reader to embark on the block quotation."

"If you insist." He sighed, rose from his desk, and went over to his computer. I sat beside him, at the chair he'd placed there for me, and watched these words appear on his monitor: "We quote the dissent, which one of us wrote—and quote it at length because we like it: . . . ."

We both laughed, and we ultimately published the passage that way, on page 230. It's one of my favorite touches in the book.

Of course, that was only one of dozens of improvements we made in the manuscript that day. We wrote several paragraphs together and made some significant progress.

The next morning, he sounded upbeat: "Bryan: Great day yesterday. Got a lot done, and I feel better about the book."

The following month, in October, we worked together again in chambers. We must have done well because the next day he wrote: "Bryan: A most productive afternoon and (especially) enjoyable evening. I am working on the stuff you assigned."

Our exchanges of material were now frequent and sometimes voluminous. One exchange stood out: on October 21, I sent him a three-paragraph debunking of some arrant nonsense that a nontextualist had written and published in a law review. Justice Scalia urged me to exclude it (I ultimately did), saying: "Just from his bumbling writing one can tell that this guy is a jerk—but I'm not sure he's the kind of jerk *we're* after—a text-distorting jerk. Anyway, an associate prof. at the Univ. of X is pretty small game for us."

An Unfunny Break

On February 1, 2011, Dallas experienced a terrible ice storm. Karolyne and I were stranded that day in Little Rock, unable to return home. A particularly dangerous type of invisible ice formed on the ground throughout the DFW Metroplex: black ice. When we returned to Dallas on February 2, on our way back from the airport, I fell on a patch of this black ice while foolishly trying to push our chauffeured car, which was stuck halfway up our driveway—a 20° incline. I suffered a serious break: my left humerus was severed clean in half. A week later, a Dallas surgeon repaired the break with a metal plate and six screws, but that surgery damaged my radial nerve, which runs along the triceps down into the hand. As a result of that nerve injury, I suffered from radial-nerve palsy, meaning that my left hand was curled up and essentially crippled. I couldn't extend my fingers. If I passed the salt, I did so with a curled-up hand, and then I couldn't let go of the saltshaker. Nor could I so much as lift my left thumb.

For nearly two years I wore a brace that kept that hand from becoming permanently crippled. It resembled a coat-hanger contraption with a rubber band extending to a small sling that enveloped the left thumb. My doctor said it was possible that the nerve would recover on its own and that I'd be fine. But over that period, there was no discernible improvement. During those months, Justice Scalia and I spent 17 days together. He was seriously concerned about the future of my hand. Coincidentally, Mrs. Scalia had suffered her own icy accident, breaking her wrist after falling on ice while trying to retrieve the *Washington Post* thrown on their front lawn. (Justice Scalia often joked later that this was good evidence of why one shouldn't subscribe to the *Washington Post*.) Her recovery was also difficult but more successful than mine.

Again and again, Justice Scalia goaded me to get a second opinion at Johns Hopkins. He was insistent, and he shared his insistence with Justice Clarence Thomas, who enthusiastically joined the campaign. In the end, after his long urging and with the kind help of Nina Totenburg (the NPR legal-affairs correspondent) and her physician-husband, I found Dr. Thomas Brushart at Johns Hopkins. On December 17, 2012, he performed a five-hour tendon transfer that would enable me to use my left arm normally, with only a slight loss in strength. It worked.

Strangely enough, as I was heavily dosed up on pain medicines, I spent much of the day after the surgery working with Justice Scalia in chambers—with my arm almost constantly raised over my head. I remained clearheaded enough, somehow, that we worked out a couple of useful passages (by then we were actually working toward the second edition of *Reading Law*), but Justice Scalia could tell I was in pain. When the doctor's office called for a midafternoon exam to replace my temporary splint, we called it quits for the day and for the year.

My eventually successful recovery was attributable in no small measure to Justice Scalia's persistent concern, empathy, and willingness to help me find the best doctor. Today my left hand functions normally. It's an outcome that even many doctors marvel at. Rarely today do I even think about the trying period in my life in which I had almost no practical use of one of my hands—a condition that might well have become permanent.

Unjust Deserts

On March 1, 2011, someone tweeted about Justice Scalia's use of the misspelling *just desserts* instead of the correct *just deserts* (what you deserve) in a newly released judicial opinion quoted in the *New York Times*. Several people sent me the tweet asking whether it was correctly quoted. So I wrote to Justice Scalia: "Nino—Today the NYT quoted you as writing 'just desserts' instead of 'just deserts.' Please assure me that they've libeled you! As ever, Bryan."

His response was almost immediate: "Bryan: I am distressed that you need to ask. My opinion said 'deserts.' I will add, in the interest of full disclosure, that my original draft of the sentence in question had 'desserts,' but my law clerk caught the error. But that is why I spend a lot of time hiring literate law clerks. (I would have put this insignificant qualification in a footnote, but e-mail does not permit footnotes.) Should I ask the *Times* to correct its error? Or why don't you do so? Nino."

"I'll be happy to," I responded.

"Excellent! You can claim standing because it denigrates our book [*Making Your Case*], which stresses the need to 'Strengthen your command of written English' (point 29). But better not to use 'denigrate,' because the hacks at the Times probably do not know its meaning. Nino."

I then composed my letter to the *Times*, using the subject line "unjust deserts":

Dear Editor:

In our book Making Your Case: The Art of Persuading Judges, *Justice Scalia and I urge our readers: 'Strengthen your command of written English.' We briefly explain some good ways to do that, including buying and using sound dictionaries of usage.*

In one of my own such dictionaries, I liken the mistaken form of 'just desserts' (for the correct 'just deserts') as a 'stage 2 misusage,' akin to a grade of D, a triple bogey in golf, or, when it comes to manners, audible belching.

Yet in today's Times *you have misquoted—indeed, maligned— my esteemed coauthor as having written 'just desserts.' He assures me that his opinion in fact says 'just deserts.' Is this an actionable libel? Perhaps. Is he a public figure under* New York Times v. Sullivan? *Perhaps. But let's not test these things. Won't you simply print a retraction and a straightforward apology? That would go a long way toward ameliorating the current state of editorial affairs.*

> Bryan A. Garner
> *Author,* Garner's
> Modern American
> Usage

Justice Scalia responded: "Bryan: Very nice. Funny enough that they may publish it." But I never saw that the *New York Times* responded in any way. The editors seem not to have run a correction.

A Schism over Isms

For the improvement of *Reading Law*, I was able to persuade West to engage five critical readers for a modest honorarium. One of these was Tony Honoré, Regius Professor Emeritus of Roman Law at Oxford University and the author of many important books. Originally South African, Tony Honoré had been Nelson Mandela's lawyer in the 1950s. I had known Honoré since 1988, and we had spent a good deal of time together in Oxford. He had been my chief source for Latin translations in *Black's Law Dictionary*, and he was unfailingly reliable. His participation in this project seemed particularly apt, since it was his collaboration with H. L. A. Hart that I offered as a model for our own when I originally pitched *Making Your Case* to Justice Scalia. After reading the manuscript in June 2011, Honoré called to say that he was sending the marked manuscript back to me—but especially he called to warn me.

"Bryan," he said in his impeccably old-fashioned British accent, "you're making a mistake with all your references to *originalism*, which is a dangerous word. It's a doctrine that isn't favorably viewed in the academy, and you'll be derided for defending it."

"But surely you don't disagree with the idea that historical meaning controls," I said to him.

"No, not really. And I think I know what you're referring to throughout the text. But I urge you to call it by a different name. Perhaps *historicism*. If you call it *originalism*, you'll be a laughingstock. A word to the wise. I'd better ring off now. Cheerio."

Naturally, this call had me worried. I discussed it with my lawyer colleagues and decided I should broach the subject with Justice Scalia. Probably 30 minutes after my call with Honoré, I called and reached Angela.

"Angela, it's Bryan. Is Justice Scalia in?"

"Hi, Bryan! One moment."

"Hello, Bryan! How are you doing?"

"Great, Nino. How is it up there?"

"Busy. Really busy. Lots of work on opinions. How's the book coming?"

"Wonderfully. It's really shaping up. Nino, we've got a potential problem that's arisen, though. As you know, we've had some scholarly readers that West is paying for their review, and one of them is Tony Honoré in Oxford. He's worried about our use of the word *originalism*."

"What?! What's the problem?"

"He thinks it has such negative connotations that we should replace it with another word, like *historicism*."

There was a cold silence. I don't think he had even registered Tony's name.

"You're absolutely kidding me," Justice Scalia finally said. "We're defending original meaning. The doctrine is called *originalism*. That's what I'm known for. Who is this idiot? And why are you listening to him?"

"Nino, it was just a suggestion."

"Are you losing your nerve? Or maybe I should say you have some nerve to call me this way with such a cockamamie suggestion. It's ludicrous."

"I'm sorry, Nino."

"You should be." He hung up the phone.

This rattled me, to say the least. It wasn't the first time that I had drawn Justice Scalia's ire, but it seemed like the most serious. I had seen his anger subside on various occasions, and I figured I'd let it happen again this time.

Given our years of friendship and work together, I thought I'd earned a charitable understanding of my words—or at least the assurance that our relationship wasn't in real peril. So I went on about my business the rest of the day, but of course I was a little concerned.

The next afternoon I received a chilling e-mail. Justice Scalia wrote that he had been "seething with anger" since our conversation. He asked who the "idiot academic" was whose advice I was contemplating accepting and whether he really thought academia would love me for peddling originalism under another "quite silly" name. He asked whether my adviser suggested that Justice Scalia change his name also "(perhaps to Posner, beloved by the dons)" so that "your interpretive views (rebaptized *historicist*) can't be thought to be mine, which everyone knows are (shudder) *originalist*."

And then, he said, he'd gotten to thinking that if I was worried, intimidated, or even perhaps ashamed to be associated with originalism, I must also be worried, intimidated, or ashamed to be associated with him in writing a book on the interpretation of texts. Indeed, there was nothing with which he was more closely identified than the "disreputable" originalism.

He opined that my adviser—the estimable Tony Honoré, though I'm sure he hadn't caught the name—was an idiot, and he said he was worried about what other ideas of my adviser I was contemplating accepting. I would not lose my prominence in the field of English usage, Justice Scalia declared, because "there is no one remotely comparable in the field." He called me "a unique word-nut," adding: "Anyway, it is not pointy-headed academics who give you your prominence (even though you suck up to them with your craven PC unisexism) but lawyers."

Then, he continued, if my adviser was an idiot for telling me this, I was an idiot for listening to it. Associating with him in a book on persuading judges was one thing, he said, but now I must have concluded that associating with his views on legal interpretation was quite another. My own proposed introduction to *Reading Law*, he said, detailed just how thoroughly nonoriginalism had swept the academy. And he said I'd constantly suggested that we take potshots at one professorial Buddha after another. How, he questioned, could I be surprised to hear that all this would make me unpopular in the academy?

The worst was still to come. If I had become newly worried about destroying my reputation in academia, he said, he most sincerely urged me to call off the project altogether. He would return the advance and be delighted to have the coming summer free. He added that, to tell the truth, since he'd learned how worried, intimidated, or ashamed I apparently was to be associated with the views that had been central to his professional career and with which he was identified in public and academic thought, he wasn't as happy to work with me as he had once been. He signed off, "Deeply disappointed, Nino."

Shaken by this message, I went to Karolyne's office, read the message to her, and discussed what to do. We decided I should promptly call him to apologize. But when I did this, I made little if any headway. He said he had to get off the line. I felt as if he was cutting me off. I waited 30 minutes and then sent an e-mail:

Nino—

Again, so sorry. I can only imagine how I'd feel if we were working on a usage project and you told me you felt doubts about being associated with "prescriptivism." After all, that's what I'm best known for. I'd be unhappy about that.

I'm entirely comfortable with our originalist positions—and of course I'm extremely proud of our association, coauthorship, and friendship. And the second book will be even better and more important than our first.

Thank you for bearing with me!

As ever,
Bryan

Thirty minutes later came his reply. He thanked me for my e-mail and said he was glad that I understood, calling my analogy to prescriptivism "just right."

Then he wrote, "All is forgiven, my friend—and I probably need your forgiveness for my overreaction."

The storm clouds had lifted. Never before in our post-call-me-Nino relationship had I felt such an ominous threat to its continuation. The reconciliation was an enormous relief.

Facing the Deadline

We were working toward a goal of having the book in print by the end of 2011. Justice Scalia's communications with me became more and more urgent. On June 29, 2011, he wrote: "I would like a new draft no later than tomorrow. I leave Friday. God, there's so much more to be done!" The draft then stood at less than half the length of the finished book—although we didn't then know how much more we'd be adding.

In mid-July, I wrote to him: "I've canceled my 18-day trip to England to focus on this project." He responded: "I'm back [from a short teaching stint in Europe] and ready to go. I'm at your disposal all summer, and will even cancel (at some risk to my marriage) my two weeks at the Outer Banks if necessary. Regards, Nino."

Our exchanges were voluminous. On July 22, he sent me a reworked batch: "Bryan: Attached, the portion I have worked on this week. As you will see, I have deleted a lot, added a lot, and reordered considerably. I anxiously await your reaction."

Three days later, he wrote to me with the subject line "Trouble." It was the second time in a week that he'd begun with "We got trouble." He said that "vast portions" of the manuscript weren't acceptable to him. "It appears that I will have to cancel my family vacation on the Outer Banks; and that you and I will have to spend many days together resolving our differences. Even then, I do not think we will be ready for an October 31 deadline. Give me a call, so that we can discuss what to do."

After our call, I booked a flight almost immediately to D.C. so that we could work out the difficulties we were encountering. Soon we agreed to push back our deadline until mid-2012. Still, we urgently needed to work out our differences.

At least half the time, some case that he'd want to cut I'd want to keep, and then we'd have a tug-of-war. In most of these instances, he'd accede to my insistence that the case was useful.

As for his reordering of material, I greeted his changes with enthusiasm: he had a gift for architecture, and his ideas about organizing and reorganizing our sections were nothing short of brilliant. For example, our lengthy treatment of originalism struck him as much too long and wide-ranging in the middle of the book. Justice Scalia suggested keeping part of it there, under the fixed-meaning canon, which reads: "Words must

be given the meaning they had when the text was adopted." Then he created two new sections at the end of the book. They became "debunking"
sections exposing 13 falsities. One was "the false notion that lawyers and
judges, not being historians, are unqualified to do the historical research
that originalism requires"; the other was "the false notion that the Living
Constitution is an exception to the rule that legal texts must be given the
meaning they bore when adopted." Allocating our discussions in this way
made a great deal of sense, and it made the book feel better-proportioned.

A Logophile's Gift

One day while we were working in chambers in late July, Justice Scalia
suggested that I join him and Mrs. Scalia at their house for macaroni. He
called Mrs. Scalia to see whether she could add me. "Excellent. We're on!"
he said.

I told him I'd brought a gift for him.

"What is it?" he asked.

"It's the new third edition of my legal-usage book." I handed it to him.
"Oxford has now renamed it *Garner's Dictionary of Legal Usage*."

"My gosh it's big!" he said, waving it up and down. "How long is it
now?"

"It's 991 pages, just a bit longer than my book on American usage."

"When did you have time to do all this?" he asked.

"I try to use every waking moment in some useful way. That's the great
thing about lexicography. If I have five minutes to kill, I can do something
useful for one of my books."

"I admire your industry," he said, thumbing through the pages. "What's
this entry, 'Lawyers, Derogatory Names for'?"

"That's an amusing one."

"*Dump truck*! 'An unmotivated criminal-defense lawyer who unskill-
fully represents indigent defendants through public subsidy.' Where'd you
get that?"

"I was teaching a seminar for some public defenders. Apparently they
use it all the time. But as you can see I found a published instance of it."

"*Jungle fighter . . . latrine lawyer . . . sore-back lawyer*. These are hilarious!"

"I had fun putting that entry together. It took lots of research over several years, as you might imagine."

"I imagine it did," he said.

"But I have a confession, Nino."

"What's that?"

"You know I think of you as an uncle. Well, I've done something in this book that I hope won't disappoint you."

"What is it? Tell me."

"You know the book is full of citations, not only of interesting and confusing words but also of mistakes. Probably 75% of the illustrative quotations are instances of mistakes by legal writers. I cite my late grandfather, Judge Meade Griffin of the Texas Supreme Court, for misusing *feoff* in place of *feoffee*. I cite my late mentor Charles Alan Wright for a mistake. And I even cite myself for a mistake."

"Are you saying you cite me for a mistake? Let's hear it. What have I done?"

"Well," I said sheepishly, "you've tended to use *thusly* as an adverb, when *thus* alone is an adverb. The *-ly* is unnecessary. Actually, you've done that a lot."

"You mean that's an error?" he asked.

"I'm afraid so. It's called a 'double adverb.'"

"I'll have to stop that," he said. "I wonder where I picked it up."

"Here's what I say in the preface. 'I persist in believing that the citations confer scholarly value on the work. And let me point out again that I have cited erroneous usages by my beloved grandfather, my great friend and mentor Charles Alan Wright, and myself. And I have cited my close friend and coauthor, Justice Scalia, unfavorably. As he might well say, "Get over it!" The purpose is never to ridicule, but to educate.'"

"Why Bryan, I think that's wonderful."

"You do?"

"Yes. It shows that you're objective and dispassionate in your approach. You're not playing favorites."

He wanted to know where I'd criticized him. I cited him a total of 25 times, but it turned out that only 1 was negative—for pretentiously using the Latinism *ex necessitate* instead of the simple adjective *necessary*. That was a pretty mild criticism, we agreed.

"You could have been harder on me," he said. "But thank you for mentioning me in the preface, in the same category as your grandfather and Charlie Wright. Say . . ." There was a pregnant pause.

"Yes?" I said, encouraging him to continue.

"What's the mistake you cited from your own writings?"

"It's really embarrassing. It dates from 1982. I used *bequest* as a verb in place of *bequeath*."

"You did *what*?"

"It was a piece on Shakespeare's Latinate neologisms—the Latin derivatives that, as far as we know, Shakespeare was the first to use in English."

"You quote the mistake here in the book?"

"I certainly do."

"Let me see." He licked his thumb and started thumbing through the pages. "Buh-buh-buh-buh. Here it is: '"And by so felicitously using the words newly *bequested* [read *bequeathed*] to English, [Shakespeare], more than any other writer of the English Renaissance, validated the efforts of earlier and contemporary neologists." Bryan A. Garner, *Shakespeare's Latinate Neologisms*, 15 Shakespeare Stud. 149, 151 (1982).' Ooh. That's bad."

"Yes," I said.

"Really embarrassing. Heh, heh, heh!"

"Yes."

"Why'd you point it out to the world?"

"For the reason you say, Nino. I shouldn't exempt anyone. We all make mistakes. I try to be a fair-minded, omniscient adjudicator of English usage. I'm sure I fail, but I try."

"I think that's the right approach," he said.

Tennis Break

The courthouse was nearly empty in the dead of the summer break. At 4:00 p.m., he suddenly remembered that he had a tennis game in an hour, and he asked me to come along if I wouldn't mind watching for 45 minutes or so before going home for dinner. I said I'd be his linesman.

In the pro shop at the Washington Golf and Country Club, I found two pullovers I thought Karolyne might like, but a purchase could be made only through a member's account. So Justice Scalia advanced me the money and put the charge on his membership account, insisting that Karolyne should have the clothes.

"We're having to give up our memberships soon," he told me.

"Why?"

"For a long time, country clubs and gyms have offered free memberships to Justices, hoping to entice them. That's coming to an end."

"But why?"

"I suppose the Court has decided that it might not be entirely proper. But of course, on our low pay we can't afford the membership initiation fee or even the monthly dues. We still pay for everything we buy, naturally. I'll be sad to give it up, but I can't afford it—even with our book royalties."

"That's too bad. Gosh. Anyway, I'll reimburse you as soon as I get back."

"Oh, don't worry about that," he said.

Justice Scalia's playing partner was a D.C. lawyer about ten years younger, perhaps in his mid-60s—a regular sparring partner. The two didn't say much. After introducing me as his guest, Justice Scalia got down to serves and volleys as a warm-up. Despite his considerable heft in the middle, his form was good. He moved around well, and he was obviously a natural athlete. His ultracompetitive nature surfaced almost immediately. In the first game, he served a shot that landed about two inches out.

"Out!" I said, taking my linesman duties perhaps too seriously.

"It was in! It was an ace!" Justice Scalia insisted.

"Yes, I think it was in," the companion said, seemingly eager to continue the atmosphere of amiability.

After that, I abstained from making any more line calls and instead just watched. It soon became apparent that Justice Scalia's rulings were in all instances final. Occasionally he'd rule against himself. One time I foreswore my resolution not to interfere: I contradicted him when he erroneously ruled against himself. Otherwise, I stayed out of disputed calls.

The games were close, but Justice Scalia won the match 6–4, 3–6, 7–5. It looked to me as if his partner was going easy on him, but Justice Scalia fought hard for every point.

Back to the Book

Soon after returning to Dallas, I expressed appreciation for his superb edits to the manuscript of *Reading Law*: "Nino—Love your edits and clearheaded revisions. Thank you." He responded: "Bryan: Glad you liked them. Forgive me for being sometimes harsh. Back to the book."

During this period, we were struggling some with each other. He wanted to truncate where I (uncharacteristically) wanted to amplify. At one point, he sent me a cover note to various cuts, telling me that I wouldn't like the changes he was sending. He didn't like repeating ideas he thought we'd already covered. He closed with: "We can't keep coming back to our vomit. Cheers."

Soon he was annoyed that I'd continued to embellish some of the more exiguous discussions of points. He was getting testy: "PLEASE, BRYAN, STOP WRITING. PLEASE. We have been working on this book for over a year, and your really worthwhile thoughts have already been incorporated. You are now dredging up the dregs. Let us spend the remaining time incorporating new thoughts suggested by others, and correcting inadequacies or mistakes that others have pointed out."

He had vowed not to work on *Reading Law* while at the Outer Banks, but I gathered he hadn't stuck to that: "I've just returned from the Outer Banks—and I am not in a good mood. I'm only about a third through, and I'll send you my suggestions (assuming they're not redundant) Monday. Regards. Nino."

A week later, his outlook was more positive: "Bryan: Yes, the book is getting better and better. I'll stay on it."

Though we continued to experience conflict on some technical points, all in all he did seem to be softening up. At one point, he said (as part of a long, complicated e-mail): "Sorry I was testy yesterday afternoon. It's been a hellishly busy couple of weeks." And he asked me how to approach the glossary. I suggested that he read the definitions only for accuracy. Then I signed off, perhaps facetiously, "Love, Bryan." I meant this with a light-hearted smile.

Without mentioning that sign-off, he responded: "I'll do what you say on Monday. Nino."

Before long, he was even more conciliatory: "Dear Bryan: I'm sorry I've been so testy. The time pressures of both the book and my cases have got to me. I know you're improving the book, and I will sympathetically review your proposed changes. Nino."

I found solace in this response. It told me that we wouldn't have lots of conflicts ahead. We were clicking again. I might expect we'd encounter minor frictions—always to the benefit of the book—but no cataclysms.

Production Protocol

We went through well over 250 drafts of *Reading Law.* I was the only one who saw them all. My associates printed out a new copy of the book every weekday when I was in town, and I'd mark it up every night or take it on a trip. I'd try to write two footnotes every morning in lieu of breakfast (by citing scholarly sources), and I'd embellish the text here and there. Every change I made would be highlighted in yellow so that when I'd send Justice Scalia a new draft—every six weeks or so—he could see precisely what I had done and focus his review. I knew he'd never tolerate a new draft every night—he'd feel inundated—but I always wanted a clean copy daily for myself.

At LawProse, we had our full complement of highly skilled staffers working on the project by the time *Reading Law* was in full swing. Our working protocol was that if I made a series of changes, or if Justice Scalia sent in additions or edits, Jeff Newman would enter them into the master copy (page proofs, actually, since our manuscript pages were the InDesign layouts), and then Becky McDaniel would verify that the edits had been correctly entered. Because Becky and Jeff are both seasoned lawyer–editors, they'd periodically do a complete citation check of all sources. Meanwhile, Tiger Jackson (LL.M.), another longtime lawyer–editor at LawProse, would hunt down potential cases for us to use and help verify quotations and citations. With all my books, this is a perpetual process until we're ready to go to press. During this period, we also had the benefit of three other lawyer–staffers: Eliot Turner, who was in between federal clerkships, Heather Haines, and of course Karolyne.

Although Justice Scalia and I wrote every word that appeared in the book, we couldn't have done it without the help of countless allies in law. Justice Scalia asked all his former law clerks to suggest useful cases for us to consider. Even a single case sent by a clerk earned that person a mention in the book. I enlisted lots of friends as well, as a result of which our acknowledgments "page" was actually two pages.

We probably considered three times as many cases as we ended up discussing or citing (667 in the published version). We took some pride in finding out-of-the-way state cases. The whole idea was to use the best teaching examples, which meant (for us) the most interesting problems that presented clean issues. Which court decided a given point didn't matter nearly as much. In fact, it didn't really matter to us whether the court got it right or wrong: we were demonstrating how legal interpretation *ought* to be done, not describing how it *is* done. So we were happy to declare that this or that court had gone wrong in some way—or to praise courts when their methods were analytically sound.

Our typical approach was to state the principle, explain its history in Anglo-American law, and then illustrate its application in a variety of cases, especially as these might provide nuance or qualification. No one had ever before taken quite this tack. Perhaps the closest forerunner had been Henry Campbell Black, the original writer of *Black's Law Dictionary*, who in 1911 had written a treatise called *A Handbook on the Interpretation of the Laws*.

As with our earlier book, the critical commenters we asked to read the manuscript were enormously helpful. Some focused on style, others on substance. We appreciated having whatever help our friends could lend.

When working together, Justice Scalia and I would normally have lunch in his chambers—a crab salad made by Fernando or Chinese take-out brought to the Court—and then we'd eat out for dinner. His favorite restaurants were Tosca and Bistro Bis, but sometimes we'd go elsewhere: Sushi Taro, the Prime Rib, the Hamilton, Plume, Central Michel Richard, or the Cosmos Club.

About a third of the time, Mrs. Scalia would join us for dinner, usually when Karolyne was in town. All four of us were epicures—we liked new restaurants as well as our tried-and-true standbys.

Oral Arguments on Obamacare

Both Justice Scalia and Karolyne had March birthdays—he on the 11th and she on the 26th. Karolyne is a splendid gift-giver, and for his birthday in 2012 she sent him three grosgrain black ties for formal events. She remembered that he'd complimented mine one time when we'd both been in tuxes and complained of his own. He was most appreciative of the gift and wanted to return the thoughtfulness. When he found out that we'd be in D.C. on March 27—the most important of the three oral-argument days for the Obamacare cases—he suggested having her as his guest, in one of his box seats.

"I still have one left. You know, it's the hardest seat to get these days in Washington."

She'd been keeping up with the lawsuit over the constitutionality of the

Affordable Care Act,[39] so I knew she'd be thrilled. Justice Scalia said he'd have her back to chambers for lunch with him after the argument.

"I've given one of my other seats to Ezekiel Emanuel. He's one of the architects of Obamacare, so he needs to be there. Even he had a hard time getting a spot. He came and asked me, and I was happy to oblige."

"That's good of you. So Karolyne may be sitting beside him!"

"Maybe."

So that was the plan. While I'd be teaching, Karolyne would be at the Court.

On the 26th, Karolyne's birthday, she and I were in New York for a LawProse seminar I was teaching. Having concluded at 4:00 p.m., we made a mad dash to Penn Station to catch the 5:00 p.m. Acela Express to D.C.—and barely made it. Once I'd sat down, I pulled out my fact sheet for the next day's D.C. seminar and saw that it wouldn't begin until 1:00 p.m. I had the morning free—something I hadn't expected.

"You think I could get a seat, Lyne?"

"Surely not, but why don't you try?"

I called Justice Scalia's chambers. "Angela, it's Bryan. Is he in?"

"No, the Justice has just left for the day. Is there something I could help you with?"

"I'm on the train now in D.C. You know that Lyne has a seat for tomorrow's oral arguments."

"Yes."

"It turns out that I'm free in the morning. I know it's a long shot, but do you think there's any way . . . ?"

"Let me call the Clerk's Office. They may still be here. I'll call you back."

In no time, my phone was ringing. "Bryan," Angela said, "we have a ticket for you. It's the very last one." She eagerly told me the story. "General Suter [the Clerk of Court] said, 'Who's it for?' I said, 'Justice Scalia's coauthor,' and he said, 'Bryan Garner? Of course we'll get him in.' But really, Bryan, this is literally the last ticket."

"You're amazing, Angela. A miracle worker! Thanks again."

At 8:00 the next morning, we arrived at the Court. Everyone was there earlier than usual for this particular argument. I sat beside Karolyne in the

---

39 124 Stat. 119–1025 (2010).

first row of the gallery, just behind the bar section. About 8:40, a marshal I'd never seen before came over to say I'd have to move back a row. "I'm with my wife," I said.

"It doesn't matter, sir. I need the rest of this bench open."

The whole courtroom was filling up rapidly. I moved back to the second row, just behind Karolyne, and ended up sitting between two famous Supreme Court advocates: Laurence Tribe of Harvard and Walter Dellinger, the former acting solicitor general. Then a group of four filed in to take the seat I had just vacated and filled the remainder of the bench. It was the attorney general, Eric Holder, and his lieutenants. I'd known Eric since we'd worked together on federal rules in the 1990s. But given that he was deeply involved in conversation with his colleagues, I decided to say nothing to him.

I shook hands with both Tribe and Dellinger, meeting them both for the first time. I'd known of Dellinger since he had served in the Clinton administration; Tribe, of course, I knew to be the foremost scholar of American constitutional law, his treatise on the subject having been a core text in the field for over 30 years. Tribe asked, "Didn't you write a book with Justice Scalia?"

"Yes, and we've just finished another—this time on interpretation."

"Really?"

"Yes, we cite you quite a bit, mostly favorably."

"I'd like to see it."

"It'll be out in June. I wonder, though: if I were to send you page proofs tomorrow, could you review it to think about writing a blurb for the dust jacket?"

"Sure I would."

"Frankly, I haven't asked anyone to write a blurb because I've dithered a little bit. I think you'd be perfect if you're willing."

"Of course I'm willing."

"The dust jacket will be final in less than a week. That wouldn't give you much time. But I'll send you the proofs tomorrow, and you can have a look. Justice Scalia and I would be most grateful if you'd do a blurb."

That's how *Reading Law* ended up with a blurb by Professor Laurence Tribe: pure happenstance. If I had kept my original seat, we might never have met.

The room was buzzing, and tensions were high. As General Suter announced the case, I saw Solicitor General Donald Verrilli take a drink of water. (This seemed advisable to me. In my book *The Winning Oral Argument*, I recommend: "Hydrate beforehand.") But it seems he gulped just as he was called to the lectern and got some water into his windpipe. "Mr. Chief Justice, and may it please the Court," he barely got out, and then coughed into the microphone. He spent much of the first minute coughing, and then took another drink. This was an unfortunate, and certainly uncharacteristic, start for such an able advocate.

He was arguing, of course, that Congress could force people to buy health insurance because it's good for them—given that everybody must buy healthcare at some point. Justice Scalia was skeptical: "Could you define the market—everybody has to buy food sooner or later, so you define the market as food; therefore, everybody is in the market; therefore, you can make people buy broccoli?" Justice Scalia asked.

Verrilli responded that buying food in the supermarket is "unpredictable and often involuntary." He never directly answered the broccoli question, except to say that broccoli is different from healthcare.

Although some commentators later objected that Justice Scalia's broccoli question was highly impertinent, it illustrated two typical Scalian moves: (1) teaching against the class—that is, upsetting settled biases with points that run to the contrary; and (2) the *reductio ad absurdum*, that is, taking a position to the extreme to show that it's untenable. He was pointing out that if the government can force people to buy things because it's supposedly good for them, there's no limiting principle that differentiates healthcare from broccoli or any other beneficial product.

In the end, of course, Justice Scalia was with the minority of four Justices who voted to overturn Obamacare. Chief Justice Roberts provided the crucial fifth vote for the majority, upholding it.

As soon as the arguments had concluded, Karolyne was off to have lunch with Justice Scalia, and I was off to teach a seminar at a D.C. firm—on the art of oral argument. While teaching that afternoon, I mentioned the argument I'd just witnessed and stressed the *beforehand* in "Hydrate beforehand." In fact, I amended it to "Hydrate *well* beforehand."

The Literary Finish Line

Three days later, on March 30, Justice Scalia e-mailed me to say that he wanted to discuss his latest edits. I responded: "Nino—Just arrived in

N.Y.C. at midnight last night, and I've reviewed your excellent edits. Yes, I'd like to discuss them. How about 3 o'clock this afternoon?"

His brief riposte: "Bryan: No. You didn't review my *latest* edits because I haven't even sent them yet. You must be referring to the last package. Three o'clock this afternoon is fine. Call me. Nino." I did, and we spent a good hour on the phone as I transcribed edits into the "BAG Master."

We worked together in his chambers twice during the week of Sunday, April 15, and had dinner together twice. On Wednesday afternoon, as we were putting some final touches on the book, he noticed that on page 211 I'd used the adjective *redoubtable* in reference to Max Radin, the great statutory-interpretation expert at the University of California at Berkeley. I'd inserted a reference to "the redoubtable Max Radin." After all, we both liked Radin a lot: he was the leading expert during the first half of the 20th century.

"Redoubtable?" he asked. "I agree that he was redoubtable. There's no doubt he was redoubtable." He paused. "No doubt about it. But didn't we use that word somewhere else in the book?"

"Maybe so," I said. I called my office in Dallas and spoke with my colleague Becky to ask her to do an electronic search of the entire 600-page book for the word *redoubtable*. She found another on page 93. We had a reference to "the redoubtable lawyer and statesman Elihu Root."

"Now Bryan, you've written more books than I have," Justice Scalia said, smiling. "You can't use a word like *redoubtable* more than once in a book—even if it were a thousand pages long. It just sticks out."

"You're absolutely right, Nino." It was a point I'd never had register so strongly on my consciousness.

"So," he said, "the question is who was more redoubtable? Or who by today's standards?"

"I think we believe Radin is more redoubtable in matters of statutory interpretation. Doubtless Root would be in matters of statesmanship."

"Then let's downgrade Root."

"How about *estimable* for him?"

"No," said Justice Scalia. "I don't like the sound of that word. *Estimable.* It sounds effete. Why not just omit any adjective?"

"We could do that. But partly what we're doing, Nino, is telling readers things they ought to know even if they don't know them. We're teaching legal literacy. We're saying, 'You ought to know this.' "

"I see your point," he said. "How about *noted*? We'll say 'the noted lawyer and statesman Elihu Root.' Should there be a comma after *statesman*?"

"No," I said, "it's a restrictive appositive. If we added a comma, it would be nonrestrictive, and we'd be suggesting that Elihu Root was the only noted lawyer and statesman—presumably ever."

"Yes, you're quite right. So no comma. It's nice having your grammatical calls on the spot like this. You know that?" I was flattered. "Now," he said, "let's talk about lexicography for a minute. *Redoubtable* . . . where does it come from, anyway? It can't mean 'capable of being doubted again.'"

"That's true. I'm willing to wager it came in through French. It's probably an old Gallicism."

"That's what you call a French borrowing? A Gallicism?"

"Yes."

"Is that in *Webster's Second*?"

"I guarantee you it is," I said, walking over to his dictionary stand.

"Please read it," he said.

I flipped to page 1028 of his beloved *Webster's Second*, and read: "'Gallicism, *n*. A word or expression peculiar to the French language, which is borrowed or adapted for use in English.' Etc."

"Is *redoubtable* in your usage dictionary? Let's find out if it's a Gallicism." He reached behind his monitor and took down the third edition of *Garner's Modern American Usage*. Meanwhile, I was looking up *redoubtable* in *Webster's Second*.

"By golly," Justice Scalia said, "you have a full entry on it. *Redoubtable* can mean either 'venerable' or 'fearsome,' and it's a 14th-century loanword from the Old French word *redoutable*."

"Yes," I said from the dictionary stand a few yards away. I summarized the entry on *redoubtable* from *Webster's Second*. "The older meaning is 'causing fear or alarm' or 'formidable, fearsome.' Over the centuries the word has undergone what linguists call 'melioration': the sense has become more favorable."

"Really? That's what it's called?" he asked.

"Yes. It's the antonym of *pejoration*, which is what happens when a word takes on very negative meanings. Like *bitch*—once a perfectly neutral word meaning a female dog. Or *notorious*. Have you ever noticed that the adjective *notorious* has undergone pejoration, while the corresponding noun *notoriety* is mostly a positive word?"

"Huh. Interesting. Is *redoubtable* related to *doughty*, meaning 'valiant'?"

"Well, no. I'm pretty sure that's Anglo-Saxon. You can tell from the spelling. But *redoubtable* is related to the military term *redoubt*, meaning 'a small fortress' or 'a secure stronghold.'"

"Well, I'm glad we caught that second *redoubtable*," Justice Scalia said. "We've just got to be careful about using words like that more than once."

"Except, of course," I said, "in a conversation like this one."

"Ha!" he laughed. "Yes, between snoots like us."

"Yep. I guess what you're saying, Nino, is that within the corpus of writings contained in this book, a word like *redoubtable* should remain a *hapax legomenon*."

"Yeah, but that's the phrase's loose sense that you allow. As you know, I think it should be a term used only once in an entire language."

"But that doesn't make a lot of sense, Nino."

"Why not?"

"Let's take a famous *hapax legomenon*. In *Love's Labour's Lost*, Shakespeare has a character named Holofernes, a pedant, use the term *honorificabilitudinitatibus*. It's made-up Latin."

"Say that again?"

"*Honorificabilitudinitatibus*."

"How do you know this off the top of your head?"

"I used to write about Shakespearean linguistics back in the early 1980s. Remember? Anyway, Shakespeare used the word only once. It's the Elizabethan equivalent of *supercalifragilisticexpialidocious*, from *Mary Poppins*."

"Right. Go on."

"Then a lexicographer records it, or a scholar refers to the word, and it's now been used twice in the language, so it's no longer a *hapax legomenon*."

"No, I don't think that's what the phrase is referring to. It means *in literature*."

"Scholarship isn't literature? We always say 'the literature' when referring to scholarship. Patent lawyers refer to 'prior art' when referring to 'the literature.' Anyway, how can a word have only one appearance in an entire language? If lexicographers are doing their job, then dictionaries account for a second appearance."

"Okay, I give up arguing about this stuff. The fact that we can spend so much time talking about these things—and I do enjoy it—means the book should be complete."

He had a point. We were working toward a June 2012 publication date, and it was mid-April. Since early March, my team in Dallas had been engaged in a massive citation check as well as preparing the table of cases and the index. The LawProse lawyers—Jeff, Tiger, Becky, and Karolyne—plus a team of four third-year SMU law students (known as Garner Law Scholars), were checking all quotations word for word, as well as the accuracy of all citations. Meanwhile, Justice Scalia and I were doing our own checks.

A few days after returning to Dallas, on May 3, I wrote to him: "Nino— Here's the current version. I'm holding off [submitting the final publishable page proofs] till Tuesday. I'll call shortly. You can proof all weekend. B."

His reply was terse: "Bryan: Not likely. I'm done. Nino."

The transmission to West took place May 8, with the expectation that we'd have bound books, with dust jackets, on June 20. That high expectation was fulfilled.

An Unexpected Mea Culpa

Karolyne and I were back in D.C. on May 23, and we arranged to lunch with Justice Scalia at Central Michel Richard, an excellent restaurant not far from the W Washington, which had become our usual haunt. We had introduced him to Central the year before, and he liked it. By the time he walked in, we had already ordered a bottle of Champagne to celebrate the publication of *Reading Law*.

"To our magnum opus," I said. We all raised our glasses.

It was a quick hour-long lunch, and I filled him in on some of the harrowing details of what our office had gone through to get the final pages into production.

With a big nod of resolve and a furrowed brow, he raised his glass and said, "To your excellent LawProse team of Jeff, Tiger, and Becky."

On our way out of the restaurant, Justice Scalia led us over to a table where four of his former clerks were sitting. He introduced me and told them what we were celebrating. He and I both shook their hands and continued our exit.

At 1:46, only 20 minutes after we had parted, I received an extraordinary e-mail from Justice Scalia. He said he had enjoyed the lunch but had suddenly been struck by the realization that he'd been rude in not introducing Karolyne to his former law clerks. He said he knew at the time they'd recognize my name, but only later did it occur to him that Karolyne is also accomplished and deserved an introduction. He had learned the lesson from experience: "Maureen gets really mad, and rightly so, when I am introduced and she is left standing like a nonentity. Please give my profound apologies to Lyne. I am a lout. Nino."

Network Negotiations

When it came to publicizing *Reading Law*, I thought that the best possible television appearance would be with CNN's *Piers Morgan Tonight*—a full hour-long interview, as he would sometimes do with major guests. The Thomson/West marketing team recommended otherwise. They wanted 15 minutes, perhaps 20 at most, on MSNBC's *Morning Joe*. I countered by arguing for a Fox News show. The marketing team—who seemed not to be Fox News enthusiasts—recoiled.

I sat in chambers with Justice Scalia and explained the impasse. He had begun getting media requests through the Supreme Court's Public Information Office. I persisted in touting *Piers Morgan Tonight* as the best down-the-middle forum. Justice Scalia had never heard of Piers. I gathered that he simply didn't watch TV news much.

"Bryan, you know a lot more about this than I do. Just tell me what we want to do."

"Piers Morgan. Full hour."

"Okay. Let's do that."

"Wait a second, though," I said. "Piers will have to commit to a full hour, and we haven't approached him yet. But I think we should stipulate that it must be a full hour."

"Why?"

"Because you're a major figure—and it slights you to have something less."

"I see that."

"Plus," I said, "what if he had you on for the first half and then Lady Gaga on for the second half—or, worse, he puts you on *after* Lady Gaga?"

"Who's Lady—Lady what?!"

"Gaga. She's a racy pop star."

"Yeah. Not good. Need to keep it dignified."

I said, "West wants to limit the time to 20 minutes. I think it's a grave mistake."

"Then tell them we'll do it only if it's for the full hour," he said. "We'll be on together, right?"

"You bet. I think that's helpful to you, Nino. Remember when Lesley Stahl kept you way overtime, in that hot room, with the camera trained on your face?"

"Yes, I do!"

"If I'm there on camera with you, I can call him out for asking an improper question. I can deflect so that you don't have to."

"I see that. But I'm pretty good at defending myself."

"Sure you are. But we have a good dynamic, and I can be a buffer if necessary."

"Well, you should be there *anyway*. You're my coauthor."

"This interview will go well," I assured him.

Although the *Piers Morgan Tonight* producers eagerly agreed to the full-hour format, they said they wanted Justice Scalia alone—no Garner.

Justice Scalia called to tell me. "Bryan, this is supposed to be about the book. You're my coauthor. I'm not going on without you. That's what I want to tell them. Do you agree?"

"I do. Thank you, Nino."

"I'll tell them."

"One more thing, though," I said. "You're scheduled to film at 5 o'clock in the afternoon, right?"

"That's what we've said so far."

"We need to limit the amount of filming. Otherwise, they'll tape more than they need, ask more sensationalistic questions, and edit things down."

"Ooh. That's right."

"They need at most 45 minutes of footage. We should agree to film no more than 55 minutes. That way, your full answers will have to go in."

"Okay. I'll add that to my usual stipulations," he said.

Two days later, Justice Scalia called to say that the *Piers Morgan Tonight* producers had agreed to all the stipulations except one: they still wanted Scalia alone, without Garner.

"Bryan, I'm going to stick to my guns. They'll cave in."

"Thanks, Nino. But let's be sure they stick to the 55-minute limit."

"Okay. I'll let 'em know. It's only right that you go on with me. I never could have done this book without you."

In the end, the producers—or, doubtless, Piers Morgan himself—

acquiesced. The interview was scheduled for July 18, well after the Supreme Court's term had ended and after the Scalias had returned from Europe, where he'd had a two-week teaching stint.

Karolyne and I spent the afternoon of July 18 with the Justice, who the night before had watched *Piers Morgan Tonight* for the first time ever.

"He's not bad," Justice Scalia said. "Seemed like a pretty good interviewer. But my friends are saying you've led me into a huge mistake."

I never found out who these friends were, but they had spooked him into thinking this might become a nightmarish experience—and he fretted all afternoon about it. Karolyne and I did our best to reassure him. "It's going to be fine, Nino," I said. "Piers will be good. I'm sure he's prepared to the hilt."

"Justice Scalia," Karolyne said, "he's sure to try to get under your skin. He does that with people he doesn't agree with. But don't let it get to you."

"That's right, Nino," I said. "You can't be irritable, no matter what. If he asks an improper question, I'll intercede."

Karolyne added, encouragingly, "Be lovable."

The Lovability Factor

For an hour before we went to the Supreme Court room where the interview was to be held, our mantra was "Be lovable!" We must have said that a dozen times in his chambers, and he repeated it after us.

"Justice," Angela said from the doorway, "Mr. Morgan's crew would like you and Bryan to have your makeup done now."

"Makeup? I don't want makeup!"

"No, Nino. We must have makeup," I said. "Remember Richard Nixon in the 1960 debates, when he didn't wear makeup?"

He reflected. "Oh, yeah. He looked terrible. Okay, we'll do makeup."

As we entered the room, we were warmly greeted by Piers and his producers. He said that it was an honor to visit the Court and to do the interview there. He thanked Justice Scalia for that.

"Of course!" said Justice Scalia. "Say, I watched your show last night. You're good!"

"Oh, well, thank you," said Piers. "First time you'd seen the show?"

"First time."

I said, "He must have been one of the few people in America who didn't know your name, Piers."

"He didn't?" Piers said with a hint of incredulity.

"No, I didn't," Justice Scalia said, "but I'm glad to know it now."

For some reason, the makeup artists took Justice Scalia away for his makeup; I sat in my seat opposite Piers. I tried to make some small talk, but he was giving his rapt attention to sheets that were being handed to him by various staffers—proposed questions, no doubt. Karolyne had gone to sit at the other side of the room with Angela.

"This will air at 9:00 p.m. Eastern Time?" I asked.

"Right," Piers said. "We have little time for editing."

"Good. It shouldn't need much."

Once the interview started, both Piers and Justice Scalia settled into a charming conversation. Piers threw me a couple of questions early on, and all was going well. But midway through, Piers started asking some edgy questions that related to the book only tangentially. "How does it feel being in the minority of the Court most of the time?"

I responded: "That's incorrect, Piers, he's in the majority most of the time."

"That's not the information I have," said Piers, looking knowingly at Justice Scalia. "You're in dissent more often than you're in the majority."

Justice Scalia said: "You've got your facts wrong. I'm in the majority far more often than I'm in dissent. That's true of all the Justices."

It took a moment for Piers to regroup. "What do you have against /**kahn**-dahmz/."

"What?"

"He's saying 'condoms,' Nino," I explained, the film still running. (An Englishman, Piers was using the posh British pronunciation.)

"Really? How did you pronounce that?"

"/**Kahn**-dahmz/. What do you have against them, when they could help prevent the spread of AIDS and other diseases in Africa?"

"Piers," I interjected, "this has nothing to do with the book."

"No," Justice Scalia stopped me. "Let me answer. I have no public position against condoms. The pope has put out several encyclicals about condoms to establish the Catholic Church's position. As a Catholic, I adhere to those views, but my private religious views don't enter my role as a judge." What followed was a brief but learned disquisition on various encyclicals, and Piers, also a Catholic, came out looking uninformed. Realizing that his question had yielded no newsworthy material—or salacious sound bites—he pivoted quickly.

There were two other points on which I jumped in to correct Piers, after he had set up a "gotcha" question on erroneous facts. When I looked down at my watch, I realized that he'd been filming us for about 75 minutes. Then he wanted a walk down the hallway of the Supreme Court for another 5-minute segment.

In the end, with almost 80 minutes of film, Piers and the producers edited out most of my participation. Piers in a way got his initial demand: Scalia, without Garner (except visually). A few of my friends wondered why I'd remained so silent—and whether I wasn't there more as a bodyguard than an interviewee. Gone were all the exchanges that put Piers in a negative light. That's TV, I suppose.

But Justice Scalia remained warm and lovable throughout, and the next day some news outlets would say that he was on a "charm offensive." The interview as aired was a big success, and everyone was happy.[40]

Just after filming, while Justice Scalia was having his makeup removed, Karolyne and I posed for a couple of photos with Piers.

Back in chambers, Angela joined Karolyne and me in congratulating Justice Scalia on such a fine interview. Karolyne asked him whether he'd like to join us for sushi before going home.

"Sushi! Of course. Will I have time to get home before the show airs? I want to watch it with Maureen."

"Yes, of course," I said. "It's 7 o'clock now, and it won't be airing for another two hours. You'll be home by 8:15."

The marshals took us to Sushi Taro, our favorite sushi place off Dupont Circle. Whenever we went there, I would invariably order for the entire table: some miso soup and edamame for starters, and then a huge boat of mostly sashimi and a few sushi rolls. His favorites were the spider roll (with soft-shell crab) and unagi sashimi (eel). We each had a Japanese beer and relaxed as we recounted some of the funny moments about condoms—and how bizarre that line of questioning had been.

---

40 The interview can be seen at http://www.youtube.com/watch?v=it7sN2jqpNs.

"Bryan," he said, laughing, "you still have on makeup! Ha! You look like you've been in drag."

"Very funny, Nino."

"You look cute," he said with a wry grin. Karolyne nodded in agreement. "They didn't give you one of those wipes to take it off?" he asked.

"No. I didn't know they had those."

"Well, of course I got one. I'm a Supreme Justice, after all."

We all laughed. He liked to invoke that self-mocking reference to explain away the special treatment he'd often receive.

8

The Fruits of Our Labors

(2012–2015)

Once the second book appeared, the deadline pressures were off, and our relationship involved considerably less strain. The first printing of *Reading Law* was barely off the press before I began working toward a second edition—almost compulsively. That's my normal routine: when a book first appears in print, I spend (one might argue masochistically) lots of time improving it in dozens of little ways—finding new sources and snippets for footnotes, burnishing the phraseology, and reworking an occasional paragraph. I especially like hunting down arcane but uncannily pertinent 18th- and 19th-century sources that other scholars seem to have overlooked. With *Reading Law*, this impulse began when we first undertook the project, and it has never abated.

After the Piers Morgan interview, each of us made a series of solo appearances to discuss the book. Mine were in Melbourne and Sydney, for courts and law schools. His were a series of television interviews: Brian Lamb (C-SPAN), Chris Wallace (Fox News), Nina Totenberg (NPR), and the Associated Press. He was always selective, and he wanted to avoid overexposure in the press.

Thomson/West was receiving many requests for Scalia interviews, not only from Charlie Rose and PBS but also from the *Colbert Report* and the *Daily Show*, neither of which Justice Scalia had heard of. When told of their nature, and perhaps after watching a bit of them on his computer, he pronounced them *infra dig* (he said *infra dignitatem*) for a Supreme Court Justice.

On August 2, 2012, he wrote a memo to our Thomson/West media-relations contact: "These TV interviews get old pretty quick. I have no intention of doing all, or even most. . . . Two more, perhaps. Three at most. . . . I would like to have Bryan take part in all the interviews." He ended up also doing interviews with Charlie Rose, the *PBS NewsHour*, and Pete Williams, turning away dozens of others. Alas, my own travel schedule precluded my participation in any of these.

My coauthor was charitable enough to be concerned that I be accorded my due, even if I didn't happen to be present. So he was sometimes extravagant in his praise. In the interview with Charlie Rose, for example, late in November 2012, he jeopardized his own credibility by saying: "Bryan Garner is a great man. He is the greatest philologist in the United States."

Justice Scalia and I didn't get reams of mail about our books. Very little, in fact. People don't write many letters these days. But we did get a few, and one especially pleased Justice Scalia. Jon A. Roberts of Oklahoma City, a nonlawyer employee of the Oklahoma Department of Environmental Quality, wrote a thoughtful page-and-a-half letter. He made two prominent points. First, he said he'd formerly believed in legislative or agency "intent," but now he'd come to realize that trying to divine a "collective intent" for any legislative body or regulatory agency is futile: there might be as many different reasons for supporting a bill as there are members casting affirmative votes. Second, he'd had an epiphany about the so-called "Living Constitution." If the Constitution changes its meaning over time, then who can possibly know what the law is at any given point in time? He quoted Justice Hugo Black, who once wrote, "Our Constitution was not written in the sands to be washed away by each wave of new judges blown in by each successive political wind."[41]

Justice Scalia felt moved to respond with a formal letter of his own. He said that the changes in Roberts's thinking were exactly, "point-for-point," what he and I had hoped to produce. It was also good to know, he said, that nonlawyers could also benefit from what we had written. He added that much of what we had said in *Reading Law* amounted to common sense.

A Pain in the Back

On Thursday, September 6, 2012, Justice Scalia and I were scheduled to give our debut presentation of *Reading Law* for the American Busi-

---

41 *Turner v. United States*, 396 U.S. 398, 426 (1970) (Black J. dissenting).

ness Trial Lawyers in Los Angeles. Each of us flew in early that afternoon, and we met downtown at the Millennium Biltmore Hotel. There's a huge banquet hall in the basement, where the Oscar ceremonies were held many times during the 1930s and 1940s. It was the same room where we'd presented *Making Your Case* in March 2009 to an audience of perhaps 500, and we knew the Los Angeles audiences to be warm and appreciative.

When Karolyne and I checked in, we had a message from the marshals that we should go by their room across the hall from Justice Scalia's once we got settled. When we reached the marshals' room about 4 o'clock, they took us across to Justice Scalia. Karolyne and I were not pleased with the cramped room he'd been given, and we immediately saw that he was in quite some pain. His back had been bothering him since the Sunday before, he said, when he'd strained it doing yardwork. After reaching the hotel, he'd started having back spasms.

"I can't go on. I just can't go on," he said, clutching his lower back. "We don't even know what material we're going to cover."

"Not to worry, Nino. I've worked that out, and I have a sheet for you—if you're able to go on. If not, I'll do it solo."

"My back is just killing me!" He groaned with every move. "I just can't do it. I can't do it!"

"Can you take ibuprofen? Remember? You took it after you fell in Providence."

"Yes, that's no problem."

"Have you eaten?"

"No," he said, "not in a while."

"Let's get some food in your stomach and then take the ibuprofen."

The lights in his room were bothering him, too, so Karolyne turned them off.

One of the marshals ran down to the kitchen to get toast, butter, crackers, coffee, and sparkling water. Within ten minutes, he was back up—a kind of U.S. marshals' room service, which was certainly more reliable and efficient than any hotel room service I'd ever seen.

Meanwhile, Karolyne went down to the banquet hall to make certain that everything was set up—and to ensure that Justice Scalia's chair for dinner and his stool onstage would be comfortable if he was able to appear.

Justice Scalia ate two pieces of toast and two crackers, and then he took an ibuprofen tablet with sparkling water. He lay back on his pillow and asked me what we'd be covering in our talk. I told him that Caroline, my daughter in New York (by this time a lawyer), had prepared PowerPoint slides for the canons of construction, and that I had decided on one-third of the book that we'd cover. We'd go back and forth, as we had in all our joint presentations. We'd share the intro, I'd do the 1st point, he'd do the 2nd, I'd do the 3rd, and so on all the way through the 70th—though skipping much in the middle, especially the arcana. He made some adjustments to the plan, and then he dozed off.

I sat silently in the half-darkness while he relaxed on his back, occasionally sighing. I was hoping that the ibuprofen would take effect and that he'd feel well enough to go on.

After ten minutes, a light knock came at the door. Karolyne slipped in and whispered that she'd switched out the chairs so that he'd be more comfortable, and she'd also changed his menu. Instead of an endive salad, he'd be having minestrone soup, and in place of chicken he'd have pasta. Closer to comfort food, they would be easier on his stomach than the typical banquet fare. The banquet captain had said the kitchen didn't have minestrone soup on the menu. She told him she hoped they'd manage to have two orders of minestrone soup ready for Justice Scalia if he needed it. Apparently the captain sent out for it—to an Italian restaurant down the street.

Karolyne left again, and I worked quietly at the computer to perfect our slide presentation and to rehearse precisely what we'd be covering so that I could prompt him, if necessary, while onstage. When I finished, he was still dozing, but his groaning had subsided. I glanced at my watch. It was 5:30. The cocktail hour was to begin at 6:00, with seating at 7:00.

"What time is it?" he asked, as he was rousing himself.

"Right about 5:30. How's the back?"

"I think it's better." He sat up on the side of the bed with little or no apparent pain. "Yes, I'm much better."

"You sound better to me. Let me show you the PowerPoints and this sheet I've prepared so you'll know which points you're covering."

"Good. Thank you."

We prepped, and he said he felt comfortable with the talk.

"This'll be more fun, I think, than *Making Your Case*," I said.

"I think so, too," he said.

"Are you sure you want to go forward?"

"Yeah, let's do it."

"Do you need my help getting dressed?"

"Of course not!"

"Okay. Just checking. Our room is down the hall. I'll be back here in 15 minutes, and then we'll head down."

Karolyne and I got dressed and went back by his room, where he was putting on his cuff links. Soon he was all spiffed up, hair combed, and we trekked down to the banquet hall with our entourage of marshals. As we got closer, of course, people recognized him, and he was drawn into conversations, just as were we. Karolyne kept a close eye on him and, without letting him be distracted too long by well-wishers, took him to the head table, where he was seated beside his (and my) old friend Judge Alex Kozinski, who was then chief judge of the Ninth Circuit. Born in Bucharest, Romania, Judge Kozinski came to the United States in 1962, at the age of 12; grew up in Los Angeles; attended UCLA for both his undergraduate and law degrees; clerked for then-Judge Anthony Kennedy of the Ninth Circuit and later Chief Justice Warren Burger; served in the Reagan administration as the first U.S. special counsel; and was soon elevated to judgeships. Although he retains a thick Romanian accent, his command of the English language is second to none, and his sardonic humor leavens both his writing and his conversation. So our dinner that evening was filled with interesting discussion. Judge Kozinski became subdued, though, when I told him of Justice Scalia's difficulties with his back.

Soon we were being introduced by David Battaglia, my old friend who had arranged the entire event. He had introduced us wittily three years before in the same banquet hall. Again, he had prepared an amusing setup, this time involving numbers:

- 5–4 (no, not a reference to a Supreme Court vote, but the number of boys versus girls that Justice Scalia had fathered);
- 51 (the number of anniversaries since Antonin Gregory Scalia had wedded Maureen McCarthy after they met on a blind date at Harvard Law School—"and don't forget," David added, "next Monday is 52");
- 18 (no, not the drinking age when Justice Scalia was a Georgetown Hoya, but the number of years since Bryan Garner had become editor in chief of *Black's Law Dictionary*);

- 75 (no, not anyone's age [Justice Scalia was 76], but the number of attorneys that were at the law firm of Jones Day when Justice Scalia joined it in 1960);
- 98 (the Senate vote on Justice Scalia's confirmation to the U.S. Supreme Court in 1986, at 98–0);
- 13 (the number of sets of procedural rules that Bryan Garner had revised, with the blessing of the courts and Congress);
- 1491 (the date of publication of the oldest law dictionary in Bryan Garner's collection);
- 236 (the number of dissents that Justice Scalia had written, among over 750 opinions—by contrast with Justice Oliver Wendell Holmes, who wrote only 173 dissents);
- 20 (the number of books written by Bryan Garner);
- 1 (Justice Scalia as the longest-serving Justice on the Supreme Court, with 9,473 days under his belt).

"And so we are pleased," David concluded, "to welcome both of them here to Los Angeles to speak about their new 567-page book, which the *Wall Street Journal* commented is 'remarkable' and 'reshapes the long-running debate about what it means to be a judge and the very role of law in our polity.'"

As we ascended to the stage and took our positions, I told Justice Scalia that perhaps we'd better stand instead of using our stools. Amid the standing ovation, he agreed, and I made sure that he was comfortable with the height of the music stand for his notes.

Then, as the applause died down, I began: "Thank you, ladies and gentlemen, for what will be the world-premiere presentation of our new book. It's an honor for both of us to be here for this special evening. It's really quite extraordinary that Justice Scalia is on this stage at all. I hesitate to tell you this, but only two hours ago, it looked as if he wouldn't be able to emerge from his room—so excruciating was his back pain. I keep telling him he shouldn't do his own yardwork. But he's better now, and he's here, and let's give him another hearty round of applause."

I had told the crowd about Justice Scalia's condition only to hedge against the possibility that his participation might be cut short if another back spasm caused him to have to leave the stage. I wanted to anticipate any rumors that might arise if that did happen. We smiled at each other, and he winked, as the crowd clapped. I saw a little sweat on his brow.

We began by explaining the three competing views of legal interpretation: *textualism*, which considers the words of a statute paramount and therefore closely analyzes the text, its structure, and its purposes (but only as purpose can be understood from the text itself); *purposivism*, which, although it considers the words, allows consideration of the legislature's broader purposes in enacting a statute to color or even override its words; and *consequentialism*, which considers of paramount importance neither the words nor the purposes but the real-world consequences of a given interpretation, and whether those consequences comport with wise policy. As Justice Scalia pointed out, *purposivism* is badly named, since textualists do take account of a statute's purpose; it's just that purposivists go outside the text of the statute—for example, looking at legislative history—to find purpose. But he said although it's a misnomer, *purposivism* is the standard term in legal circles.

"All statutes," he said that evening, "have as their purpose the promotion of good and the deterrence of evil. But if you take 'purpose' at the highest level of abstraction, or you allow judges to weigh consequences, then you substitute the judge for the legislature. You make the judge into a policy-maker, and the whole balance of government is shifted."

Our foundations having been laid, we traded points—just as we always had in teaching *Making Your Case*. (But we reversed the order: for *Reading Law*, he wanted me to take the odd-numbered sections so he could have the even-numbered ones.) He was in good form that evening, gesturing with great animation, orating with verve, and good-naturedly taunting me—all to the audience's delight. He was obviously enjoying this subject matter more than I'd ever seen before. His adrenaline had kicked in, and the back pain seemed to have vanished.

"Let's take questions," he said at the end. "I'm sure there are questions."

One of the questions had to do with something that almost always puzzles people: what is the difference between *textualism* and *originalism*? "*Textualism* is the much broader doctrine," Justice Scalia answered. "It says that a judicial interpreter should be guided by the text, structure, and purpose of a statute. *Originalism* is simply a gloss on textualism: it says that the statute—by which, you understand, we mean any enacted text—the statute must be understood as it would have been understood by competent users of the language at the time of enactment."

I chimed in: "Originalism rarely comes up—perhaps in 1% or 2%

of the cases, most often in constitutional cases. Textualism, by contrast, comes up in every single instance of judicial interpretation."

Justice Scalia took over again: "As we say in the introduction, every judge is a textualist. All judges say, 'We look first to the text of the statute.' Those who say that usually end up going far afield. [*laughter*] A pure textualist begins and ends with the text."

When we were finished, we received another standing ovation—or, rather, he did, and I just happened to be standing on the stage with him. Afterward, various audience members came up to thank and congratulate us. Somebody told me we resembled a comedy duo made up of Don Rickles and Kelsey Grammer—which seemed an apt comparison.

We had been finished barely five minutes when Karolyne came to tell me she was concerned about his back. I went over to him and said, "Nino, let's get you to your room!"

"No! Come with me. Get Lyne. We're going in the car."

"What?"

"Don't ask questions. Just come with me. The marshals are taking us."

Once we were in the car, he told us: "We're going to see Placido Domingo. He's expecting us at the Los Angeles Opera."

"You're kidding me," I said. "He's just meeting us there?"

"No. It's a dress rehearsal for the Verdi opera *The Two Foscari*. Placido has the lead, and it's a closed rehearsal. But he wants us to come."

"You know him?"

"Of course I do. We've met. I'm an opera aficionado, and he's the greatest tenor ever."

"How's your back?"

"I'm just fine. No pain at all."

"I hope you don't mind what I said at the outset of our presentation."

"Not at all," he said. "You did just right."

"This is exciting," said Karolyne. "I can't believe we're going to meet Placido Domingo."

It turned out that an L.A. lawyer named Don Erik Franzen, an L.A. Opera board member, had attended our event that evening. He had called ahead to the opera to see whether Domingo would like to have Justice Scalia come over. The answer, of course, was yes because the two had known each other for some time. Franzen had introduced himself after the presentation and told Justice Scalia about the possibility of attending the rehearsal. The whole thing had been instantly arranged, and soon we were being ushered to the opera.

We met Franzen at the opera house and walked in as the dress rehearsal was in progress. It was a stunningly good performance—and, essentially, a private one. After an hour or so, the performers took a break. Domingo came into the audience to meet us all, and he and Justice Scalia exchanged warm greetings. It turned out that Domingo's wife, Marta, had been sitting right behind us, and she was as happy to see her distinguished guest as her husband was. After a 15-minute visit, Justice Scalia declared that he must get back to the hotel to sleep a little before his early-morning flight back to Washington. On the way back, he remarked that he was relatively pain-free. He thanked us both for all that we'd done that day. We all agreed that it had been a day like no other.

The Posner Book Review

Less than two months after the release of *Reading Law*, Judge Richard A. Posner of the Seventh Circuit in Chicago published a lengthy review in the *New Republic* under the title "The Incoherence of Antonin Scalia." The insulting title was intended, I suppose, to mirror an article in the same publication from five years before: "The Arrogance of Justice Anthony Kennedy." But with the Scalia piece, the dignifying title "Justice" was omitted.

The gist of Judge Posner's criticisms I would never have predicted. I had been certain that he'd argue that although Scalia and Garner array an impressive number of authorities, they chase a formalist will-o'-the-wisp in thinking that legislative words can ever result in such a degree of linguistic determinacy that judicial discretion is much constrained. I thought he'd say that the open-textured nature of language makes it necessary for judges to engage in glossing statutes and even nudging them toward the better policies that judges, with the benefit of hindsight, can perceive (as opposed to legislators, who work only with foresight).

Instead, he took a tack that I'd have thought impossible: in what my colleague Tiger called a "hysterical outburst," he accused us of writing a book that was riddled with errors and misrepresentations of the cases we discuss.

When the *New Republic* asked me to respond, I welcomed the opportunity. It was a lengthy response in which I detailed some of the fact-checking lengths to which my staff and I (as well as Justice Scalia) had gone. I mentioned that I'd had four lawyer–colleagues at LawProse undertake extensive fact-checking, and I argued that the allegations of error were themselves false.

In further response to this, Judge Posner essentially accused me of lying about my fact-checking protocol ("I have trouble believing Garner")—and wondered why I hadn't mentioned my lawyer–colleagues in the acknowledgments. In fact, they were all listed there as my colleagues but not identified as lawyers. I was astonished at how quickly the whole affair descended into incivility.

In a telephone call with Justice Scalia, he could tell how unhappy I was about the brouhaha. He acted mildly surprised at this.

"Nino, he's called me a liar."

"You're mad at him?"

"Of course I am. He called me a liar about something that's easily verifiable."

"Don't you ever say 'Our Father'?" (Of course, in this conversation, I couldn't see the capitals and the quotation marks.)

"What do you mean?"

"Don't you ever say 'Our Father'?"

"You mean the Lord's Prayer?"

"Exactly. Forgive those who trespass against us. Forgive him."

"Of course I'll forgive him, Nino, in time. But right now I'm feeling indignant. I never imagined he'd resort to an argument like *sloppiness* or *dishonesty*."

"I'm telling you, you'll be happier if you just forgive."

More Work, More Invitations

Invitations to make joint presentations of one or the other of our books rolled in pretty steadily. During these years, Justice Scalia and I spoke jointly at more than 40 events across the United States and Asia. His on-stage personality was typically warmer when we were together than when he was at a lectern alone: we could engage in banter, and I could evoke humor from him. When he was solo, he tended to read speeches, and he was often placed at some remove from the front of a stage—sometimes 35

feet from the closest audience members—making him seem a distant figure. Like any other speaker suffering from poor stage management, he was
at the mercy of event organizers. When we appeared together, Karolyne
would always check the stage setup on-site beforehand, including lectern
placement, stools, music stands, water within easy reach, and lighting. Her
attention to these subtle details made our events go smoothly in all sorts of
noticeable ways—and in other ways that were more subliminal.

When we spoke together for the Supreme Court Historical Society, our
lecterns in the Supreme Court chamber were separated by only two inches.
We'd never been standing quite so close. Much to the audience's delight,
Justice Scalia elbowed or nudged me a couple of times when he took mild
issue with something I'd said, which of course got both of us laughing. He
really seemed to like the physical proximity. From that point on, we'd ask
to have our lecterns all but touching (without adding the explicit rationale
that this would enable him to elbow me at will). The Historical Society
event was supposedly filmed by C-SPAN, but I've never seen the film, and
it was never broadcast.

Lawyer groups often tried to use me as a conduit to Justice Scalia. That
was understandable, I suppose. Most would invite us jointly, but we all
knew that the entire event hinged on whether Justice Scalia would accept.

Interestingly, the only hitch that ever came up in the negotiations was
from one of Justice Scalia's former law clerks who questioned Karolyne's
requests for Justice Scalia. First class for the Justice?! Why?! A suite in a
hotel?! Why?! And on and on. The former clerk overcame his initial resistance. But he remained stubborn about wanting to remain onstage after
introducing us. Our settled practice was to take the stage and handle the
presentation ourselves—even questions from the audience, which I'd field.
But this former law clerk wanted all the onstage exposure he could get.
(Actually, this wasn't uncommon.) In the end, Karolyne insisted that he
must leave the stage after the introduction, and he reluctantly agreed to
do so. If he hadn't, he'd have been nothing but a distracting unused prop.

Fellow Curmudgeons

For some reason I can't recall, in December 2012 I sent Justice Scalia an
e-mail asking an autobiographical question. I was perhaps curious about
what influences led him to textualism when I'd never heard him talk about

this or that professor who professed such an approach. So I asked him what, in his background, made him a textualist.

He paraphrased my "silly question": "What made you believe that a text means what it says?" After all, no one ever asks, "Why do you use a glossary for Shakespeare?" What needs explaining, he said, is what makes anyone a nontextualist. If the nature of textualism weren't enough, of course, "one would be driven to textualism by the chaotic and undemocratic consequences of all other approaches."

That same month, a reporter with *Business Insider* interviewed me for a piece she was writing on my friendship with the "famous curmudgeon." Her lead was appropriate: "Bryan A. Garner, a lawyer and writer, and Justice Antonin Scalia are, on the surface, an odd pair of friends. Garner is pro-choice and supports same-sex marriage, while Scalia is a conservative Catholic whose comments about homosexuality have outraged gays. But the two became tight after collaborating on two different books about the law."[42]

I told her, "We've become so close that he's like an uncle to me."[43]

She mentioned an instance in which Justice Scalia had lamented the poor grammar of flight attendants. Unsurprised, I told her: "If you think that certain minimum standards of behavior are good and important, then when people fall below these standards it's disappointing—not in an officious way, but you wish it were otherwise."[44]

Citing the example of how irritated Justice Scalia and I both get at men wearing their hats while eating in restaurants, I blamed our parents for inculcating in us both the bedrock idea that this is absolutely forbidden behavior—a badge of sheer boorishness. And I noted that he and I rubbed off on each other, or at least he did on me: "Garner's wife says he gets more curmudgeonly after spending time with the Justice."[45] Karolyne always said that not resentfully, but affectionately.

I tried to end the interview on something less hopeless than completely pessimistic resignation. I was trying to explain an attitude that Justice Sca-

---

42 Erin Fuchs, "Scalia's Close Friend Tells Us Why the Justice Is Such a 'Famous Curmudgeon,'" 24 Dec. 2012, http://www.businessinsider.com/bryan-garner-talks-about-scalia-2012-12.

43 *Id.*

44 *Id.*

45 *Id.*

lia and I shared: "The world changes. Of course the world changes. But that doesn't mean all change is good. I think a lot of change is retrograde. That's the definition of a curmudgeon: someone who says harrumph about changing social conventions."[46]

A Second Dallas Visit

The following month, in January 2013, Justice Scalia came to Dallas for a joint lecture we were to deliver at SMU. The trip was the first of several times he stayed with Karolyne and me at our house. We knew, of course, that breakfast was important to him, and in preparation Angela mentioned to Karolyne that he would often have a bagel or muffin after reaching the office. We stocked up with pastries, bagels, and a pie—together with plenty of coffee.

After our first breakfast together, Justice Scalia told me how dissatisfied he was: "I need a full American breakfast! I need eggs and bacon and toast!" He wasn't angry so much as disappointed, and I appreciated his willingness to be candid.

After that misunderstanding, Karolyne and I—who both normally skipped breakfast in those days—made a full breakfast each of the two remaining days. As I was cooking over-easy eggs the second morning, Karolyne was frying the bacon and making toast. Justice Scalia was standing right between us in the kitchen, scrutinizing my technique.

"Bryan, those eggs are looking good, but you're not timing this well at all!" he said.

"What do you mean?"

"By the time the bacon's ready, your eggs will be cold. You have to *time* your cooking just right. That's something Maureen is great at."

"Okay, Nino. I'll eat these eggs cold and have another fresh batch ready for you as soon as the bacon and toast are served."

"Good. That's better," he said with a chummy smile.

He and I were equally amused by our playful banter in the kitchen—and the intrinsic humor in the roles we were playing as he supervised my egg-frying technique. Soon we were enjoying a delectable breakfast that gratified us all.

Several events had been scheduled for this trip: an SMU-sponsored

---

46 *Id.*

party at our house; a Scalia talk with foreign law students; the keynote event, a joint lecture in McFarlin Auditorium, the largest venue on campus; a Scalia talk at a constitutional-law class; and a dinner with the Dedman family, the greatest benefactors to SMU Law.

About 100 local lawyers and judges attended the cocktail party at our house. The marshals had vetted our list of invitees. It was a festive event: people were excited to be able to meet and chat with Justice Scalia, and many enjoyed seeing my library for the first time. But one prominent local lawyer was a little boisterous when she arrived late in the evening. She walked into the library and loudly proclaimed, "I paid for this! I paid for this library!"

A little taken aback, I stood by as someone asked her what she meant. "I hired Bryan Garner to lecture at my department, and we paid his big fee! So I paid for part of this library!"

Her husband seemed to be trying to rein her in, so I decided to leave the room and find Justice Scalia, who was on the back porch enjoying a cigar with two of our other guests. He suggested that I have one. We had a chuckle when I recounted what had just happened in the library. Midway through our cigars, she found her way out to the patio. I warned him as she approached, and within moments she was accosting Justice Scalia with aggressive questions. "How can you explain *Bush v. Gore*?!"

"I explained it in my opinion," Justice Scalia said. "Go read it."

"You don't represent me!" she said loudly and sloppily. "Your vote doesn't represent me!"

"What do you mean?" he asked, growing noticeably disdainful and impatient.

"You're supposed to represent everybody, including me, on the Court, but you do a lousy job representing me." Now she was getting even more careless in her posture and demeanor.

"My job," Justice Scalia said patiently, "isn't to represent you or anyone else. I represent the law. I don't have a constituency."

"I think you should represent *my* voice!"

"This is tiresome," he said. "It's getting late." He put out his half-smoked cigar.

Fortunately, the woman's husband swooped her away, and she was soon out the front door.

"Is she actually a *lawyer*?" Justice Scalia asked me.

"Yes, believe it or not. She's fairly prominent."

"It's hard to believe."

"I know. Believe me, she wasn't on my invitation list. She must have been invited by somebody else. Nobody could have predicted that." I was sure he'd seen much worse.

Changing the "Living Constitution"

The next afternoon, we were at my kitchen counter preparing for our big event at McFarlin Auditorium. It was to be a packed house, and we planned to cover all 70 sections of *Reading Law*, from beginning to end in nearly two hours without intermission. I made a suggestion to him: "Nino, I think you should stop criticizing the Living Constitution."

"What?!"

"I just mean the term. Find another name for it."

"But everyone calls it the Living Constitution."

"I know. But it was a name chosen by your intellectual enemies, and it advances their cause. In the early 1960s, William O. Douglas wrote a book called *The Living Bill of Rights*."

"So what's the problem?"

"You lose the debate in the minds of the American people. They don't want the opposite of a Living Constitution."

"I've sometimes joked," he said, "that the Constitution is dead."

"Right. And that joke is turning people against you. Remember section 21 of *Making Your Case*?"

"No. What?"

"Control the semantic playing field," I reminded him. "Names have power."

"How so?"

"'Living Constitution' is just a euphemism for a Constitution that morphs year by year without amendment. It's the euphemism devised by people who tout it—your nemeses."

"Are you saying I've made a mistake over the past 30 years by using their terminology?"

"I do think so. You've sometimes called it the 'Evolving Constitution,' which is better, but you usually say 'Living Constitution.' And that's the term we used in *Reading Law*."

"Yes, it is," he said.

"If you asked the American people whether they'd rather have a stable Constitution or a highly volatile one that morphs without amending it, what would they say?"

"Stable, no doubt," he said.

"Right. I suggest that, from this day forward, you stop attacking the Living Constitution. Attack the Morphing Constitution instead."

"I don't like the word *morph*. It's newfangled and tendentious. How about the Changing Constitution?"

"That's much better. Can we change all the references in *Reading Law*?" I asked.

"Let's have a look."

We sat down and examined all the references in the book to "Living Constitution," and we both thought the passages read much better with "Changing Constitution." We agreed to make those edits in the second edition.

"I can't believe I've never thought of this before," Justice Scalia said.

"It's a subtle point how names can affect a public debate," I said. "Think of *pro-life* vs. *pro-choice* or *anti-life* vs. *anti-choice*. As we say in *Making Your Case*, if you can get your adversary to use your terminology, you're often halfway home to winning the argument."

That evening, I paid close attention to what Justice Scalia said when we were talking about the fixed-meaning canon. Naturally so, given our talk earlier in the day. I remember it distinctly: "I used to say that the Constitution is not a living document. It's dead, dead, dead. But I've gotten better. I no longer say that. The truth is that the Constitution is not one that morphs. It's an enduring Constitution, not a changing Constitution."

We stayed late in the auditorium that night to sign books as audience members formed a long line, coming up to us on stage left and exiting stage right. It was another assembly-line autographing of books on the half-title page without inscriptions. Because it was a Dallas audience and I knew many of the attendees, I briefly introduced those I knew to Justice Scalia. Good-naturedly, he called me (once again) Chatty Cathy. He was in high spirits.

On our way home with the marshals, I asked, "Would you like a glass of grappa on our back balcony? The weather is beautiful tonight."

"That would be lovely," he said. "Do you have any cigars?"

"No, I'm out. Let's stop and get some. Lyne, would you like a cigar as well?"

"I don't think so, no. But I'll join you on the balcony."

I asked the marshals to make a quick stop at Pogo's, a liquor store, and got two cigars while Justice Scalia and Lyne waited in the car. When we reached the house, we saw that two marshals had already established their watch in the front yard—or perhaps they'd been there all the time we were away.

Soon all three of us were upstairs on the back balcony, toasting our friendship and looking out on the lighted pool in the backyard. Justice Scalia had to show me how to get my cigar going because I'm pretty unfamiliar with the practice. Soon I was coughing as I took my first puffs—prompting from Justice Scalia some mischievous glee.

"That was quite a performance you two gave tonight," said Karolyne.

"I certainly enjoyed it," said Justice Scalia. "Just look at this view back here. That's an enormous backyard."

"It's unusual for the center of Dallas," I said. "There are eight of these big lots on our street. I've wanted to have one since the early 1990s."

"And now you do," said Justice Scalia. "Do you trim all those hedges yourself?"

"Oh no," I said. "I couldn't possibly."

"I like to do my own yardwork," he said. "I mow my own grass and clip my hedges."

"I know. Every time I call you on a Saturday afternoon, Maureen says you're out working on the lawn."

"I just love it."

"Bryan's contribution," said Karolyne, "is murdering weeds in the drive. He loves spraying weed-killer on the little weeds coming up between the bricks."

"Oh, that *is* fun," said Justice Scalia. "Say, Lyne, how long have you been a lawyer?"

"Since 2006," she said.

"Why don't you become a member of the Supreme Court Bar? You could come up for the swearing-in. It's a beautiful ceremony."

"Actually, the Clerk of Court, General Suter, said something about it last year. He offered to sponsor me."

"I'll tell you what. *I'll* sponsor you. Bill Suter can be my cosponsor."

"Wow," she said. "What an honor, Justice Scalia. You can do that?"

"Of course. It would be my honor to do that. We'll arrange for a day before the end of the term."

"It's General Suter's last term," she said.

"Oh, that's *right*. Let's do it in April or May while he's still Clerk."

"That's so kind of you to think of it, Nino," I said.

"You'll have to move her admission, Bryan," said Justice Scalia. "Neither Bill Suter, as Clerk of Court, nor I, as a Justice, can do that. How long have you been a member of the Supreme Court Bar?"

"Twenty years, I think," I said.

"Didn't you like the ceremony?" he asked.

"I didn't attend, I'm afraid. I regret that. This will be my first participation in the ceremony."

"Oh, you should have gone. When Lyne does it, I'll have you both back to chambers afterward. We'll toast the newest member with Champagne. That'll be fun."

"Thank you, Justice Scalia," said Karolyne, a little choked up.

"More grappa?" I asked.

"No," said Justice Scalia, snuffing out his cigar. "We should call it a night. I have to teach tomorrow."

And teach he did the next day at SMU: an hour on comparative law with foreign students, an hour on administrative law, and a late-afternoon hour on constitutional law. Each hour was brimming with fascinating observations. In comparative law, he said: "Just as you don't understand your own language until you study a foreign language, you don't understand your own legal system until you study another." He added that the big difference between common-law countries and civil-law countries, such as those of Europe and Asia, is that common-law judges aren't career bureaucrats who swallow everything that the government does. And then a frisson for the French: "French judicial opinions are bloodless and dull: no intelligent person would want to read them."

The theme for the administrative-law class was that "there's no such thing as government by experts." He said that the "headless fourth branch of government"—the collection of federal agencies—isn't really headless at all: it's run by Congress. Apropos of something, he quoted Chief Justice Rehnquist's view as being, "Don't worry too much about the wording of the holding. Just make sure the judgment is correct. We're not going to pay attention to the holding in the next case anyway!"

In the constitutional-law class, many of his comments were quotable:

- "The cases I'll fall on my sword for are the structural cases, involving separation of powers."
- "I couldn't care less what a legislature intended. I care what they adopted."
- "Sign me up for original meaning. I urge you to abandon original intent."
- "God does natural law. I do American law."
- "The only way to run a sensible judicial system is a government of laws—what does the text say?"

At one point, he brought up *New York Times v. Sullivan*,[47] the freedom-of-the-press case that established the actual-malice standard for defamation claims by public figures. He said it was an example of judge-made law that was flat wrong. I then spoke up and asked whether it should be followed by later Courts, even though it was initially wrong. "Yes," he said, "I think so. That's our system of stare decisis, and there are all sorts of people who now rely on that holding."

I stayed with him throughout the day. After a faculty lunch, we decamped in a faculty lounge and napped before the final class. The lectures were impromptu but well-thought-out, as he'd given versions of them dozens of times. He particularly shone, though, when responding to questions. He always had the audiences laughing, at least as much because of his own risibility when delivering his lines as because of the iconoclastic nature of the utterances.

"Dead, Dead, Dead" Comes Back to Life

The next day the *Dallas Morning News* ran an article about the event two nights before. It quoted Justice Scalia as saying about the Constitution: "It's not a living document. It's dead, dead, dead." End of quotation. When we saw that after breakfast, we weren't happy about it. I told him I'd write a letter to the editor objecting to the mischaracterization. (See the bottom

47 376 U.S. 254 (1964).

half of page 202 for the actual words.) When I did write the editors, though, things still weren't put entirely aright.

After reading my letter the next day, Justice Scalia wrote to say that it should make the editors blush, adding: "Apparently the print media in Texas are as biased as the print media elsewhere." He said he enjoyed his stay with Lyne and me and thanked us. Nothing about the controversy had soured his experience: "I thought our presentation was the best. Regards. Nino." More than three weeks after the misleading story, the *Morning News* (page A2) ran an anodyne "correction":

> *An article in the Jan. 29 Metro section misspelled the name of a new book by U.S. Supreme Court Justice Antonin Scalia and Bryan A. Garner. It is* Reading Law: The Interpretation of Legal Texts. *The article quoted Scalia as calling the U.S. Constitution "dead, dead, dead." He went on to say he believes it is not a document that "morphs" but rather an "enduring" one.*

The new item still didn't give the words with which he had prefaced "dead, dead, dead."

When I sent the "correction" to Justice Scalia, he responded curtly: "A pox on all of them!"

Some of the later reporting of the event, meanwhile, was much fuller and more favorable. I had been wrong in thinking that only one news outlet had been present. Mark Curriden, a noted legal reporter with the *Texas Lawbook*, covered the event and wrote a pretty thorough piece. Fortunately, he quoted snatches of the unfilmed repartee:

> *While the book is good, the live version of Justice Scalia and Garner was so much better. For more than 90 minutes, the duo talked about whether roosters are animals, death-ray technology, whether the Constitution is living or dead and a lengthy discussion of what the meaning of "into" is. . . .*
>
> *"My political beliefs are greatly different from Justice Scalia," Garner told the audience, receiving a splattering of applause. "I deplore the Second Amendment. I'm in favor of gun control. I favor gay marriage. Still, we worked through 700 decisions, and we have yet to find a single decision on which we disagree with each other."*

"I had to bring you kicking and screaming," replied Justice Scalia. *"You're a bleeding heart."*

The bleeding-heart line was one that Justice Scalia frequently used after that event. He always said it with a smile, never a sneer, and audiences liked it.

For his part, Curriden faulted Justice Scalia's stipulation that the event be unrecorded. He wrote: "Justice Scalia reportedly didn't allow it. He didn't want any television cameras or recording devices. Anyone claiming that a newspaper didn't print a long enough article or didn't publish Justice Scalia's complete quote [he meant me, obviously] needs to first answer why they didn't vigorously advocate for a full and public recording of the event."

Fair enough, I suppose. Perhaps I was somewhat naïve about it, but I did encourage filming the event—just not very energetically. Justice Scalia said no. His policy was to disallow all recordings except when he had high trust in the organization, such as the Supreme Court Historical Society or the Newseum.

Curriden's final point contained an insight that I hadn't before fully recognized (in the final sentence of this quotation): "The event was terrific. Most of those attending got their first Bryan Garner experience, and they were overwhelmingly impressed. They also got to witness Justice Scalia at his best. Unfortunately, the benefits are forever limited to the 1,500 [the dean had told me 1,700] in McFarlin Auditorium last week. Justice Scalia is sometimes misunderstood. And some of those times, such as this, he has no one to blame but himself."

Although I shared Curriden's remarks with Justice Scalia and with Kathy Arberg of the Supreme Court's Public Information Office, the no-recording policy remained part of Justice Scalia's standard stipulations, with rare exceptions.

A Surprise in Chicago

In early April 2013, Karolyne and I were in Chicago for two nights before I was to teach a seminar. The first evening, we arranged dinner with my old friend Frank Easterbrook, chief judge of the U.S. Court of Appeals for the Seventh Circuit, which is based there. Because Karolyne wasn't feeling well, Frank and I dined alone. Frank, of course, had written the foreword to *Reading Law*. He was such a thoroughgoing textualist that Justice Scalia had often said that if he could choose a successor for himself on the Supreme Court, it would be Frank.

Much to my surprise, Frank told me that evening that he'd be introducing Justice Scalia the next day at the Lawyers Club of Chicago. Justice Scalia was to discuss *Reading Law*. Frank said we'd be welcome to attend as audience members.

Later that night, after discussing Frank's kind invitation, Karolyne and I decided we'd stick to our original plans and spend our day off at the Shedd Aquarium and the Field Museum. Frank's invitation was necessarily last-minute because it was the merest coincidence that I was in the same city at the same time. Anyway, we resolved to relax instead. We slept in and had a room-service breakfast.

At 10:36 a.m., as we were finishing getting dressed to leave for the Shedd Aquarium, an e-mail came through on my phone. It was Frank: "Bryan: Nino's flight has been delayed, and he may not make the lunch. Any interest in standing in for him and talking about *Reading Law*? Frank."

"Of course! We must go!" Karolyne said. "This is the only time you'll get to stand in for a Supreme Court Justice."

We dressed again, this time in business attire, and arrived at 11:45 at the Union League Club, where the Lawyers Club was meeting. At the corner of Dearborn and Jackson, the Union League has one of the grandest ballrooms in America. Some 500 lawyers and judges were packed into the sumptuously decorated hall. During the meal, Frank was getting updates on Justice Scalia's whereabouts every ten minutes or so from the U.S. Marshal's Office. By the time I began speaking at 12:15, Justice Scalia's flight had landed, and he was being whisked to the site. I had spoken about the Scalia–Garner collaborations for only about 15 minutes when out of the elevator, which was visible from the rostrum, strode Justice Scalia with a small retinue of marshals behind him.

"Here's the great man now! I yield the floor," I announced.

"Bryan!" he shouted boisterously from the back of the room as he headed toward the front. Everyone stood and applauded for a solid minute. He shook my hand, and Frank's, hugged Karolyne, and took the lectern. I retreated to my seat at the table just in front of him. He spoke for about 20 minutes and then answered several questions with his usual

Working in chambers on *Making Your Case*.
(Washington, D.C., November 2, 2007)

Working in chambers on the second edition of *Reading Law*.
(Washington, D.C., February 12, 2015)

With Karolyne before a presentation of *Reading Law* to the State Bar of California.
(San Diego, September 11, 2014)

Presenting *Reading Law* to the Supreme Court Historical Society.
(Supreme Court Chamber, June 3, 2013)

Presenting together to the American College of Trial Lawyers.
(Naples, Florida, March 2, 2013)

Working together in chambers the day after my five-hour
tendon-transfer surgery at Johns Hopkins.
(Washington, D.C., December 18, 2012)

Justice Scalia inspects our Samuel Johnson–themed wedding-cake base.
(Newport, Rhode Island, August 8, 2010)

Justice Scalia hugs the bride.
(Newport, Rhode Island, August 8, 2010)

My groomsmen and the officiant.
(Newport, Rhode Island, August 8, 2010)

Karolyne's and my rehearsal dinner.
(Pawtucket, Rhode Island, August 7, 2010)

Lecturing at SMU's McFarlin Auditorium.
(Dallas, January 28, 2013)

Onstage at the Burton Awards.
(Library of Congress, June 15, 2009)

Backstage at the Burton Awards with Chief Judge Judith Kaye of
New York and her son Jonathan.
(Library of Congress, June 15, 2009)

In chambers, consulting *Garner's Modern American Usage*.
(Washington, D.C., February 2008)

Photo by Thomas C. Leighton

ABOVE: Justice Scalia tried on my reading glasses just before going onstage at the Chinese University of Hong Kong. (February 2, 2016)

RIGHT: Karolyne and Justice Scalia roar in front of Stephen, the famous shrapnel-scarred HSBC lion. (Hong Kong, February 1, 2016)

verve. Afterward we autographed books together for about 30 minutes. At 2:30 he was off to the airport again. This kind of in-and-out trip was fairly typical for him. He was always much in demand, and he did his best to accommodate reasonable requests.

As he headed to O'Hare to fly to his next destination, Karolyne and I went to the Field Museum, musing over our unexpectedly eventful day.

Some Tosca Substitutes

Occasionally when I was in Washington, Tosca would be closed. Although Justice Scalia liked his regular places, he'd be willing to try something new with me. In 2013, after sessions in chambers, we tried two offbeat Italian restaurants—Obelisk and the Ristorante La Perla, an old-fashioned Italian restaurant. At Obelisk, on the second floor of a brownstone off Dupont Circle, seemingly none of the staff recognized my companion, even though Angela had made reservations under the name Scalia. But a father and son approached our table, and the father asked Justice Scalia if he could take a picture of the Justice with his son. Justice Scalia was usually happy to do this kind of thing, even in the middle of a meal. He never resented it.

At the end of our meal, during which we continued our conversation about the work we'd done that day, Justice Scalia noticed that he'd dropped red calamari sauce on his tie in two places. He did that kind of thing often, and he'd always become annoyed at himself.

"Dammit, I've ruined this tie. Once you take a tie to the cleaners, it's definitely ruined. I've never gotten a tie back from the cleaners in good shape."

"Neither have I. Why not try a Tide stick?"

"What's that?"

"It's a new device to remove stains."

I'd learned of it recently from Karolyne. Remembering that I just happened to have one in my pocket, I tried to show him how to use it. One of the stains was too close under his chin for him to see it easily, so I got up from my side of the table, went beside him on the banquette, and applied it while he looked up at the ceiling.

"You're sure this works?" he muttered with a funny grimace, eyes aloft.

"If it doesn't, I think nothing will."

"Okay. I'm trusting you."

"You got some on your suit as well. Let me take care of that."

"I'm a slob. I'm just a slob. Wait—you can use it on wool, too?"

"I do it all the time. Works wonders."

Soon it was finished and dry, and he was all but incredulous that no traces of the stains were left. "Great device. Where can I get one?"

"Any pharmacy or grocery store. But here, take this one."

"I don't want to take yours!"

"I insist. I have two others in my travel bag. Lyne won't let me travel without one. Seriously."

"Well, thank you. This is really going to come in handy."

As we got up to leave, a waitress from another station came up to me and said, "May I just say what a good-looking couple you make? You two look very happy together."

"You're funny," I told her, smiling.

As we were preparing to get into the marshals' car, I chuckled and told Justice Scalia what the waitress had just said. His only reaction was a loud, hearty "Ha!"

"Have you ever been to Second Story Books?" I asked.

"No. What's that?"

"It's my favorite secondhand bookshop in D.C."

It was just across the street. Upon deciding to go, he told the marshals we'd be back in about 15 minutes. Inside, I showed him the law section and the rhetoric section, as well as some of the finer antiquarian books. "This is where I do a lot of our research, Nino—used-book stores. It's a great way to see whether we've covered all the bases. It's a necessary supplement to university libraries."

"This is quite a place. I didn't know it was here."

"Why don't you find a book to take to Maureen?"

"I think I will!"

We browsed for five minutes or so. We both found a couple of books we wanted, and we paid and left. The marshals were waiting just outside to take him home. "Would you like a ride?"

"Sure."

"What's your hotel?"

"The W Hotel at 15th and F."

"Very well." Then he directed the driver to swing by the hotel to drop me off—a thoughtful convenience.

As usual, we talked about the day's work during the five or ten minutes it took to reach my hotel. Whatever my hotel might be—the W, the Willard, the Mayflower, the St. Regis, or the JW Marriott—I'd typically know the doormen because I'd been frequenting these places for over two decades. I'd ask Justice Scalia if he'd like to meet James (or whoever the doorman might be). Every time he'd say yes. So I'd get out from the seat behind the driver, walk around the back of the car, hail James, and Justice Scalia would roll down his window. "James," I'd say, "please meet Justice Scalia of the Supreme Court."

"Good to meet you, James. Take care of this fellow!"

"It's an honor to meet you, sir."

Those interactions were a pleasure to him.

Some weeks later we dined at La Perla—Justice Scalia, Karolyne, and I had the place almost to ourselves at 6:00 p.m. We wanted an early dinner so he could get back home to Mrs. Scalia. Again, Angela had made the reservations under the name Scalia. Unlike our experience at Obelisk, here the managers and staff greeted us with no small fanfare. I must have heard the name "Justice Scalia" a dozen times before we were seated. Of course, he had long been revered in the Italian community.

"You know," he said, "I never knew how much it would mean to Italian-Americans to have an Italian Supreme Court Justice. When I was nominated, the outpouring of support and sentiment was incredible. There were baskets and baskets of notes and cards. At first I told my assistant I wanted to read every one of them, but in the end that was unrealistic."

"Did you continue reading a choice few?"

"Yeah, she'd pick out the best ones, and I'd read two or three a day for my first six months on the Court."

"That doesn't happen with every Justice," I said.

"I don't think so. For Italian-Americans, it was a matter of suddenly achieving real respectability. There had been a sense of shame within the Italian community over the Mafia, mob bosses, and so on. That's what we were known for, primarily. With a Supreme Court Justice, the feeling changed. I was amazed at how much it meant to people. You can have an Italian governor, but he can be corrupt. A Supreme Court

Justice symbolizes both integrity and intelligence. It was important to Italians."

How to Succeed

Shortly after the dinner at La Perla, Justice Scalia and I were working once again in his chambers toward the second edition of *Reading Law*. He warned me that we'd have a 4:00 p.m. interruption. About five minutes before the appointed time, Angela came into the room and said, "Justice, the students are now in the Lawyers' Lounge—ready for your 4 o'clock."

"What is it, Nino?" I asked.

"Some high-schoolers from New Jersey. I have to give a little talk."

"May I come along?"

"You want to watch?"

"Absolutely."

"Okay. Then we can resume our work about 4:45. We'll leave for dinner at 6:00."

Angela handed Justice Scalia a thin folio, and we walked through the courthouse corridors to the portrait-adorned conference room known as the Lawyers' Lounge—the very room where I'd interviewed him seven years before.

After the teacher leading this field trip introduced Justice Scalia to the students, he put down his folio (never opening it) and started in. He explained federalism in a nutshell, assuring the students that their state high court's rulings affected their lives more pervasively than the rulings of the U.S. Supreme Court.

Then he said: "Let me ask you a question. What makes the American system of government so great? Why is it so widely admired? And how do the American people remain free?"

The students offered various answers, to each of which Justice Scalia gave the same answer.

"The Constitution?" No.

"The judiciary?" No.

"The presidency?" No.

"States' rights?" No.

"The military?" No.

Everyone was stumped, but I'd heard this speech before.

"What makes our government so remarkable is a feature that our Founders built into it: the separation of powers! They wanted to ensure that no single person in government, and no single department of government, had too great a concentration of power. That's the only way to prevent tyranny."

He continued: "Our Constitution isn't the best, if you judge it by its guarantees. Frankly, the old Soviet constitution was better, and it was full of all kinds of grand guarantees. Instead of our Fourth Amendment guarantee of protection against unreasonable searches and seizures, the Soviet Union's constitution's guarantees were much more explicit and extensive. For example, 'Citizens are guaranteed inviolability of the person. . . . Citizens are guaranteed inviolability of the home. No one may, without lawful grounds, enter a home against the will of those residing in it. The privacy of citizens, and of their correspondence, telephone conversations, and telegraphic communications is protected by law.' But this Soviet constitution was just a piece of paper: there was no independent judiciary to back it up."

He paused, as if for dramatic effect, and then continued: "I wouldn't trade our old Constitution for the Soviet constitution in a million years. A bill of rights has value only if the main articles of the constitution truly constitute the organs of government—establish a structure that will preserve liberties against the ineradicable human lust for power. It is the separation of powers that makes it impossible for any element of government to obtain unchecked power."

The students listened with great interest. At the end, he took questions. One in particular elicited a great answer. "Justice Scalia, what do you think it takes today for a young person to succeed?"

"I think it takes what it's always taken," he answered. "Make a habit of excellence. No matter how menial or trivial the task before you may seem—whether you're stapling papers or washing dishes or flipping burgers or painting a room—do your dead-level best. Do it excellently. If you do that with the little things, you'll probably soon find that you're getting more and bigger responsibilities. Then perform those with excellence. If you do this day in and day out, you'll stand out from the crowd who are pleased with their own mediocrity; they do just what's barely good enough. Your career will be better, and you'll thrive. Just commit yourself to excellence in all things. That's what I'd say."

Karolyne's Swearing-In

Karolyne had arranged to be sworn in on April 29, 2013, as a member of the Supreme Court Bar. That gray, rainy morning, we arrived at the Clerk of the Court's Office at 9:15. General Bill Suter greeted us warmly and said that the Court would be announcing two decisions that day at 10 o'clock. Then I would move Karolyne's admission.

"Normally," General Suter said, "we go in alphabetical order. But not today. Karolyne will be first. It's not often that Justice Scalia sponsors somebody."

"I'm honored, General Suter," she said.

"Bryan," he said, "here's the script. You can't depart from it one jot. The only thing you can add are the two words *my wife*. You can say '*my wife, Karolyne H. C. Garner*.' Otherwise, word for word. The Chief Justice insists."

"No departure at all?"

"Not one syllable. You can just read it."

"I couldn't possibly just read it. I'm a professional public speaker. I don't just read things. Besides, remember what Justice Scalia and I say in *Making Your Case*? 'Never read to the Court.' "

"You'll have plenty of time to memorize it. It's not long."

Other movants and candidates came into the room, and soon we were all being directed to go into the Court. I was seated at the front and center of the bar section, just behind the counsel table. Karolyne was seated to the left, near the press section to the Court's right—close to Nina Totenberg.

The Clerk of the Court gaveled in the Justices and called out, "All rise. The Honorable, the Chief Justice and the Associate Justices of the Supreme Court of the United States. Oyez, oyez, oyez! All persons having business before the Honorable, the Supreme Court of the United States, are admonished to draw near and give their attention, for the Court is now sitting. God save the United States and this Honorable Court!"

"Be seated," said Chief Justice Roberts. "Justice Alito will announce the decision in *McBurney v. Young*."

Realizing I still hadn't memorized my script, I took it from my pocket and started reading. I read it twice. Suddenly Justice Alito was finished speaking, and Chief Justice Roberts announced that there would be motions before the Court. He called out my name.

I stood, walked up to the lectern, and said: "I, Bryan A. Garner, a member of the Bar of the Supreme Court of the United States, hereby move the admission of my wife, Karolyne H. C. Garner, to the Bar of the Supreme Court of the United States. I am satisfied that the applicant possesses the necessary qualifications."

"Thank you," said the Chief Justice, calling the next movant. As I left the lectern, Justice Scalia and I exchanged smiles and nods. Then I looked at Justice Ginsburg, who smiled with her eyes and nodded at me.

Once all the motions had been made, the Chief Justice administered the oath to all the applicants collectively, saying: "Please repeat after me. 'I,' state your name, 'do solemnly swear . . . that as an attorney and as a counselor of this Court . . . I will conduct myself uprightly . . . and according to the law . . . and that I will support the Constitution of the United States.'" He then pronounced them members and congratulated them.

A marshal approached me with a handwritten note from Justice Scalia asking us to join him in chambers afterward for a Champagne toast. As usual, Angela met us at the Marshal's Office and took us back to chambers.

"Congratulations, Lyne!" Justice Scalia greeted her.

"Thank you."

"Excellent job, Bryan! Is that your first appearance before us?"

"Yes. I must say, it all happened very quickly. I had only about 60 seconds to memorize that motion."

"You did fine. Listen, Lyne, isn't Veuve Clicquot your favorite Champagne?"

She lit up. "It is. I'm flattered you remembered."

"I brought a bottle with me this morning. We've been chilling it, and I think it's cold enough." Raising his voice, he said, "Fernando—please bring in the Champagne!"

Angela walked in. "Justice, Professor and Mrs. Abraham are here as well. And the Court photographer." In walked the venerable law professor Henry J. Abraham, then 91, and his wife, Mildred. He had taught with Justice Scalia years before at the University of Virginia Law School. This was the first time Karolyne and I had met them.

Fernando brought in five glasses with the chilled Champagne. Justice Scalia uncorked the bottle and carefully poured the glasses, serving the women first. When all the glasses were filled, he raised his, saying, "To Karolyne H. C. Garner, the newest member of the Supreme Court Bar."

Everyone clinked glasses. Steve Petteway, the Court photographer, documented the celebratory event.

"Thank you, Justice," said Karolyne, obviously moved. "This is an honor. And thank you for the Champagne."

"Happy to do it," he said with obvious pleasure. "Oh, I have something for you." He went around to his desk and picked up a Supreme Court notecard on which he'd written with a fountain pen: "April 29, 2013. To Karolyne Cheng Garner—Admitted to the Bar of this Court on this date. Warm congratulations. Antonin Scalia." She got tears in her eyes when she read it, hugged him, and thanked him again.

"So what's next for you two?"

"We're off to L.A. at 3 o'clock," I said.

"Really? You don't have time for lunch?"

"I'm afraid not."

"That's okay. I have opinions to work on. You flew in just for this?"

"Yes," said Karolyne. "It was the only day we had available before the end of the term—while General Suter was still the Clerk."

"What's going on in L.A.?"

"I'm teaching a seminar for a law firm tomorrow."

"Boy, you must rack up those airline miles."

"Bryan's at nine million miles now with American Airlines," Karolyne said.

"I don't know how you do it," he said, shaking his head.

"You travel a lot, too, Nino, with all your speeches. Are you ever going to slow down?"

"I doubt it. I hope not." He beamed.

Hecht Yes!

Justice Scalia and I saw each other a couple of times during the summer of 2013. We made presentations on *Reading Law* in Washington and Brooklyn, and we spent some time in August working in his chambers on the second edition.

On September 10, Governor Rick Perry promoted our friend Justice Nathan Hecht of the Texas Supreme Court to chief justice. Shortly after, I received a call from Justice Hecht to ask whether I could help enlist Justice Scalia to travel down to Texas to swear in both him and Justice Jeff Brown, who were being installed at the same time. The scheduling was flexible, he said, according to Justice Scalia's calendar.

When I called to ask, Justice Scalia enthusiastically accepted the assignment, and we blocked out November 11. He would fly into Austin on the 10th, we'd have dinner, and then the swearing-in would be the afternoon of the 11th. As it happened, the new chief justice arranged for a dinner at a steakhouse the night before, with Justice Scalia, members of the Texas Supreme Court and their spouses, Karolyne, and me. Our group had a private room. It was a long festive evening—the kind that flies by despite efforts to savor every moment.

The next day, in the packed chamber of the Texas House of Representatives, Governor Perry introduced Justice Scalia, reading a prepared speech. He pronounced the first name as "Antone"—a mispronunciation reminiscent of President Reagan's introduction of "Antoine Scalia" when he nominated him to the Supreme Court.

In response to a note I wrote him that afternoon in which I mentioned Governor Perry's mangling of his first name, Justice Scalia wrote to me: "I really liked Governor Perry, despite what he did to my first name. Maybe that is just one of many respects in which he resembles the Gipper. Too bad he screwed up the presidential run so badly. I'm afraid it's irreparable."

A Word About Introductions

Over the years, Justice Scalia and I had many introductions—more than 40 of them. He liked them short and sweet, and he'd get restless and impatient if they dragged on, as they typically did: "Justice Scalia truly needs no introduction," followed by "He was born in Trenton, New Jersey . . ." and then a detailed excursus. If it was to be a long intro, it could be justified only by wit, as with the Battaglia introductions quoted earlier.

Judge Carlos Bea gave us a fascinating introduction in San Francisco on August 21, 2013, by reporting some data on *Reading Law*. During its first year in print, the book had been cited in 74 appellate decisions. By contrast, he said, a book on the same subject by a former colleague of Justice Scalia on the D.C. Circuit—a book in print for more than 15 years at the time he spoke—had been cited only 9 times by appellate courts. Judge Bea was a charming introducer, and he'd done his homework.

One of the most memorable introductions we ever had was the worst.

It was a law-school dean who sat with us beforehand, in the greenroom, but said nary a word. Mostly, Justice Scalia and I traded remarks about what was about to happen before the large audience that awaited. When the time came for us to begin, the aloof academician went out to introduce us. We stayed behind the curtains, as usual: we always liked to be offstage during introductions. The dean went through Justice Scalia's bio and then began introducing me. "Bryan Garner is the editor in chief of *Black's Law Dictionary*, the bane of every law student." The dean waited for a laugh, but there was only silence.

Backstage, Justice Scalia became incensed. "The bane?! The bane?! *Black's Law Dictionary* is the *blessing* of every law student! What kind of intro is *that*?"

Some in the audience could hear these offstage remarks. But Justice Scalia was never much concerned about whether something he felt strongly about might embarrass someone else—in this case the dean. He'd have thought the embarrassment deserved.

Another time it was my turn to be embarrassed.

Once when we were introduced at an event in Washington, D.C., we were handed nicely wrapped boxes. As soon as we finished and returned to the greenroom, Justice Scalia wanted to see what the gift was—in this case a dozen Honduran cigars, which delighted him. I stuck my box unopened into my suitcase.

Immediately after the event, I flew back to Dallas, where Karolyne and I were hosting an event for our friend Frank Stevenson, who was running for president of the State Bar of Texas. After introducing him, I announced to the 120 lawyers present: "This morning I gave a speech in Washington with my coauthor"—I didn't have to mention the name. "As a gift, we each received a dozen Honduran cigars. Anyone who'd like a cigar should join me on the terrace in ten minutes." When the moment came, eight or so people joined me on the terrace as I unwrapped the box.

But when I opened the box, it had only one cigar inside! One. My box was perfectly identical to Justice Scalia's, but while he'd gotten a dozen, I'd received one. I felt like Rodney Dangerfield. That's an occupational hazard for a Supreme Court coauthor. My compatriots that evening all thought it was hilarious. But no one laughed more robustly than Justice Scalia himself when he later heard about it. Several times he asked me to repeat the story for others, who always found it amusing as well.

Francis Ford Coppola's Food and Wine

While preparing for a presentation of *Reading Law* at the University of San Francisco, the organizer, an alumnus named Joshua Rosen, called my office to inquire whether Karolyne and I thought Justice Scalia might like to have lunch with Francis Ford Coppola. I relayed the query to Justice Scalia, who bellowed: "Of course! The first and second *Godfather* films are the best ever made." Soon it was all arranged: on January 30, 2014, we'd be having lunch at Coppola's San Francisco restaurant, Café Zoetrope.

The two men sat opposite each other at our table of ten, which in a way was fitting because they seemed so different in their views. Early in the conversation, Coppola brought up global warming. Probably eager to "teach against the class," Justice Scalia expressed doubts.

Maybe thinking he had the trump card, Coppola said, "If we're not sure about global warming, then what's the harm in acting to mitigate its effects?"

Justice Scalia responded, "At what cost to the American economy, or to economies around the globe? How many hundreds of billions of dollars are you willing to spend to affect the earth's temperature by perhaps half a degree over the next century?"

That pretty much ended this thread of the conversation. Justice Scalia appeared warm, jovial, amiable, and relaxed. Coppola seemed to me to be friendly, but reserved and a little standoffish. Perhaps I was misreading him at the outset, but that's how I saw him.

Things soon changed, though. Rosen stood at the end of the table and asked each of us to introduce ourselves and say something about our background and how it affected our current creative endeavors. I cringed because I was certain that Justice Scalia would react negatively to this request and simply wouldn't play along. But I couldn't have been more wrong. After five people went through a brief recitation, Coppola talked about his father's professional flute-playing with the NBC Orchestra (he and I both had professional flutists[48] as fathers), his upbringing in Queens,

---

48 Some might ask whether that shouldn't be *flautist*. In fact, *flutist* is the much older word in English (dating from the 17th century), and it predominates in both American print sources and World English print sources by a 2-to-1 margin. See *Garner's Modern English Usage* 397 (4th ed. 2016). Justice Scalia raised this point of usage over lunch,

and the rich artistic environment of New York City. Justice Scalia then reminisced about his own upbringing in Queens as the son of a Romance linguist, and how not only his parents but also his aunts and uncles had closely cultivated his education in every way. He had no cousins, he explained, so he was doted on by a very large family who kept him on the straight and narrow and wanted to ensure that his mind was thoroughly enriched.

I asked the two men whether, in Queens, they'd seen the old Italian parades of the kind depicted in *The Godfather*, with hundred-dollar bills stuck onto the Virgin Mary: "Absolutely!" said Justice Scalia. "And I've never seen a more accurate portrayal than in Francis's films!"

"Were you aware of Mafia bosses who extorted protection money from local businesses?" I asked.

"I knew absolutely nothing about that," said Justice Scalia. "I suppose I led a sheltered existence."

Coppola had thawed by now, and the two men were trading stories of their youth. Only three years separated them, Justice Scalia being the senior. The two had grown up only a few neighborhoods away from each other. Coppola professed that his politics were far to the left. But as with many others I'd seen, Coppola seemed disarmed by just how taken he was with Justice Scalia—a man who, from press accounts, he might have imagined to be a reactionary throwback.

A Third Book Together?

Soon after *Reading Law* appeared, I proposed to Justice Scalia that we should complete our trilogy with a book about judicial precedent. After all, we'd ended *Reading Law* with several pages devoted to the doctrine of precedent, and this subject did seem to be the final piece. We talked about it over several meetings. While I was enthusiastic, he was noncommittal— but then again that seemed to be our usual startup routine.

"Send me an outline," he said, "and I'll think about it."

It took me many months to prepare the outline, but finally I did. It had 188 sections—compared to 115 for *Making Your Case* and 70 for *Reading*

---

correctly supposing that *flutist* was the preferred form before I pronounced on the subject.

Law. The proposed 188 sections were research-intensive: I knew it would be a hard book to write.

I sent Justice Scalia the proposed outline. Then I called him.

"Nino, did you see the outline I sent?"

"Yes, Bryan, it's very impressive. Looks like a hell of a lot of work."

"Well, it will be."

"I think it's too hard. No way the two of us can research and write that."

"That's a shame. Did you see the publisher's offer?"

"Lookit, Bryan. You know I don't do these things for the money. I do them for the bar. I do them for the law. I do them because I enjoy working with you."

It was a firm no, which of course disappointed me. He said we could continue working together by keeping our other books up to date.

A couple of hours afterward, I had a small brainstorm, and I called him back.

"Nino, what if we tried something different here? What if we brought on a dozen or so state and federal appellate judges and had them draft 30 sections apiece? Then I'll do my own research and writing, and I'll edit their material, and then you'll scrutinize the result of that work so that you'd feel comfortable signing off on it—and you'd rework whatever you want to."

"You think circuit judges would go for that?"

"Sure they would. To be coauthors with you? Absolutely!"

"Who would you get?"

"Gorsuch of the Tenth Circuit."

"Oh, he's excellent."

"Bea of the Ninth Circuit."

"Excellent."

"And of course Alex Kozinski. And your former clerk Jeff Sutton of the Sixth Circuit."

"That's 4 of the 12 right there. You think they'd say yes?"

"I do—barring some unforeseen problem."

"Let me think about it."

I followed up this conversation with a letter in which I said: "We'll try to enlist people with clean prose styles compatible with our own. All the coordination will occur on my end, making more work for me and my staff. But it's work that I find most congenial. If we start with a good first draft, the painful part of book-writing will be minimized."

Justice Scalia took many months to mull over this fallback proposal. I tried not to rush him.

He called me in April 2014.

"Bryan, since 2008 we've talked about your helping me compile and edit my speeches into publishable form. Are you still willing?"

"Of course, Nino! I'm honored. Just have Angela bundle them all together and send them to me."

"Oh yes. I haven't gotten around to that."

"I can't wait to see them."

"I think you're going to like them."

"I'm sure I will. I'll dive right into that work, Nino . . . Have you given any more thought to our precedents book? We shouldn't let that project stall."

"If you're helping me on my speeches"—I felt it coming—"I don't want to do the precedents book."

"Okay," I said with resignation.

"The important thing is that we continue working together," he said. "We have to keep working together."

"Yes. We do like that, don't we?"

"It makes us happy." He liked that simple expression of sentiment, but he usually said *me*, not *us*. This was the first time I'd heard him say *It makes us happy*.

"You won't mind if I go it alone with the judges on the precedents book, will you? I haven't asked anyone yet. I was waiting for you."

"Of course I don't mind."

"Will you help me think of the people I should ask?"

"Sure. Gorsuch is on your list, right? Boy, I like him."

"Yes."

"And Alex Kozinski."

"Yes."

We spent perhaps ten minutes going through my list of possibilities. Sometimes, Justice Scalia would say, "No way! He doesn't believe in the doctrine of precedent!" Or: "Absolutely! Excellent." Or: "Are you kidding? Horrible."

He agreed with me that it should be a list of judges nominated by presidents from both parties—that the only defining characteristics should be a first-rate mind, a good prose style, and an abiding respect for precedent.[49]

---

49 In the end, my coauthors were Justice Neil M. Gorsuch (Justice Scalia's successor), Judge

Winners and Losers

In May 2014, Justice Scalia and I tried something new when appearing before the Federal Judges Association in Washington, D.C.: after our normal 90-minute presentation on 25 or so canons of construction, we gave the 200 participants a quiz, with prizes for correct answers. The plan was to pose realistic problems of statutory construction and to ask the participants to give both the correct answer and the correct rationale. Justice Scalia and I both had some trepidation about whether federal circuit and district judges would willingly submit to raising their hands, answering, and being declared, on the spot, either right or wrong. Perhaps Justice Scalia's worries were greater than mine, because I was the one pressing for this innovation in our lecture plan.

But it ended up working beautifully. I posed the problems on Power-Point slides so that the audience would both see them and hear them. Justice Scalia and I had worked out all the problems and solutions in advance—many of them in the book itself. When someone would volunteer an answer, Justice Scalia would declare it correct or incorrect (there were several of both types). Somewhat surprisingly, there were many hands in the air for each problem. The first correct answer for each problem won a copy of *Making Your Case*, and the winning judges were just about as excited as game-show participants. Everybody seemed to have a great deal of fun.

The problems we posed give some flavor of what our collaborative presentations were like. You might try your hand at them, though admittedly the correct rationales will be harder for someone who hasn't just sat through a presentation of the canons of construction providing the rationales. The correct answers follow, but for now, just focus on the questions.

Carlos Bea of the Ninth Circuit, Chief Justice Rebecca White Berch of the Supreme Court of Arizona (retired), Judge Harris L Hartz of the Tenth Circuit, Chief Justice Nathan L. Hecht of the Supreme Court of Texas, Judge Brett M. Kavanaugh of the D.C. Circuit, Judge Alex Kozinski of the Ninth Circuit (formerly chief judge), Judge Sandra L. Lynch of the First Circuit (formerly chief judge), Judge William H. Pryor Jr. of the Eleventh Circuit, Senior Judge Thomas M. Reavley of the Fifth Circuit, Judge Jeffrey S. Sutton of the Sixth Circuit, and Chief Judge Diane P. Wood of the Seventh Circuit. *See* Bryan A. Garner et al., *The Law of Judicial Precedent* (2016).

1.   A state contract freely permits a company to remove "gravel, sand, earth, or other material" from state-owned land. May the company harvest timber from state-owned land?

2.   A state constitution declares that superior-court judges are to be elected by both branches of the legislature. The state legislature enacts a statute allowing the governor to appoint superior-court judges. Is the statute constitutional?

3.   A 2008 statute makes it a felony to sell or offer to sell certain controlled substances. A 2011 statute makes the identical act a misdemeanor, which carries a less severe punishment. Is the act both a felony and a misdemeanor, or is it only a misdemeanor? What if the 2008 statute made it a misdemeanor and the 2011 statute a felony?

4.   The Hawaii Legislature enacts a statute irrevocably dedicating 25% of all state gasoline excise taxes to a special fund for construction of roads and bridges. A later statute diverts those tax receipts in the future to different purposes. Is the later statute effective?

5.   An 1884 constitutional charter for a university states: "Men and women are eligible to become members of fraternities and sororities." Last year, several women sued to become members of fraternities, and several men to become members of sororities. No precedent exists. How should a trial judge rule on a motion to dismiss, and why?

A judge who goes by the text, of course, would try to give the words their fairest reading, using well-recognized rules of interpretation. A purposivist or consequentialist would ask, in one way or another, how best to solve the problem, giving much less weight to the words—perhaps even in defiance of the words.

Here are the textualist's answers:

1.   No. The company may not harvest timber. The applicable rule is the *ejusdem generis* canon, which implies the word *similar* after the word *other*. This rule is treated in section 32 of *Reading Law*.

2. No. The statute is unconstitutional. The constitution specifies how superior-court judges are to take office—not including gubernatorial appointment. The governing rule is the negative-implication canon, which is treated in section 10 of *Reading Law*.

3. Although repeals by implication are disfavored (section 55 of *Reading Law*), a later statute that flatly contradicts an earlier one prevails. Here, the two provisions, and their concomitant penalties, are utterly inconsistent. Hence the later one prevails. The rule of lenity has no applicability because of the lack of ambiguity.

4. Yes. The earlier statute's prescription of irrevocability is invalid under the repealability canon: no legislature can bind its successors. This rule is treated in section 45 of *Reading Law*.

5. Dismiss the lawsuits. They are nonmeritorious under both the fixed-meaning canon (section 7 of *Reading Law*) and the distributive-phrasing canon (section 33). That is, (1) from 1884 to the present day, no one ever attributed the meaning that these students are now trying to attribute to the charter, and the meaning doesn't "evolve"; and (2) with the syntax and sense of the problem, the word *men* goes with *fraternities* and the word *women* goes with *sororities*.

The enthusiasm of our judicial participants dispelled any doubts we had about the value of ending with a participatory quiz. In fact, from that day on, we began our presentations by using the old joke that there would be a quiz at the end, but then insisting that we were entirely earnest in saying so. Every audience, whether judges or lawyers or law students, relished these little exercises.

By the way, our intent here wasn't to say that textualists invariably arrive at one and the same answer. That may be true *most* of the time, but admittedly it isn't true *all* the time. Our exercises posed straightforward questions that should yield consistent answers—unless, of course, the "interpreter" uses criteria other than textual ones.

The Appellate Judges Education Institute

We used the same technique later in 2014 at an annual summit for judges—this time held in Dallas. The interim dean of the SMU School of Law and a Fifth Circuit judge had come by my office some months earlier to see me about what might be the best approach for writing to invite Justice Scalia. After listening to possible scenarios to approach him, I said, "Why don't I call him now to see whether he's willing?" They were surprised but eager. I went back behind my desk to the phone and dialed not Angela's number, but the private number he'd given me—the one that rang only at his desk.

"Nino. It's Bryan. How *are* you?"

"Hello, Bryan! Long time no see."

"Did you get those reviews I sent you?"

"I *did*. Thank you. Are you coming up? When can we get together?"

"Not anytime soon. That's what I'm calling about. I have in my office the SMU law dean and Judge X of the Fifth Circuit."

"What do they want?"

"They want us to appear together."

"Good! When?"

"November 15 of this year. It's in Dallas."

"What's the group?"

"It's the Appellate Judges Education Institute—they go by the initialism AJEI."

"Good for you not calling that an acronym."

"Yes. We snoots know it's an initialism."

"Right, because the letters are sounded out individually. Is it a good group?"

"Quite reputable. I've spoken to them before. It's state and federal appellate judges. They'll reimburse you for expenses, of course, and I've told them you'll stay with Karolyne and me."

"I'd prefer that. We'll have more time together that way."

"Yes. And I'll personally cook your eggs for you."

"Ha! Excellent. November 15?"

"Right."

"I'm free. I'm putting it on the calendar. I have something here in D.C.

the 14th, so I may not get in until late on the 14th. Maybe quite late. Is that okay?"

"Of course, Nino. I'll stay up and wait for you. You're like an uncle to me. I've got to be sure you're comfortable."

"We'll do our normal routine on *Reading Law?*"

"Yes, with our normal deviations—to make it a little more fun."

"Looking forward to it. Hey, listen! Did I tell you I called Dick Posner?"

"No, why?"

"I hired one of his clerks, and I always give a courtesy call to the circuit judges whose clerks I hire just to let them know—and to have a friendly chat."

"Was it awkward at all?" I asked.

"No. Just like old times. Dick and I are friends. I like the guy—just not his style of judging!"

"Are you sure it's wise to hire one of his clerks? Is the clerk a textualist?"

"He's definitely a textualist—solidly in my camp, not in Posner's. Believe me, my current clerks vetted him thoroughly."

"Good. And I'm glad to hear you've spoken so warmly with Dick."

"It was a good feeling."

Within moments the dean and the judge had their headline event, and they seemed ecstatic.

When November 14 came around, Justice Scalia was to arrive at our house about 9:00 p.m. Karolyne and I would have just finished hosting a wine-tasting and library tour for AJEI participants at our house.

But Justice Scalia didn't arrive until 1:30 a.m. Exhausted, he went straight to bed and asked me to wake him up at 8 o'clock for breakfast.

As usual, I cooked the eggs, and Karolyne handled everything else. Justice Scalia came downstairs in his full suit, ready for a public appearance.

"How do you like your eggs?"

"I want *snotty* eggs—over easy," he said. "I like them snotty."

"Okay. That's the first time I've ever had that request. You want two or three?"

"Two will be perfect, Mr. Chef."

"And I'll time them well. I haven't forgotten that you like your eggs well timed." He was right there with me in the kitchen, standing beside me again as I heated the skillet. "Snotty eggs, huh?"

"That's what I always call them."

"It reminds me of a country-music song," I said.

"Which one?"

"Have you heard it? It's a love song. 'If my nose was running money, I'd blow it all on you. But honey, it's snot.'"

"Ha! That's funny. Where'd you get that?"

"No idea."

Over breakfast, I mentioned that we needed to sign two boxes' worth of books in the library before leaving for our presentation at a downtown hotel. The AJEI had sent them over so that board members could receive autographed copies. Of course, we'd also be staying for autographs after our session.

When we walked into the library, Justice Scalia immediately noticed something different.

"What have you done here?"

"I was wondering whether you'd notice."

"It's something, but the splendor of this room is so overwhelming I can't say exactly what it is."

"It's the 58 portraits newly hung around the base of the gallery. You see them?"

"Yes, that's beautiful. Who are they?"

"On the south side are 29 legal and literary figures—Shakespeare, Ben Jonson, Milton, Samuel Johnson, Dickens, Goethe, Galileo, Bentham, Emerson, and so on. I even have Samuel Pufendorf there at the end. But can't you recognize the portraits on the north side here?"

"Who are they?"

"I know you've had cataract surgery. With your new lenses, you should be able to see better despite your age," I joked.

"You had to mention that, didn't you?" he said, grinning. "Let's see, those are Supreme Court Justices."

"Right. But it's a select group. These are the 32 pre-1890 Supreme Court Justices whose opinions you and I cite with approval most frequently in *Reading Law*."

"You can't be serious," he said, gaping up at the portraits.

"It's true. And notice there are two portraits of John Marshall—and none for Taney."

"No Roger B. Taney?"

"I blackballed him because of the *Dred Scott* case," I said.

"He was a distinguished Justice otherwise," he said.

"Yes, but you know he played a big role in precipitating the Civil War. *Dred Scott* is a major blot on his record."

"Bryan, this is a one-of-a-kind display," he said warmly.

"Yes, the greatest 19th-century textualists."

"How did you get them?"

"Karolyne bought the portraits for me—a whole set of engravings done by Max and Albert Rosenthal of Philadelphia—father and son artists. During 1889–1890, they did etchings of all the Justices up to that time."

"Amazing. I don't think I've ever seen them," he said.

"I framed only about a third of them—only the ones you and I cite favorably."

"My goodness."

"The whole art installation was completed just this week, in time for last night's wine-tasting and library tour."

"You really do like *Reading Law*, don't you?"

"It's my favorite of the books I've worked on," I said.

"You can't be serious. *Black's Law Dictionary*? Your usage book, which is really your magnum opus?"

"Yes, but *Reading Law* is even more fun. I get to work with you."

"Well." He hesitated and cleared his throat. "Thank you. Let's get these books signed, and then we have a show to put on."

It was a big event in downtown Dallas, and the line for autographs was long. Afterward, he came back to the house for a couple of hours before flying to Boston. He wanted to read briefs among the *Reading Law* Justices in my library.

"I'm getting ready for a moot-court competition tomorrow at Harvard."

"Can I help you?" I asked.

"How could you possibly help me?" he asked.

"I can show you how to tell instantly whether they've followed our advice in *Making Your Case*."

"How can you possibly do that?"

"First, you look at the questions presented. If they're one-sentence *whether*-questions, they're probably incomprehensible. If they're set out briefly in separate sentences, as we recommend, the whole brief is likely to be pretty good."

"Seriously?"

"Yes. Second, you look at the table of contents. All you have to do is glance at the point headings to see whether, when the argument section begins, they're typeset in down-style, not initial caps or all-caps—and whether they're comprehensibly phrased. And see whether the page is attractive."

"We do say that in *Making Your Case*, don't we?" he asked me.

"Of course we do!" I answered. "Third, you glance at the conclusion. See whether it says, 'For the foregoing reasons,' or whether it gives a short, fresh summation."

"I can see what you're driving at," he said, nodding.

"Yes. Now, let's look at these two briefs you're reading. Aha! The petitioners have issue statements in sentence fragments beginning with *Whether*—they're incomprehensible. The respondents have reasonable-looking issues in a few succinct sentences. They're instantly readable. The petitioners have an awful table of contents. Look at that! It looks like a ransom note!"

"Ha! You're right."

"The respondents have a good table of contents," I said. "Now let's look at the conclusions. Ah. Just as I suspected. Both sides have perfunctory closers. That's the way it's taught at Harvard—almost as a dogma."

"How do you know that?"

"That's been the case for years. I've seen their moot-court materials."

"I should encourage them to change that. This is amazing. We've literally spent no more than two minutes with these briefs, and I can already tell that the respondents are the better writers."

The Original Originalist

After that visit, I kept up my usual travel schedule, visiting D.C. six times over the next four months. I saw Justice Scalia on all but one of those trips. When we'd have in-chambers time together, we'd eke out a difficult paragraph or two—almost always on *Reading Law*, as opposed to *Making Your Case*.

One afternoon in April, I asked him what he thought of the new stage play depicting him. It was called *The Originalist*, and both the lead actor (Ed Gero) and the play itself had received lots of national attention—mostly, it's fair to say, acclaim.

"It's *really* good," Justice Scalia said. "You ought to go see it. The actor who plays me, Ed Gero, has all my mannerisms down—the gestures, the walk, everything. His ancestors come from the same part of Italy as mine."

"Amazing. You've seen the performance?"

"No, but I've met the guy, and I really like him. I've had some clerks go, and one of my sons went."

"Is it a sympathetic portrayal?"

"Let's put it this way. Anyone who goes into the theater, whether they like me or hate me to begin with, leaves thinking better of me. That's all that matters to me. That's about as fair as you can get."

"That's good."

"You want to go?" he asked.

"Lyne and I could go tonight, but we're leaving tomorrow."

"Let me call and see whether I can get tickets. It's been sold out, you know."

He went over to his desk, picked up the phone, and said, "I think I've got his number here." Within seconds, he had Gero on the line: "Ed, it's Nino. My coauthor, Bryan Garner, is in town, and he and his wife would like to come see the play tonight. Can you help them get tickets? *Excellent.* They'll pay full freight, but get them the best tickets you can . . . Right. They'll pick them up at the box office. What's that? . . . Bryan, can you stay and meet him in his dressing room afterward?"

"Sure," I said.

"He can do that. Yes. Thanks, Ed."

It was an excellent performance. I could see why the play was so popular. Gero had indeed mastered many Scalian mannerisms: the protruding lower lip, the folded arms with hands grasping elbows, the determined walk with palms facing backward, the eyebrows going very high and very low. Afterward, Karolyne and I talked with Gero in his dressing room as he was taking off his makeup. He had pictures of Justice Scalia with all kinds of expressions posted around the dressing room; I took him to be a method actor.

Gero was affable and charming, and we exchanged contact information. He told me that in a few weeks, he'd be going skeet-shooting with Justice Scalia and his law clerks. I told him he'd love it.

When I called Justice Scalia the next day from Dallas, I told him how much Karolyne and I liked the play—and that I agreed with the assessment he'd been given. But I had two other reasons for calling. First, I wanted to schedule another work session on June 3. I had that full day free in D.C. He said he couldn't do it because he'd be taking his clerks skeet-shooting.

"With Ed Gero?" I asked.

"Yeah. It's going to be fun. Say, why don't you come along? The clerks would like that."

"Sure. I can make it."

The second reason for the call was that a *Dallas Morning News* reporter who was writing a profile of me wanted a comment from him.

"She wants to know why you like working with me."

"Why I like working with you?"

"Assuming you do. If you're willing. I know you're really busy, and I hesitated even to mention it."

"No, I'd like to make a statement about that. Can I just put it in an e-mail?"

"Sure."

"I'll have it to you shortly. Let me write it out now. You can forward it to her."

"That's very kind of you, Nino."

"Glad to do it. See you soon. Goodbye."

In about 30 minutes, his comment popped up in my mailbox.

Why do I enjoy working with Bryan Garner?

Several reasons: Perhaps most important of all, we agree on what is the object of textual interpretation. And I do mean entirely. He is the original Originalist.

Secondly, he makes me work hard. He is a tireless worker. I cannot imagine how he manages to write and edit all the books he does—and all of them first-rate.

And third, he is good company. Not only knowledgeable, but interesting and witty. Not what one expects of a philologist.

I sent this response on to the reporter, who then wanted me to interpret the first part of his answer, about being the "original Originalist," for a newspaper audience. My decoding: "Like me, Bryan is committed to the idea that judges should interpret and apply statutes and contracts as written—and as understood at the time they were written. Judges shouldn't imbue legal documents with their own visions of wise policy or economically efficient outcomes. To interpret isn't to distort or contort the words."[50]

Rainy Days

On June 2, the day before the scheduled skeet shoot, I taught a half-day writing seminar for a government agency and met Justice Scalia for lunch at the 701 Restaurant on Pennsylvania Avenue. Sitting at a secluded table when I arrived, he seemed downcast as I walked up to shake his hand.

"Hi, Bryan." He sounded gloomy.

"Hello, Nino. Everything okay?"

"I've already ordered you a glass of white wine. I hope you don't mind."

"Not at all."

"Listen, I've had to cancel the skeet shoot tomorrow," he said. "We'll be rained out."

"That's a shame," I said.

"Yeah, we'll have to reschedule for this year's clerks."

"Too bad. I guess I'll just miss out. I was looking forward to it."

"You're going to be in town tomorrow?" he asked.

"I have all day free," I said, "and then I teach again on Thursday."

"Why don't you spend the day with me in chambers? Do you have something for us to work on?"

"Sure. I've identified about five little problems I'd like to write something about in *Reading Law*. They need your close attention. And then I'd like us to look through *Making Your Case*."

"Yeah. We never go back to that book."

"Every time we do, we like what we see," I said, raising the glass of wine that had silently appeared before me.

"Right," he said, raising his, and then sipping.

"There's only one section that desperately needs your amplification," I said.

"What's that?"

"How to handle hypothetical questions at oral argument. I've heard

---

50 Cheryl Hall, "Expert Makes a Case to Clarify Fine Print," *Dallas Morning News*, 26 Apr. 2015, 1D, at 12D.

you say so much about it in speeches and conversation, yet in the book we devote only a measly half-page to it."

"Is that all we have? We should expand it. I agree."

We ordered lunch. He was more reticent than usual, his damp and pendulous lower lip protruding more than usual. He seemed dejected.

"Bryan, I want your advice about something."

"Sure."

"You know I can't talk about cases, and I never would."

"I know."

"I'm thinking about criticizing a colleague's writing style. You're something of an expert on judicial opinions. Do you think that sort of commentary is permissible?"

"Nino, for a stylist like you, it's almost irresistible," I said, "as it would be for me. That's especially so if the bad writing you're criticizing reflects bad thinking. You're a snoot. So the temptation is great."

"I'm thinking about saying I'd be mortified to join in such a badly written opinion."

"What?"

"I'm thinking about saying I'd rather put my head in a bag than join in such a badly written opinion."

"In those very words?" I asked.

"Yeah," he said.

"Ooh. That stings. Let me say this, Nino. I've never purported to advise you on things. You've been on the Court for 28 years. In your later years on the Court, you don't want to sound bitter. If you sound like a bitter old man, people will discount what you say. You *must* be magnanimous."

"I suppose you're right."

"I'm sure you think about your legacy sometimes. Direct insults can't be good—even if you're right on the merits. You should find a way to sound magnanimous."

"I'll think about it," he said.

Naturally, I was curious about what the opinion might be. Two weeks later, when I was back in my office in Dallas, Justice Scalia called with some other news about legal style: "Bryan, listen, I wanted you to hear it first from me. I'm going to be issuing an opinion with all citations in footnotes—your technique. It really does work well."

"Wonderful!" I said.

"I'm not adopting the technique across the board. In fact, it's just for this one opinion."

"Why are you doing it?"

"Because it'll be printed in newspapers, and I want people to *read* the damned thing. Citations would just get in the way. So I'm adopting your system in this one case. I thought you'd be pleased."

"I really am, Nino. It's a start toward getting you to see how much better it'd be if you did it in all your opinions."

"I'm not there yet."

"I know. But thanks for letting me know."

As it happened, these stylistic points all related to the same dissenting opinion, in the same-sex marriage case known as *Obergefell*. He ended up putting all his citations in footnotes. In the end, too, he couldn't resist the head-in-a-bag comment, although he relegated it to a (textual) footnote:

> *If, even as the price to be paid for a fifth vote, I ever joined an opinion for the Court that began: "The constitution promises liberty to all within its reach, a liberty that includes certain specific rights that allow persons, within a lawful realm, to define and express their identity," I would hide my head in a bag. The Supreme Court of the United States has descended from the disciplined legal reasoning of John Marshall and Joseph Story to the mystical aphorisms of the fortune cookie.[51]*

This made me think of the great laughter that Justice Scalia and I had enjoyed just four months earlier, when we opened fortune cookies after having Chinese takeout food for lunch in his chambers. His fortune had said, "Your coworkers take pleasure in your great sense of creativity." Somehow, I imagined that a majority of his coworkers *didn't* take great pleasure in this rhetorical rebuff.

The Meade Griffin Citation

The day after our lunch at 701 Restaurant, when he'd asked for my thoughts about the head-in-the-bag comment, we were working together in his chambers on *Reading Law*. I suggested that we begin by reviewing

---

51　*Obergefell v. Hodges*, 135 S.Ct. 2584, 2630 n.22 (2015).

all our additions to the book since the first edition was published in 2012. Then we would set to work on the heavy lifting, tackling some new legal puzzles I'd brought with me that day. He stopped pretty early in the preface.

"Bryan, you're including some unnecessary citations!"

"I don't know what you mean, Nino. It's all pertinent, and it adds scholarly depth."

"For example, you've added this Texas Supreme Court case to the preface. Cut it! We don't need a state supreme court."

"Nino, that's my grandfather—my mother's father. Notice that the citation says 'Griffin, J.' at the end. My grandfather, Meade Felix Griffin, was on the Texas Supreme Court for 20 years." Justice Scalia was listening intently. I continued: "A couple of months ago, I decided to see whether my grandfather ever said anything about statutory construction. He was a conservative judge. He believed in stare decisis. It's not a perfect sentence that he wrote, but it's pretty good in saying that the court shouldn't rewrite statutes: 'It is not the duty of the court to write the laws of our state, but the proper function of the courts is to enforce the laws as made by the Legislature.'[52] Please, Nino, let me cite my grandfather."

"Well, I see now. If my grandfather had written anything on statutory construction, I'd damn well want to cite it. Of course we'll keep it."

"Thank you for understanding, Nino."

"You've done well. Judge Griffin must stay." We smiled at each other.

Doppelgänger

That evening, I had planned dinner with Ed Gero, the actor in *The Originalist*, at the Cosmos Club—just the two of us. In the middle of the afternoon, as Justice Scalia and I were writing some tricky paragraphs, I asked him whether he'd like to join us. Yes, he said. So at 6:00 p.m. the marshals took us to the Club—a place where Justice Scalia had lived for six months during the Nixon administration—and we met up with Ed for a lively evening of conversation about theater and the law. The high point

---

52 *Central Educ. Agency v. Independent Sch. Dist. of City of El Paso*, 254 S.W.2d 357, 361 (Tex. 1953) (per Griffin J.).

came when two elderly couples were leaving. Justice Scalia was facing them, and Ed's back was to them as they walked by. Upon seeing Justice Scalia, one of the women stopped and said, "Forgive me for interrupting, but I want you to know how much I enjoyed your show. You were really good!"

Laughing, I said: "This is Justice Scalia himself. And here's the actor over here—Ed Gero."

The three of us laughed over that, and so did the woman, who lingered for a moment after I told her that Justice Scalia hadn't seen the play. She reassured him that it was a most endearing representation of him.

A Hack Job

I didn't see a great deal of Justice Scalia during the summer and early fall of 2015. In July, he sent me his *Daily Missal* for repair: it's an early-20th-century book full of Latin prayers he'd say each day. That explained to me, for the first time, why he was so conversant with Latin, particularly spoken Latin: he was reading it—and probably reading it aloud—every single day. His leatherbound missal had become frayed, and the leather had separated from the boards. Knowing that I had various book presses and book-repair materials, as well as friends in the book-repair business who could help if necessary, he sent me the book. This was an easy job I could do on my own, requiring only some special book glue and some time in a book press, together with some careful trimming with fine scissors. I soon returned it to him as good as new.

On August 25, he wrote to me: "Bryan: Many thanks for the wonderfully restored Missal. I will try to make it last for the time left. We don't have a gig together until November. I hope we will see each other before then. I miss you guys. Regards to Lyne. Nino."

After we arranged two dinners in D.C. in early October, on the 4th and the 6th, a funny thing happened. He received a bizarre e-mail message from me, with the subject line "Trip." It was strangely written and mispunctuated (replete with typos and a comma splice):

I really hope you get this fast as I could not inform everyone about my trip to Philippines for a conference. I had my phone and other items stolen from me here on my way back to my Hotel room, I've tried to sort

thing out with the necessary authorities but my return flight will be be
[sic] *leaving soon. I need an urgent assistance from you. Let me know if*
you can be of any help.

                                                            Bryan

Shortly after receiving this, Justice Scalia responded, asking whether I'd
sent it. "Sounds like a scam," he said.

That day, I was teaching in South Carolina, and I didn't receive his
e-mail message for several hours. He followed up with a phone call to
LawProse, telling Karolyne he was concerned that he hadn't heard back
from me. It was the first she had heard about my Philippine escapade.
Justice Scalia said he'd happily do anything he could for me, including
wiring money. He mentioned that the message seemed very unlike me,
even if I were sending it from a jail cell in Manila: he couldn't imagine
my committing such grammatical blunders even if I were in extremis.
Karolyne assured him that my e-mail account must have been hacked,
and that my biggest worry that day was extricating myself from the
Charleston floods. She told me later that day that he'd sounded seriously
concerned, and she could hear the sigh of relief when he found out I was
all right.

Scalia on Law, Civics, and Religion

Not long after this, Justice Scalia finally sent me all his speeches to collect
and edit—nearly 200 of them. I soon set to work sorting them into three
broad categories: law, civics, and religion. They were stunningly good, and
I thought they'd make an excellent three-volume boxed set. Perhaps we'd
come out with one volume per year, selling them individually, until we
had the full set for bundling. In my judgment they surpassed in quality
any collection of speeches I'd seen published before. But some didn't have
titles, and they needed at least a little bit of his attention. We talked several
times about my plan, and he agreed in principle with my categories and
with the idea that the volume on religion should come last—probably posthumously. Although I told him that I'd do the editorial work as his friend,
he insisted that I should receive part of the royalties.

"It's a lot of work!" he said.

"We'll see," I responded. "Just help me with titles and see whether you like the order I've put them in."

"You like the speeches?"

"They're brilliant, Nino. I've never seen anything like this collection of speeches. And I have probably 500 volumes of collected speeches."

"Okay, I'll get on it this summer. They are good, aren't they? Heh, heh. I do work hard on the speeches I give."

9

Preparing for Asia

(2015–2016)

Karolyne and I had traveled to Hong Kong in 2010, 2012, and 2014. Just as Justice Scalia liked to regale us with brief accounts of his international travels, to Galway or Innsbruck or Florence, we'd tell him about ours—especially the ones to Hong Kong, involving Karolyne's many aunts and uncles there, the superb cuisine, the excellent shopping, and the tailor-made clothing.

Beginning about 2013, he told us that he wanted to travel with us to Hong Kong. At first I suppose we thought of this as idle talk or remote reverie, but soon it became a recurrent topic of conversation. Finally he said, "I *really* want to go to Hong Kong with you. We could do a speaking tour." As in that very statement, the speaking engagements were an afterthought—a kind of excuse to make the trip.

I said I'd try to line up something through our publisher, Thomson Reuters. Unfortunately, my first phone call with their head of legal marketing in Asia—carefully arranged through American channels—proved futile. He was German, and he seemed completely uninformed about American law and the U.S. Supreme Court—and perhaps a little anti-American. "You have an American judge who wants to speak in Asia? There are lots of American judges, I'm sure, but what makes you think an Asian audience would have any interest?"

I answered: "He's not just *an* American judge. He's probably the most famous judge in the world. People turn out everywhere to hear him." Although I may have sounded hyperbolic, I also felt certain I was speaking truth.

"I can't imagine moving forward on this," he replied. "It wouldn't be profitable for the company, and American law is *very* different from Chinese law. Totally different system. But thank you for your interest."

The call was so perplexing and dumbfounding that I never told Justice Scalia about it. Our American contacts at Thomson Reuters suggested that we make a joint appearance in London. That would be easy to arrange. I called Justice Scalia to suggest it.

"I don't want to go to London," he said. "I can always go to London. I want to go to Hong Kong with you and Lyne. I want to meet her family there and see how it's changed in the quarter century since I was last there. I want to get tailor-made suits there."

"Okay, Nino," I said, "I'm working on it."

As luck would have it, in the fall of 2014 Justice Scalia received an invitation from Simon Chesterman, dean of the law school at the National University of Singapore. He wanted Justice Scalia to speak in late 2015 or 2016. When Justice Scalia showed me the letter in chambers one day, he suggested that we coordinate the trip with our long-desired week in Hong Kong. Although the invitation was for Justice Scalia alone, he said he'd like to see whether we could arrange a joint presentation for the two of us in Singapore. And soon he had done so: the Supreme Court of Singapore, at the suggestion of Dean Chesterman, invited the two of us to speak about *Making Your Case* in the Court's huge auditorium.

In the end, we settled on dates in late January and early February 2016. That timing was convenient for his Court schedule, for Karolyne's family, and for Karolyne and me with our LawProse commitments. It was also right before the Chinese New Year celebrations, meaning that we'd see lots of festooned streets and buildings, but we'd be gone before all the mad revelry itself would begin.

Soon, with the help of Tom Leighton at Thomson Reuters (no longer working through the head of Asian marketing), we also had invitations from both the University of Hong Kong and the Chinese University of Hong Kong to make presentations. At the latter affair, I would be interviewing a retired justice of the High Court of Hong Kong along with Justice Scalia. Our third presentation in Hong Kong was to be at the offices of Thomson Reuters, where we would discuss book authorship and the nature of our collaborations.

Tailoring Our Plans

About six months before the trip, I told Justice Scalia that we must find a good D.C. tailor.

"Why?"

"We need to get shirts made."

"But why?"

"So copies can be made in China."

"Aren't the Chinese tailors going to measure us?"

"Yes. That's for suits. For shirts, it's better to have them made in advance."

"I don't understand."

"We'll spend about $200 on a tailor-made shirt in D.C., and we'll get it made exactly as you want it—an inch longer than usual, French cuffs if you like, the precise style of collar you'd like, the extra button on the arm vents, and so on."

"Why can't we do that in Hong Kong?"

"We could, but that would cost about $100 a shirt. Lyne's aunt Jenny can go into mainland China and have ten of these shirts made—precisely to your specifications—for $200."

"You're kidding."

"And they're the finest fabrics—all whites and blues, but superbly woven cottons. My favorite is Egyptian cotton."

"Why not just send her our measurements?"

"That's risky," I said. "It doesn't work, I promise you. It's better to send them a well-tailored shirt that they can mimic in every detail. That way it'll be perfect for you."

"Huh."

"You'll have ten tailored shirts for $400—$200 for the first shirt here, and $200 for the ten in China. Otherwise, it'd cost you over $2,000."

"Won't I have eleven, counting the one I get made here?"

"No. That one will be destroyed in preparing the pattern for the other ten."

"But why can't we do it all there? I want to see the whole process!"

"No, you don't, Nino. It'd waste a whole day, and you'd have to get a special visa for mainland China. The way we're planning it, Jenny will have our shirts ready for us when we arrive. We can wear them to our events in Hong Kong."

"Ah. And they're only 10% of the cost of American-made shirts?"

"If they're tailor-made, right. Karolyne's mother, Sandra, gives me shirts like that every Christmas. One year, we sent only the measurements, and the shirts didn't fit at all. They were comically bad. We have to send tailor-made shirts for the pattern."

"But I don't have a tailor in D.C."

"I'll find one for us. Mine is in New York, but we're not going there together anytime soon. Let me find a tailor for us in D.C., and we'll do it together. It'll be fun. Just one more little adventure."

On a flight to D.C., a month or so later, Karolyne and I sat near Ben Barnes, the former lieutenant governor of Texas and an old acquaintance of mine. We struck up a conversation at the baggage claim, and I asked the well-accoutered man about his tailor. He recommended Christopher Kim on M Street.

One afternoon, while Justice Scalia and I were working together in chambers on the second edition of *Reading Law*, I suggested that we go to Mr. Kim's to get our shirts made before meeting Karolyne for dinner. He was enthusiastic. Angela called ahead so that Mr. Kim would be expecting us. The large shop was crammed full of racks of suits, shirts, and fabrics, and we were the only customers there for a full hour. We both chose white shirts with the same style of collar, and we each bought two—one to wear and one to be copied in China. We had one of Justice Scalia's shirts sent to my office so that I could send it on to Jenny with one of mine.

Looking at some suits, Justice Scalia asked whether our Hong Kong suits would be as well made as Mr. Kim's. Yes, I assured him, at a third of the cost—or maybe less.

"I've never had a bespoke suit," he said. "I'm excited about Hong Kong."

"Me, too," I said.

San Antonio

In November 2015, Justice Scalia and I made a joint presentation in San Antonio for the annual conference called the General Counsel Forum, at La Cantera Hill Country Resort. Karolyne and I took an early flight from

Dallas on the morning of the presentation and met Justice Scalia for breakfast in the resort's restaurant.

"Long time no see!" he said as we approached him. He was having coffee. "I'm just trying to decide what to have for breakfast. It's the most important meal of the day, you know."

"You've indoctrinated me to that point of view," I said. "I'll bet you can get a Mexican breakfast here. That's the best."

"No way. Too mushy! I don't like mushy!"

"Then go for American. But snotty eggs seem pretty mushy to me! How's the term shaping up?"

"It's going fine. What have you been working on?"

"Apart from the second edition of *Reading Law*? I'm closing in on the precedents book, which should be out next year. You know, it's the one you backed out of," I said, nudging him with my elbow. Karolyne smirked.

"You're almost done with it?"

"Almost, and it's going to be superb. You won't believe the amount of research that my twelve coauthors did. It's going to be over 800 pages."

"Lookit, Bryan, if you're trying to make me jealous, it's not working."

"Come on, Nino. It's nothing like working with you. I haven't had any sessions at all with them personally—except two hours with your former clerk Jeff Sutton. It's all been through e-mail."

He was silent. I was sensing jealousy. I added: "You know, Nino, nothing else in my life could be like working with you. Our sessions together have been the experience of a lifetime. You've changed my life. I'm the only person in the history of the nation who's coauthored a book with a sitting Justice. Uh, make that two books. And of course you've changed Lyne's life."

"Just knowing you," Karolyne said.

"Well, I've appreciated being close to both of you. Have you decided on breakfast? I'm *hungry!*"

"Just don't be *hangry*," I said. "You know that word?"

"What? *Hangry*? Angry because you're hungry?"

"Right. It's a portmanteau word."

"Okay. *Let's order!*"

We did. Soon we were talking about our Hong Kong trip, just two months away.

As we finished our breakfast, I changed the subject.

"Nino, Lyne brought along 42 books to sign. You know how people are always asking us to sign books."

"Where are they?" he asked.

"In her purse," I said.

"You're joking," he said, turning to Karolyne. "What's he talking about?"

"I ordered some bookplates that we can use in a pinch," she said. "Why don't you two sign them while I go check on the room?"

So we did. We were both using fountain pens. His was black, mine red. When he saw that, he said, "Don't you have another color? Red's no good for signing books." So I changed to blue for my last 38 signatures.

"I don't know what you have against red," I said. "It's a great color."

"I don't want to sign in black," he said sportively, "alongside a coauthor who signs in red. You might as well wear two-tone shoes when we lecture together."

Our San Antonio presentation went smoothly, and soon we were saying goodbye. It was perhaps the shortest meeting we ever had on the day of a joint presentation. But it was still enjoyable, and we all left feeling enthusiastic about our trip to Singapore and Hong Kong.

Change of Travel Plans

On the morning of Thursday, January 21, four days before our departure for Asia, a call came into the office. "It's Justice Scalia," my assistant said. I picked up, and it was Angela.

"Hi, Bryan. This is Angela. Please hold for the Justice."

"Sure."

With hardly a pause, he came on: "Hi, Bryan! Listen, I've got a problem. The blizzard is coming into Washington, and if I don't get out of here on Friday, I may not make it out at all. The airport's probably going to close tomorrow afternoon, and then our whole trip may have to be postponed."

"Come down to Dallas early. Fly down tomorrow morning."

"Would that be okay?"

"Sure. We'll just have an extra day together here in Dallas. Karolyne and I are hosting a reception at the house tomorrow night, and then of course on Saturday we're having dinner with Chief Justice Hecht of the Texas Supreme Court and Harriet Miers. You know Harriet."

"Yes. Sounds good."

"Otherwise, we'll just do whatever you like—perhaps work on *Reading Law*. I have a few little assignments for you."

"I can do a little of that, but you know I have work to do on opinions."

"I'll set you up in the library. And we can do some last-minute things to get ready for the trip. This'll be great. How soon can you get here tomorrow?"

"I'm checking. But if this snowstorm shuts down the airport before I get out, everything's going to be thrown off kilter."

"Let's get you out of there early."

Karolyne teamed up with Angela, and soon Justice Scalia was set to fly the next day.

I knew that U.S. marshals would be coming by the house: this would be the third time that Justice Scalia had stayed with us. But unlike the other times, we had no events scheduled for him in advance, apart from Saturday's Hecht–Miers dinner. Karolyne and I would have to keep him productively entertained and otherwise well rested. The Sunday flight to Hong Kong would be in business class, so the seats would lie flat for sleeping. Even so, 16 hours on a transpacific flight to Hong Kong—followed by another 4-hour flight to Singapore—would tax anyone.

Oh, and breakfast! His most important meal, as we well knew: we must have eggs and sausage for Saturday and Sunday. And oh again! We must find a Sunday Mass for him. We'd have two Sundays with him, in Dallas and in Hong Kong, and he'd want traditional Masses—preferably in Latin, if we could find them.

On Friday, Justice Scalia would arrive just before midday. Karolyne and I spent the morning at LawProse. For me, it was snoot-time: this was the final window of opportunity to approve page proofs for my new book, *The Chicago Guide to Grammar, Usage, and Punctuation*. I was eager to show it to Justice Scalia. Along with tables, sentence diagrams, and other graphic elements, the book sports many Scalia-inspired shaded boxes: choice quotations from scholarly literature interspersed throughout the text.

"Bryan, you're going to be late!" Karolyne said about 11:15 a.m. "The Justice will be landing any minute!"

"Have you verified that with Angela?"

"No, I checked the flight status online. Go home!"

"I just have to get my final printout of *The Chicago Guide* to show him.

You know it's going to press today. We're sending it through to Chicago now."

"I'll bring your copy home with me. Go! Make sure his room is ready. Make sure he has shampoo and conditioner."

Justice Scalia's Arrival

My dash home took ten minutes. No marshal was out front. I went straight up to the second-story pink bedroom where Justice Scalia always stayed. The window looks out onto the front yard. Once there, I saw that now there was a marshal's car in our front cross-drive near the street. I made sure Justice Scalia had plenty of bottled water, and I noticed that Karolyne had put a bottle of Campari on his side desk. Shampoo? Check. Conditioner? Check.

I walked out the front door to see the marshal. He emerged as I approached his car.

"Hello," I said. "Good to have you here. I'm Bryan Garner." We shook hands. He was a young marshal I hadn't met before, perhaps in his mid-30s. "Is he close yet?" I asked.

"He just landed. He'll be here about seven minutes after he gets into the car." The marshals always had precise times, down to the minute.

"Excellent. Let me know what I can do for you while you're here. Do you need water? Would you like a Diet Dr Pepper? I have plenty of those."

"No thank you, sir. We have everything we need."

"Will a marshal be here at all times?"

"Yes."

"Front and back? Is there somebody stationed in the alley?"

"Intermittently. We'll be checking on the house, but we won't disturb you."

"Do you sleep in the car out here?"

"No, sir. We take shifts. We're set up in a hotel room nearby, so we get to sleep. But when we're here, we're awake and alert."

His phone rang. "Roger." It was 11:35.

"He's on his way."

"Thank you. I'll be right out when he drives up. Thanks for your help this weekend."

"No problem, sir."

I went in, made some coffee, plumped the couch pillows, and otherwise made ready. I had prepared two matching accordion folders of 23 law-review articles for us to review together: one labeled "Justice Scalia—Asia 2016" and the other labeled "BAG—Asia 2016." The contents were identical. The articles contained commentary on *Reading Law*, some laudatory and some critical. I figured these articles would give us plenty of fodder. Mind you, we had already added some 55 pages of new material for the second edition of *Reading Law*, so at this point we merely needed to add finishing touches. We planned to bring out the second edition in the fall of 2016.

As his car pulled up in the front drive, I walked out.

"Hello, Bryan!" He was in a full suit, as always, with a dapper gold-and-blue tie. He looked as if he might have shed some weight. His complexion was rubicund from the cheeks down, a little whitish in the forehead.

"Hello, Nino! How was your trip?" We shook hands and walked into the house to the front foyer, accompanied by two marshals.

"Good, but that food on Virgin America isn't what it's cracked up to be."

"No? That's a shame. What was it?"

"Some kind of curry. I didn't like it. Mushy. Boy, I got the last flight out of D.C. The very last one. I think they shut down the airport ten minutes after we took off. I'm really, really lucky to have gotten out."

"You wouldn't believe it from the weather here in Dallas, would you?"

"It's beautiful here. A world of difference. I built a fire for Maureen. It should last her at least 36 hours. It's a big one. I hated leaving her. I feel bad about it. At least I built a fire."

"Excellent."

"Where's Lyne?"

"Still at the office. She has lots to do this afternoon before we leave."

"What are we going to do?"

"On this extra day? Guy stuff, I figure. Maybe you need a haircut."

"A haircut? Are you serious?"

"You're getting a little shaggy, and so am I. Let's get a haircut." The truth was that I needed one badly—but I could see that he did, too.

"Okay. Nobody but my regular guy in Washington has cut my hair in, let's see, 30 years."

"I've got a great barber. It's an old-fashioned barbershop. You'll like it."

"But I'm a little tired after that flight."

"You want a nap?"

"I want a nap," Justice Scalia said emphatically, stressing each word. He would often respond to a question in just that way, echoing the question but with avuncular, jovial emphasis. "When can we get a haircut?"

"How about tomorrow morning?" I said.

I turned to Ralph Tenorio, the senior U.S. marshal in the area, a man I'd known for years. Ralph wanted to know the particulars about the barber and the shop so he could make arrangements. Justice Scalia listened as we went through the immediate itinerary.

"We'll be having dinner here tonight. I have three guests coming at 5:00 p.m. for wine and cheese, and then we have a Trinity University alumni reception at 7:00."

"Am I expected to go to *that*?" Justice Scalia objected. "An alumni reception?"

"No, Nino. We've just had it on the books for quite some time."

"Well, I don't want to be part of that. Is it a fundraiser?"

"Yes."

"I *can't* do that. I'll work in my room. I have opinions . . ."

"Of course. We'll be having barbecue, and we'll bring a plate to your room. How does that sound?"

"Barbecue? Sounds good."

"It's from Sonny Bryan's. You'll like it. Promise."

"So you won't be leaving the house tonight?" Ralph asked.

"Right. We're set for the afternoon and evening."

"What about tomorrow morning?" Ralph wanted to nail down all the logistics.

"We'll have breakfast at Angela's Cafe, just 300 yards to the south of us. Is 8 o'clock okay for breakfast?" I asked Justice Scalia.

"Sure."

I turned to Ralph. "Then we'll leave about 9:50 for a 10:00 haircut. I'll get you information on the barber first thing in the morning. You can make sure his chair is open at 10:00, I think."

"Right." The U.S. marshals always needed to know our movements an hour or so in advance, especially for restaurants. I figured I'd call Ivan, my barber, to tell him what was going on.

"So we'll get our hair cut, Nino, and then we'll have lunch. If you need anything for the trip, we can pick it up. Then, in the afternoon, we'll work on *Reading Law.*"

"Oh, great."

"I have a few difficult problems for us to work through."

"I need a nap."

"Sure. You're in the pink bedroom, as usual. Let me take that." I reached for his garment bag.

"I can carry that!"

"Well, then, let me put your suitcase and briefcase on the elevator. And your garment bag, too. It'll all go up together, just outside your room."

"Thank you, men," Justice Scalia said to the marshals.

I led him up to his room. "I have to say it again, Bryan: this is a beautiful house."

"Thank you."

He paused on the top landing to see the Supreme Court bobbleheads. "I have those, you know. I keep them all together on a windowsill in my office."

"I've seen them."

"I keep your bobblehead behind my computer," he said. "You're not a Justice, so you're not on the windowsill. But I see you more frequently there by my computer screen."

"That's touching. Here's the picture where you married us. Remember that great day?"

"I do indeed! What's this over here?" He was looking at a framed note on the wall. "Is that my handwriting?"

"That's a note you sent down from the bench—a note to Karolyne to come back and see you in chambers at an oral argument. It was shortly after you married us. She was so proud to get that note that she framed it."

"She's really sweet. Now let me get some sleep. Oh, when will I see her?"

"About 5:30."

He gave a single nod and said, "When I get up I'll need to call Maureen. I want to make sure the fire is doing well."

Frozen Shoulder

With Justice Scalia ensconced in his room and marshals out front, all was quiet. I went to the library to figure out precisely which statutory-interpretation problems we most urgently needed to work through for *Reading Law*. There was no doubt: the series-qualifier canon (for example, in *unreasonable searches and seizures*, the adjective *unreasonable* modifies both nouns—*seizures* as well as *searches*) and the so-called rule of the last antecedent (if the phrase were *searches and seizures that are unreasonable*, would *that are unreasonable* modify only *seizures*, or would it also modify *searches*?). We had encountered some scholarly criticism for aspects of our treatment of these issues in the first edition, and we intended to improve our analysis in the second edition. We had our work cut out for us. I put four articles in order for him.

At 3:30 he was stirring. I knocked on his door. "Nino, you need anything?"

"No, I'll call Maureen and be out in about 15 minutes."

"Sure thing."

Rarely do I find myself just doing busywork, tidying up the library and so on, but at moments like this, with Justice Scalia in the house, I felt as if I was in a holding pattern. He emerged just before 4 p.m. saying that he'd hurt his shoulder.

"I have frozen shoulder. I've been diagnosed. I don't have much range of motion. Look at this: I can't serve a tennis ball." He pantomimed a tennis serve and then grimaced in pain.

"I know all about frozen shoulder," I said. "My dad had it. He cured it through simple exercises. I do them every day. Did your doctor show you how?"

"Yes, progressively up the wall?"

"Right. Would you like a little workout?"

"I think I need one."

"I'll be your trainer."

We walked downstairs to the workout room. "This is a great gym," he said.

"Thanks. We've gotten some new equipment since you were here last. But this exercise requires no equipment—just a door opening. Did your doctor show you how to start with your hand here and go up a little at a time?"

"Yes." He tried the exercise, but he was rushing it.

"Slow down. Put slow but constant pressure as you lean forward, like this." I showed him, and he tried but was obviously in pain.

"Don't rush it, Nino. You know, my father is a band and orchestra conductor. In the early 1990s, he developed frozen shoulder. There are little adhesions, bony adhesions in the shoulder, that have to be broken a little at a time. With the exercises, it might take over a year for them to break. With my father, it took 15 months. If that doesn't work, they'll put you under and violently break the adhesions. But exercise is better."

"Put me under and break them! I want it fixed now."

"Believe me, the exercises are better. It may be a bit painful, but slow and steady every day will get the job done."

He was impatient. "I've had enough," he said after about 60 seconds. "What else do you have?"

"Here's a medicine ball. Try this." I handed it over. "Can you go from side to side?"

"Sure. No problem." He moved it back and forth just above waist level. "Can you raise it beside your head? Do it slowly." On the left side he could do it, but not on the right. He was exasperated, and he tended to try to jerk the ball up.

"Slow and steady, Nino."

"I can't lift it on the right! I just can't do it. What else do you have?"

"This is an elliptical machine. Why don't you try it?" I figured he'd seen one before, but they're not all the same. He tried it for 30 seconds but was soon off.

"I don't like that."

"Good thing I didn't buy you one of those. Do you remember I was going to get you one?"

"You were?"

"Yes. But we agreed it might be embarrassing to disclose that as a gift— and you said you might not use it anyway."

"Yeah, that's right."

"There's a recumbent bicycle you could try, and a treadmill, but why don't we try some weights?"

On the weight machine, he had no trouble pulling weights from side to side or even pulling them down, as long as he didn't have to reach as high as his head. I put it on the lightest weight possible.

"This is really good! This is what I need." He did five reps.

"I need more of it myself. I wish I spent more time in here."

"Enough of this. What's next?"

"I have three friends coming over for wine and cheese. They're partners at a major firm here in town. They're literary guys, and we get together every so often just to talk about literary things. I hope you'll join us. They proved very useful when you and I were working on *Reading Law*. I ran lots of ideas past them. I think you'll like them."

"Good. I'll do that. But the fundraiser I can't do, so I'll be in my room for that."

We went down to the wine cellar to pick a bottle of wine—an Italian red—then back up to the kitchen. I had bought some artisanal cheeses. As I prepped the cheese and uncorked the wine bottle, Justice Scalia sat at the bar sipping club soda. I told him about our guests—Steve Fink, Herb Hammond, and Bruce Sostek—and explained that we'd spend an hour or so talking in the library. I left Justice Scalia to sample the cheeses while I went outside to tell the marshals the identities of our three guests. Not that our guests would be stopped as they approached, but I figured the marshals would prefer to know who would be coming in. I also took a roster of the Trinity University alumni who would be attending that evening and told them the name of the valet company that would be parking cars.

Steve and Herb arrived promptly at 5:00, and soon after came Bruce—on crutches. He was still recovering from hip-replacement surgery, and sadly, he wouldn't be able to take up running again. As we stood in the kitchen sampling cheeses, Bruce regaled us with a story about the surgery and the pain meds that kept him delirious for several days afterward. Bruce's wife, also a lawyer, had to keep him from trying to work while he was more or less hallucinatory. As we walked into the library, Justice Scalia asked Bruce several questions about the surgery. Then he talked about his shoulder problem, saying he might not be able to continue playing tennis if it didn't get fixed.

We also spoke of law, law practice, legal interpretation, the marshals parked out front, and the upcoming trip to Asia. Soon Karolyne arrived home and got hugs from everyone. Justice Scalia told her, "I've been wondering when I'd see you!"

Toward the end of our visit, I mentioned Justice Scalia's experience as a teenage etiquette maven on New York City television during the 1950s. "Yeah," he said, "they'd put up four of us teenagers at the Algonquin Hotel on 44th Street. We were local celebrities. They'd give us a situation involving teenage behavior and ask our opinions about it. Who knows, if

I'd stuck with television, I might have amounted to something!" Everyone laughed.

By 6:30, the valets had arrived, our servers were bustling in the kitchen, and an early contingent from Trinity had arrived. "We'd better get you up to your hideout," I said to Justice Scalia. On the way out of the library, he briefly greeted President Danny Anderson of Trinity, said goodbye to our three guests, and then ascended to his room. Soon the house was filled with 35 or so guests, and Karolyne and I had assumed our hosting duties.

About 8:00 p.m., I went to Justice Scalia's room with a plate of barbecue, but he was on the phone. I decided to wait. Soon most guests had left, and I returned to his room with food. All was silent. I knocked but heard nothing. I knocked again and said, "Nino?"

He growled a little: "What is it?"

"I have food for you."

"I'm not hungry anymore. I'm sleeping."

"Sorry. See you in the morning."

I learned later that he had received some sad personal news. He needed time alone to think and to pray.

Ivan the Barber

The next morning at 7:30, Karolyne and I were downstairs making coffee. Justice Scalia came down dressed in a golf shirt and khakis. As we sipped coffee, I asked whether he'd rather ride with the marshals to the restaurant down the street, or walk. He decided to walk the 300 or so yards to the restaurant. I went out front to tell Ralph Tenorio (who had two cars ready) that we'd be walking through the back gate and down the back street—not really an alley, but a small side street. I opened the gates so the marshals could pull through the drive.

Justice Scalia walked between me and Karolyne, with a sprightly step. "The morning air is so good!" he exclaimed. "Just what I need." The marshals drove slowly behind us, at perhaps one mile an hour.

A lot of neighbors walk their dogs on this street, and one couple pointed, seemingly worried, and said to us, "Do you realize there's a car following you?"

"Yes," I said, "they're with us. No worries." They seemed perplexed. We walked on as they stared.

When we were finished with breakfast, Ralph reminded me that I still hadn't given him the barber's information, and I realized that I hadn't gotten around to calling Ivan. I looked it up on my phone under Ivan. Nothing. So I told him, "It's Lovers Lane Barber Shop. The guy closest to the window is Ivan. I think he'll remember me. It's on Lovers just past Douglas." Ralph said he had enough information to go on.

We paraded back home, two slow-motion vehicles behind us. The joggers and walkers we passed seemed bemused, but no one said anything.

As we went into the house to freshen up, Ralph said we should leave at 9:55. When the time came, we drove over with two cars—ours and a chaser car. As usual, I sat behind the driver and Justice Scalia sat behind the front passenger seat. We talked about our planned work that afternoon: the series-qualifier canon and the last-antecedent canon.

When we got to the barber shop, I hopped out briskly to alert Ivan to what was happening. The moment he saw me, he exclaimed that he couldn't cut my hair. "Can't do it. The place is surrounded by federal marshals." He was frazzled.

"I know, Ivan, I've brought Justice Scalia here for a haircut."

"*You* brought him here?"

"Yes, he needs a haircut, and you're the best around."

"What will I say to him?"

"Don't worry. Just be yourself."

Knowing all the barbers at this shop to be reliable, I took an available chair two down from Ivan's so we'd be finished about the same time. A thin man perhaps in his mid-50s, with gray hair flowing over the back of his collar and a close-cropped beard, Ivan was noticeably nervous through the beginning of the haircut, and other than asking how Justice Scalia wanted his hair, he remained reticent through most of the cut. I made some small talk, telling Justice Scalia that this barbershop was among the oldest in Dallas. On the television above the mirrors, at low volume, reruns of the 1960s Western series *The Rifleman* seemed fitting. Two other customers who were waiting in line joined in the conversation. The shop has a small-town feel—about as close as you can get to TV's Mayberry within a major American city.

As we finished, Ivan overcame his unwonted taciturnity and asked for a photograph with Justice Scalia, who patiently obliged as I snapped one. A fourth-grader accompanying her father asked for a photo as well. Justice

Scalia said he'd agree on one condition: "Can you name the three branches of American government?"

"Yes," she said confidently. She had just been studying them. "The president, Congress, and . . ." It was a long pause, and she seemed stumped. "Judges?"

"Excellent!" exclaimed Justice Scalia. "Of course I'll take a picture with you."

"Where are you going next?" asked Ivan.

"We'll have lunch," Justice Scalia responded. By then it would be about midday.

"Where?"

"I don't think Bryan's decided where yet."

"Why don't you go to Kuby's?" Ivan suggested to me.[53]

"Great idea," I said. It's an old-time German restaurant in Snider Plaza, about a block from the SMU Law School. I knew Justice Scalia had never been there, and I thought he'd like it: it has a traditional butcher shop, and the food is first-rate. But first we needed to stop by the pharmacy to get him some compression socks for the long plane trip we'd be making the next day.

The Drugstore

The marshals drove us to my neighborhood CVS. As we walked in, we were flanked by two marshals. I asked Justice Scalia whether he needed anything other than the socks, and he said: "I need deodorant. Not antiperspirant. It can't be antiperspirant. It has to be deodorant."

We went for the socks first. A CVS employee directed us to one section and then another, and it took several minutes to find compression socks. Meanwhile, I had grabbed the roll-on deodorant as we passed down one of the aisles.

As we were heading to the checkout counter, I noticed an African-American man walking erratically and excitedly down the aisle next to

---

53 For a humorous television account of this haircut—which aired more than two weeks after it occurred—go to http://www.nbcdfw.com/news/local/Justice-Scalia-Suprises-North-TX-Barber_Dallas-Fort-Worth-368249691.html. The reporter had no idea why Justice Scalia happened to be in Dallas.

ours. He had spotted Justice Scalia. As we approached the counter, the man started saying to me, "Is that Scalia? Is that Scalia?!" in a high, excited voice.

I nodded.

"Well, I just want to shake his hand! I just want to shake his hand!"

Justice Scalia heard this and walked toward the man, who now had a marshal beside him. "He wants to shake your hand," I said.

"I just want to shake the hand [*Justice Scalia took his hand*] of the *biggest bigot* on the U.S. Supreme Court!" he shouted in a crackly, high-pitched voice.

Justice Scalia just smiled and walked back to the cash register. "Please get away," I told the man. A marshal stood between the man and me, and without touching him, essentially escorted him to the back of the store— using nothing but body language.

As we were leaving, I said, "I'm sorry that happened, Nino."

"I didn't even understand what the guy said. Are you ready for lunch? Is Lyne joining us?"

"No, she's seeing her grandmother and putting flowers at her father's grave. He died when she was ten, and he's buried here in Dallas. She visits the grave periodically."

"That's touching. Filial piety is so important in Asian cultures."

"Yes. It has its advantages. The downside, though, is that obligations to one's elders can sometimes become stifling coercion. Lyne has friends whose parents demand payments from their adult children as soon as they start working. 'I want $5,000 now: I've raised you, and you're working.' Some parents use filial piety almost to extort money from their children."

"At this stage in my life," Justice Scalia responded with a smile, "that doesn't sound bad at all. I think I'd like that system."

Wurst and Kraut

We got out of the car at Kuby's and were briskly escorted by the marshals to a back seat—a communal bench, really. Justice Scalia and I sat across from each other; each of us had about three seats open to the side of us. The marshals sat at the next bench. We had seating for six, but no one else was at our table. Almost instantly, a friendly waitress came by and began explaining the menu. I suggested the sausage sampler to start, and Justice

Scalia said he'd like a beer. We asked her to bring us two glasses of a German pilsner. Soon she arrived not just with the beer but also with slices of bratwurst, knackwurst, wienerwurst, and Polish sausage, together with red cabbage and sauerkraut. Justice Scalia chose the Polish sausage and the sauerkraut; I went for the red cabbage.

An odd-looking couple, in their mid-60s, came in, looked around, headed back toward us—passing several empty tables on their way—and sat down at our table, he beside me and she beside Justice Scalia, who of course was facing me. The husband was a huge disheveled man with a ponytail, dressed in overalls. She was a frumpy blonde with a strange knitted cap made of orange yarn: cat ears on the top and long earflaps that extended down to her shoulders, with pompoms on the end. It seemed almost as if someone had tipped off this bizarre pair that Justice Scalia would be going to Kuby's. Both were stealing glances at Justice Scalia, who seemed oblivious of it. The marshals looked at me and raised their eyebrows. Perhaps the CVS experience had made me extra alert.

"Do you see that to your left?" I whispered to him.

"Yep," he said, turning to his right.

The woman turned to Justice Scalia and said, "Sir . . . Sir . . . Sir."

"What is it you need?" I asked.

She ignored me and kept trying to get Justice Scalia to respond to her. "Sir . . . Sir." He didn't look at her. He kept his eyes focused straight ahead, either on the food or on me.

Squeaky Fromme came to mind—the Charles Manson family member who tried to assassinate President Gerald Ford in 1975. The woman looked about as I'd imagine Squeaky might look today. I knew that Squeaky had been released from prison and that she had served time in Fort Worth.

Finally, she looked at me. "I just want to know what he's having."

"Please talk to the waiter." It goes against my instincts to cut someone off so abruptly, but nothing about this circumstance was normal. She kept reaching into her calico homemade purse on her lap, rummaging around, and I was watching her hands, ready to leap over the table if necessary. I nodded at the marshals, who looked on, but her back was to them and they couldn't see her hands. She kept fooling around inside her purse for about 60 seconds, which seemed to me like an eternity. Then she put down her purse, having taken out nothing.

She said something to her companion. Meanwhile, Justice Scalia and I were making small talk about German beer gardens and Bavarian cuisine. I was trying to avoid saying anything that might reveal the identity of my friend: nothing about law.

The waitress came to take our main order, since we'd shared the appetizer. "You know," said Justice Scalia, "I think we've had just the right amount before we get down to work."

"I agree. Just the check, please."

I summoned Ralph Tenorio with my hand and had him lean over to my left. "Watch this couple closely. We're going to get up and leave. Please pay our bill with this." I handed him a $50 bill. "We'll walk out through the meat shop. Don't let her close to him."

Adjoining the small restaurant is a butcher's shop. I asked Justice Scalia to come around to my side of the table. Then I pointed the way, staying between him and the couple every step of the way. This was perhaps the first time that I truly felt as if I was somehow directly taking part in Justice Scalia's security detail. The feeling would continue in Asia, where I'd essentially be his *only* bodyguard.

The strange couple were doubtless just local eccentrics. But one never knows.

In the old-fashioned meat shop, Justice Scalia was interested in their house-made offerings, such as freshly cut steaks, sauerkraut, and beef jerky. We walked through at a steady pace. About a third of the people did a double take.

As we got in the car, I said, "Well, there have been lots of Justice Scalia sightings up and down Lovers Lane today. Maybe we'd better retire to the house for a low-key afternoon of work." That's what we did.

An Awkward Visit

At 4:30 I received a text message from a friend—a political-science professor who happened to be in town: "Where is your house?" Suddenly I remembered that I had agreed some weeks before to have this friend stop by at 4:30. He was having relationship troubles, and I had wanted to offer whatever help I could. Meanwhile, my doctor, who had once spoken on the phone to Justice Scalia about a sore knee when he and I were working in D.C., was to come by at the same time because he was a fan. The doctor had wanted to meet Justice Scalia in person, and I was also hoping that even though this was a casual visit, he might give Justice Scalia a once-over and help with any advice he might need before the Asia trip, especially regarding his back and knees.

"Oh, no, Nino. I'm sorry, but I'd forgotten that I have the doctor coming over at the same time as a professor friend. You know that Chief Justice Hecht and Harriet Miers are coming over at 6 o'clock. Well, I didn't plan this very well. But I agreed weeks ago that my old friend, a professor of political science, could stop by for a brief visit."

"When will he be here?"

"Now, I'm afraid. It totally slipped my mind. I can either put you and the doctor in a separate room, and he can talk with you, or else we can open a bottle of wine and all sit down together."

"I guess let's sit down together," Justice Scalia said.

The doorbell rang, and on the front step were both the professor and my doctor. I welcomed them in, introduced them to Justice Scalia, and rushed to the wine cellar to grab a bottle of Italian red. The conversation seemed to be going smoothly when I returned, although instinctively I knew this would be a strange mix of people. The professor was pretty clearly left-leaning; the doctor was right-leaning (and a Scalia fan).

We sat down in the back of the library, and I thought I'd start things off with an icebreaker: "Tell us about your newest book," I said to the professor. It was a biography of a Washington diplomat of Justice Scalia's acquaintance. The professor went on at great length about the man's life—in much more depth, and at much greater length, than I'd expected. He detailed the degree of access that he had to papers, the number of interviews he'd conducted, and the overall approach to the biography.

Finally, after 15 long minutes or so on this one topic, Justice Scalia asked: "Is the biography positive or negative?"

"Well, it's mixed, I'd say," responded the professor. "Everyone has a bad, dark side, and I try not to sugarcoat that. He has warts. But overall I'd say the reader gets a positive impression."

Justice Scalia seemed none too pleased. Perhaps sensing the tension, the doctor tried to change the subject: "I hear you're about to go to Asia." It was an awkward transition, but then all the transitions had been slightly uncomfortable in this exchange. I tried to steer things back to something that might interest Justice Scalia, but it wasn't working. Still, he gamely listened and made a little conversation himself. We talked some about what we'd been working on that afternoon.

Karolyne walked in and joined us, meeting the professor for the first time. She shook his hand.

"Bryan says he admires your scholarship," she said.

"That's very nice, but it's nothing compared to all Bryan's books. Right now I'm interested in gun rights and the havoc they're wreaking on American families."

I chimed in: "You know, Justice Scalia wrote the groundbreaking *Heller* decision."

"That's right," he said with what seemed like hesitant realization. "Yes, I'm aware of that. But I'm interested not in the Founders' vision, which is quite arguable as you know, but in the policy behind our current framework for gun rights and the way it's affecting inner-city families especially—and how different this is from families elsewhere in the First World. Essentially, . . ." During the three-minute screed that followed, I watched Justice Scalia, arms crossed, looking up at the ceiling.

I circled back to one of his earlier statements: "I for one don't think the Founders' vision is arguable. I'd be in favor of repealing the Second Amendment, but I think the *Heller* decision was correct about its meaning."

"You'd repeal the Second Amendment?" said the doctor. "I'm a hunter. I like the Second Amendment."

"Yes, I would," I said.

The professor again: "Well, *Heller* is shaky as a matter of history—as many scholars have said—but that's not what I'm interested in."

"Lookit," Justice Scalia interjected. Experience had taught me that "lookit" signaled his growing impatience. "The historical evidence was overwhelming," he said. "The reference was to *the right of the People. The right*—not *a right*. The idea was that there was a preexisting right in English common law. And indeed there was. But my opinion speaks to that. There's no reason to rehash it here."

"The *Heller* opinion gives an exhaustive history," I said, "and it's compelling."

"However that may be," said the professor, "my focus is on the American family and the ravages of widespread gun ownership."

The whole thing was odd, and I thought my professorial guest was being cavalierly disrespectful. As we'd begun, the oddity involved having a person of great eminence in our midst, yet we were either making small talk or focusing unduly on the academic interests of the professor. Many will read this and think that there's nothing wrong with that. But I'd never been in quite this situation before. Most people would focus their curiosity on Justice Scalia, but that wasn't happening here. Then the oddity intensified when we shifted from pretty much ignoring Justice Scalia to having the professor disparage one of his most important judicial opinions.

In retrospect, I realized that I should have trusted my instincts, putting the doctor and Justice Scalia in one room to discuss medical issues while I joined the professor for a brief chat in another.

The four of us had finished off our bottle of wine—Karolyne was abstaining—when the doctor shifted the conversation back to Justice Scalia's work with me. It was 5:30 now, and we talked a little about *Making Your Case*. Justice Scalia seemed agreeable enough until I rose and suggested that he and I sign a book for our two guests. "I don't think so, I'm tired," Justice Scalia said, starting toward the staircase to go to his room.

"Come on, Nino, let's find a couple of copies and autograph them."

"No, I'm going to my room." Then to the guests: "Nice meeting you." He walked up the stairs to his room.

It was an uncomfortable moment. Maybe I'd erred by suggesting the autographs when they hadn't even been requested—but then I knew that the doctor would appreciate it. Doubtless Justice Scalia was annoyed by the *Heller* discussion. Unable to find a copy of *Making Your Case*, I signed two copies of *Black's Law Dictionary*. Then Karolyne and I sent our visitors on their way.

We walked to the kitchen, where Karolyne started prepping our salads for that evening. I'd be grilling steaks. She said she had enjoyed most of the conversation.

"Gosh, did you hear what he said about *Heller*?" I asked.

"Yes, that seemed unnecessary and disrespectful," she said.

"Bryan," Justice Scalia called from the den. He'd come downstairs and was waiting for me, so I walked to the next room.

"I'm not happy!" he said emphatically, with a big frown. At this point he was whisper-shouting: "You just wasted an hour of my life! I don't appreciate it. You shouldn't waste my time!"

"I'm sorry, Nino."

"I could have been working on opinions!"

I was speechless and flushed.

"When are Harriet Miers and the chief justice getting here?" he asked, still angry.

"Six o'clock."

"I'll be in my room until they arrive."

"I'm really sorry, Nino."

He turned, walked back toward the library stair, and went up to his room. He didn't exactly slam his door, but the firmness with which he shut it expressed his vexation with no less clarity. I sat glumly in the living room for a few minutes, looking out at the marshals' car parked in the cross-drive of the front yard and pondering how I'd set in motion the convergence of events that culminated in this calamitous faux pas.

Then I went into the kitchen, where I figured Karolyne had just over-heard the exchange. She'd heard nothing. So I told her, adding: "I think he'll be fine."

"I'm sure he will," she said. "It's a shame that happened."

A More Cordial Visit

At 6:00 p.m., I saw Chief Justice Hecht and Harriet Miers drive up. I knew from earlier conversations with Justice Scalia that he didn't really know Harriet at all. This would be a good opportunity for them to talk—not necessarily about the Court, but about things in general. Once nominated by President George W. Bush for the Supreme Court, Harriet is a wise, kind, gentle, centered person with eminently sound judgment. I knew Justice Scalia would enjoy having a meal with her. And of course he'd known Chief Justice Hecht for many years, from the time in the late 1980s when Hecht first became a justice on the Supreme Court of Texas. Their friendship had grown over the years, especially when Justice Scalia came down to Texas in November 2013 to conduct Hecht's swearing-in as chief justice.

As Karolyne and I greeted our guests, Justice Scalia appeared atop the front staircase and silently started descending. Both our guests approached him warmly, and he was all smiles as he said hello. This apparent harbinger of his changed attitude proved correct: he was again charming, spirited, and characteristically witty. He stayed that way throughout the evening.

During dessert, when the five of us had had our fill of steaks and baked potatoes, none of us wanted the conversation to end. I said as much, and we continued talking until about 9:30. About that time, our concern became finding a Catholic church where Justice Scalia could attend Mass the next morning. Harriet suggested Christ the King Catholic Church not far from the house. So we found a weekly Mass that would give us plenty of time to leave for the airport at 10:45.

Sunday Morning

The next morning, Karolyne made a hearty breakfast of Nueske's bacon, snotty eggs, and coffee. Justice Scalia pronounced it excellent. Afterward, Ralph Tenorio rang the doorbell and told us he needed our passports and all the luggage we planned to check. We went upstairs to get them. I told Justice Scalia just to put his bags on the elevator, next to his room, so that we could send them down—so much easier than lugging them down the stairs. It took us just a minute or so to move the bags onto the elevator.

Karolyne and I noticed that Justice Scalia was planning to carry a garment bag. "I have to do that," he said. "Otherwise, my suits will get wrinkled."

Karolyne said, "Oh, that's going to be hard for you, Justice Scalia." (She still didn't call him "Nino," even though he signed notes to her that way.) "We can fold it up like Bryan's garment bag and put it into my bag. I have room."

"Well, I have room," he said, "but I just don't want the suits getting wrinkled."

"Bryan's are always fine. Let me show you." She folded the garment bag over, opened her bag, and put it on top of her own clothes. Then she closed the bag.

"You're crushing the suit. It'll get wrinkled."

"Trust me, with the garment bag, you'll be okay. Bryan does it on every trip, and his suits look fine. If you were to carry your garment bag on a 16-hour trip to Hong Kong and then another 4 hours to Singapore, you might leave it on the plane. It's easy to forget things like that. We'll have everything pressed when we get to the hotel."

"Okay. If you say so."

Karolyne had convinced me of this technique, and I'd been using it ever since.

The marshals loaded our bags and took our passports, saying they'd be back with our boarding passes. For our 11:30 flight, we'd leave the house at

10:45. They had timed everything perfectly. Although we had been all over North America with Justice Scalia, we'd never been on the same flight. This time we were traveling internationally together. Ralph explained that our security clearances would be taken care of in advance: the marshals would have our boarding passes at 10:20 or so. There would be no need for TSA screening: the marshals were taking care of that, with State Department clearance for me and Karolyne.

We were preparing to attend Mass, and Justice Scalia had already dressed comfortably for our flights. For this long trip, he wore khakis, a light-brown short-sleeve shirt, untucked, and a navy zip-up sweater. He had a black travel pouch hanging from his neck and falling to his abdomen; it would hold important documents such as boarding passes and his passport. I was dressed in a suit, having figured (incorrectly) that Justice Scalia would be as well. "You're going to travel wearing a tie?" he remarked.

"No, I'll change when we get back from church. It's just that my grandmother taught me always to wear my Sunday best when going to church."

"How are you going to change? Aren't we going straight to the airport?"

"No. We'll have 15 minutes at the house after church to cool our heels."

At precisely 9:18, one marshal headed for the airport while three others loaded us in for the ride to church. The three of us were in an SUV, and there was a chaser car in front. The marshals had already figured out precisely which entrance we'd use for Christ the King, and access would be no problem: as hundreds of others hunted for parking spots, we drove straight into a portico that had a door to the nave of the church and went inside. (This wasn't a matter of privilege, mind you, but of security.) We found a pew near the center, where during the entire Mass we remained unnoticed. Unfamiliar with the service ourselves, Karolyne and I followed Justice Scalia's lead on standing and sitting. Afterward, he expressed surprise at how much he liked this Catholic service in Dallas. "Come on, Nino," I said. "Dallas is quite a sophisticated city."

After we returned to the house, Karolyne and I changed into comfortable travel clothes. Justice Scalia spent a few minutes in the exercise room lifting weights. When I joined him, I had him try the doorsill exercise for his shoulder again. He lasted only 45 seconds at that.

"Did you put on your compression socks? Did you take an aspirin?" I asked.

"Compression socks . . . yes. Why an aspirin?"

"It's good before a long flight. Don't you take a baby aspirin every day?"

"Oh yeah, I do that at night. My doctor told me to."

"Good. Let's take another baby aspirin now. You don't take any other blood thinners that would cause a problem, do you?"

"No."

"Good. I'll be right back." I got him a baby aspirin and some tonic water. I thought the quinine in the tonic might do him some good, since it's supposed to help with muscle tone.

Karolyne joined us at the breakfast table as he quaffed some tonic water and then said, "Ahhhh. This is really good. Hey, listen. My head gets cold sometimes on flights. Do you have a watch cap? Something like a knit cap?"

Karolyne surprised me by saying we did. She went up to her closet and returned about a minute later with just such a cap.

"Wonderful." He tried it on. "May I borrow this cap for the trip?"

"Of course!" said Karolyne. "You look a little like Mickey from *Rocky*!"

He chuckled and finished his tonic water wearing the cap.

Karolyne said, "Justice Scalia, you haven't gotten our Christmas present yet, but can we show you what it is? We're still waiting for it to come in. The woman who's making it takes her time."

"Do we have the time now?" Justice Scalia asked.

"Sure, Nino," I said. "We still have ten minutes. I think you'll like it."

Lyne went upstairs to get it. In her Boston College undergraduate handbook, she'd found a prayer by St. Thomas Aquinas and asked me to write it out in my finest penmanship. I read it to him as we sat around the breakfast table:

Give me, O Lord, a steadfast heart which no unworthy thought can drag downwards; an unconquered heart which no tribulation can wear out; an upright heart which no unworthy purpose may tempt aside. Bestow upon me also, O Lord my God, understanding to know thee, diligence to seek thee, wisdom to find thee, and a faithfulness that may finally embrace thee; through Jesus Christ, our Lord.

—*St. Thomas Aquinas*

"It's an excellent prayer," said Justice Scalia. "Very nice. I don't recall seeing it before."

"We've made it into three handkerchiefs for you," said Karolyne. "One says 'A steadfast heart,' one says 'An unconquered heart,' and one says 'An upright heart.'"

"That's so very kind of you. My Christmas present?"

"Yes," said Karolyne.

"And I'll have these when I get home?"

"We'll send them on as soon as they arrive—probably as soon as we get back from Hong Kong," said Karolyne. "We know you've always been partial to Sir Thomas More, but I'm partial to St. Thomas Aquinas. I repeat these three phrases whenever I feel overwhelmed."

"That's really thoughtful. I'll use them. Aquinas was splendid, and I'm glad to know about this prayer. I'll remember it."

The doorbell rang. Justice Scalia put both the prayer and his knit cap into his briefcase with his iPad and a few other loose papers, and we were all soon in the marshals' car and off to the airport.

When we arrived, we actually walked in the "out" way at security. The marshals whisked us through with no wait at all. We walked about 50 yards from the entry point and went straight onto the American Airlines plane as soon as boarding began. The marshals accompanied Justice Scalia down the jet bridge until the moment he boarded.

10

The Asia Trip

(Jan.–Feb. 2016)

As we boarded the plane in Dallas and said goodbye to the marshals, it suddenly occurred to me that we were now on our own: Karolyne and I would now be responsible for Justice Scalia, except at the airports, where the State Department would take charge. We probably both felt a little nervous.

Our flight left on January 24 at 11:30 a.m., arriving in Hong Kong on January 25 at 6:35 p.m. Justice Scalia and I sat just opposite each other in row 4, with a partition between us; we lowered it so that we could talk easily and hand things back and forth—mostly articles that I was asking him to read on the subject of statutory construction. We had some Champagne, tried the excellent business-class fare, and chatted for the first couple of hours. Then he wanted to see a movie, and I went to sleep listening to my iPod. After that, it was mostly Karolyne that he talked with, as one or the other of them would walk up or down the aisle to see what was up.

But this leg to Hong Kong was just en route to Singapore. Our flight to that city didn't leave until 1:50 a.m. (for arrival in Singapore four hours later). During our seven-hour layover in Hong Kong, we waited in a Chinese-government VIP lounge, where we were looked after by two staffers from the U.S. Consulate in Hong Kong. We were the only people in the lounge, which had lots of comfy chairs and two couches, as well as two adjoining bathrooms. The Consulate had prepared briefings for us on Asian news: folders containing news clips about all sorts of things affecting U.S. relations with Asian countries, especially China. The biggest news at the time was that a Hong Kong bookseller who sold banned books had mysteriously disappeared.

Mostly we slept in the lounge on the couches, though at intervals Justice Scalia, Karolyne, and I would all be awake. The staffers from the Consulate brought us tea and dim-sum dumplings.

At one point we did a little work on the second edition of *Reading Law*. I trotted out a law-review article criticizing the decision in *FDA v. Brown & Williamson Tobacco Corp.*,[54] in which the Supreme Court, in an opinion by Justice Sandra Day O'Connor, held that cigarettes aren't drugs and therefore aren't subject to the jurisdiction of the U.S. Food and Drug Administration. Justice Scalia had joined in the opinion. The law-review writer argued that because nicotine is a drug, cigarettes should fall within the definition of "a drug-delivery device"—something used to deliver a drug to the human body. I asked Justice Scalia how this could possibly have been in line with his textualist philosophy, given that nicotine is a drug that is delivered by means of cigarette paper. He grew contemplative and asked me to read the relevant passage, which I did. He sighed heavily, as he often did in deep thought, and proclaimed: "Nobody ever thought that that provision in the Food and Drug Act gave the FDA the power over such a well-known phenomenon as cigarettes. There are lots of other statutes dealing with cigarettes as such." He also thought that *drug* was being used, contextually, in a therapeutic sense, not in the broader sense of substances that have no beneficial effect. We spent probably 15 minutes discussing the case, and he persuaded me that *drug* must have been meant in a therapeutic sense.

I mentioned that I hadn't seen him smoking in at least a couple of years. He smiled, putting his headphones on, and said he'd given up even the occasional cigarette. Then he dozed off listening to Mozart.

Singapore

When we finally arrived in Singapore on January 26 (we had lost a full day), we were met by a U.S. Embassy representative named Nick, who looked and acted the part of a career diplomat. About five feet ten inches, of medium build, he was conservatively dressed, with a short haircut. Tortoiseshell glasses straddled his aquiline nose, and he had rapid, intelligent-sounding speech. He was studiously apolitical but exceedingly well informed, and he was refreshingly candid about the local political situation.

---

54 529 U.S. 120 (2000).

Our local guide and caretaker, meanwhile, was a National University of Singapore representative named Johann, a native Singaporean who had spent a good deal of time in Europe. His job was to organize special events at the university and to handle special visitors. He was earnest, thoughtful, well organized, and eager to please. He'd be our university escort for the entire stay.

Right off the jet bridge, we were taken by bus to a VIP lounge, where we waited for our bags. Nick began briefing us all on U.S. Embassy views on Singapore. When our bags finally arrived, we boarded a bus, and Nick continued briefing us all the way to the Shangri-La Hotel. Upon arriving, we thanked him and said goodbye with the understanding that we'd see him again upon leaving Singapore and also upon his return to the States from service overseas.

Although Justice Scalia's beautifully outfitted three-room suite was ready upon arrival at 7:30 a.m., our room wouldn't be ready until 1:00 p.m. at the earliest. Justice Scalia kindly offered to have us wait in his suite until our room was ready. We demurred but took our bags there to freshen up. Then the three of us went to the hotel restaurant for breakfast. The offerings included not just a buffet but also an à la carte Singaporean breakfast, an Indian breakfast, and a Japanese bento box. That first morning, Justice Scalia ordered an all-American breakfast with scrambled eggs. Beginning the next day, he branched out with the bento box—featuring grilled fish, pickled vegetables, rolled omelet, dried seaweed, and sticky rice—and didn't again revert to American fare until we reached Hong Kong.

After breakfast, Karolyne arranged to have Justice Scalia's suits steamed, and then she and I went to the spa for a few hours while Justice Scalia rested. He was to meet with Prime Minister Lee Hsien Loong from 5 to 6 o'clock at the Istana, his official residence. Several times before the trip, Karolyne and I were told that this meeting, as well as the meeting with the president of Singapore University, would occur with Justice Scalia alone. Karolyne and I were decidedly *not* invited. When we saw Justice Scalia at 1:00 p.m. to get our bags to take them to our room, he was reading Court-related work.

Because we'd have only one opportunity—that afternoon—to do any shopping in Singapore, we had arranged for Johann to pick us up at 1:30. We asked him to take us to a good street-shopping spot. I asked for the antiques district, but he said there was none. Instead he explained that there was a style of ceramics and other crafts called Peranakan; it was peculiar to Singapore. Very special, he said.

Intrigued, we decided to go. We dressed informally, but none more so than Justice Scalia, who wore a navy golf shirt, seersucker shorts, light-brown socks, and brown dress shoes. Johann, despite the humidity and heat (which he was used to, since Singapore stays at 95° Fahrenheit pretty much year-round), was dressed in a suit and tie. When we got to the small Peranakan shop, none of us liked what we saw. We didn't want to buy anything there. I told Johann that we wanted a big street full of all types of different shops: silks, rugs, dresses, art, sculpture, and so on. There had to be such a place, I assured him: every major city has one. Johann was reluctant at first to bring up Arab Street because he thought it wouldn't be good enough for us—but in fact it was just what we wanted. While we were there, Justice Scalia bought a pink silk scarf for Mrs. Scalia.

He also came close to buying a three-by-four-foot Persian rug. I bargained for him, trying to get it down from $2,000 to $450 U.S., but the dealer stopped at $550 U.S. Good thing, too, perhaps: Justice Scalia was concerned about such a major expenditure on something that Mrs. Scalia had never seen. He *thought* she'd like it, and he imagined she wouldn't say otherwise. In any event, we both felt a little skittish when we couldn't get the price we sought.

When we returned to the Shangri-La, Justice Scalia said he didn't want to go to sleep before meeting the prime minister, or else he might not be able to get up when Johann arrived to transport him. Instead, we opted for a late lunch at the hotel's international buffet. Justice Scalia and Karolyne, both adventurous foodies, enjoyed exploring the fare and made many trips back to the little stands together.

Jet Lag Catches Up

Karolyne and I were to meet Justice Scalia and Johann in the lobby at 6:30: they would swing by to collect us for a dinner hosted by Chief Justice Sundaresh Menon, along with four other Singaporean judges and a New Zealand High Court judge. So Karolyne and I decided to go to our room to take a nap. I set my alarm for 6:10 so that we'd have 20 minutes to prepare. Soon I was utterly unconscious—and so was Karolyne. The next thing I knew, our room phone was ringing. I picked up: "Mr. Garner, Justice Scalia is waiting for you here at the reception area."

"I'll be right down!"

I looked at the clock and panicked. It was 6:43. We were 13 minutes late. Karolyne jumped up and we got dressed in less than two minutes. I tied my tie in the elevator. It was 6:46 before we got downstairs. By then I had discovered that I'd set the alarm for a.m., not p.m. That old pitfall.

When we got into the lobby, I hurriedly approached Justice Scalia and profusely apologized that my alarm hadn't gone off—and that jet lag had sent us into a deep slumber. I felt certain that he would be irked by our late arrival.

But no. Tom Leighton of Thomson Reuters had just arrived in Singapore and was in the lobby entertaining Justice Scalia, who greeted my apology with joviality. "That's okay, Bryan, we've got plenty of time to get to dinner." He seemed carefree, and on the way out to the van he enjoyed regaling us with the political astuteness and wide knowledge of the prime minister. The two had hit it off splendidly, and they enjoyed talking about the 2016 presidential election. Mostly, Justice Scalia said, he listened while the prime minister gave him his penetrating analysis of American politics in particular and world politics in general.

After we said goodbye to Tom at the hotel's entrance, Johann took us to Corner House, a restaurant in the Singapore Botanic Gardens. As it happened, we were among the first to arrive. There were formal introductions all around: Justice Scalia, five other judges, and Karolyne and me. At dinner, I was sure to sit away from Justice Scalia, as I normally did, so that others would have a better chance to interact with him. At his end of the table, there was frequent laughter. Like Justice Scalia, Chief Justice Menon was both good-humored and gregarious.

A Full Day Ahead of Us

We agreed to meet for breakfast the next morning at 9:00. Our itinerary was full. Johann would pick us up at 10:30 a.m. for an 11:00 a.m. law-school class on constitutional law, a 12:40 p.m. lunch with the entire Supreme Court of Singapore at the Court's dining room, a 2:00 p.m. meeting with the Court's law clerks, a 5:00 p.m. talk in which Justice Scalia and I would make a joint presentation on *Reading Law* at the Supreme Court's auditorium, and finally a 7:00 p.m. dinner hosted by Justice Quentin Loh and Dean Chesterman at an Italian restaurant named Forlino.

On this second morning, January 27, Tom joined us at breakfast. He would accompany us in most of our activities for the rest of the trip. In his mid-50s, he was quite fit, a former navy man with a buzz-cut. His dry sense of humor, often self-deprecating, made him a great companion. Although Justice Scalia didn't know him well at first, Tom soon became an integral part of our little troupe, and he fit in perfectly. Over breakfast, Tom explained something about what, from the publisher's perspective, we might try to accomplish with this book tour for *Reading Law*. He had brought several boxes of giveaway books for the judges and other dignitaries we'd be meeting.

After breakfast, we went to our rooms to freshen up, having agreed to meet in the lobby at 10:30 for Johann to fetch us. Karolyne and I arrived at the lobby a few minutes early and met Tom there. I asked whether he had brought books down with him. He hadn't, so I suggested that he grab a few quickly before we left. He called an elevator, and just as his elevator left Justice Scalia stepped off another one, saying, "Let's go!"

"It'll be just a minute, Nino. Tom is grabbing a few books to give away."

"He's late?!" He furrowed his brow.

"No, he was here. I just sent him to his room to get a few books."

"And I have to wait again? This isn't good. You don't make me wait!"

"It's my fault, Nino. I'm sorry. Let's go out to the car. He'll be down in 90 seconds. He knows it's urgent."

With a grand harrumph, he strode through the marble entryway and toward the van in front. He was clearly annoyed. We got into our seats and waited about another minute for Tom, who of course was unaware of what had happened. When he got into the van, Tom and Karolyne engaged in some lighthearted jocularity, and soon the unpleasantness evaporated.

As we entered the university grounds, we saw a huge sign with a picture of Justice Scalia and the title of his public-lecture series: "Judicial Interpretation of Legal Texts."

"Stop the bus!" I said.

"Why?" said Justice Scalia impatiently.

"Nino, get out and pose for a photo beside the sign."

"I'm not going to do that," he said, probably from a sense of modesty.

"Oh, come on! This will be your only chance."

"Okay. I guess I will."

He posed alone, pointing at the photo of himself and giving the old-fashioned "okay" sign with his right hand. Then he posed for a photo with Karolyne. He was delighted—glowing, in fact.

When I asked what he'd be speaking about to the class, Justice Scalia said he wasn't quite sure what the format would be. He'd give some remarks from one of his "stump speeches" and then invite questions. He was an old pro at this kind of forum, and it always went off well. We speculated about how good the students' command of English might be and whether he should speak a little more deliberately than he would with an American audience. "I'm not going to do that. The bright ones will get it."

When we arrived at the law school, we were greeted by Dean Chesterman, a thin, fit, bespectacled Australian man in his early 40s. Quick-witted and charming, he is an expert in international law, public authority, and data protection. We would later find out that he was once a Rhodes Scholar and that his wife is the daughter of Singapore's president, Tony Tan. He made us feel at home in the academic environment of a Singaporean law-school class, and his introduction of Justice Scalia was deft and short. He'd arranged for a third-year student to lead a question-and-answer session with the Justice. As it happened, all the students we heard from were impressive. They asked intelligent, thoughtful questions about particular American cases, such as *Obergefell* (the same-sex-marriage case), and Justice Scalia answered with characteristic panache.

One student asked how, at oral argument, an advocate should respond to a judge's questions from the bench. Justice Scalia advised that an advocate should never view questions as interruptions, but instead as indications of real interest and attention. "Answer the questions directly!" he said. "If it's a yes/no question, there are only four possible answers—and you must say one of these at the outset of your answer: 'Yes,' 'No,' 'I don't know,' or 'I'm not telling.'" This line was a crowd-pleaser.

Lunch at the Court

The excursion to the Supreme Court of Singapore was fascinating. First we met in chambers with Chief Justice Menon. From his office we could see much of Singapore. The Chief Justice enjoyed explaining the highlights of the skyline, including the beautiful Marina Bay Sands Hotel, which is designed to look like a boat atop three office towers. Chief Justice Menon told us that we should go to the restaurant at the top if at all possible. That was the one request that Justice Scalia would later make of Dean Chesterman.

Then we went to a grand conference room for lunch with all the appellate judges. Once a week, the full court lunches together, and two of the judges are designated hosts. We had traditional Singaporean food: soup, curried chicken, mushrooms, bok choy, tofu, and fresh fruit. After dessert, Justice Scalia and I each said some words of thanks to those assembled around the huge conference table. Tom gave out a dozen or so copies of *Reading Law* as gifts—the books that had delayed our departure—and Justice Scalia and I inscribed one for each judge.

At 2 o'clock, in a packed conference room, Justice Scalia addressed all the law clerks of the Singapore courts. To Justice Scalia, Karolyne, Tom, and me, it seemed highly considerate of the Singapore judges to want their clerks to have a session of their own with Justice Scalia. He began his talk by stressing how important clerkships are both for the judges and for the legal system as a whole. He explained how clerkships in the U.S. circuit courts, such as the D.C. Circuit where he once sat, differ from those at the Supreme Court. In the latter, clerks must spend a great deal of time deciding which cases to hear. That's not true in the circuit courts, which don't enjoy discretionary review. He remarked that former law clerks in any American court are held in high regard throughout the legal system, drawing a laugh with his reference to his own "clerkarati" (his own neologism, a portmanteau of *clerk* and *literati*).

He asked me to comment on my own experience clerking for Judge Thomas M. Reavley, and I did so briefly. No small degree of wonderment came across the room when Justice Scalia noted that upon departing from their one-year stints at the Supreme Court, most clerks immediately get paid more than the Justices themselves.

Reading Law Presentation

Afterward, we went back to the Shangri-La for a two-hour break. Justice Scalia wanted to review each point we'd be covering later that day in our *Reading Law* talk at the Singapore Supreme Court. It was to be a 40-minute talk, followed by a 15-minute Q&A session. Working together in his room, we agreed that we'd give our five-question test at the end (see pp. 224–25). We'd therefore have to be sure to cover those points in our main lecture. We further marked up the "cheat sheets" we habitually used, with diagonals from G to S and back to show how we'd divvy up the material. Mostly he was nervous about precisely how we'd deal with the introductory materials in the book, but by this point in our experience I was always happy to simply wing it: together, we'd cover everything essential, and it always worked best when it was spontaneous. When I reminded him of that, he felt comfortable and ready to go.

Before leaving, I brought up a touchy subject. "Nino, there were a couple of points of usage that came up in your remarks this morning."

"Really? Did I say something wrong?"

"Would you want me to tell you if you did?"

"Of course!"

"You were in great form, of course, so I feel churlish isolating a mistake in usage."

"Out with it! Give it to me!"

"In reference to the death penalty, you said something about prisoners who were *hung*. It really should be *hanged*."

"Really? With executions, prisoners are hanged?"

"Strictly speaking, yes. Coats are hung; prisoners are hanged."

"By golly, I didn't know that. I'm glad to know that."

"In *My Fair Lady*, even Henry Higgins got it wrong."

"Really?"

"Yes. He said something about people who should be 'hung for the cold-blooded murder of the English tongue.' Totally out of character, Lerner and Loewe were going for the rhyme of *hung-tongue*."

"Okay. What's the other one?"

"*Contra proferentem*." That's the Latin name for the doctrine that a contract, especially a consumer contract, will be construed most strictly against the party that prepared or drafted it. The doctrine is invoked all the time against insurance companies.

"*Contra proferentem*. What's the problem?" he asked.

"You just said it properly. But this morning you said *preferentem*."

"*Preferentem*? I did not."

"Well, I'm sure you did."

"It's /proh/! *Proferentem*!"

"Right. I just thought I'd mention it before the other one becomes habitual."

"That's good. Thank you for that. Prisoners used to be hanged. *Contra proferentem.* I'll remember those."

"It's always awkward correcting someone."

"C'mon! Not between us! I appreciate that. I need you for that."

Soon we were at the Supreme Court of Singapore being introduced by Justice Andrew Phang of the Court of Appeal, who was generous in his remarks. Our presentation went well, and the quiz questions were impressively answered. A correct answer to any of our five questions won the participant a signed copy of *Reading Law.* After the presentation, many attendees lingered to speak with us. Soon Dean Chesterman was herding us toward our transportation to Forlino, the Italian restaurant in which he'd arranged a private room with a huge round table for 11—the 4 of us (Tom Leighton now being a regular part of our quartet), 1 judge, 3 professors, and 3 local lawyers.

Afterward, Dean Chesterman took a small group of us to Spago, a rooftop bar at the Marina Bay Sands. When we got there, Justice Scalia called his chambers. Then he told me he must excuse himself. He needed privacy.

He was gone for 30 minutes or so, in a secluded room I helped him find in the rooftop lounge. When I saw him emerge from the door, I went over to get him. He looked somber, his lower lip protruding. "It was a death case from Texas," he said.

"A last-minute motion for stay of execution?" I asked.

"Yes. The man will be executed later today. My law clerk has been scouring the record to help me decide whether there is any merit to the motion. We discussed it at some length. Unfortunately, it has no merit."

"Persuading you was his last hope, I suppose," I said. As the Justice assigned to the Fifth Circuit, he was the one to hear emergency motions from Texas, Louisiana, and Mississippi. If he didn't see a reason for review by the full Supreme Court, that essentially put an end to the matter—and the execution would go forward. The full Court would see his memo, and all the Justices would vote on the order denying review, but considerable deference is normally given to the Circuit Justice's view.

"This is the gravest function I have as a judge," he said, sighing.

When he rejoined the party, he smiled and chuckled less than usual, and he spoke in low tones, as if something had caught in his throat. He seemed to have been deeply affected by the decision he'd just made. It was no different from reviews done by many judges before him, both state and federal. But his decision was essentially the last stop. Only Karolyne and I knew the cause of his reserve. He remained taciturn and somewhat distracted until we said goodnight.

National University of Singapore

The next morning Justice Scalia had a private meeting with the president of the National University of Singapore and other university officials. Tom and I joined him for lunch with the law faculty, while Karolyne ducked out for a quick shopping excursion. She came back with a traditional Singaporean blouse for Mrs. Scalia.

In the afternoon, Justice Scalia was to give his keynote address, entitled "Judicial Interpretation of Legal Texts." For this purpose, he decided to adapt one of his favorite speeches, called "Mullahs of the West: Judges as Moral Arbiters." Beforehand, he had about 30 minutes to review his speech, which he'd given many times but which needed tailoring, he thought, to the Singaporean audience. Karolyne, Dean Chesterman, and I were with him in a large, multiwindowed conference room as the students amassed in the auditorium. Justice Scalia showed what I took to be mock-irritability as the time approached. "Leave me alone to study my speech!" he demanded with a smile.

The three of us retreated to a nearby sitting area where Justice Scalia was still in view. We watched as he whispered parts of the speech and gesticulated with muted animation.

The point of the speech was that during the first half of the 20th century, a headless fourth branch of American government had been created—namely, the alphabet soup of federal agencies (EPA, FDA, FTC, etc.) supposedly to be run by "experts," who could be expected to be mostly apolitical. He called the experiment a "grand failure," observing that most questions to be decided by the agency experts have no right or wrong answers, but merely social preferences. He also noted that policy questions cannot be divorced from politics: because Congress controls the agency purse strings, the so-called "executive" agencies are subservient to Congress, and agency heads are no longer removable by the elected president.

In a surprising twist, Justice Scalia said that he believed in natural law—meaning a universal moral law derived from a sense of human nature or divine justice. (I would have thought he didn't.) He said he was sure that it exists, yet he said that his own sense of it would be different from that of others. So the only way to implement natural law, for moral questions such as abortion and the death penalty, is to let the *people's* sense of natural law be determinative—as expressed through their elected representatives. He cited example after example of courts as maverick moralizers. Then he tied this theme to textualism and originalism: "Why have judges not *always* been such pioneering policy-makers? The answer is that until relatively recently, the meaning of laws, including fundamental laws or constitutions, was thought to be *static.*" He noted that in 1920, when there had come to be a general agreement that women ought to be able to vote, the Supreme Court didn't declare that the Equal Protection Clause had "acquired new meaning" that it hadn't borne before, but instead the people adopted the 19th Amendment, requiring every state to give women the franchise.

He tied this point back to the agency experts, saying that judges are no more qualified to give people answers to moral questions than the technical experts are. And he noted that if judges engage in freewheeling social regulation by departing from original meaning, the appointment-and-confirmation process for judges will be more political than ever. He ended by saying, "I'm not happy about the intrusion of politics into the judicial-appointment process in my country, but frankly I prefer it to the alternative, which is government by judicial aristocracy."

It was an excellent speech, with powerful points, but he looked withdrawn onstage: he read the whole thing at a lectern that was 25 feet back from the front of the stage, and the lighting for that part of the stage was poor. Laughter was relatively infrequent and muted, and the applause at the end was only polite, not enthusiastic.

The 45-minute speech was followed by a 45-minute onstage interview by Dean Chesterman—and then questions from the audience. One of those questions was especially pointed: "What do you think if your comments in dissents, such as those in *Obergefell*, suggest that the Court is engaged in illegitimate exercises of power, and therefore the Court's stature is lowered in people's eyes?"

Justice Scalia's answer stunned me, and I'd never heard him say anything like this before: "Maybe the Court's stature should be lower in people's eyes, if a majority of my colleagues are going to behave that way."

Some Wrinkles in the Return to Hong Kong

Although Justice Scalia and I had only three speaking engagements during our six days in Hong Kong—at the Chinese University of Hong Kong, the University of Hong Kong, and Thomson Reuters—our schedule was pretty well filled. It included a reception at the American Consulate, sightseeing most mornings, dinner with Chief Justice Geoffrey Ma of the Court of Final Appeal, a tour of the courthouse, two shopping excursions, two tailoring appointments, and two family dinners. Yet we had paced things reasonably well.

Although Justice Scalia seemed to experience a relatively stress-free trip, Karolyne and I found it perhaps the most stressful one we'd ever taken. We were his "handlers"—the only ones he had except at airports—and we remained at his beck and call to ensure that he had what he needed and was happy at all times. Karolyne took on the role of general concierge and "Supreme Scheduler" (as Justice Scalia dubbed her). I took on the roles of footman, bodyguard, and occasional jester—or straight man, as the situation might require. Tom played the crucial roles of Zen master, amiable companion, logistical factotum, and frequent adjunct jester.

The departure from Singapore was auspicious. Before leaving, Karolyne had assured Justice Scalia that she'd steam his suits upon our arrival in Hong Kong—so he needn't worry about wrinkles. We had plenty of time, after all. Hence she folded his suits again and packed them in her suitcase. Before we left for the airport, she asked us to exchange the Singaporean pocket money she'd given us for our Hong Kong pocket money.

"My goodness," said Justice Scalia. "You're so well organized. Is she always like this?"

"Yes, she is," I said. Karolyne just smiled.

Nick, our State Department aide in Singapore, saw us off. Justice Scalia enjoyed his briefings and offered him a visit to the Court and a box seat for oral arguments when he returned to the United States.

After the pilot said we'd be delayed, Justice Scalia caught my eye and beckoned me. I went up the aisle to see him.

"My iPod isn't working." He handed it to me.

"It's out of juice," I said. "Use your other one—the one that Lyne and I gave you. I'll charge this one on the flight."

"Okay. I guess it's in my briefcase."

Of course, he couldn't get it out of the overhead bin because of his bad shoulder. I took it down, opened it, and there the iPod was, tucked neatly into a leather pouch.

"Here it is, Nino."

We were talking over a woman in the aisle seat next to him, but she had headphones on and seemed happily unaware of us.

"You want Mozart?"

"Mozart's good."

"Okay, there are more than 200 pieces by Mozart on here. I'll set it on shuffle songs, and you'll hear a great variety of pieces by Mozart."

"What do you mean?"

"Just try this. You'll love it. You won't have 20 harpsichord pieces in a row. It'll be varied. Just put your headphones on now and lose yourself in the Mozart. We'll be in Hong Kong before you know it."

"Thanks, Bryan."

He closed his eyes, and I went back to my aisle seat two rows back. Our flight was delayed for well over an hour.

The bigger delay, though, was in receiving our luggage in Hong Kong. Once again we were taken to the Chinese-government VIP lounge, where Alissa Redmond from the State Department looked after us. A friendly, mild-mannered midwesterner in her early 30s, she had had several years of experience with the State Department in Africa and Hong Kong. Because the bags were delayed, we spent an inordinate amount of time in the VIP lounge, while she waited just outside.

Alissa explained to us that Clifford Hart, the consul general, would be greeting us with a reception at his official residence—the former embassy—soon after we checked in at the hotel. When the British handed over Hong Kong to the Chinese government in 1997, the embassy was downgraded to a consulate and the ambassador became a consul general.

"My suits are going to be wrinkled, and there'll be no time for Lyne to steam them," Justice Scalia said. "Wouldn't you know this would happen!"

Justice Scalia fretted about this all the way to the hotel. By this time we were already an hour late to the consul general's reception, with 80 or so guests waiting, when we arrived at the Ritz-Carlton. The hotel was festooned with Chinese New Year decorations, and the drive-up was impressive. Technically in Kowloon, not central Hong Kong, the Ritz-Carlton is housed atop the International Commerce Center (ICC), which is the tallest building in the metropolis. Check-in is on the 103rd floor—which we were told was a world altitudinal record for hotel lobbies.

As soon as we arrived at the reception desk, Karolyne helped Justice Scalia check in as I checked in to our room. Karolyne had made the reservation under a slight alias, "Gregory Scalia" (using his middle name), so as to attract less attention among hotel staff. She and I took a room on 116, one floor above Justice Scalia's and Tom Leighton's rooms.

We accompanied Justice Scalia to his room, where, upon entering, he gave me a key to his room in case I might need it for any reason. We opened Karolyne's suitcase to get his suits out, and he was exceedingly upset when he saw how wrinkled they were. "What am I going to wear?"

"Nino, wear these dress slacks with the blazer you have on, and put on a tie," I said. "There's no time for steaming now."

"Dammit! This is exactly what I was trying to prevent by originally carrying my suits on board instead of checking them!"

"I know. We didn't expect the delay. You'll look great in the blazer."

"I will not, dammit!"

"How long before we meet you in the lobby, Nino? Fifteen minutes? Say 3:30?"

"I'll be there in 15," he grumbled.

When the 15 minutes had passed, Karolyne, Tom, and I had already been waiting in the lobby for 5. He didn't come at 3:30. At 3:40, I called his room. The consul general and his invitees had now been waiting 90 minutes for us.

"Nino, we're waiting in the lobby."

"I'm waiting here in my room."

"Waiting for what?"

"They're coming to pick up my suits for pressing."

"We can't wait for your suits to be pressed, Nino."

"They're just going to pick them up. They'll be pressed by the time we get back."

"Who knows how long it'll be before the guy gets there, Nino? The ambassador [I upgraded him] has been waiting for more than an hour and a half!"

"I'm tired of having wrinkled suits. I'm not standing for it."

"Bring them down. I'll leave them with the concierge."

"They're coming, and I'm waiting."

I couldn't get him to budge. Tom and Karolyne were concerned. Alissa was waiting with them, and I simply said there had been an unexpected delay. Finally, at 3:48, Justice Scalia emerged from an elevator wearing a blazer with a red tie. He was angry: "I look like a goddam yabber! [This, once again, was the Scalianism meaning "boor"—a major pejorative.] This is an insult to the ambassador for me to show up this way!"

It was the lengthiest episode of extreme pique that I ever saw him in—lasting perhaps 15 minutes, until we (Alissa included) pulled up to the consulate. Karolyne, Tom, and I were all seriously worried about what might happen upon our arrival. We heard "goddam yabber" about ten times on the van ride to the consulate, and I couldn't get the anger to subside. It only made him angrier when I told him he looked fine.

"This was an unpredictable thing, Nino, having so many delays," I said.

"Justice Scalia," Karolyne said, "I'm genuinely sorry. It's my fault. I was sure I'd have time to steam your suits. I'm so sorry."

He said nothing for a minute or so, and then broke the silence: "I look like a goddam yabber. They expect a Supreme Court Justice, and they get a yabber."

His reddish, stern countenance concerned all of us. We stayed quiet until we approached the consul general's imposing residence, a white-stoned colonial edifice on a hill in central Hong Kong. Alissa said, "That's Consul General Hart waiting outside."

I jumped out immediately to greet him and to announce Justice Scalia, who was suddenly congenial and charming—as he remained throughout the rest of the afternoon. Among the guests were employees of the consulate and local lawyers. The event was beautifully catered, and both Clifford Hart and Justice Scalia eloquently addressed the assembly. Justice Scalia introduced me, Karolyne, and Tom, and he explained that he and I would be making three appearances in Hong Kong in relation to our coauthored books. To look at photos of the event, you'd swear that he was wearing a suit, the only giveaway being the gold buttons on his blazer. He looked perfectly dapper.

One thing I learned from the experience is that Justice Scalia would never have been happy wearing a suit in the condition in which I habitually wore suits. I also learned that the one subject on which I couldn't possibly placate him, under any circumstances, was wrinkles.

First Visit to the Tailors

Upon our leaving the consulate, Alissa accompanied us to the International Financial Center, where Yuen's Tailors were located. Although they specialize (oddly enough) in Scottish kilts and other tartan apparel, they also make traditional suits, often for members of the bar. The owners, brothers Bonnie and Johnny, had done work for friends of Karolyne's aunt Jenny, who lives in Hong Kong and is doubtless the most stylish member of Karolyne's large family.

Jenny and Sandra, Karolyne's mother, met us at the Four Seasons Hotel and walked us briskly through the maze of shops to Yuen's. Jenny walked beside Justice Scalia and chatted with him through the breezeways and corridors. They had met years before at the wedding. Karolyne walked with her mother, and I walked with Tom. I watched not only Justice Scalia but also the pedestrians all around. At one point, a friendly-looking man walked up to Justice Scalia and said, "Excuse me, are you Justice Scalia?"

"I am indeed."

"It's a pleasure to meet you. I'm a law professor visiting here this semester, and I thoroughly enjoy teaching your opinions."

"Good to meet you, Professor. We're on a mission, so we must press on."

That was the first of several times that someone on the street recognized him. We arrived at Yuen's in no time. Jenny made introductions and waited outside with Sandra.

Following the normal practice with Hong Kong tailors, Bonnie took 24 measurements of Justice Scalia; he would call them out while Johnny wrote them down. Meanwhile, Johnny prepared an assortment of woolen fabrics to choose from.

"I need something that'll breathe," Justice Scalia insisted. "I sweat a lot. If the fabric won't breathe, I don't want it."

I added, "We also want something that doesn't wrinkle easily." Justice Scalia and I traded smiles.

He picked two fabrics, and then waited patiently with Karolyne while Tom and I went through the same process.

While Bonnie was measuring me, a 30-something American man came in to get his tartan kilt for a costume party. I started chatting with him and found out that he'd been in Hong Kong for only six months as an investment banker.

"Wait a second," he said, looking at Justice Scalia. "Are you Judge Scalia?"

"I am."

"Wow. What are you doing in Hong Kong?"

"I'm giving a couple of speeches here with my coauthor—the man with whom you've just been conversing."

"I've heard a lot about you, sir. It's an honor to meet you." He paid and was soon gone.

Bonnie and Johnny said we wouldn't need to pay until our final fitting, which we scheduled for the night before we were to fly back to the United States.

Jenny and Sandra took us to have dinner with Ivan, Jenny's husband, a computer-science teacher at the University of Hong Kong; Jennifer, Jenny's daughter; and Jennifer's boyfriend, Will. It was an enjoyable dinner at a brand-new restaurant, the entrance to which was garlanded with dozens of flower arrangements given by friends and well-wishers.

Among other courses, we had two orders of whole steamed fish. The waiter carefully prepared the fish for us, deboning the filets and apportioning them among us.

"May I present the head of the fish as a centerpiece?" the waiter asked, looking toward Justice Scalia and me. Perhaps Sandra had told him that we had an honored guest. I nodded. He then prepared the head on one end and the tail on the other, with a small heap of bones and scraps in between, and said: "In Chinese tradition, we present not only the head but also the tail. We believe that what has a good beginning must also have a good end." He then placed it in the middle of the table.

Justice Scalia was sitting beside me on one side and Will, a young barrister, on the other. From Will he elicited a good deal of information about the nature of legal work in Hong Kong. But soon he was asking about Will's relationship with Jennifer. How long had they been dating? About a year and a half. What did Jennifer do? She worked in procurement for Christian Dior. She was a lovely young woman, Justice Scalia said, and she had a charming smile and a demure but confident way of carrying herself. At the end of the dinner, Will was eager to pose for a photograph with Justice Scalia, saying that his colleagues in chambers simply wouldn't otherwise believe that he'd had this experience.

After dinner, Jenny surprised us with two bags, each containing ten shirts copied in China from those we'd had made by Mr. Kim in Washington. We both expressed profuse gratitude. Justice Scalia insisted on paying for his, but Jenny even more forcefully insisted that the shirts, both his and mine, were gifts from the family.

As we walked through the mall back toward our hotel, Justice Scalia asked me why Will hadn't proposed to Jennifer after 18 months. He was worried that he might be treating her unfairly—"wasting her time"—if he didn't intend to propose. I said I didn't know. It was my first time to meet him as well.

When we got to Justice Scalia's floor, we said goodnight and agreed to meet at the gym the next morning at 7:00. We'd have breakfast after our workout.

Morning at the Gym

Twice in Hong Kong we went to the workout facility before breakfast. (Tom, being a fitness fanatic, was there every day.) On the first of these two mornings, Karolyne and I walked into the gym to find Justice Scalia deep in conversation with an attendant. "They're saying I have to change my shoes, but this is all I have!" He pointed at his brown dress shoes, exasperated.

"We have other shoes," the attendant said.

Karolyne helped the attendant get the right size, and then Justice Scalia sat on a bench and changed into tennis shoes.

"Now I'm ready!" he announced to me.

"You want me as your trainer again?" I asked.

"You're my trainer. But first I want to get on this bicycle for a while."

"Ten minutes," I said. "I'll be on the elliptical machine just over there. Don't overdo it, Nino."

I wasn't really worried about him. But I did want to be sure he didn't overexert himself. After about eight minutes on the recumbent bicycle, as he was watching a tennis match, he was huffing and puffing a little while eagerly following Serena Williams and others in the Australian Open. I went over to him.

"You okay?"

"I'm fine," he said, breathing heavily. "Two more minutes. I want to see the end of this match."

I went back to the elliptical, watching him pretty closely. He seemed fine. Soon he got up, sweating a little, and said, "Okay, what's next?"

"Let's take a drink of water," I said.

"Boy, look at Karolyne running on the treadmill," he said. "She's quite fit."

"Yes. Why don't we try your frozen-shoulder exercise?"

"All right. Let's do it."

Once again, the gentle lean against the wall, with the palm of the right hand going progressively as high as he could reach, proved painful for him. We worked on the left shoulder instead, but soon he lost patience: "My left shoulder isn't the problem!"

"Nino, you need to work on that one as well—for preventive reasons. If you don't, you'll wind up with two bad shoulders."

I noticed that within two minutes after getting off the bicycle, his breathing was back to the normal resting rate.

"Let's do something else. How about these machines?"

The exercise machines were a little different from the machines in Singapore, and there were fewer to choose from. We tried the leg curl, the medicine ball, the lat machine (a bit), the shoulder press (a tiny bit), and the chest press—all at low weights. I tried to talk him out of the lat machine, saying he might hurt his shoulder even worse. He insisted on two reps, though, at ten pounds. Pulling down wasn't painful—just going up.

"This is what I need, you know. I need to do this regularly," he said.

"So do I. Do you have any good equipment at home?"

"Nothing I like."

"Remember, a few years ago I was going to buy you an elliptical machine?"

"Boy, the press would have fun with *that*."

"We need to find some cardio equipment that you'll use."

"I'll do better. I'll use what I have. When I get back, I'm going to exercise more!"

The Ritz Lounge and Bar

We soon established a routine of meeting in the lobby on 103 and taking an escalator down to 102 for breakfast (or late-night drinks) at the Lounge and Bar. The lounge provides a panoramic view of commercial Hong Kong, with its two dozen or so dazzlingly lit-up buildings giving off

Chinese New Year messages. You could also see hundreds of apartment buildings teeming on the hillsides of Hong Kong Island. We estimated that 200 vessels could be seen in the harbor at any given time. When we'd see an interesting ship, cruise liner, barge, or tugboat going in or out of the harbor, we'd comment on it and check on its progress from time to time.

Meanwhile, the Lounge and Bar had its own charming feel inside, with two enormous 25-foot catenoidally shaped glass chandeliers descending from the 30-foot ceiling. We habitually sat at either of two corner tables where we could best take in the scenery, both interior and exterior.

We marveled not only at the view each morning at breakfast but also at the culinary offerings. In the 7,500-square-foot restaurant were seven sumptuously outfitted stations: a noodle bar, a dim-sum bar, a pastry station, a congee (rice-porridge) station, a fruit-and-salad station, an omelet station, and a hot-food station. This was a breakfast like no other. Because breakfast was included in our room charges, and because Justice Scalia, of course, insisted that breakfast was his favorite and the most important meal of the day, we dutifully met there every morning.

Despite his adventurousness with Singaporean breakfasts, the first day in Hong Kong Justice Scalia reverted to a conventional American breakfast of ham and eggs. Tom ate fruit. Justice Scalia kidded me about my selections: "Noodles for breakfast, Bryan? You're having noodles?! And what are those lumps on your plate?"

"They're dumplings, Nino," I said, smiling. "These things are collectively called dim sum, and they're the greatest breakfast foods ever devised by any culture. I can't believe you're having an American breakfast despite all these splendiferous choices."

"There he goes," he said to Tom and Karolyne. "Splendiferous!"

Using some serving chopsticks, I put some noodles on his plate. "Okay," he said, "let me try those!"

Karolyne showed him how to use the chopsticks with pan-fried angel-hair noodles, which present a different challenge from sushi. Despite the thickness of his hands and fingers, Justice Scalia was dexterous and coordinated. He got the hang of it pretty quickly.

"You're holding them too close to the tips," said Karolyne gently. "Refined Chinese hold the chopsticks toward the far end, away from the food."

"Oh." Justice Scalia laughed, adjusting his grip. "I want to be refined!"

With shu-mai pork dumplings, he adopted a different strategy altogether: after splattering one of his shirts when a dumpling fell into soy sauce, he resorted to impaling the dumpling with a single chopstick and lifting it into his mouth. "Say," he joked, "these are awfully good!"

As I was leaving the table to get a bowl of congee, I said, "I'll bring you a small plate of those noodles."

"Please do!"

Just as in Singapore, Justice Scalia switched to local fare after the first breakfast and never looked back. The second day, he tried dim sum, and the third day congee with pickled vegetables. Finally, on the fourth day he sampled the soupy noodles: "Who would think of soupy noodles for breakfast?" he said. "But these are really good! Can't believe I skipped these the first three days."

After the first day, he sampled all the fare *except* the American items. Even so, he and Karolyne would split a few pastries at the end of each breakfast.

One of the appealing points at the Ritz Lounge and Bar was that the chef alternated many of his dishes day by day—angel-hair fried egg noodles one day, spaghetti-sized fried egg noodles the next, and thick udon noodles the next; or Japanese fried rice one day, Korean-style kimchee fried rice the next, and Chinese pork-fried rice the next. This kept our foursome on a daily breakfast adventure as we discovered differences. It was Justice Scalia who first noticed the shifting fare.

"Hey," he said to me one morning, "where's my angel-hair? I loved that yesterday. I want my angel-hair."

"Well," I said, "today they have only spaghetti-sized noodles."

"I guess I'll try these," he said with resignation. But soon he decided he liked them even better.

"It all started here, you know," I remarked.

"What do you mean?"

"Italian pasta—your favorite food from the time you left the cradle."

"You mean Marco Polo? Yeah, he brought noodles back from the Orient."

"Isn't that an urban legend?" Karolyne asked.

"I think it's true," I said. Justice Scalia nodded that he did, too.

"Let's find out," said Tom, taking out his iPhone. Within seconds, he'd found a reliable-looking website confirming Karolyne's doubts. Italian pasta occurred in total isolation from China centuries before Marco Polo had sailed home to Venice in 1292.

"Well, what do you know?" said Justice Scalia. "I'm glad my forebears invented it on their own."

"But China was in fact earlier," said Tom, still swiping screens on his iPhone.

"Even so," said Justice Scalia, "Italians came up with it independently. You can't keep a good idea down."

A Full Day in Hong Kong

On our first full day in Hong Kong, a Saturday, we had breakfast and then met our guide, Polly Lin, a diminutive, bright woman with a ready smile and the metabolism of a hummingbird. She took us to the Hong Kong History Museum on the Kowloon Peninsula. Then we took a 15-minute helicopter tour of Hong Kong starting and ending at the Peninsula Hotel. The helicopter ride was fascinating. We wore headphones, and the pilots pointed out major landmarks as we went. Justice Scalia was jovial and playful. As I snapped a few photos of him strapping himself into the seat, he looked across at me and stuck his tongue out for the camera.

We flew all around Hong Kong Island, and we had a superb view of the tallest building, the ICC, where our hotel was located. From the air we could see the building's overlapping windows, designed to mimic the scales of a dragon. In fact, the enormous skyscraper was meant to suggest a dragon heading toward heaven. The views were breathtaking.

During lunch at Spring Moon, the Michelin-starred restaurant at the Peninsula, the waiter brought to our table some glistening, gelatinous-looking strands.

"What's this?" Justice Scalia asked Karolyne.

"Can you guess?" she said.

"No idea."

"It's jellyfish."

"Jellyfish! Well, let me try that."

"Nino," I said, "that may be a bit adventurous for you. I don't eat jelly-fish. You know, it might sting your tongue."

"Ha!" he said. "Say, this is excellent. I like the texture of it. I really like it. I'm just more adventurous than you, Bryan. You see? Here, Tom, try some of this jellyfish." He served Tom with his own chopsticks. Tom tried it but humorously scrunched up his nose: no more jellyfish for Tom.

But jellyfish soon became a leitmotif during the rest of our stay. At every lunch or dinner, if it was a Chinese restaurant, Justice Scalia would add, "Oh, and please bring me a generous side of jellyfish." Then he'd add, "My uncle here"—gesturing at me—"doesn't eat it, but I do like jellyfish." That was the first of many times that he called me "uncle" on the trip.

Despite the slippery nature of jellyfish, Justice Scalia generally had no problems delivering it to his mouth via chopsticks—though occasionally, very occasionally, he'd help the food into the tweezing side of the chopsticks with his left forefinger and thumb.

At the end of our meal at Spring Moon, the waiter brought a yin-and-yang chocolate mousse. Justice Scalia liked the look of it so much that he posed for a picture while holding it. The waiter explained the meaning of yin and yang to his (mostly) Western guests. He told us that in Chinese culture yin and yang are symbols of the many complementary dualities that pervade our lives, such as light and dark, expansion and contraction, fire and water, male and female.

Shopping on Hollywood Road

Toward the end of the meal, I asked Justice Scalia whether he'd like to go to the antiques district of Hong Kong—at Hollywood Road, on the west side. At first, he wasn't interested because he didn't care for antiques.

"It's not just antiques, Nino. They have lots of interesting things—even dinosaur eggs."

"Dinosaur eggs? Are you kidding me?"

"No."

"How do you know they're dinosaur eggs?"

"Wait till you see them. You'll see that they're fossilized. They're rock. They're mostly hadrosaurus eggs from the Henon province. They have them throughout the antiques district."

"Doesn't sound interesting to me."

"You'll find things there for Maureen. I promise."

"Like what?"

"Gewgaws."

"Gewgaws? Who uses a word like that?"

"I do. You know I use words like that."

"Yes, unfortunately, I do. Okay, let's go to Hollywood Road."

So we did. We took a cab from the Peninsula Hotel to Hollywood Road. Justice Scalia, Karolyne, and Tom followed me through various antiques shops as I examined vases, jewelry, and dinosaur eggs—at least two dozen sets of them. I thought most items seemed overpriced, and I forbore negotiating for anything.

Justice Scalia was fascinated by Chinese dragons. At one shop, he found a jade dragon that he especially admired and pointed it out to the shopkeeper.

"How much will you pay?" asked the shopkeeper.

"Let me ask my uncle," said Justice Scalia, turning to me. When it turned out that the dealer wanted more than $2,000 U.S. for the dragon, Justice Scalia politely declined. "My uncle says it's too much." We walked away with a smile and a wave.

"So I'm your uncle?"

"You're my uncle!"

"You're getting that from me. You know I've often said you're like an uncle to me. I do feel that way."

"I've heard you say that," he said, smiling, as we nudged shoulders while walking down the sidewalk.

One shop had hundreds of busts of Chairman Mao. The raspy-voiced seller had sold me an 18-inch-high bronze bust of Confucius six years before—the only likeness of Confucius he had. But likenesses of Mao pervaded every nook of his shop.

In front of his shop were hundreds of bronze animals representing birth years in the Chinese zodiac. I was born in 1958, the year of the dog. Karolyne figured out Justice Scalia's birth-year animal: born in 1936, he was year of the rat. Tom, born in 1960, was also year of the rat. So we needed a good dog and two good rats, as well as a rooster (for Karolyne's birth year).

Halfway through the search, Justice Scalia took me aside. "I wish I weren't a rat. I could be anything but a rat. I just don't want to be a rat."

"Nino," I said, laughing, "facts are facts. You're a rat."

We narrowed the choice down to three bronze rats. Justice Scalia took one sitting atop a nut, with coins on the side. Tom took one of the others. Justice Scalia and I posed for a photo—each of us holding our birth-year animals.

Then the four of us walked down the lane, past sellers of counterfeit American coins—19th-century Morgan dollars seemingly made out of tin and obviously fake Washington quarters with oversized busts of Washington on the obverse.

At the end of the street, we found what looked like a reputable store full of beautiful old vases. Inside the shop, two dusty old moon vases were tucked away on the bottom shelf of a seldom-opened case. The seller told us that they dated from the 1600s. In any event, I knew that with Chinese antiquities, 17th-century items aren't considered particularly old. He wanted $8,000 U.S. for the pair. I was skeptical about his dating. I thought they were probably modern replicas made to look old. In the end, I negotiated a price of $1,900 U.S. Because he could speak no English, the negotiation took place entirely by typing numbers into his calculator. When we finally got to the stopping point of $1,900 U.S. (we were using Hong Kong dollars on the calculator), the seller accepted but acted extremely agitated by the price. But he agreed to that number.

"Nino, you could take one, and I could take one, for $950 U.S. apiece. We'd have matching Ming vases."

"You'd have one, and I'd have one," he said. "I like the idea."

"You can see that they're unusual. We've looked in 20 shops already, and we've seen nothing like these."

"I agree."

"And they're very appealing aesthetically," I said.

"I think so," Justice Scalia said. "I'm willing to do it."

"Would Maureen like them? It's a big expenditure if she doesn't."

"I think she would."

Then Karolyne walked in from the sidewalk and said, "Bryan, what are you *doing*?"

"I think we're going to buy these vases."

"Don't do it. You've gotten enough already."

"Darling, I've bargained the guy down by 75%. I think it might be a good deal."

"Let me see them . . . How much?"

"They're $1,900 U.S.—for the pair."

The seller took some water out for a demonstration. He put droplets on the vases, and the water instantly disappeared—either through absorption or by instantaneous evaporation. He did it repeatedly. It was astonishing how quickly the water vanished.

"That's impressive," I said.

"What does that show?" asked Justice Scalia.

"I have no idea," I said, laughing. "What does that show, Lyne?" Then Karolyne spoke with the seller in Cantonese.

"He says that it shows how good the vases are," Karolyne said, "and that they're genuine. But I don't think you should get them."

"Why not?" I said.

"Just a feeling," she said.

Justice Scalia said, "If Lyne thinks we shouldn't, then we probably shouldn't."

I said, "That's why I call her my *arbiter elegantiarum*," I said. "She talks me out of things like this when she needs to."

Second Full Day in Hong Kong

Sunday would be our last day in Hong Kong without a scheduled speaking engagement. Justice Scalia and Tom, a fellow Catholic, had agreed to attend an early Mass that would allow them to return to the Ritz-Carlton by 9:00 a.m. It was the only time they had been without Karolyne to help them navigate and communicate, and it reportedly involved some nervous moments on the iPhone. But they had successfully returned for breakfast.

That morning Polly took us on the tram to Victoria Peak to see the finest view of Hong Kong, and then to Aberdeen Harbour, where we rode on a sampan boat and took a tour of fishermen's houseboats. We wore traditional sampan hats, which looked like upside-down wicker bowls. We all enjoyed a good laugh at how silly we looked—especially Tom, whose hat sported a vibrant multicolor chin-strap. Polly then took us to Stanley Market, where we shopped awhile at the array of small stores.

At 1:00 p.m., Polly dropped us off for lunch with Karolyne's family— dim sum at the Sheraton Hotel. Once again, Will sat beside Justice Scalia. While the lazy Susan was turning to pass food around the table, the subject of marriage somehow came up. "You're being awfully slow, dating Jennifer for 18 months," said Justice Scalia. "Do you intend to propose?"

"I don't know yet."

"Well, be fair to her. Don't waste her time. Eighteen months is a long time if you're not serious about pursuing the relationship."

Will asked how long Justice Scalia had known his wife before proposing. Three months. What about me? Six months. What about Tom? Eighteen months—but his excuse was that he was still in law school at the time, and broke.

"Will, I think you have been given judicial direction," I said.

He said he'd think further on the matter.

We left the Sheraton Hotel in taxicabs to meet at the jade market in Kowloon. Justice Scalia's announced purpose was to find a jade bracelet for Mrs. Scalia, as well as a dragon for himself. He said he'd always had a fascination with Chinese dragons. Karolyne and I simply liked going to such markets for whatever might strike our fancy—and for the experience of haggling with the sellers. Our own jade expert, revered in the family, was Karolyne's eldest aunt, Dai Yee (or Dai Yee Ma, as Karolyne and I call her), who speaks perhaps only four expressions in English: *good morning, hallo, money,* and *thank you.*

The Jade Market

The Hong Kong jade market is really a series of covered bazaars with dozens of stalls inside—a dusty place with concrete floors and all sorts of wares besides jade, such as bronze figurines, exotic stones, pearls, and various kinds of jewelry. The aisles are narrow and the stalls crammed. As you walk through, sellers scramble for your attention, hawking their items. Justice Scalia was being attended to by Karolyne, Sandra, Jenny, and Dai Yee, not to mention Tom, so I left them with their jade sellers to go in search of a dragon for Justice Scalia. I found what I thought to be the best of its kind—a 13-inch-long greenish dragon for sale by a seller I came to know as Wong Kam Wa.

He also had several glow-in-the-dark natural-stone spheres about five inches in diameter. He demonstrated their phosphorescence by putting one of the orbs under a tablecloth, where it plainly emitted a greenish light. I decided to think more about whether to buy one of them later, but first I wanted to negotiate the price of the dragon.

He wanted $65 U.S. in the beginning, but readily went down to $45. I countered at $18. He then went to $35, saying that was his absolute minimum. I then mentioned that it was only a four-claw dragon, not five. Four-claw Chinese dragons like this one, I said, are more common and really nothing special. It's five-claw dragons that are traditionally reserved for members of the extended royal family. I said $19 was the most I'd be willing to pay. When he balked at that, I smiled and said goodbye in the most genial way I could. I walked to the next stall, picked up an item there, and Mr. Wa came over to say $25 would be his very best price. I smiled and said I'd already decided against it. Then he offered it for $20. I accepted and shook his hand, telling him that I must go and get my friend. I knew I was bargaining for Justice Scalia, and if he didn't like the dragon, I'd have to buy it myself.

When I reached Justice Scalia, he said, "Bryan, I got the bracelet! You'll never believe what happened. Karolyne's aunt [Dai Yee] slapped the man twice on the cheek with two $500 bills! I've never seen such a negotiating tactic in my life. She slapped him twice! She's some lady."

"Did she get the price she wanted?" I asked.

"No. He wanted $1,000, and she was demanding $800, so she slapped him."

"Did he budge?"

"No—we paid $1,000."

"U.S. dollars?"

"No. Hong Kong dollars, so divide by eight."

"That's a great price for a jade bracelet."

"I'm *very* pleased. Maureen is going to love it! And it was only about $120 U.S."

Our entire group was abuzz about the slapping incident.

"Nino, I found a dragon for you."

"You did? Let's see it."

"It's the one I like best. There are many dragons like this," I said, pointing at one in a stall beside us. "But come back here to see this other one! You'll like it better."

We walked back about 20 paces to Mr. Wa's stall. Justice Scalia looked at Mr. Wa, pointed at me, and said, "My uncle here thinks I should buy something from you."

"Here it is, Nino. Look at this."

"It's perfect. How much does he want?"

"He wanted $65 initially, but I negotiated him down to $20."

"U.S. dollars?"

"Right."

"That's a good deal."

"It took a little doing. Guess what. He also has phosphorescent balls."

"He has what?"

"He's selling phosphorescent stone balls. They glow in the dark."

"Jeez. I thought you were describing a medical condition!"

We both laughed. "Seriously, Nino, look at this ball." I held it under the tablecloth, in the dark.

"That's not glowing!"

"It is, Nino! Are you even looking at it?"

"Then it's probably radioactive."

"You think so? Maybe I shouldn't have it in my bag."

"I still don't think it glows in the dark," said Justice Scalia.

By now, Mr. Wa had taken out a flashlight and shone the light directly on part of the ball. Then he put it under the table.

"Yep," said Tom, who had now joined us. "It definitely glows in the dark."

"Let me see again," Justice Scalia said.

Meanwhile, I asked Mr. Wa what he'd sell it for. He wanted $75 U.S. but would let it go for $65. I countered at $25. Then Karolyne entered the fray, saying we wouldn't pay more than $20 for the ball. She said, "I agree with Justice Scalia that it might be radioactive." I figured she was posturing for negotiating purposes, but I couldn't be certain.

"Okay, Nino, let's get down to business about your dragon. You want it?"

"I want it." Then he turned to Mr. Wa and said, "What's the price my uncle negotiated? Twenty dollars?"

"Yes," said Mr. Wa, and the transaction was concluded. "Let me sell you the ball," he said to me. "It glows for you."

"My wife says $20, no more. I'm sorry."

"Okay. I'll take that."

So we left the jade market with a bracelet, a dragon, a phosphorescent ball, and various baubles that others in our contingent had acquired in similar mini-expeditions. Tom left with two jade crosses.

Dai Yee's Condo

As we were leaving the jade market, Dai Yee asked us, through Sandra's translation, to her condominium on the 72nd floor of the Arch, a fashionable high-rise connected to the Ritz-Carlton. She wanted to serve us some of her special health-giving broth.

"We may as well, Nino," I said. "It'll probably be your only chance to see home life in Hong Kong—even if it's not 'typical' home life. It's an apartment in the Arch, after all."

"Sounds good to me. You want to come, Tom?"

"Sure," Tom said. "I'm game."

Dai Yee, Sandra, Jenny, and Karolyne were happy to have us up to the condo. Once we entered the commodious three-bedroom lodgings, we all took off our shoes and were greeted not only by our hosts but also by dozens of jade Buddhas and Guanyins. On the balcony were a Taoist shrine, potted plants, and drying laundry. Taken by the view and the fresh air at this altitude, Justice Scalia was amused by my acrophobia, which caused a palpable dread as I approached the railing. Nevertheless, I posed for a photo with him on the balcony, as did Tom. Soon all three of us were at the dining table quaffing bowls of Dai Yee's fish air-bladder broth in the Asian way—straight from the bowl and not with a spoon.

Then Dai Yee suddenly appeared with a bowl of large mushroom caps and a single toothpick. She thrust one in front of Justice Scalia's mouth, saying in Cantonese, "Please try this. It's good. It's good for the body."

I told him, "She wants you to eat it." He had little choice but to chomp on it. Then she fed one to me, and then to Tom—all from the same toothpick. Then back to Justice Scalia, who balked this time. But she didn't understand English and impetuously insisted that he take it. He did. Three rounds for each of us.

"Well, guys," I said, "now we've shared the same toothpick three times over. I think Dai Yee has cured me of my germophobia."

"It's about time, Bryan!" said a smiling Justice Scalia. "What can we do for your acrophobia?"

"Nothing, I assure you."

Dai Yee tried for a fourth round, but Justice Scalia said to Karolyne across the room, "Please tell her that we're stuffed."

Dai Yee was happy. So were we all.

When Justice Scalia, Tom, Karolyne, and I returned to the Ritz-Carlton, we decided that after those mushrooms, no dinner would be necessary. "Besides," said Justice Scalia, "I want to see Serena Williams win the Australian Open! She and her sister Venus are two of the best athletes in history. I really like watching them."

We turned in early before our tour the next day with Polly.

Third Day: Chinese University of Hong Kong

Justice Scalia was uncharacteristically late for our 8:00 a.m. rendezvous in the lobby. At 8:05, I told Karolyne and Tom that I'd go to his room to check on him. Although I had a key, I knocked—of course—and heard "Coming!" from within.

"Ah, good morning," he said.

"Good morning."

"Come in while I finish dressing. Sorry to hold you up. I guess I overslept."

"I just wanted to be sure you were all right."

"I'm fine. Did you see that tennis match last night?"

"I missed it," I said.

"It was a heartbreaker. Serena lost to Kerber, a virtually unknown German player, in the final set, 6–4. What an exciting match."

"Too bad Serena lost."

"Yeah."

Soon we'd caught up with Karolyne and Tom in the lobby, and their worries evaporated.

At breakfast, I asked Justice Scalia whether he'd seen the "Cockney Trump" video, in which the comedian Peter Serafinowicz had overdubbed a Trump speech with a deep voice and a tough-guy cockney accent. He hadn't. So we watched the 90-second video together, as Trump was heard dropping his H's: "I'm beatin' 'illary, I'm beatin' 'illary, and I 'aven't even focused. We 'aven't even focused on 'illary." We both thought it was hilarious, and brilliantly done.

"It's amazing," Justice Scalia said, "how readily Trump's speech patterns fit into a cockney accent."

After breakfast, we met Polly at the entrance to the Ritz. We were to tour the bird market and the fish market in Central Kowloon and then have lunch at a restaurant called Duddell's. Because it was rainy that day, we each carried an umbrella. While Justice Scalia took many photographs of fish in aquariums and fish in water-filled plastic bags hanging from aluminum lattices, I took photos of him taking those photos. The fish are all sold as pets—not as food. Until you've seen it, you wouldn't believe the magnitude of the fish market, with shop after shop. The four of us marveled at it.

The same could be said for the bird market, which had endless shops, in street after street, with caged songbirds and exotic birds to be kept as pets. For lunch at Duddell's, we ate (appropriately) pigeon. The whole bird was served up, including its head decoratively placed on the serving platter.

After lunch, we had a little time to rest before the afternoon event at the Chinese University of Hong Kong. I was to moderate a discussion between Justice Scalia and Justice Kemal Bokhary of Hong Kong's Court of Final Appeal. The title was "Judges and Democracy," and the event was nicely covered by a reporter for the *Hong Kong Lawyer*.[55] She wrote: "Professor Garner's personal and professional relationship with Justice Scalia added a layer of intimacy, as the two affectionately ribbed each other and often finished each other's sentences."[56]

My notes for conducting the interview consisted of nine words: "Stop at 6. Justice. Human rights. Dissents. Purposive/textual." I wrote them during the 20 minutes when Justice Scalia, Justice Bokhary, and I sat in a conference room across from the lecture hall as the audience gradually took their seats. Justice Scalia and I had already been briefed about Justice Bokhary: he was known for liberal leanings and purposive interpretation, as opposed to textualism. A thin, mild-mannered man who seemed sensitive and introspective, he was also known for legal cartooning, and he had developed an amiable crocodilian character named "Crocky." On the chalkboard in the conference room that we were using as a greenroom, he drew Crocky and various judge caricatures. It took him only seconds. He graciously presented us with copies of his book *Recollections*, which we gratefully received.

When the starting time came, we walked into the packed law-school classroom and were warmly greeted by applause from the 120 or so attendees. Justice Scalia and I both noticed Consul General Clifford Hart and his colleague Alissa Redmond—who had twice taken care of us at the airport and would soon be doing it again. We both gave little nods to those we knew, including Karolyne and Tom. After introductions by Dean Christopher Gane, a charming Scotsman, I dove immediately into the first question: "Justice Scalia, didn't you once say that judges shouldn't be con-

---

55 Cynthia G. Claytor, "An Evening with Justice Antonin Scalia and Justice Kemal Bokhary," *Hong Kong Lawyer*, March 2016, at 14ff.

56 *Id.*

cerned with pursuing justice when interpreting statutes and constitutional provisions? What did you mean?"

"I never said *that*," Justice Scalia responded with theatrical flair.

"I think we both said that in our book," I said in reference to *Reading Law*. "Or maybe I wrote that part of the book."

It was a warm audience, and they laughed. As their laughter subsided, Justice Scalia continued, "Well, I was not the first to say it, I'll put it that way." He cited a famous incident in Massachusetts, on the evening of December 3, 1902, when Justice Oliver Wendell Holmes was about to be seated on the United States Supreme Court. An audience member shouted, "Now justice will be done in Washington!" to which Holmes is said to have called back, "Don't be too sure. I am going there to administer the *law*."[57]

"That is my answer, really," Justice Scalia said. "Justice in a democracy is what the people deem to be just. Very often my notion of what is just or what is good differs from the people across the U.S.—which is to say the members of Congress. Where there is a difference, it is *their* notion of justice that should prevail." He went on to say that he often has to reach results that he considers quite unfair. "But if that's the law, then in my system of democracy, that is the result I must reach." Without this view, he said, you can't really have a democratic system.

Justice Bokhary's answer was shorter: that people go to law with the expectation that they will receive justice according to law.

I then asked both panelists: "Should a judge at times be unhappy with his or her decisions?"

Justice Scalia answered first: "You show me a judge who is always happy with the results he reaches, and I will show you a bad judge. That means he is applying his own notion of what the result ought to be, instead of the notion of what is required under law."

Justice Scalia cited another example, saying that his adherence to originalism sometimes forced him to take legal positions that went against his ideological grain. He mentioned *United States v. Eichman*,[58] in which he joined the majority's 5–4 decision holding that burning the American flag is protected speech under the First Amendment to the U.S. Constitution. "If it were up to me," he said, "I'd have them put that person in jail right

---

57 Fred Shapiro, *The Yale Book of Quotations* 368 (2006).

58 496 U.S. 310 (1990).

away. I am a very conservative person, but that is just not what our First Amendment says. It protects freedom of speech, including expressive conduct."

At one point, he raised the example of *King v. Burwell*,[59] the Obamacare case in the Supreme Court. "There was a provision of it," he said, "which said that the individuals who registered for medical insurance with 'exchanges established by a state'—that was the language of the statute, 'exchanges established by a state'—would get subsidies.

"Well," he continued, "as it turns out, many of the states did not establish exchanges. And the system would not work if so many people did not get subsidies. So my Court said, well, by golly, this thing would not work unless we read 'established by a state' to mean 'established by the federal government,' and that is how the Court read it. That is purposivism, and that is a good example of how a purposivist would reach a different result."

Justice Scalia said that he was adamantly against interpreting the statutory language that way: "If the statute will not work, that means that Congress wrote a bad statute. It's not my job to improve the statute. They wrote what they wrote. Many thought, of course, that what happened is the members of Congress were hoist by their own petard because they were trying to force the states to establish exchanges, and it didn't work. So should we revise the statute? No, I don't think so! I dissented in the case."

Taking this opportunity for a smooth transition, I next invited the distinguished panelists, both famous for their dissenting opinions, to talk about what value dissents have.

Justice Scalia answered first: "Judges have different attitudes." He disagreed with people who think you should refrain from dissenting unless it's a really important point in a really important case—especially at the Supreme Court level. "I've never signed my name to an opinion that I didn't think was correct, not only in the result, but in every aspect of its reasoning. If there is one aspect of the reasoning that I disagree with, then I'll say, 'I join in the opinion except for that.'"

That way, he pointed out, you can hold your judges' feet to the fire: "I can be criticized not just for the opinions I have written but also for the opinions that I have joined. That is good. You ought to hold your judges to principle. You want to hold them to be consistent, and that can only be

---

59 135 S.Ct. 2480 (2015).

done if you let them dissent and expect them to dissent when they don't agree."

And dissents serve other purposes as well, he said. "For instance, I am never more confident of my opinion when I'm writing for the majority than when I have a dissent. When the opinion is unanimous, there is nobody to point out potential flaws in my opinion. When you have a dissenter, the dissenter will poke holes in your weak arguments and you can retrench. And that often happens."

Justice Bokhary agreed with Justice Scalia, adding that sometimes what begins as a dissent may bring colleagues around so that a different majority is formed.

At the end of the session, a student asked whether Justice Scalia thought it wise to include references and allusions to literature in his opinions—such as Shakespearean quotations.

I quickly interceded, figuring that my doing so would give Justice Scalia a little more time to reflect on his answer. "Justice Scalia has already used a Shakespeare quotation tonight, by using a famous phrase from *Hamlet*. Does anyone know what it was?"

"I don't even know," Justice Scalia said, provoking laughter. Nor did anyone else.

"You said 'hoist by his own petard,' a phrase used by the character Hamlet himself. Most people don't know what a *petard* is."

"Well, I just used the phrase, and I know its meaning broadly speaking—'causing your own downfall'—but for the life of me I couldn't tell you precisely what a *petard* is."

"Can anyone?" I asked, giving everyone in the audience a chance. No one knew.

"It's a bomb," I said. "So it means 'blown up by your own bomb.'"

"Really?" Justice Scalia said with a quizzical expression. People were chuckling.

"Yes," I said. "There's actually a debate among Shakespeareans about whether it's *petard* or *petar* (without the final *d*), and people wonder why Shakespeare didn't write *hoisted* instead of *hoist* for the past-tense verb. And then there's the question whether it's *hoist with* or *hoist by*. You said *hoist by* even though Shakespeare wrote *hoist with*. But in literary expression today, *hoist by* predominates, so you're on firm ground."

"Are you making this up? Is that all true?" asked Justice Scalia.

"All true, I promise."

"That's why I keep this guy around," Justice Scalia said. "He's a philologist, and he's such a pain in the neck. He knows all sorts of stuff like that."

The audience seemed to enjoy our repartee.

"But let's get back to the young man's question," I said. "Is it desirable to use literary allusions and references in judicial opinions?"

"If they're pertinent, and they add insight or interest, I think they're good," Justice Scalia answered. "I like them. But for literary references to work, we must expect educated people to have a shared knowledge. And in the age of MultiCulti"—he said it with some derision—"we're losing the literary core that *every* educated person was once expected to have mastered. I frankly lament that loss."

"Me, too," I said.

Justice Scalia added that he liked literary references and allusions primarily in dissents: "It's important to make dissents interesting. So I will quote Shakespeare. I will use Bugs Bunny. I will use whatever will attract the attention of law professors and law students."

A judge from the Isle of Man asked both Justice Scalia and Justice Bokhary whether they thought the need politicians have to run for re-election makes it hard for them to make unpopular but correct decisions. Yes, both said. Justice Scalia mentioned that many American states still elect their judges, some even with partisan elections, and that that kind of system doesn't encourage good judging. But he added that if the judiciary is wholly independent, without significant fear of political repercussions, correct but unpopular decisions aren't particularly difficult.

After Dean Gane's brief closing remarks, the audience applauded heartily. Justice Scalia bolted into the audience to thank Consul General Hart and Alissa for coming. A minute later, though, Dean Gane beckoned him back to the front of the room for photos and the presentation of gifts. This interruption annoyed Justice Scalia, who had been exchanging warm greetings with the group from the U.S. Consulate. In the photos that were snapped after he'd been told to come back, he can be seen frowning with displeasure.

But when the photo session was over and we were back in our holding room with Karolyne across the hall, he said, almost boyishly, "Hey, what'd we get? Let's open our presents."

And so we did. His gift was a Chinese chess set; mine was a miniature Chinese screen to put on a desk or shelf.

"What's this?" Justice Scalia said. "I think I like yours better. I wish I'd gotten that screen instead."

Karolyne told him, "It's a Chinese chess set. I'll teach you how to play. It's a great intellectual exercise."

"Okay. Thank you, Lyne." He still seemed a little disappointed.

Justice Bokhary joined us and talked with us until Dean Gane escorted us down the hall to a reception for students and faculty. Strangely, as we stood amid dozens of students and faculty, no one said a word to us. Justice Scalia, Tom, Karolyne, and I stood there for several minutes while our erstwhile audience members chatted in small groups.

"This is ridiculous," said Justice Scalia. "Let's go to dinner now. I'm hungry."

"I'll tell the dean," I said. Wandering off, I returned a few minutes later with the dean only to find Justice Scalia and Karolyne having fun at my expense. "There he is," Justice Scalia said, "Chatty Cathy! Lyne called you that first," as they both suppressed a laugh. Whenever she invoked that moniker, any annoyance he felt at my social volubility gave way to amusement. Anyway, I'd located the dean even if I'd spoken briefly with others along the way.

Soon Dean Gane led us down two sets of escalators to a dinner in a restaurant housed in a connected building. The dinner got off to a rocky start. We were late—something Justice Scalia deplored. And when we arrived, there were no introductions: we were simply taken past the other tables. This seemed like a social blunder. We were in a private room with perhaps five tables. We were seated at the head table—Justice Scalia beside Karolyne and Dean Gane but opposite me at a huge round table for 10 or 12—and no waiters came around. They were on the periphery of the room doing what appeared to be busywork. They didn't approach our table, and after three minutes Justice Scalia was irate.

He said to me across the table, "Where are the waiters! I'm ready to order a drink." Justice Scalia went over to the corner where the waiters were huddled and asked them to take our drink orders. He came back and sat down, obviously perturbed because we didn't even have our water yet. As the waiters tarried, he said, "I've sat here for five minutes!"

I looked around the room, stood, and summoned the waiters to tell them they should visit our table immediately—but, inexplicably, to no avail. The dean sat impassively at first but became concerned as Justice Scalia's ire intensified. "What kind of place is this?!" Justice Scalia said.

I jumped up, took a bottle of wine, and instructed the waiters to pour immediately. A waiter kindly took the bottle from me, and I sat back down. She started pouring, but at the front tables where people had been only incompletely seated. So I jumped up again and asked her to start with my table, and specifically with the man on the far side—Justice Scalia. Once she had done so, all was well, and the rest of the evening went smoothly, with a fair amount of academic talk at our table.

Going Walkabout on February 2

On Tuesday, our group of four again met in the gym at 7:00 a.m. Justice Scalia and I went through the same routine as we had before: ten minutes on the recumbent bicycle, shoulder exercises, and then light weights. "Let's do this leg-extension machine today," Justice Scalia said. "Why didn't we do it the other day?"

"We shouldn't do that one, Nino. We've both had our knees scoped."

"No, it's fine," he said. "You just have to do it right."

"My knee doctor told me not to under any circumstances."

"I've looked into this," he said. "You just have to start with the machine farther up. Don't do it with your leg cocked back."

"Really, Nino, I think it's unwise for either of us."

"Come on. Get on." He pushed me a little, and I relented. "Look, we set the machine so that your leg starts out almost fully extended, and then you take it up the last bit. Do five reps."

I did it, reluctantly. Meanwhile, I was curious about how he knew so much about this one machine when I had needed to show him how to use all the others. But I was humoring him. Then I got off, and he did the same.

It wasn't until we were walking out to the elevator that I realized that my right knee, the one I'd had scoped, was aching—suddenly pretty badly. I mentioned it at breakfast, jovially, noting that it wasn't a good day for knee aches, given the walking tour we had ahead of us. "Oh, you'll be fine," Karolyne said reassuringly. She had stressed to the tour company that we wanted a light walking tour—no serious hoofing around the city.

Our walking tour of Hong Kong's Central District was to be led by an Englishman with supposedly strong walking-tour credentials. The day got off to a shaky start, though, as the tour guide—I'll call him Basil

Middlemiss—was late. We were downstairs in front of the Ritz-Carlton, just where we had always met Polly, at the appointed time of 9:00 a.m. No guide was in sight. By 9:10, Justice Scalia was getting unhappy, and so was I, so I walked outside to check with each of the three van drivers to see whether any of them worked with Basil. The last one said he did, and he pointed back inside where we had all been standing. I went back in.

Back inside, I reported, "I think he must have gone to the restroom, Nino."

"That's ridiculous. He should have done that before arriving."

I looked around the large foyer, and far off in a corner, near the entrance to the Elements mall, I saw a disheveled man talking to himself while typing something into his handheld device. He was a man of perhaps 60 with gray thinning hair. His tinted glasses mostly hid his eyes. He carried a backpack and wore dingy, frayed jeans, a flannel shirt, and a bright-red windbreaker. I walked over to him, some 30 steps. "Are you Basil Middlemiss?"

"Why yes! You must be Mr. Garner!"

"Yes. We've been waiting for you at the door, just there, for about 15 minutes. Didn't you think to look for us?"

"Ah, well, I knew you'd find me. Right! Let's get going. We have a full walking tour ahead of us—the peripatetic delights of Hong Kong, as I like to call them."

I took him over to meet the rest of our disgruntled group. He launched into a spiel, sounding almost like a lower-middle-class Monty Python character. "Today, lady and gents, we shall have a walking tour of Central, the primary business district of Hong Kong, located on the north shore of the island, across Victoria Harbor from Tsim Sha Tsui, which is the southernmost—"

I broke in, given that we were still just standing in the front foyer of our own hotel: "Basil, let's get going."

"I just wanted to explain—"

"Please explain in the van. It's 9:20, and we need to get a move on!"

"That's right!" said Justice Scalia, marching toward the exit. Then he whispered to me, "What was his explanation for being late?"

"He had none, Nino. He said he was sure we'd find him."

"He's an oaf."

Even though I had introduced Justice Scalia to Basil as "Justice Scalia,"

Basil asked for his first name. He was using first names. "Just call him Justice," I said. "His first name is 'Justice.'"

Basil seemed to have no idea about his audience. In his mind, he was leading four Americans on a tour. Just a routine thing.

As Justice Scalia was getting into the van, I stood right at his door as usual. "Stop babying me! Get in on your own side!"

"Not until the 60% rule is satisfied. Please get in with at least 60% of your buttocks on the seat. Remember Providence?"

Tom and Karolyne chuckled. "Oh, all right," said Justice Scalia with resignation. He got in.

As I walked behind the van, I took Basil aside and said, "This walking tour won't be strenuous, will it? Not too much walking?"

"Not at all, Bryan."

"You have Justice Scalia on this tour. Do you know who he is?"

"He's a judge, I think you told me. I had a judge recently from New Zealand, and I must say he—"

"Basil, please focus. Your primary mission is to satisfy him."

Justice Scalia shouted from inside the van: "Get in, Bryan! No more delays!"

"Remember, Basil," I said, "this is a *light* walking tour."

"Yes, sir!"

I went around to my side and got in. Justice Scalia said, irritably, "What on earth are you doing?! Let's get this show on the road!"

"This guy's going to be a challenge, Nino," I said just before Basil got in.

"Right!" announced Basil. "As I was saying, the Central District of Hong Kong, which is where we will be walking today, is bordered on the westernmost side by Sheung Wan, marked by Aberdeen Street (which is known to locals as Wing Kut Street). It is bordered on the east by Admiralty, on the south by Midlevels, and on the north by Causeway Bay, which . . ."

He continued droning on in this way, only barely audible to any of us. "I miss Polly already," muttered Justice Scalia.

We started out in Statue Square, near the Court of Final Appeal. As Basil kept up his voluble commentary, we were standing, standing, and then standing some more. Basil was giving what was patently his standard shtick, and he was delivering it in a way that we didn't find endearing, with a fair number of lame puns and standard jokes. "Hey, Justice," he said loudly as Justice Scalia and I started drifting away, Karolyne and Tom being too polite to do so—"Hey, Judge, there are lots like you who sit right there in this building," he said, pointing at the Court of Final Appeal. "It's the court of last resort in Hong Kong, although I'm told by visitors that the place isn't at all like a resort. Ha! Ha! Now laugh at that, guys! Have a sense of humor!"

"How did we end up with this joker?" said Justice Scalia.

"I have no idea. I'm sorry, Nino. You want me to cancel this right now?"

"No. Let's give him a chance. I think he's trying."

I went over to Basil and said, "Please try to keep us on the move and not standing for too long at a time. I hurt my knee this morning, and standing makes it worse."

"Sorry to hear that," he said.

"I know we have to stop for us all to hear you, but please make your remarks more succinct. Just the highlights, please."

"All right, Bryan." Then in a loud voice: "Right! If I may have every-body's attention: we're going to cross the street to the HSBC Bank Building, where you will see the historic shorelines of the ocean. Most interesting."

"Shouldn't that be *historical*," said Justice Scalia to me, "not *historic*?" Of course, Basil couldn't hear us.

"Yes," I said, "unless the shorelines were important to history. Maybe it's arguable, but I think you're right."

The group followed Basil across the street, where he introduced us to Stephen and Stitt, the two famous HSBC bronze lions cast in Shanghai in 1837. Stephen is roaring; Stitt is calm. Stephen is racked with shrapnel holes acquired from the Japanese forces during World War II. Karolyne and Justice Scalia posed for a couple of photographs in front of Stephen— in both of which they pretended to roar mightily. Basil hadn't dampened their spirits much: Karolyne and Justice Scalia were almost childlike in their playfulness.

Soon we crossed Queen's Road, where Basil said we'd be ascending the steps to the original building of the Court of Final Appeal and what's called the Olympic Amphitheatre (even though the city has never hosted the Olympic Games).

"We're going up all those steps?" asked Justice Scalia.

"It's not that far!" insisted Basil. "Just up there." He started climbing the steps.

"Is your knee going to be all right, Bryan?" asked Justice Scalia.

"I'll be fine. It's hurting some, but I'll be okay."

"Then come on," he said, "let's get going."

I stayed just behind Justice Scalia on the way up, to ensure that he wouldn't fall. He was perfectly steady, but after the first part he was huffing and puffing. He stopped at a landing halfway up—after 52 steps—to catch his breath. He was leaning against a concrete orb on the capital of the balustrade.

"Are you okay, Nino?" I asked. Tom and I were right with him now.

"I didn't know we were going to be doing all this climbing!" He had become annoyed. We waited 30 seconds or so, while he caught his breath, both hands on the concrete ball atop the wall. He turned, looking over Queen's Road, and shouted, "Glow in the dark!" He had us laughing. I whipped out my camera to film him saying that twice more. He was joking, of course, about the phosphorescent stone ball I'd bought three days before.

"Seriously, Nino, are you okay? Do you need to stop?"

"I'm fine. Just needed a second wind."

We embarked on the remainder of the climb. Karolyne had stayed with Basil, who was no doubt blathering on, and they were already at the top. But we soon realized that after 52 steps up, we were barely halfway. We had many more steps to reach the top.

Justice Scalia was seriously irked when we finally reached the top.

"This is supposed to be a *walking* tour, not a *climbing* tour!" said Justice Scalia. "Basil, nobody said anything about lots of climbing."

"I always come this way. Most people enjoy a bit of exercise. Right! This"—he pointed to an orange-brick building behind him—"is the original Court of Final Appeal, but before that it was the Mission Étrangères, built in 1917."

An upward slope took us to the front of the building. Farther on, to the right, was a yellow cathedral that caught Justice Scalia's eye. He and I went straight over there, leaving Karolyne and Tom to listen to Basil. When we reached the entrance to the cathedral, we learned that it was St. John's—the oldest Anglican cathedral in Hong Kong, with a beautiful, multicolored stained-glass window behind the reredos.

Justice Scalia crossed himself as we entered. A funeral was underway, the pews half full. A large photo of the deceased stood on an easel beside the altar. A full choir was behind the altar, singing. We watched from the back for a minute or so. Justice Scalia crossed himself again, turned, and saw an offertory box. He pulled out a Hong Kong banknote of $100 (equivalent to $12 U.S.) and put it in. I made an offering as well.

Across the lane was St. Michael's Chapel, where Justice Scalia pointed out to me that the charity shop was called "Castaways." "What a funny use of that word," he said to me. "Do you think it's a pun?"

"Maybe," I said. "I think it's referring to the discarded items donated to the church. Anglicans don't pun much in church-related matters. I'd wager that it's a very literal and old use of a word that we think of as invariably metaphorical. The literal sense of *castaway* is dead in American English."

"I'm sure you're right," he said.

He seemed to have caught his breath. Perhaps, I thought, it was simply that the unexpected exertion with the first half of those steps had caught him unprepared. We soon reached Basil, Karolyne, and Tom, who had moved on down the lane.

"And now," announced Basil, "we're going to walk up there to the Peak Tram Entrance"—the place where we'd been dropped off two days before when we took the tram up to Victoria Peak. "Then across to the park."

I said: "More uphill walking, Basil?! This isn't easy for all of us." Of course I was concerned mostly about Justice Scalia, but my knee was aching from the ill-advised leg extensions that morning.

"I don't like all this climbing, Basil!" said Justice Scalia.

"It's really not that hard," said Basil. "Right! Let's just step across the street here." He really did seem like a bungler to me—a character that might have been played by Michael Palin of the Monty Python troupe.

"I want Polly back," Justice Scalia said to me as he trudged across the road, and I limped.

"Me, too!" I said.

Basil hadn't prepared us for the climbs still ahead: 47 stairs up to Hong Kong Park, and an additional 86 stairs up to the base of the Vantage Point Observatory. I stayed with Justice Scalia the whole way, as Karolyne and Tom, who stayed well ahead with Basil, glanced back at us with some frequency. Although my knee was in constant pain, I tried to conceal it. Justice Scalia's difficulties seemed to have subsided. He was just unhappy about the arduousness of this "walking tour."

When we reached the base of the observatory, Basil announced that we could ascend its steps to have the second-finest view in all Hong Kong.

"What's the finest?" asked Justice Scalia.

"Why, Victoria Peak, of course!" answered Basil.

"We saw that yesterday," said Justice Scalia. "How many steps up that tower?" he asked.

"Precisely 123, if memory serves, Your Honor!" said Basil.

"Do I look as if I want to climb another 123 steps for the second-finest view, when I've already seen the finest?"

"I would say that you do *not*, sir. Perhaps you could sit on that bench while the others might join me in taking in the splendid panorama atop the tower. Any takers?"

Holding my knee, I said, "You're telling me that we just climbed all those steps—there were 86 of them—to get to the base of a tower that nobody in our group wants to go up?"

"I'm sorry if you don't," said Basil. "The good news is that it's all down-hill from here."

Justice Scalia muttered to me, "It's been all downhill since we found this guy."

"Right!" said Basil—in the British way, responding to nothing. "From here we get to see both the aviary and the park. Let's continue." He marched forward as if everything was going just as he'd planned.

We had to descend 90 steps to the Olympic Amphitheatre, which was being disassembled for renovations, and another 12 down to Hong Kong Lake. The descending steps were harder on my knee than the ascending ones. Justice Scalia, meanwhile, seemed fine.

"Hope your knee's okay!" he said. "You really should work out more often."

"You're one to talk, Nino. How could you say such a thing to your trainer?"

"My trainer needs to be more fit," he said. "That's not my fault. Hey, look at that naked man!"

"Basil," I said, "this is the second naked-man sculpture we've seen on this trip. They seem identical."

"This, American friends, is one of 31 fiberglass-and-iron statues placed all around the city. Look at that rooftop there,"—he pointed—"and over there." Several naked-man sculptures were in sight. "This is part of a city-wide art installation by Antony Gormley, a British artist. It's entitled *Event*

Horizon, and apparently some people like it. Each statue is a life-size body cast of the artist."

"Do you like it, Tom?" Justice Scalia asked.

"I *really* do," he said facetiously. To everyone's amusement, Tom walked up to the park statue, took it by the hand, and posed for photos with the look of a simpleton.

"Nino," I said, "go hold its hand for a photo."

"I'm *not* doing that . . . Well, it is kind of funny . . . No, I can't pose for that picture. Let's move on!"

"You're very lucky to see Antony Gormley's work," said Basil. "This art installation was delayed for more than a year after it was first put up and then removed. An investment banker leapt to his death—a suicide. Then people thought that all these naked men were actual people on the verge of suicide, and alarms were raised all over the city. So the installation had to be taken down. Now, though, it's back up. The artist has realized his dream of having replicas of his naked self placed all over the city—an unusual exhibition."

"Or exhibitionism," Justice Scalia said. I grinned at him.

We looked at the Asian carp in Hong Kong Lake, which is really more of a pond, and then Basil announced, "I'm happy to say our descent will be quite easy, since there are escalators all the way down."

"And *up*, too, presumably?" asked Justice Scalia.

"Yes, but it's less scenic."

"You mean we could have taken escalators up and walked *down* the steps?" Justice Scalia persisted.

"I suppose, yes, but I never do it in that order."

We followed Basil to the top of the first escalator. Justice Scalia was incensed all the way down. "This is an outrage!" He was fairly snarling. "He made us climb those steps unnecessarily!" "You could have hurt your knee even worse!" "And he promised a 'light' walking tour!" "Dammit. He's a fool. A damn fool."

Tom and I muttered various things in agreement. Karolyne, well ahead with Basil, doubtless thought she could help most by keeping Basil away from Justice Scalia, and she did so as Basil babbled on.

"And now, American friends," he said at long last, "it will soon be time for me to leave you as you enjoy your midday meal at Mott 32. But I will escort you to the entrance of this fine establishment."

We were standing in front of the Standard Chartered Bank Building, which has an unusual architectural feature: you have to walk up 38 stairs to get to the main floor. Then, to reach the basement where the restaurant is, you must go down a long escalator.

"I'm not climbing one more stair!" said Justice Scalia. "In fact, I'm not taking one more step! I'm not moving from this spot." He was scowling at the staircase as we stood on the sidewalk of a major street, Des Voeux Road, cars and buses noisily passing.

"It's just a few more stairs for lunch," said Karolyne. "Just think: jelly-fish is right inside there, and roast suckling pig."

"Well . . . okay. Dammit."

"We'll get a cab afterward, Nino," I said. "We won't walk any more than necessary."

"This is truly unfathomable!" said Justice Scalia as we ascended the granite steps. "I just can't believe we're having to go up to go down!"

I said: "It's a miniature reenactment of our whole morning: steps up, escalator down. Escalators all the way down. Kind of like turtles all the way down."

"Ha! Is your knee okay?" he asked.

"I'll be fine. Are you okay?"

"Sure. I'm in better shape than you, with your gimpy leg!"

"That's just because you made me do the leg extensions this morning. I told you I wasn't supposed to do it."

"You just didn't do it right!" he declared. He had an impish frown on his face.

When we got to the entrance of the Mott 32 restaurant, Basil said, "Right! And now, American friends, I bid you all adieu. May the rest of your stay in Hong Kong be excellent. It's been a pleasure to be your guide."

We all said thank you to Basil. As he walked off, Justice Scalia said to me, "You know, he's not such a bad guy. Basil Middlemiss was growing on me there at the end. But I'm glad we'll have Polly again tomorrow."

After lunch and a brief rest, we met with Chief Justice Ma for a tour of the Court of Final Appeal. The main courtroom has finely carved brown-wood paneling that isn't so different from that in Justice Scalia's own chambers. Once in the courtroom, Justice Scalia took the lectern for a moment, as if he were an advocate. I said, "Nino, declaim for us! I want a photo." And he posed by pretending to pound the lectern, as if delivering an old-fashioned forensic oration. Unfailingly gracious, Chief Justice Ma was generous with his time that afternoon.

Reading Law at the University of Hong Kong

Later that day, at the University of Hong Kong, there was concern over student protests. A week before our appearance, students had besieged a meeting of the university's governing council and trapped members for several hours. We'd been warned by the State Department, which sent a security detail to accompany us—at least one that we knew about. He was a former air marshal who seemed ultraprofessional. Always alert, he was exceedingly courteous and impressively knowledgeable. He was a fan of Justice Scalia's, and he was interested in the subject of our presentation on *Reading Law*. He stayed near us all the time we were on campus. But no protesters ever came into view.

Our late-afternoon event that day was to be a joint talk on legal interpretation. Backstage, the dean, Michael Hor, asked us to take our seats onstage before the introduction. Karolyne said no: we'd wait till the introduction was finished and then walk out during the applause and take our places. The auditorium was packed as Dean Hor walked out to introduce Justice Roberto Ribeiro of the Court of Final Appeal. He in turn introduced us while we were sitting backstage.

"I was just thinking, Nino," I said.

"Yes?" he said.

"Here you are—making one of countless appearances touting textualism, your brand of judicial decision-making. You're hoping to sway the audience to your point of view."

"Of course."

"And presumably Justice Breyer and Justice Ginsburg are out doing the same, promoting their methods."

He stroked his lower lip with his middle finger, contemplating what I'd said, and then answered: "I don't think so. No. I'm the only one promoting a judicial method. They don't really have one to promote. So-called 'pragmatism' is just saying 'trust me to do the right thing.' That's not a method . . . Hey, wait a second, I left my reading glasses at the hotel! Now I can't read my notes!" He was exasperated, and with his abrupt change of topic we never resumed our conversation about other Justices' trying to spread the ideas underlying pragmatism.

"Here. Use my reading glasses."

"Let me try them." He tried them on.

"They look great!" said Karolyne while snapping a photo as Tom did the same. It was the quintessential photo of the trip: he was posing for Karolyne, and Tom captured the three of us as Karolyne's photo was being taken. He liked the glasses, and we agreed to share them as necessary. But when we emerged from the curtains amid enthusiastic applause and took our seats, Justice Scalia sitting to my left, he laid down the glasses to his left—well out of my reach. Then, much to my surprise, he never touched the glasses throughout our presentation. At least they gave him the security he needed: they were available if necessary.

"Ladies and gentlemen," I began, "we're here to talk about our second book, *Reading Law*. It took us three and a half years to write, and it's fair to say that it's the most comprehensive treatment of textual interpretation ever written for lawyers and judges."

Then he jumped in: "It's the first hornbook-style treatment in more than a century. Henry Campbell Black wrote a hornbook on legal interpretation in 1911, but no one else has even tried since."

"That's right."

We gave what had become our standard performance, discussing one-third of the canons in *Reading Law* and then administering our five-question quiz to the audience. A member would have to solve a posited problem of statutory construction and cite the correct textualist rationale. The answer would always have to do with how a reasonable person would interpret statutory words, never how a reasonable person would solve the problem (which would involve the judge's policy preferences). That's the basic distinction between a textualist and either a purposivist (who asks what the legislature would have wanted) or a consequentialist (who asks about the preferred outcomes).

At the end, we had time to take questions. Perhaps the most difficult question Justice Scalia ever received from an audience member arose that evening at Hong Kong University. It was a question that I had posed to him several times privately after being prompted by Sir Christopher Ricks. The question is this: what if *meaning* is stable and fixed, but not its *application*? The word *cruel*, let's say, meant "intentionally causing pain and suffering" or "willfully brutal" in the 18th century, and it means the same thing today. But our understanding of what constitutes cruelty has changed over time. The meaning is the same, but not its application to real-world referents. How do we solve this problem of originalism?

It's a question that Senator Joe Biden asked my coauthor in 1986, during his confirmation proceedings. In that year, before the Senate Judiciary Committee, he responded: "I think that there are some provisions of the Constitution that may have a certain amount of evolutionary content within them." He said he hadn't firmly made up his mind. But 30 years later, he *had* made up his mind when it came to the Cruel and Unusual Punishments Clause. If lashing or notching of the ears wasn't cruel and unusual in the 1780s, then it's not a violation in 2016. "We just hope," he said, "that the legislature doesn't revive those practices."

So Justice Scalia came to dismiss the conundrum as mere wordplay. "It's nonsense," he said, "to say that the meaning and its practical application are different. If they *were* different, it would be a verbal free-for-all: each generation gets to decide for itself what's cruel and has to engage in all sorts of hand-wringing over whether applications have changed. Then there's no real permanence of meaning at all. Applications and meaning are convertible."

The Cruel and Unusual Punishments Clause is a special case, as Justice Scalia noted that evening. The Fifth Amendment contains three separate passages in which the acceptability of the death penalty is contemplated, and the Fourteenth Amendment contains another:

- "No person shall be held to answer for a *capital*, or otherwise infamous, crime, unless . . . ."[60]
- "Nor shall any person be subject for the same offence to be twice put in jeopardy of *life* or limb."[61]
- "Nor shall be . . . *deprived of life*, liberty, or property, without due process of law."[62]
- "Nor shall any State *deprive* any person of *life*, liberty, or property, without due process of law."[63]

---

60 U.S. Const. amend. V.

61 *Id.*

62 *Id.*

63 *Id.* amend. IV.

To a textualist, if the text itself conveys permissibility, then the death penalty can't, over time, evolve into per se prohibited status—not if the Constitution is a document that we're interpreting. Justice Scalia was delighted when I once presented him with a passage in which Chief Justice Burger had made just this conclusive point. To prohibit the death penalty, he'd said, we'd need a constitutional amendment.

Justice Scalia liked to point out to audiences, as he did at Hong Kong University, that no fewer than four colleagues with whom he had served on the Supreme Court—Justices Brennan, Marshall, Blackmun, and Stevens—had adopted the view that the death penalty is in all instances unconstitutional, despite the text's own clear implication that it's entirely allowable. He cited this as evidence that what they were actually doing was "constitutionalizing" their own policy preferences instead of interpreting a written Constitution.

The audience was warm and receptive, and they seemed every bit as informed as an American audience.

Immediately after, we were met by a minibus to transport eight of us to our dinner destination. The dinner that evening at Peking Garden Restaurant, in Alexandra House, was excellent, and the service was impeccable. We had interesting conversations, and Dean Hor remarked on how dramatic our entrance had been: by waiting until we were announced to come onstage as opposed to sitting there throughout the introductions—we created a much more dramatic effect and, he thought, generated more applause.

About 30 minutes after appetizers were served, a local lawyer who had come just for the dinner announced that he would have to leave. He was dressed in jeans and a sweater. He was a Westerner, and his native language was English. Once he had the entire table's attention, he said: "Justice Scalia, thank you for coming. I didn't attend your lecture because I'm really busy. And now I must go to my daughter's field-hockey game. So forgive me for leaving. But thank you for coming."

That was an odd moment, and the man struck me as a boor—or perhaps a yabber. Justice Scalia smiled graciously and wished the man all the best for his daughter's field-hockey team. He asked how old she was. The answer was 12. "Yes, attend to your daughter," Justice Scalia said, "because these years will be fleeting. She needs all the attention you can give her."

Antonins and Ninos

Karolyne and I had a friend, the distinguished German lawyer Anton Maurer, who was in Asia at the time of our trip. Anton decided to attend our lecture at the University of Hong Kong, and he stayed at the Ritz-Carlton for several days—often having breakfast across the room from us. At one point I introduced Justice Scalia to Anton at the omelet bar. Once we were out of Anton's earshot, Justice Scalia said he was most curious about why a lawyer from Stuttgart would travel to Hong Kong to see one of his lectures. "Nino," I said, "we have the Deemster who came from the Isle of Man to see you. In Anton's case, I'm sure he wanted to see us perform together to find out whether I've been exaggerating about how we work together!"

"Nice fellow," Justice Scalia said.

Gradually, Anton became a quasi-member of our group. At breakfast on the next-to-last day, Justice Scalia said, "Pull up a chair, Anton, and join us."

Soon we were talking about Anton's international legal work and Justice Scalia's knowledge of German law—and the funny story about how, when he was first promoted to the D.C. Circuit, Justice Scalia's European friends thought something had gone wrong with his career. Continental law professors, he explained, are revered while judges are held in fairly low regard; in the United States, by contrast, both are respected but judges are particularly exalted.

Once he'd gotten to know Justice Scalia better, Anton wanted to know how "Antonin" became "Nino." Where did the *o* come from?

"That's easy," said Justice Scalia. "I had an Uncle Antonino, and my nickname came from him. For some reason, my parents named me Antonin instead of Antonino. Maybe they thought it was more anglicized."

"You're probably the most famous Antonin who ever lived," I said. "I'd say you outrank Dvořák."

"You think?" he asked.

"I do. Can you think of any other famous Antonins?" I asked.

"Come to think of it, I can't," he said.

"And no other famous Ninos, either," I said. "When I interview you about your life, I'm going to ask you all about your uncle Antonino. He had a bad temper, didn't he?"

"How did you know that?" Justice Scalia looked baffled.

"I have my sources," I said, grinning.

The reference to my interviewing Justice Scalia was about our planned series of biographical interviews. Over ten or so 60- to 90-minute filmed segments, I would ask all about his life, his interests, and his beliefs. This plan had been hatched over dinner in 2013 when he told me he'd never write an autobiography, and we agreed that the painless way to do such a work would be through these interviews—and that I'd publish the book posthumously, or earlier if we agreed to it. We reconfirmed the plan several times and agreed in Hong Kong to begin shortly after our return.

Some Unsettling Soothsaying

On this Wednesday, our last full day in Hong Kong, we were scheduled for a tour of the Chi Lin Nunnery (Buddhist) and then the Wong Tai Sin Temple (Taoist). As we got into the van, I followed the usual protocol of ensuring that Justice Scalia had satisfied the 60% rule. Once I was in, I said to Polly, with artificial drama, "To a nunnery, go, and quickly too! Get us to a nunnery!"

"Are we in a hurry today?" Polly asked.

"No," said Justice Scalia. "He's just having fun paraphrasing Shakespeare."

"You know which play, Nino?" I asked him.

"Of course I do. *Hamlet.*"

"Yes," I said, "it's that painful scene with Ophelia in which Hamlet says, 'Get thee to a nunnery, farewell. Or if thou wilt needs marry, marry a fool, for wise men know well enough what monsters you make of them.' Don't worry, Lyne, that's not really true."

"How do you know the lines so well?" asked Justice Scalia.

"I acted in *Hamlet* in high school. I was Polonius. 'Neither a borrower nor a lender be, for loan oft loses both itself and friend, and borrowing dulleth the edge of husbandry.' And so on. Did you ever act in Shakespeare?"

"Yes," said Justice Scalia. "I was Macbeth."

"Wow. The lead role," I said.

"Yes. 'Is this the dagger which I see before me, the handle toward my hand?'" He was using the low, gravelly voice. "'Come, let me clutch thee.' I made a pretty good Macbeth."

"I'll bet you did."

"You know," I continued, "you've been calling me your *uncle*. If you want to be Shakespearean, you should call me your *nuncle*."

"*Nuncle?*" he asked. "My nuncle?"

"It sounds the same as *mine uncle*. Hamlet says that: 'I'll have these players play something like the murder of my father before *mine uncle*.'"

"Well, does he say *mine uncle* or *my nuncle?*"

"I can't remember. But *nuncle* is used elsewhere in Shakespeare, I promise. I think it's in *King Lear*."

"Okay, *nuncle*. You're now my *nuncle*."

"'Mark it, nuncle,'" I said. "'Have more than thou showest, speak less than thou knowest.'"

"So true, nuncle," he said. "So this place we're going . . . why do they call it a nunnery? Why not a *convent* or an *abbey?*"

"Maybe those words are too closely associated with Catholicism," I said. "This place is Buddhist."

"Yes," Polly said, "it's a Buddhist nunnery."

"Hong Kongers really do use a lot of old-fashioned English words," I said.

Once we arrived, Justice Scalia took many photographs of buildings, walls, fences, and fountains. I took photos of him taking photos. What sounded like a monk's voice was coming over a loudspeaker throughout the nunnery, and he and I were pretty certain it was a recording—until, in one of the rooms, we actually saw the nun (it turned out to be a female voice!) chanting into a microphone.

At the colorful Wong Tai Sin Temple, we saw dozens of Taoists kneeling and practicing sortilege: shaking sticks out of tubular containers—the traditional Taoist method of divination by consulting the *I Ching*. Polly told us, with great earnestness, that people come to this temple to help them make decisions—whether to marry, whether to divorce, whether it's a propitious time to get pregnant, and so on. Having seen this sort of thing before in Asia, I had more fun watching Justice Scalia soak in the experience than I had watching the superstitious folk.

"Do you believe in this, Polly?" Justice Scalia asked.

"Yes, I do," she said.

"So you're a Taoist?"

"I'm both Buddhist and Taoist."

"Do you come here to shake out the sticks?"

"No, I don't do that. But I do believe in it."

Justice Scalia's eye caught a sign: "Soothsayer's Stall."

"Look at that! They have a *soothsayer*. Now that's a word you don't see every day."

"True," I said. "*Sooth* is an Anglo-Saxon word meaning 'truth.' It's literally a truth-teller, but really, as you know, it's a fortune-teller."

He snapped several pictures of the sign, and I photographed him doing it.

"Let's go see the soothsayer," I said.

"What does he do?"

"He probably reads palms. Karolyne, let's go get our palms read!"

Polly added that the soothsayer reads not only palms but also faces, and he interprets the sticks that get shaken out by those engaged in the sortilege.

"Are you serious?" asked Justice Scalia. "You're going to get your palms read?"

"Sure. I've done it before. Apparently I have good palms—if I pay enough money."

The five of us walked through an arcade to the soothsayer's stall. There were two palm-readers, a man and a woman. Karolyne asked the price for two palms, and the man quoted a fee amounting to about $10 U.S.

I went first. He said, in fairly good English, that I would have a good life. I figured it would all be generalizations of this kind. Then he said that I have two children, both daughters. The correctness of that point was surprising. Then he said I'd live to be 89—"easily."

As for Karolyne's palm, he correctly said that she had no children. She would have a good life, never be in want, and live to be 88—"easily."

Each act of palm-reading took only about two minutes.

"Nino," I said, "get your palm read."

"No," he said.

"I'll pay for it. Come on! Let's see if he knows how many children you have."

"No," he said adamantly, walking away with determination.

"Come on, Nino!" I said, following him back out. "It's like the carnival, where they try to guess your age or weight. Let's see if he knows how many children you have."

"No! I don't want to know when I'm going to die."

That stopped me in my tracks. "Okay. I'm sorry, Nino," I said, trying to catch up with his brisk exit. I had no idea he'd take it so seriously. The date was February 3, 2016.

You Call Everybody Darling

We walked outside where there were twelve enormous bronze sculptures of animals representing the Chinese zodiac. I posed with the dog, Karolyne with the rooster, and both Justice Scalia and Tom with the rat. Justice Scalia wanted to know the zodiac animal of his wife, Maureen. Karolyne and Polly figured out that it was the rabbit. He lingered with the smiling, anthropomorphic rabbit sculpture for quite some time, touching its arm and posing for photos. He got choked up when he laid hands on the rabbit. As I walked up beside him, he said, "I miss Maureen."

As we got into the van, Justice Scalia remarked how crowded the temple was. "Is it packed like that every day?" he asked Polly.

"Yes, it stays crowded most days—except in bad weather," she responded.

"Too many people," said Justice Scalia. That reminded me of a Paul McCartney song of that name.

"Nino," I said, "I want you to listen to a song. Perhaps I've finally found a rock song you might like. Do you remember when I tried to play 'Nothing Is Easy' for you on my iPod?"

"That's my motto!" he said.

"I know, and when I saw the sign your clerks made for you, I played the Jethro Tull song 'Nothing Is Easy' for you in your chambers."

"Did I like it?" he asked.

"No, you didn't," I said, "even though it's a great song based on your motto. Let's try another."

"What is it?"

" 'Too Many People,' by Paul McCartney and Wings."

Tom was quicker on Google than I was, and he began playing it. Unfortunately, it was a recording of a live performance in which the raucous electric-guitar lead-in was rather extended. With mock-annoyance, Justice Scalia said, "Turn that off! Why would you think I'd like that?" The music stopped.

"It's called 'Too Many People,'" I said, "and it's a clever little song with interesting lyrics and a good tune—if we'd only gotten that far. I can see why you didn't like the guitar in that particular version."

"Lord, no!" said Justice Scalia. Tom and Karolyne, both smiling, seemed to be enjoying the exchange. He continued: "What I like in pop music is a good tune with a nice lyric. There's this old song." He started singing, "You call everybody 'Darling,' and everybody calls you 'Darling,' too. You don't mean what you're saying, it's just a game you're playing, but you'll find someone else can play the game as well as you . . ."

"You've got a good voice, Nino," I said.

"You're quite a singer," said Tom.

"Thank you. I was in the glee club in college, you know. Say, Tom, see if you can find a recording of 'You Call Everybody Darling.'"

Within seconds, Tom had found a recording of the song, and Justice Scalia sang along with it on the ride back to the hotel. If he'd miss the beginning of a line, the singers would prompt him and he'd join in quickly, smiling and serenading the rest of us through the simple 1940s-style ditty: "If you call everybody 'Darling,' then love won't come a-knocking at your door. And as the years go by, you'll sit and wonder why nobody calls you 'Darling' anymore."

When it was over, he remarked, "Now that's a good song. And it has a good message for people, too."

"That's true," I said.

Divining Words

Still riding in the van, I changed the subject to words—always a favorite for Justice Scalia. I asked him whether he knew the technical term for palm-reading.

"There's a technical term for it?" he asked.

"Sure," I said. "There's a whole list of words, dozens of them, ending with the same suffix that denotes divination by certain means. You don't know it?"

"I'm afraid I don't know it," he said curiously.

"It's called 'chiromancy,' also known as 'palmistry.' *Chiro-* for hand, as in *chirograph*, the handwritten legal instrument such as an old deed; and *-mancy*, meaning divination, or foretelling the future."

"Are you serious?" said Justice Scalia.

"Sure," I said. "The ancient Romans had all kinds of divination. With *necromancy*, they foretold the future by supposedly speaking to the spirits of the dead. With *aleuromancy*, they somehow used flour to tell the future."

"How do you know this stuff? Are you an occultist?"

"Of course not! I'm a lexicographer. When I was a teenager, and I first discovered the suffix *-mancy*, I spent a week or so finding every word I could in *Webster's Second* ending with that suffix. I had a language note-book full of interesting things like that."

"You were a precocious snoot," Justice Scalia said.

"Tom," I said, "Google the suffix *-mancy*, and you'll find lots of them."

"I found some," said Tom. "The suffix comes from the Latin word *mantis*, meaning 'prophet or soothsayer.'"

"Yes," I said, "as in 'praying mantis.'"

He started calling them out while Justice Scalia, Karolyne, and I tried to guess what the word might mean based on the etymological roots: *aeromancy* (divination by means of observing atmospheric conditions), *arithmancy* (by means of numbers), *capnomancy* (by means of watching smoke rising from a fire), *geomancy* (by means of configurations of earth), *hieromancy* (by means of sacred objects), *hydromancy* (by means of watching water), *myomancy* (by means of watching the movements of mice), *omphalomancy* (by means of examining an umbilical cord—although we guessed navel), *oneiromancy* (by means of dreams), *pyromancy* (by means of fire or flames), *rhabdomancy* (by means of a wand), *stichomancy* (by means of books), and so on. I let Justice Scalia and Karolyne have the first guesses, since I recalled most of them, and they did remarkably well. Only *capnomancy*, *myomancy*, *rhabdomancy*, and *stichomancy* stumped them, and of those I got only *myomancy* and *stichomancy*. How Justice Scalia came up with the correct answer to *oneiromancy* is anyone's guess.

"This is amazing!" said Justice Scalia.

"You see," I said, "there are lots of ways to tell the future, if you believe in that sort of thing. You don't really believe in chiromancy, do you?"

"No, but I just don't want to hear people predicting the time of my death. You understand that."

"Of course." I hesitated. "I'm surprised Tom didn't find the one about cutting open animals to examine their entrails. That was a favorite means of Roman divination."

Tom Googled it. "Hey," he said. "That's called *haruspicy*." He spelled it out letter by letter. "How do you say it?"

"/huh-ROO-spi-see/," I said. "Good word. And do you know the word for shaking sticks out of the container?"

"No. What kind of *-mancy* is that?" asked Justice Scalia.

"It's not a *-mancy* word. It's more of a fancy word: *sortilege*, which means divination by lots or sticks."

"Are you sure you don't believe in the occult, Bryan?"

"Not a bit of it," I said. "I just love all these words. But I wish I'd had Google in 1974. When I was a kid, I spent probably two weeks chasing down all these words in *Webster's Second* and the *Oxford English Dictionary*. They're not all collected in a single place."

"You must have been a nerdy kid," said Justice Scalia, "like me. But I have to say I didn't go to those lengths." He grinned. "Why'd you do it?"

"You've never heard the story about how I fell in love with words, and why I was copying words out of *Webster's Second*?"

"Oh," said Karolyne. "Wait till you hear this."

"I'm sure I've heard this before. But remind me," he said.

"It was an attempt," I said, "a silly attempt to impress a girl. When I was 15, she complimented me by saying I had a big vocabulary. 'Oh,' I thought, 'she likes a big vocabulary. Well, I can make it even bigger.' And so I spent months copying out what I considered interesting, useful words."

"Did she notice?" asked Justice Scalia.

"I don't think so."

"Did you ever call her or send her flowers?"

"No. I was probably too shy. Anyway, I soon forgot about her and realized I was in love with words."

"Great story," he said.

Soon we had arrived at the Ritz-Carlton, and we said our final goodbyes to Polly. She received warm hugs, and we posed for photographs with her. We were all a little sad to say goodbye to her.

Karolyne had arranged for us to have lunch at Tosca, a Michelin-starred Italian restaurant at the Ritz. (How wonderful, we thought, that it bore the same name as our favorite Italian restaurant in Washington, D.C.) It was the only Italian meal we had in Hong Kong, and it was uncanny just how Italian it was. We shared a bottle of Sicilian wine that Justice Scalia picked out—in homage to his Sicilian ancestors.

In the afternoon, we went back to the Central District for our presentation at Thomson Reuters. The format was an interesting one. The local head of the company introduced us, and then we essentially interviewed ourselves about book authorship and how we worked together. We briefly described our reasons for writing the books and our methods.

"What made it easy," I said, "was that our literary styles are perfectly compatible."

"Perfectly," Justice Scalia said. "I can't imagine a better fit."

I drew a laugh by saying, "Justice Scalia showed great magnanimity toward me. At the beginning of our partnership, he said, 'Bryan, I want to make clear that you're my coauthor, not my law clerk. You and I are equals—for purposes of this book only.'" No one laughed more heartily than Justice Scalia himself. He had in fact said all but the last six words.

"I never could have written these books without Bryan. He's absolutely tireless, and both books required a great deal of research."

An audience member asked a question: "What are the two of you collaborating on now?"

Justice Scalia said: "We've almost completed a second edition of *Reading Law*. And Bryan is helping me assemble my speeches into a three-volume set."

"Yes," I said, "Justice Scalia has a great storehouse of excellent speeches he's given over the years. It's going to be a great set of books. Otherwise, we're going to be doing new editions of our two books."

As part of this "self-interview," I mentioned that we'd been musing about what we might say to the constitutional framers if we could time-travel for five minutes to speak with them. How would we try to influence them to make some adjustment to their planned Constitution? Justice Scalia said he would advise them not to make the Constitution so very difficult to amend. "It shouldn't be easy to accomplish," he said, "but the fact that it's so very difficult has made people impatient with the process, so today we've gotten into the habit of asking the Supreme Court to amend it under the guise of 'interpretation.' That's very bad. Anyway, the Constitution should be somewhat easier to amend."

Final Fittings and Family Fete

After the post-talk cocktail party, we rushed from Thomson Reuters to Yuen's Tailors for our final fitting. When we arrived, brothers Johnny and Bonnie were all smiles, and so was Justice Scalia as he tried on his half-made jacket. It was perfectly fitted. For the trousers, we encountered a problem: the tailors' shop was so cramped that there was no dressing room. So Tom, Karolyne, and I formed a visual barrier at the front window—a kind of human curtain—so that Justice Scalia could take off his trousers. Karolyne kept her back to him.

But of course I peeked. "Nino, you wear sock-garters!" I had never seen that before, on anyone.

"You bet I do! Keeps the socks up."

The trousers fit just as well as the jacket, so Johnny and Bonnie got the go-ahead to complete the suits and mail them. They wanted photos with the Justice, so I took them.

"We'll hang your picture on our wall," said Bonnie. Justice Scalia seemed flattered and amused as we left the shop.

This was our last evening in Hong Kong. A family dinner had been planned to celebrate the Chinese New Year. It was a joyous event with 20 of us at Prince's restaurant in the Elements mall below the Ritz-Carlton. It was Justice Scalia's first time to meet many in the Woo family, including Karolyne's eldest uncle, Stephen, who had long before taught English in Hong Kong. Stephen's brand of English was old-fashioned and hyper-formal. He would say to a waiter, "We shall have the fried crab. And furthermore, we shall have fried rice." Justice Scalia sat between Stephen and me, but there was a good deal of shifting of seats at dinner—so at various points he was sitting beside Karolyne, Tom, and Anton Maurer. The musical chairs made the dinner more fun.

At the end of the evening, as we were walking through the huge mall back to the hotel, Justice Scalia said: "You know, what really strikes me about Karolyne's family is how much they *like* each other. They don't just love each other; they genuinely enjoy each other's company. That's a great thing to see in a big family. I'm so glad to have been a part of this. It's just like my kids. When they're together, it's as if they haven't missed a beat. They really like being together."

Goodbye, Tom

Over breakfast the next morning, Justice Scalia said, "I've joined a hunting society—an ancient and noble group called the International Order of St. Hubertus, who was the patron saint of hunters."

"You have?" I said with only a moderate degree of interest. I've never had any passion for hunting.

"Yes, I have. I think it's going to be rewarding. They promote hunting ethics and wildlife conservation. I don't join many new things, but I think this'll be good for me. We have a hunt coming up soon. You know, it's based in Europe."

"You're going hunting in *Europe*?"

"No, this hunt is in Texas. But the organization is a European knightly order—with connections to royalty in Spain, Austria, and Hungary."

"Wow. I'll be curious to know how you like it," I said noncommittally, looking down at the harbor. "Look at those barges. It's going to take that tug forever to move them very far."

With that abrupt change of topic, we never again discussed his new hunting society.

After breakfast, on the elevator ride up to our rooms, I asked whether he was all ready for the trip back.

"Not yet. Lots of packing to do."

"I could help you," I said.

"I'll be fine," Justice Scalia said. "I need to do it myself."

"Tom," I said, "I need to get the *Reading Law* manuscript back from you. Did you look at it?"

"Yeah," said Tom. "It's amazing all the additional work you've done."

"We've been working hard," said Justice Scalia.

Because Justice Scalia's room was on the same floor as Tom's, and closer to the elevator, Justice Scalia invited us in while we waited for Tom to retrieve the large binder with 700 pages of proofs.

"I've got to pack up my C-PAP," he said. It was on his bed. "Hey, Bryan, did you ever get tested for sleep apnea?"

"Yes, I did, but the results were inconclusive."

He looked at Karolyne. "Does he snore?"

"Yes!" she said. "Keeps me awake sometimes."

"Bryan, you've got to get one of these." He came toward me and stuck the two curled tubes up his nose. "It fits in just like this. It's easy. You'll sleep like a log—and Maureen says I don't snore anymore." He looked a little funny speaking with the device on.

Then he removed it from his nose and came closer to me. "Here, try this."

I moved back in resistance.

"No, really, try it!" he said, gesturing that he wanted to insert the tubes into my nostrils.

"Nino, I'm not sticking your tubes up my nose! I love you, Nino, but . . . Come on, you know I'm a germophobe."

"Oh yes, the great germophobe," he said sarcastically while stepping back. "Always washing your hands! 'Oh, don't let me get any germs!' You know you're weakening your immune system."

"I think I've saved you from many colds by sharing my hand sanitizer, after we've shaken hundreds of hands. Why expose yourself needlessly to other people's germs?"

Just then Tom knocked at the door, and Karolyne let him in. He handed me the big binder containing the manuscript for the second edition of *Reading Law*. "Thanks for letting me see this," Tom said. "It's great. You think it's ready to publish?"

"We're ready," I said.

"We're ready," Justice Scalia agreed.

"We've added lots of new material—all the text highlighted in yellow," I said.

"Then I'll get the gears working at Thomson Reuters," said Tom. "What do you see as the publication date?"

"We can have final proofs to you in May, with the redone index and bibliography, all ready to print," I said. "So an August 2016 pub date is entirely workable."

"I can do that," said Justice Scalia.

"Good," I said. "Now Tom's going to the train station downstairs. Lyne and I are going to see him off. We leave here for the airport in two hours. Do you want to come downstairs and see Tom off?"

"You bet I do," said Justice Scalia, grinning. "Tom, you've been an excellent travel companion. I'm glad that you came along."

"It's been such a privilege for me, Justice Scalia."

He was still using that formal title—but then again, so was Karolyne. He never told either one to call him "Nino," so they didn't.

After saying goodbye to Tom, we rode the elevator back to the top of the Ritz-Carlton. "You know," he said to Karolyne emphatically, "I don't want to go back. I resent having to go back. I just can't see going back to Washington. This has been the most remarkable trip. I really don't want to go back to work."

"That's so sweet," said Karolyne.

"Do you often feel that way after a vacation?" I asked.

"No. Not really."

Now we were at his floor. "Rest up a little, Nino, and we'll see you at 11 o'clock."

The Chinese VIP Lounge

Soon we found ourselves back at the Hong Kong airport, in the same VIP lounge where we'd waited en route to Singapore just 12 days before. Once again we had green tea, and some servers brought us an assortment of Chinese dumplings.

Justice Scalia was now dressed in a button-down shirt and a blazer. I asked him why. He said he was returning to his home turf, where people would recognize him. He smiled and said, "I'm a Supreme Justice, you know."

"Nino," I said. "What's going to happen to your papers?"

"I don't know. I haven't made any plans. They're a mess. Most of them are down in the basement of the Court. The Chief has said he'd pay to have someone get them in order for me."

"That's a good idea. But what about placing them? They could have a lot of historical value—or even historic value."

"I suppose they'll go to the Library of Congress."

"Hmm. You know there are great libraries that pay large sums of money for the papers of important writers and political figures. Lyne serves on the board of the Harry Ransom Center in Austin."

"I do," she said, "and we acquire literary archives—like the David Foster Wallace papers. Those are much in demand among literary scholars. They're used all the time."

"You mean I could sell my papers?"

"It's a possibility," I said. "It depends on what you've kept. I've always had the sense that you throw a lot of stuff away."

"I do."

"That's a shame. Even my letters to you?"

He smiled. "Oh, I think I've kept some of those."

"I trust that you've kept the letter that George H. W. Bush wrote to Maureen about the flag-burning case."

"The one where he defended me because he'd heard that Maureen was unhappy with my vote?"

"Right."

"Oh, we have that one at home."

"If I could time-travel and advise you at the outset of your career," I said, rehearsing a familiar fantasy of mine, "I'd tell you to file everything meticulously."

"Well, you can't, now, can you?" he said.

"What about seeing whether a university library has any interest in paying to acquire your papers? Maybe Harvard will have an interest. Maybe Texas."

"Could you look into it?"

"I will. Are you officially retaining me?"

"I hereby retain you officially."

"Okay, I'll be acting as your agent in seeing about placing your papers. I'll start with some informal inquiries. Perhaps I'll begin by calling some literary archivists I know."

"Sounds good."

"Depending on what you have, we might place your papers in a way that would make them well maintained and at the same time bring in some money for your family."

"You mean my colleagues have been foolish to put their papers in the Library of Congress without compensation?"

"I don't know. I don't know what the rules are about what you own and what the government owns."

"I think the papers are mine to dispose of as I please—just like a president's papers. But I'd want a moratorium in place. No one should see my papers until after the death of the last colleague with whom I've served. I didn't like what happened with Thurgood Marshall's papers. That was atrocious."

He was referring to the upset caused to members of the Court when no provision had been made to seal Justice Marshall's papers for any period after the Justice had died. So within six months of his death, all sorts of Court memos that might have been seen as confidential were immediately opened up to public access. In 1993, Chief Justice Rehnquist had written a stinging letter about it to the Library of Congress—to no avail.

"Do you have a literary executor?" I asked.

"No," he said.

"Don't you think you need one?"

"I don't know."

"You do have a will, don't you?"

"Of course. Maureen and I both do."

"There was a Texas Court of Criminal Appeals judge many years ago, a friend of my grandfather's, who died intestate. It was a major problem for his widow, who was his second wife. Anyway, it sometimes happens that judges, of all people, die intestate. The British scholar Jarman, who wrote the big two-volume treatise *Jarman on Wills*, died intestate."

"He did?" Justice Scalia asked.

"He did. Anyway, now that you have literary property—our two books—you probably need to name a literary executor."

"Hmm." He was silent for 15 seconds or so, rubbing the cuticle of his thumb on his lower lip.

"I'll do something about it when I get back. It's called a 'literary executor'?"

"Right. The point is that you need someone who can make good decisions about your literary property. Plus, you'll have your published speeches soon, and all the interviews that we'll soon be doing about your life—and the book that will come from that. This is all pretty important."

"I'll get right on it."

"Well, of course there's no rush. It won't affect anything for another 22 years, since you'll live past 100."

"I do hope. How's the book on precedent coming—with the circuit judges?" He switched the subject abruptly.

"It's going to be excellent," I said. "I'm just struggling right now with organization."

"What do you mean?" he asked.

"It needs the benefit of your kind of architectural genius. I'm consolidating here and there, and reorganizing. I'm trying to do what you would do. I just don't have your gift for structure."

"How long is it?" he asked.

"It'll be about 900 pages—a third longer than *Reading Law*."

"I could spend some time with it this summer. How long do you think it would take me?"

"At least a week, Nino. Could you actually spare that time?"

"For you, I'd be happy to. Of course."

"My goodness." I got a lump in my throat knowing the commitment he was making in time and effort. "Are you sure?"

"You say it needs my help. I'll give it a week. I'll see what I can do. It's an important project. What's a week between friends?"

"Thank you, Nino. I'll get it into the best shape I can before I send it to you."

Our State Department handler, Alissa, came in and told us we should move on to the van, to go to the terminal. She said our bags had already been loaded, so all we had to do was be driven to the terminal. She added that we were short on time.

The Flight Home

When we got to the terminal, I suggested to Justice Scalia that we should get some duty-free Scotch. "That sounds good. But we can get Scotch back in America."

"Yes, Nino, but sometimes they have Scotches not available domestically, and it's usually at pretty good prices."

"Do we have time?" Justice Scalia asked.

"Let's make time," I said, perhaps overconfidently. "Alissa, let's find a duty-free shop."

"We're boarding in 15 minutes," said Justice Scalia.

"We'll be fine, Nino. Boarding *starts* in 15 minutes, at 12:50, but the gate won't close until 1:20—that's 45 minutes from now. We have time. The gate is just 50 yards that way."

We had to walk about 100 yards the other way to get to the duty-free shop. Karolyne was worried, but Justice Scalia was game. As we walked, I took his briefcase and put it on my rolling briefcase, leaning against the long handles, so he'd have both hands free. "Be careful with that," he said.

"Of course, Nino."

We strolled briskly down to the duty-free shop. Once there, we started looking together at some of the liquor they offered.

"Bryan, we're walking to the gate in five minutes," said Karolyne.

"Fine. I see what I want. We'll have time to spare. Good thing you don't smoke anymore, Nino. They sell lots of cigarettes here. I haven't seen you smoke in a very long time."

I rolled my briefcase over to Alissa's assistant and said, "Please watch this. Just keep it like this." The handle was angled toward her so that Justice Scalia's briefcase would remain securely on top. I picked out a single-malt whisky and a tawny port and then asked Justice Scalia whether he wanted anything. He said no. I pulled out my credit card to pay.

Suddenly there was a small thud a few feet away. Alissa's assistant had let go of the handle on my rolling briefcase, and Justice Scalia's briefcase had fallen to the ground.

"I knew that was going to happen! Dammit!" Justice Scalia was furious.

"It shouldn't have happened. Here, please give that to me," I said to the demure assistant as I reached for Justice Scalia's briefcase. I'm sure she was mortified.

"No, give it to me, dammit. Maureen's bracelet is in there, and it's surely broken!"

"It'll be fine. I'm sure it's not broken."

He was fuming. I called off the transaction, and we started toward the gate.

"They're already boarding!" said Karolyne. "You and your Scotch! You had to get your Scotch."

"The bracelet's broken," Justice Scalia said. "I know it's broken," he said as the five of us marched toward the gate.

"Well, let's open the briefcase and check right now," I said.

"No. I'll check after we board. It's broken. I know it."

"I'm pretty sure it isn't. We'll know soon enough."

"What if it is?"

"Then we'll get an exact replacement. But again, I think it's going to be fine."

He shook his head and grew quiet, his shoulders hunched. All his body language radiated anger as he stomped alongside me toward the gate. Alissa got us to the front of the business-class line. The gate agent scanned our boarding passes, and within seconds we were on the jet bridge.

"What seats are we in?" I said.

"Let's see," said Justice Scalia. Suddenly the anger seemed to have disappeared. "I'm in 14J."

"Bryan, we're in 4E and 4H," said Karolyne. "Why don't you take my seat again, Justice Scalia?"

"No," he said jovially, "Bryan gives me too much work!"

As we boarded, I accompanied him back to 14J. We opened up the briefcase together. "It had better be okay!" he said in a monitory tone. It was. Karolyne had wrapped it in tissue paper, and it was perfectly preserved.

"Again, I'm sorry, Nino. I can't believe she let it fall that way, but I shouldn't have entrusted her with it. At least we're in good shape, everything's fine, and Maureen's going to love that bracelet."

"You think she will?"

"I'm sure of it."

"I really hope it fits her. It's beautiful, isn't it?"

"It's beautiful, Nino. What will you need for the trip? Let's get it out now, and then I'll put up your briefcase." By now we had been reminded many times how painful it was for him to try to reach up to the overhead bin.

"I've been thinking," he said. "You know that stone ball you bought?"

"Yes."

"If it really does glow in the dark, I think you got your money's worth."

"Believe me, Nino, it does. Funny you should bring that up. It glows."

He was soon settled, so I went up to 4E to get myself situated for the flight. The three of us had identical lie-flat seats, television monitors, and headphone sets. Within a couple of minutes, he was up beside Karolyne, since they were on the same aisle. "Lyne, I need to get something else out of my briefcase. I forgot the knit cap. Can you help me?" She went back to his seat to get his briefcase down. She suggested keeping it in her own overhead bin, but he insisted that it be in his.

I slept most of the flight. Twice I woke up and went back to check on Justice Scalia. Both times he was sitting upright, knit cap on his head, noise-canceling headphones on, mouth open, snoring just a bit. Karolyne would tell me later that while I was sleeping, he came up to check on us three or four times. One time she was sleeping with her monitor on, and he shook her arm. Here's how she reported it to me:

"What are you watching?" he asked, still wearing his headphones.

"Oh, some trashy movie. I was just dozing. How are you?"

"Good flight, isn't it? Ooh, I watched a good movie," he said. "The one with Tom Hanks in it."

"*Bridge of Spies?*"

"Yeah, that's the one. You ought to watch it. It's great on attorney–client privilege. It's just a great lawyer film. I love Tom Hanks."

"Me too," she said. "I'll watch it."

"He's out like a light, isn't he?" Justice Scalia said, nodding at me. "I'll check on you later. I'm going to see what other movies they have."

Finally, after 15 hours in the air, we landed at Dallas–Fort Worth International Airport. Everyone scrambled to get things out of the overhead bins and get off the plane. The crowded aisles made it impossible for me to get back to Justice Scalia. Karolyne handed me his suit bag. "Let's meet him on the jet bridge," I said. But I would have to meet her there as well because even though we had been seated beside each other, we were on separate aisles.

Being among the first two or three off the plane, I waited a few feet away in the little bulge in the jet bridge. Karolyne soon came off and said she'd go out to the gate to meet the marshals—doubtless the same ones who had dropped us off 12 days before. She took the suit bag outside with her. It took about three minutes for Justice Scalia to come into view from the door. He came off and said, "Did Lyne get my suit bag?"

"Yes, she took it on out. Safe and sound."

"I need to get into my briefcase," he said, handing it to me. We propped it on my knee as he opened it. He said, "Oh no! I've forgotten something."

"Nino, the bracelet is right here. You've got both your iPods. Is it a document?"

"No, it's not that." People were flooding past us. "I've got to go back to my seat."

"What is it, Nino? Let's get out to the marshals. They can get whatever it is."

"No. I have to go back and get it."

"There are still 200 people trying to get off. What is it? I'll go get it."

"Never mind. I've got to go back."

He wouldn't tell me what it was he'd left behind, and now he was fighting the crowd to get back to his seat, some six seats back from the plane's entrance, on the far aisle. I wondered what this mysterious thing was. It took 60 seconds for him to get back to the far aisle, turn right, and disappear from my view. Two flight attendants were telling everyone, "Thank you for flying American." Again and again.

I knew the marshals must be wondering what was going on. If I was worried with what little information I had, they must have been really worried. I texted Karolyne that Justice Scalia had gone back onto the plane to retrieve something. After three minutes with no sign of him, I urgently told one of the flight attendants: "I need your help. There's a United States Supreme Court Justice on board. Actually, he needs your help. He's trying to get something from his seat: 14J. Please go back and help him. I don't know what's wrong. It's Justice Scalia."

Seeing my distress, and concerned herself, she went back down the far aisle, going against the onslaught of exiting passengers. No one getting off seemed concerned about having seen something troubling, so I felt comforted by that. "Where is he?" Karolyne texted me.

"Back at his seat," I replied. "Flight attendant helping."

After what was probably another 90 seconds but felt like an eternity, he came into view again, smiling. "I've got it!"

"What in the world was it?"

"Your knit cap!" He pulled it from behind his back with a flourish.

"Oh, goodness, Nino. You had me really worried."

"I said I'd borrow it, and I had to return it!"

We walked off the jet bridge, where Karolyne was standing with four U.S. marshals, including Ralph Tenorio. Justice Scalia handed the cap back to her. "Your cap, madam!"

Last Embraces

We strode toward the nearby exit. "You really had me worried, Nino. We didn't need that cap back."

"I couldn't not return it to you. I wasn't raised that way. It would have disappointed my mother."

"Well, thank you." I paused. "Nino, we've gotten you safely back to U.S. soil. The whole way, none of us got sick—not even a cold."

"You know, that's right," he said.

"We're all healthy," I said, "and you've made a little progress on that frozen shoulder."

"Not much on the shoulder. But it has been a great trip. This has been wonderful."

Ralph explained that we'd have to go retrieve our bags with two marshals, who would recheck Justice Scalia's bags to Washington, D.C. But Justice Scalia would be going to a holding room near his gate.

"This is as far as we go," Ralph said.

"So it's time to say goodbye?" I asked.

"It's so quick, isn't it?" Karolyne said to Justice Scalia.

"It really is," he said.

"Goodbye, Nino," I said, with my arms outstretched for a hug. I don't think I'd ever hugged him before. It was a little awkward for him, but we embraced. Then he gave Karolyne a big hug and said goodbye.

"Thank you both for everything," he said to us. "And say thanks again to your family, Lyne."

"We love you, Nino," I said. He paused but said nothing. He seemed a little choked up.

"We love you," Karolyne said.

"It's been a great trip," Justice Scalia said. "I'll see you both again soon."

He turned in the direction that one of the marshals motioned toward. Karolyne and I waited as he walked some 100 feet down the hall, rounded the corner, and disappeared from our sight.

Telephone Volleys

He called us the next day, on Friday, February 5, to report that Mrs. Scalia's bracelet didn't fit. He was crushed. Karolyne joined me on the speakerphone and said she had another jade bracelet more oval in shape. We sent it by FedEx that afternoon for Saturday delivery.

He called again on Saturday and left a voicemail. The oval one didn't fit, either. He suggested exchanging the bracelet for a jade necklace. He asked us to assure the jade dealer that he would pay any difference in cost. Karolyne called her aunt in Hong Kong to arrange the exchange.

Sunday afternoon, I called and left a voicemail. I said that arrangements had been made with the jade dealer. I also asked the Scalias to have dinner Monday night, since I'd be in Washington that evening before an all-day Tuesday seminar for a D.C. law firm. I never heard back about that.

But Wednesday morning, February 10, when I was back in Dallas, Justice Scalia called my cellphone. "Bryan, you're in town!"

"No, Nino, I'm afraid not. I'm back in Dallas. I was in Washington Monday evening."

"Oh, I was up in New York giving a talk."

"Traveling again so soon? You need to rest up," I said.

"I know, I know," he said. "Listen, I have something important to tell you." I was listening intently. "The world of tennis has lost a great competitor."

I was at a loss. Serena Williams had died? Roger Federer?

"What do you mean?"

"My doctor tells me I won't ever play tennis again. It's a torn rotator cuff that's already been fixed once, and it's no use operating a second time."

"What?! I had you doing exercises for what we thought was a frozen shoulder. That's not what it was?"

"That's not what it was," he said solemnly.

"I may have made things worse with all that stretching!"

"No, not at all. I'm fine. I just won't ever be able to serve a tennis ball again. As I say, the world of tennis has lost a great competitor."

"Well, you certainly were that. You remember when I watched you play at your club? You were a fierce competitor. I'm sorry, Nino. I know how much tennis means to you."

"I'll just have to live without it," he said matter-of-factly.

We spoke more about the jade necklace, about the three volumes of his speeches I was editing for him, and about the final strokes we needed to complete the second edition of *Reading Law*. He thanked me again for my role in arranging the trip to Singapore and Hong Kong.

I noticed an unusually crusty quality in his voice.

"You sound as if you have a cold," I said.

"Yeah, I came down with it over the weekend. Just some crud in my throat."

"That's too bad. Rest up."

I wish I had been more insistent about rest. His domestic travel schedule was typically one event after another. He said nothing in that conversation about preparing to leave shortly for his Texas hunting trip.

Epilogue

Justice Scalia died two days later, in his sleep, on the first night of the hunting trip.

It was a wrenching moment when I found out, and the wrenching moment turned into a wrenching month and a wrenching year. Life hasn't been the same.

What began as an interview request, prompted by David Foster Wallace, evolved into a joint writing project. Back in 2006, I thought it would be a fascinating diversion. But soon my life had been transformed. Justice Scalia had befriended me, and his loss has caused a more profound hurt than I could have imagined.

Of course, loss is a familiar story. Someone you love and cherish is there one moment and gone the next. As Gertrude, Hamlet's mother, says callously to her son about her late husband's death, "Thou know'st 'tis common: all that lives must die, passing through nature to eternity."

"Ay, madam," says Hamlet. "It is common."

But hurts of this kind are always particular. I miss him terribly. I lost a coauthor, an adoptive uncle, and a dear friend I never expected to make. Having reached midlife by 2006, I never thought I'd strike up a new friendship that would alter the course of my life—especially when all I sought, initially, was a videotaped interview with a person of great eminence, and the interview itself seemed unattainable.

The closeness that developed between us surely took us both quite by surprise. We had conversations that only the two of us could have—Nino and me. I can't have those conversations anymore, with anyone.

🐾 🐾 🐾

The only thing that brought Justice Scalia and me together, in the beginning, was our love of words—the same thing that, improbably enough, brought me together with David Foster Wallace. I suppose that Justice Scalia found something in me—a love of language—that reminded him of his father, the professor of Romance languages. What strengthened our bond, of course, was our joint literary enterprises. And food, wine, and conversation. And argument. And, in the end, Karolyne.

In retrospect, the friendship that developed between us seems to have been simultaneously both impossible and inevitable. As different as we were in some respects—you'll have gleaned as much from this narrative— we were also very much of one mind.

Gone is the nucleus of a small society of snoots who were confederates and mutual admirers. He was a passionate man who, because he thrived on argument, imbued almost every situation with some degree of drama and tension. Soon after starting our collaborative work I came to love the man, and our continuing projects—appearance after appearance together both onstage and offstage—only intensified that feeling.

To have him snatched from this world, at the height of his powers, was tormenting. It still is. It's not that so many projects were left uncompleted. Not that. It's that he himself has vanished—this man so unlike any other, who made the most of his considerable gifts, whose uncommon blend of qualities will never be replicated.

I miss him. Terribly.

I don't care if he despised one-sentence paragraphs, or for that matter contractions.

To use a snoot's metaphor, he was truly a *hapax legomenon*.[64]

Beyond Personal Loss

America's loss, too, is a particular one. We lost our most consequential, powerful snoot: the connoisseur of language whose pronouncements about words had the greatest, most far-reaching impact on the world.

Stated differently, America lost its leading textualist: its leading legal exponent of the straightforward idea that words deliberately written typi-

---

64 In the strict sense of the word (which, of course, is the sense that he preferred [see pp. 36–39]).

cally have an ascertainable meaning, certainly those included in legal instruments such as contracts, rules, regulations, statutes, and constitutions; that they can and should be given a fair reading; that legislatures should be taken at their word; and that, equally to the point, our Founders knew what they were doing when they committed their Constitution to written words.

Within American legal academia today, believe it or not, it takes courage to take such positions. The modernist orthodoxy is that words are notoriously indeterminate; that there is an amorphous constitution that exists outside the written Constitution; that all judges are inevitably political, and that therefore we should allow them to be openly political; that the people as a whole can't be trusted to make wise decisions for themselves, and that therefore a kind of judicial aristocracy is preferable to democracy, which is slow and messy; that progressive thinkers know best what paths society should take, not society itself—so that judges should go around and behind the words of governing texts to enact their own visions of what they consider wise policy.

Straw-man positions, you say? No. These are all but dogmas.

Antonin Scalia set his face against all these notions. He thought that if the Constitution needs to change, it must change through amendment— the very mechanism for change provided for in the charter itself. He didn't believe that it can truly evolve on its own, or on the whims or desires of five unelected judges who decide it's time for a new constitutional policy. Likewise, according to his convictions, statutes can be changed only by amendment, not by judicial alteration.

But don't we leave the difficult decisions to judges if the legislature can't work them out? Not always, in the view of a textualist such as Justice Scalia. What's not in the Constitution simply isn't in the Constitution. And what's not in a statute simply isn't there. The people will need to act democratically to add things, if additions are needed. The Constitution has a provision saying how it can be amended, and that provision says nothing about having judges graft new provisions onto the document. (This point isn't without difficulty, since the amendment process, with its required supermajorities and voting by states, is arguably undemocratic.) Whether you like that position or not, it's a principled one.

If Justice Scalia was widely misunderstood, that fact was attributable, I think, to three things. First, he had an inveterate tendency, dating back to his professorial days, to "teach against the class"—to voice positions that listeners were almost certain to disagree with in order to generate a better discussion. He would therefore frequently play the devil's advocate in an argument to test the limits of a position with an extreme hypothetical case. Second, he was linguistically conservative (and, I think, naïve) enough to adopt prevalent labels that had been devised by those he opposed: *Living Constitution*, *pragmatism*, *purposivism*, and *realism*. To him, these words connoted disreputable things. In one way or another, they represented bad, unprincipled judging, and he could make a compelling case for why that was so. But for people unfamiliar with his arguments, these words—and therefore the ideas they represent—have positive associations. So he and his audience often had a kind of semantic mismatch. Third, because most people never get past the headlines, most knowledge of Justice Scalia was filtered through reporters who weren't sympathetic with the conservative results often reached by his brand of textualism. Besides, most Supreme Court outcomes are reported as if the judges are freewheeling policy-makers who are unconstrained by method. Justice Scalia's teach-against-the-class habit made him a target of parodists. Hence, unless you were a pretty serious student of the Court, you'd hardly know that he was a towering intellect.

He was. And we are unlikely to see his like again. I know I won't.

An Explanatory Analogy

How, exactly, did this whole relationship change my life? That's hard to explain. I might have thought the general idea to be obvious, but as with so many profound personal experiences, it seems impossible to convey its full significance in any effective way—or even to comprehend it myself.

Analogies appealed to us, Nino and me, so let me try with an admittedly imperfect one that just may get the idea across. Envision yourself as a youngish, minor singer–songwriter in 1971. A prominent musician who's a friend of yours says you should get together with John Lennon. And so, with some difficulty and a little luck, you arrange a meeting. To your delight, you discover that Lennon is vaguely a fan of your work, and the two of you hit it off remarkably well. You feel a visceral bond. You keep in touch. Soon you begin writing songs together. After a turbulent start, you grow quite close and compose and record some of the best work that either of you has ever done—on two albums. The prolonged recording sessions are exhilarating. Fans of Lennon laud the recordings; your own small cadre of fans seem almost as excited about the collaboration as you are.

You have endless jam sessions whenever you're in the same town. You even start touring together and soon learn that Lennon actually prefers performing with you to appearing solo. The crowds overflow with enthusiasm. You well understand that you're the sidekick, not the superstar. The extended standing ovations are for him, not you. But he insists that you're his partner and deserve equal recognition: during performances, he routinely alternates the lead with you. You love almost everything about his personality, his humor, his tastes—just being with him—and your feelings seem to be fully reciprocated. He wants to travel with you and your spouse on a two-week trip half a world away, just the three of you (along with your record-company exec), traveling more or less incognito. You play a few private gigs, but otherwise this trip is just for pleasure. The adventure is transformative, at times almost otherworldly. The three of you fly back home, happy and in good health.

Then, just shy of the tenth anniversary of your friendship, he dies unexpectedly. He's gone, and you have almost nobody to grieve with except your loving spouse—and, in a much more abstract and universal sense, Lennon-lovers everywhere.

Why should that change a person? I don't know. It just does. It's hard to understand, and even harder to express, without an analogy. I'm sure Nino, after careful contemplation of his ceiling, would have hit on—no, *upon*—just the right words. He always did. I also suspect that he might not appreciate *my* draft, associating him in this way with one of those "rock-'n'-rolly" Beatles. Perhaps it's the subversive in me, but it seems apt. Anyway, it's the best I can do. After all, I was the sidekick—an honor I shall forever cherish.

Postscript

This story began with three professional snoots—a linguistic triumvirate, of sorts, in different fields: a novelist, a lexicographer, and a textualist judge.

By late 2008, there were but two.

By early 2016, there was but one—and the least one at that.

He is grateful that the other two considered him worthy of their company.

He remains a devotee of *Charlotte's Web*, by the redoubtable E. B. White. The moral of that story, of course, is that it isn't often that someone comes along who is both a good writer and a true friend.

Acknowledgments

I wrote this book for several reasons. First, it was therapeutic. As best I could, I wanted to make sense of the experiences recorded here, and writing about them has certainly helped. Second, I couldn't *not* write the book. I'm a writer, and writers write. Third, I felt and continue to feel certain that Justice Scalia would have liked having our story told. We had an agreement that the first of us to die would receive a tribute from the survivor—though, I'm sure, when we had that discussion on more than one occasion, neither of us figured it would be a book-length treatment. In any event, he would have insisted that every word of it must be true, as I have faithfully tried to make it. Fourth, when I considered the possibility of keeping it all to myself, that course of inaction seemed like a dereliction to posterity and to the pursuit of knowledge. Unlike a Court employee, I'm not bound by a code of silence. Although that certainly doesn't relieve me of a duty of discretion, it does mean that writing an intimate memoir entails no conflict of interest.

My debts are many. My wife Karolyne, who was directly involved in so much of the story, helped me reconstruct innumerable snatches of dialogue. Her readings of the manuscript proved invaluable. My daughter Caroline was similarly helpful with the early portions of the book. My team at LawProse—Jeff Newman, Tiger Jackson, Becky Moler (formerly McDaniel), Ryden McComas Anderson, Christina Gigliotti, Elizabeth Nanez, and Alyssa Bolin—read and commented on dozens of drafts, improving it each time. Several long-standing friends of Justice Scalia's suggested improvements. So did friends of mine: J. P. Allen, Herb Hammond, Ryan Killian, Brian Melendez, Judge Thomas M. Reavley, John Scanlan, and Randy Tietjen. My friend Judd Stone, one of Justice Scalia's last law clerks, pored over the manuscript twice to make dozens of enhancements. My longtime friend and colleague John Trimble, whose name comes up in the book more than once, skillfully line-edited a draft. So did my editor at Simon & Schuster, Mitchell Ivers. My agent, James Levine, suggested the final title. To say I had a little help from my friends would be a severe understatement.

Among all my various books, this one was particularly challenging and emotionally difficult. Now that it's done, a melancholic milestone has passed—but the melancholy persists. I'm reminded that the pain of grief is the price we all pay for having loved.

B.A.G.

23 August 2017

Index